Praise for *The Mommy Myth*

"In sharp, funny, fed-up prose . . . *The Mommy Myth* takes such a cathartic bite out of the celebrity-mom mystique, you can save that backup carton of Coffee Heath Bar Crunch for a different emergency."

—*The San Diego Union-Tribune*

"A full-on feminist attack on the way the media portrays mothers, done in a manner reminiscent of Susan Faludi's *Backlash* . . . *The Mommy Myth* provides a sprightly and thought-provoking tour through the last thirty years of feminist attitudes toward motherhood."

—*The Washington Post Book World*

"In smart, sardonic prose, the authors demonstrate how much moms are up against today, from the impossible-to-achieve advice of child care experts to the increasing list of mothering no-no's to the anxiety that you can't ever let your kids out of your sight."

—*Brain, Child—The Magazine for Thinking Mothers*

"Witty and well researched. . . . What we learn about motherhood from Susan Douglas and Meredith Michaels is that motherhood is still very much a battleground."

—*Chicago Tribune*

"The chapter 'Attack of the Celebrity Moms' is alone worth the price of the book for its dead-on analysis of the ways stars and the people who write about them constantly harp on the pleasures of family life."

—*The Baltimore Sun*

"*The Mommy Myth* is a fun read and a smart one, too. . . . Witty, engaging, and backed by a lot of research."

—*The Nation*

"Lively and smart and irreverent. *The Mommy Myth* is a healthy indicator that feminists are sick and tired of being beaten up on and are fighting back. It pokes fun at airbrushed profiles of celebrity moms and pokes holes in the media panics about child safety, including a fascinating demolition of the "epidemic" of crack babies, an alarmist falsehood from start to finish.

—*The American Prospect*

"Written with verve and a healthy dose of humor, this book says the best role models are everyday women who ignore the pressures of the new momism as they manage their families." —*The Hartford Courant*

"In this insightful, critical look at modern motherhood, the authors debunk the mythological mother created by the media in the past three decades." —*The Arizona Republic*

"In *The Mommy Myth,* authors Susan Douglas and Meredith Michaels harness the anger of Cathi Hanauer's *The Bitch in the House* and the critical prowess of Ann Crittenden's *The Price of Motherhood* in a witty look behind popular images of motherhood. . . . Speaking as two sardonic mamas and savvy media consumers, the authors lead us on a whirlwind romp through the magazines, movies, television shows, and political debates about motherhood over the past thirty years." —*The Progressive*

"This funny, angry book is making waves." —*The Guardian* (London)

"Our sisters stateside have done it again, hit the nail on the head: the latest book of popular feminist controversy is called *The Mommy Myth*. Its authors dissect beautifully the dilemma of modern motherhood: despite increasing pressures on our time, we are confronted with ever escalating visions of maternal perfection. If motherhood is as good as apple pie, why do we all feel so bad?" —*The Western Mail*

"Clever and provocative. . . . Arms akimbo, with a jaundiced eye turned to the gritty reality of mothering, Douglas and Michaels wisecrack their way through an explication of the evolution of motherhood in the media during the final third of the twentieth century." —The Mothers Movement online

"Ultimately, the authors provide a clearly delineated explanation of how feminism became a dirty word in our culture, and their book should be required reading for all students of American history, breeders or not." —*Bust* magazine

"Insightful and backed up with compelling evidence. . . .The authors drive home excellent points in this myth-bashing look at motherhood."

—Minneapolis *Star-Tribune*

"A highly readable send-up of the 'new momism' . . . written in a crystal-clear and approachable style."

—*Ann Arbor News*

"[The authors'] passion and sense of humor are undeniable."

—*Library Journal*

"In the idealized myth, mothers and babies spend their days discovering the wonders of life, reading, playing, and laughing. Mom wears her baby in a sling, never raises her voice, and of course has unlimited time and patience. Baby grows up safe, happy, and respectful. In real life, however, it's a different story. Douglas and Michaels will blow the lid off 'new momism,' 'a set of ideals . . .that seem on the surface to celebrate motherhood, but which in reality promulgate standards of perfection that are beyond [a mother's] reach.'"

—*Publishers Weekly*

"Fascinating, funny, smart, scary, and long overdue, *The Mommy Myth* debunks the next big myth that's gotta come down: that of the Perfect Mother. Do not, I repeat, DO NOT SKIP THIS BOOK."

—Cathi Hanauer, editor of *The Bitch in the House* and author of *My Sisters' Bones*

"I have one word for *The Mommy Myth*: FINALLY! With humor, wit, and solid information, Douglas and Michaels take on the sentimentalized, privatized moralism of contemporary motherhood and show how it harms both women and children."

—Katha Pollitt, author *Subject to Debate: Sense and Dissents on Women, Politics, and Culture*

THE
MOMMY
MYTH

The Idealization of Motherhood and How It Has Undermined All Women

Susan J. Douglas and Meredith W. Michaels

FREE PRESS

New York   London   Toronto   Sydney

FREE PRESS
A Division of Simon & Schuster, Inc.
1230 Avenue of the Americas
New York, NY 10020

First Free Press trade paperback edition 2005

Photo Insert Credits:
Giant babies from Johnson and Johnson courtesy of the authors. Meredith Tax cartoon, courtesy of Meredith Tax. Ad for Schlafly's anti-daycare book "Who Will Rock the Cradle" courtesy of Labadie Collection, Special Collections Library, University of Michigan. Feminists demonstrating with signs for daycare centers courtesy of Bettmann/Corbis. *One Day at a Time* courtesy of Movie Stills Archives. *An Unmarried Woman* courtesy of Movie Still Archives. *Alice Doesn't Live Here Anymore* courtesy of Movie Still Archives. Clair and Cliff Huxtable from *The Cosby Show* courtesy of Movie Still Archives. Princess Diana and sons on a log ride courtesy of Stan Roberts/Collier Photos/Corbis Sygma. Princess Diana and sons sitting in the sand courtesy of Tim Graham/Corbis. Martha Stewart image courtesy of John Dominis/Getty Images. New Traditionalist courtesy of the authors. Mary Beth Whitehead with baby courtesy of The Record/Corbis. Crack baby in incubator courtesy of Ted Thai/Getty Images. Richard Nixon courtesy of John Olson/Getty Images. Marian Wright Edelman courtesy of Dirck Halstead/TimeLife Pictures/Getty Images. *Hand That Rocks the Cradle* courtesy of Movie Still Archives. *thirtysomething* courtesy of the Movie Still Archives. *Married with Children* courtesy of the Movie Still Archives. *Roseanne* courtesy of the Movie Still Archives. Susan Smith in handcuffs courtesy of Najalah Feanny/Corbis Saba. Andrea Yates with cop courtesy of AFP/Corbis. Dr. Laura courtesy of Dave Burton/Corbis Saba.

FREE PRESS and colophon are trademarks
of Simon & Schuster, Inc.

For information regarding special discounts for bulk purchases,
please contact Simon & Schuster Special Sales at 1-800-456-6798
or business@simonandschuster.com

Manufactured in the United States of America

10 9 8 7 6 5 4 3

Library of Congress Cataloging-in-Publication
Data Control Number: 2004299458

ISBN 0-7432-5999-8
    0-7432-6046-5 (Pbk)

CONTENTS

INTRODUCTION

The New Momism

It's 5:22 P.M. You're in the grocery checkout line. Your three-year-old is writhing on the floor, screaming, because you have refused to buy her a Teletubby pinwheel. Your six-year-old is whining, repeatedly, in a voice that could saw through cement, "But mommy, puleeze, puleeze" because you have not bought him the latest "Lunchables," which features, as the four food groups, Cheetos, a Snickers, Cheez Whiz, and Twizzlers. Your teenager, who has not spoken a single word in the past four days except, "You've ruined my life," followed by "Everyone else has one," is out in the car, sulking, with the new rap-metal band Piss on the Parentals blasting through the headphones of a Discman.

To distract yourself, and to avoid the glares of other shoppers who have already deemed you the worst mother in America, you leaf through *People* magazine. Inside, Uma Thurman gushes "Motherhood Is Sexy." [1] Moving on to *Good Housekeeping*, Vanna White says of her child, "When I hear his cry at six-thirty in the morning, I have a smile on my face, and I'm not an early riser." [2] Another unexpected source of earth-mother wisdom, the newly maternal Pamela Lee, also confides to *People*, "I just love getting up with him in the middle of the night to feed him or soothe him." [3] Brought back to reality by stereophonic whining, you indeed feel as sexy as Rush Limbaugh in a thong.

You drag your sorry ass home. Now, if you were a "good" mom, you'd joyfully empty the shopping bags and transform the process of putting the groceries away into a fun game your kids love to play (upbeat

Raffi songs would provide a lilting soundtrack). Then, while you steamed the broccoli and poached the chicken breasts in Vouvray and Evian water, you and the kids would also be doing jigsaw puzzles in the shape of the United Arab Emirates so they learned some geography. Your cheerful teenager would say, "Gee, Mom, you gave me the best advice on that last homework assignment." When your husband arrives, he is so overcome with admiration for how well you do it all that he looks lovingly into your eyes, kisses you, and presents you with a diamond anniversary bracelet. He then announces that he has gone on flex time for the next two years so that he can split childcare duties with you fifty-fifty. The children, chattering away happily, help set the table, and then eat their broccoli. After dinner, you all go out and stencil the driveway with autumn leaves.

But maybe this sounds slightly more familiar. "I won't unpack the groceries! You can't make me," bellows your child as he runs to his room, knocking down a lamp on the way. "Eewee—gross out!" he yells and you discover that the cat has barfed on his bed. You have fifteen minutes to make dinner because there's a school play in half an hour. While the children fight over whether to watch *Hot Couples* or people eating larvae on *Fear Factor,* you zap some Prego spaghetti sauce in the microwave and boil some pasta. *You* set the table. "Mommy, Mommy, Sam losted my hamster," your daughter wails. Your ex-husband calls to say he won't be taking the kids this weekend after all because his new wife, Buffy, twenty-three, has to go on a modeling shoot in Virgin Gorda for the *Sports Illustrated* swimsuit issue, and "she really needs me with her." You go to the TV room to discover the kids watching transvestites punching each other out on *Jerry Springer.* The pasta boils over and scalds the hamster, now lying prostrate on the floor with its legs twitching in the air. "Get your butts in here this instant or I'll murder you immediately," you shriek, by way of inviting your children to dinner. "I hate this pasta—I only like the kind shaped like wagon wheels!" "Mommy, you killded my hamster!"

If you're like us—mothers with an attitude problem—you may be getting increasingly irritable about this chasm between the ridiculous, honey-hued ideals of perfect motherhood in the mass media and the reality of mothers' everyday lives. And you may also be worn down by media images that suggest that however much you do for and love your kids, it is never enough. The love we feel for our kids, the joyful times we have with them, are repackaged into unattainable images of infinite patience and constant adoration so that we fear, as Kristin van Ogtrop put it movingly in *The Bitch in the House*, "I will love my children, but my love for them will always be imperfect."[4]

From the moment we get up until the moment we collapse in bed at night, the media are out there, calling to us, yelling, "Hey you! Yeah, you! Are you *really* raising your kids right?" Whether it's the cover of *Redbook* or *Parents* demanding "Are You a Sensitive Mother?" "Is Your Child Eating Enough?" "Is Your Baby Normal?" (and exhorting us to enter its pages and have great sex at 25, 35, or 85), the nightly news warning us about missing children, a movie trailer hyping a film about a cross-dressing dad who's way more fun than his stinky, careerist wife (*Mrs. Doubtfire*), or Dr. Laura telling some poor mother who works four hours a week that she's neglectful, the siren song blending seduction and accusation is there all the time. Mothers are subjected to an onslaught of beatific imagery, romantic fantasies, self-righteous sermons, psychological warnings, terrifying movies about losing their children, even more terrifying news stories about abducted and abused children, and totally unrealistic advice about how to be the most perfect and revered mom in the neighborhood, maybe even in the whole country. (Even *Working Mother*—which should have known better—had a "Working Mother of the Year Contest." When Jill Kirschenbaum became the editor in 2001, one of the first things she did was dump this feature, noting that motherhood should not be a "competitive sport.") We are urged to be fun-loving, spontaneous, and relaxed, yet, at the same time, scared out of our minds that our kids could be killed at any moment. No wonder 81 percent of women in a recent poll said it's harder to be a mother now than it was twenty or thirty years ago, and 56 percent felt mothers were doing a worse job today than mothers back then.[5] Even mothers who deliberately avoid TV and magazines, or who pride themselves on seeing through them, have trouble escaping the standards of perfection, and the sense of threat, that the media ceaselessly atomize into the air we breathe.

We are both mothers, and we adore our kids—for example, neither one of us has ever locked them up in dog crates in the basement (although we have, of course, been tempted). The smell of a new baby's head, tucking a child in at night, receiving homemade, hand-scrawled birthday cards, heart-to-hearts with a teenager after a date, seeing *them* become parents—these are joys parents treasure. But like increasing numbers of women, we are fed up with the myth—shamelessly hawked by the media—that motherhood is eternally fulfilling and rewarding, that it is *al-*

ways the best and most important thing you do, that there is only a narrowly prescribed way to do it right, and that if you don't love each and every second of it there's something really wrong with you. At the same time, the two of us still have been complete suckers, buying those black-and-white mobiles that allegedly turn your baby into Einstein Jr., feeling guilty for sending in store-bought cookies to the class bake sale instead of homemade like the "good" moms, staying up until 2:30 A.M. making our kids' Halloween costumes, driving to the Multiplex 18 at midnight to pick up teenagers so they won't miss the latest outing with their friends. We know that building a scale model of Versailles out of mashed potatoes may not be quite as crucial to good mothering as *Martha Stewart Living* suggests. Yet here we are, cowed by that most tyrannical of our cultural icons, Perfect Mom. So, like millions of women, we buy into these absurd ideals at the same time that we resent them and think they are utterly ridiculous and oppressive. After all, our parents—the group Tom Brokaw has labeled "the greatest generation"—had parents who whooped them on the behind, screamed stuff at them like "I'll tear you limb from limb," told them babies came from cabbage patches, never drove them four hours to a soccer match, and yet they seemed to have nonetheless saved the western world.

This book is about the rise in the media of what we are calling the "new momism": the insistence that no woman is truly complete or fulfilled unless she has kids, that women remain the best primary caretakers of children, and that to be a remotely decent mother, a woman has to devote her entire physical, psychological, emotional, and intellectual being, 24/7, to her children. The new momism is a highly romanticized and yet demanding view of motherhood in which the standards for success are impossible to meet. The term "momism" was initially coined by the journalist Philip Wylie in his highly influential 1942 bestseller *Generation of Vipers,* and it was a very derogatory term. Drawing from Freud (who else?), Wylie attacked the mothers of America as being so smothering, overprotective, and invested in their kids, especially their sons, that they turned them into dysfunctional, sniveling weaklings, maternal slaves chained to the apron strings, unable to fight for their country or even stand on their own two feet.[6] We seek to reclaim this term, rip it from its misogynistic origins, and apply it to an ideology that has snowballed since the 1980s and seeks to return women to the Stone Age.

The "new momism" is a set of ideals, norms, and practices, most frequently and powerfully represented in the media, that seem on the surface to celebrate motherhood, but which in reality promulgate standards of perfection that are beyond your reach. The new momism is the direct descendant and latest version of what Betty Friedan famously labeled the "feminine mystique" back in the 1960s. The new momism *seems* to be much more hip and progressive than the feminine mystique, because now, of course, mothers can and do work outside the home, have their own ambitions and money, raise kids on their own, or freely choose to stay at home with their kids rather than being forced to. And unlike the feminine mystique, the notion that women should be subservient to men is not an accepted tenet of the new momism. Central to the new momism, in fact, is the feminist insistence that woman have choices, that they are active agents in control of their own destiny, that they have autonomy. But here's where the distortion of feminism occurs. The only truly enlightened choice to make as a woman, the one that proves, first, that you are a "real" woman, and second, that you are a decent, worthy one, is to become a "mom" and to bring to child rearing a combination of selflessness and professionalism that would involve the cross cloning of Mother Teresa with Donna Shalala. Thus the new momism is deeply contradictory: It both draws from and repudiates feminism.

The fulcrum of the new momism is the rise of a really pernicious ideal in the late twentieth century that the sociologist Sharon Hays has perfectly labeled "intensive mothering."[7] It is no longer okay, as it was even during the heyday of June Cleaver, to let (or make) your kids walk to school, tell them to stop bugging you and go outside and play, or, God forbid, serve them something like Tang, once the preferred beverage of the astronauts, for breakfast. Of course many of our mothers baked us cookies, served as Brownie troop leaders, and chaperoned class trips to Elf Land. But today, the standards of good motherhood are really over the top. And they've gone through the roof at the same time that there has been a real decline in leisure time for most Americans.[8] The yuppie work ethic of the 1980s, which insisted that even when you were off the job you should be working—on your abs, your connections, your portfolio, whatever—absolutely conquered motherhood. As the actress Patricia Heaton jokes in *Motherhood & Hollywood*, now mothers are supposed to "sneak echinacea" into the "freshly squeezed, organically grown orange juice" we've made for our kids and teach them to "download research for their kindergarten report on 'My Family Tree—The Early Roman Years.'"[9]

Intensive mothering insists that mothers acquire professional-level skills such as those of a therapist, pediatrician ("Dr. Mom"), consumer products safety inspector, and teacher, and that they lavish every ounce of physical vitality they have, the monetary equivalent of the gross domestic product of Australia, and, most of all, every single bit of their emotional, mental, and psychic energy on their kids. We must learn to put on the masquerade of the doting, self-sacrificing mother and wear it at all times. With intensive mothering, everyone watches us, we watch ourselves and other mothers, and we watch ourselves watching ourselves. How many of you know someone who swatted her child on the behind in a supermarket because he was, say, opening a pack of razor blades in the toiletries aisle, only to be accosted by someone she never met who threatened to put her up on child-abuse charges? In 1997, one mother was arrested for child neglect because she left a ten-year-old and a four-year-old home for an hour and a half while she went to the supermarket.[10] Motherhood has become a psychological police state.

Intensive mothering is the ultimate female Olympics: We are all in powerful competition with each other, in constant danger of being trumped by the mom down the street, or in the magazine we're reading. The competition isn't just over who's a good mother—it's over who's the best. We compete with each other; we compete with ourselves. The best mothers always put their kids' needs before their own, period. The best mothers are the main caregivers. For the best mothers, their kids are the center of the universe. The best mothers always smile. They always understand. They are never tired. They never lose their temper. They never say, "Go to the neighbor's house and play while Mommy has a beer." Their love for their children is boundless, unflagging, flawless, total. Mothers today cannot just respond to their kids' needs, they must predict them—and with the telepathic accuracy of Houdini. They must memorize verbatim the books of all the child-care experts and know which approaches are developmentally appropriate at different ages. They are supposed to treat their two-year-olds with "respect." If mothers screw up and fail to do this on any given day, they should apologize to their kids, because any misstep leads to permanent psychological and/or physical damage. Anyone who questions whether this is *the* best and *the* necessary way to raise kids is an insensitive, ignorant brute. This is just common sense, right?[11]

The new momism has become unavoidable, unless you raise your kids in a yurt on the tundra, for one basic reason: Motherhood became one of the biggest media obsessions of the last three decades, exploding especially in the mid-1980s and continuing unabated to the present. Women have been deluged by an ever-thickening mudslide of maternal media advice, programming, and marketing that powerfully shapes how we mothers feel about our relationships with our own kids and, indeed, how we feel about ourselves. These media representations have changed over time, cutting mothers some real slack in the 1970s, and then increasingly closing the vise in the late 1980s and after, despite important rebellions by Roseanne and others. People don't usually notice that motherhood has been such a major media fixation, revolted or hooked as they've been over the years by other media excesses like the O. J. Simpson trials, the Lewinsky-Clinton imbroglio, the Elian Gonzalez carnival, *Survivor,* or the 2002 Washington-area sniper killings in which "profilers" who knew as much as SpongeBob SquarePants nonetheless got on TV to tell us what the killer was thinking.

But make no mistake about it—mothers and motherhood came under unprecedented media surveillance in the 1980s and beyond. And since the media traffic in extremes, in anomalies—the rich, the deviant, the exemplary, the criminal, the gorgeous—they emphasize fear and dread on the one hand and promote impossible ideals on the other. In the process, *Good Housekeeping, People,* E!, Lifetime, *Entertainment Tonight,* and *NBC Nightly News* built an interlocking, cumulative image of the dedicated, doting "mom" versus the delinquent, bad "mother." There have been, since the early 1980s, several overlapping media frameworks that have fueled the new momism. First, the media warned mothers about the external threats to their kids from abductors and the like. Then the "family values" crowd made it clear that supporting the family was not part of the government's responsibility. By the late 1980s, stories about welfare and crack mothers emphasized the internal threats to children from mothers themselves. And finally, the media brouhaha over the "Mommy Track" reaffirmed that businesses could not or would not budge much to accommodate the care of children. Together, and over time, these frameworks produced a prevailing common sense that only you, the individual mother, are responsible for your child's welfare: The buck stops with you, period, and you'd better be a superstar.

Of course there has been a revolution in fatherhood over the past thirty years, and millions of men today tend to the details of child rearing in ways their own fathers rarely did. Feminism prompted women to insist that men change diapers and pack school lunches, but it also gave men permission to become more involved with their kids in ways they have found to be deeply satisfying. And between images of cuddly, New Age dads with babies asleep on their chests (think old Folger's ads), movies about hunky men and a baby (or clueless ones who shrink the kids), and sensational news stories about "deadbeat dads" and men who beat up their sons' hockey coaches, fathers too have been subject to a media "dad patrol." But it pales in comparison to the new momism. After all, a dad who knows the name of his kids' pediatrician and reads them stories at night is still regarded as a saint; a mother who doesn't is a sinner.

Once you identify it, you see the new momism everywhere. The recent spate of magazines for "parents" (i.e., mothers) bombard the anxiety-induced mothers of America with reassurances that they can (after a $100,000 raise and a personality transplant) produce bright, motivated, focused, fun-loving, sensitive, cooperative, confident, contented kids just like the clean, obedient ones on the cover. The frenzied hypernatalism of the women's magazines alone (and that includes *People*, *Us*, and *InStyle*), with their endless parade of perfect, "sexy" celebrity moms who've had babies, adopted babies, been to sperm banks, frozen their eggs for future use, hatched the frozen eggs, had more babies, or adopted a small Tibetan village, all to satisfy their "baby lust," is enough to make you want to get your tubes tied. (These profiles always insist that celebs all love being "moms" much, much more than they do their work, let alone being rich and famous, and that they'd spend every second with their kids if they didn't have that pesky blockbuster movie to finish.) Women without children, wherever they look, are besieged by ridiculously romantic images that insist that having children is the most joyous, fulfilling experience in the galaxy, and if they don't have a small drooling creature who likes to stick forks in electrical outlets, they are leading bankrupt, empty lives. Images of ideal moms and their miracle babies are everywhere, like leeches in the Amazon, impossible to dislodge and sucking us dry.

There is also the ceaseless outpouring of books on toilet training, separating one sibling's fist from another sibling's eye socket, expressing breast milk while reading a legal brief, helping preschoolers to "own" their feelings, getting Joshua to do his homework, and raising teenage boys so they become Sensitive New Age Guys instead of rooftop snipers or Chippendale dancers. Over eight hundred books on motherhood were published between 1970 and 2000; only twenty-seven of these came out between 1970 and 1980, so the real avalanche happened in the past twenty years.[12] We've learned about the perils of "the hurried child" and "hyperparenting," in which we schedule our kids with so many enriching activities that they make the secretary of state look like a couch spud. But the unhurried child probably plays too much Nintendo and is out in the garage building pipe bombs, so you can't underschedule them either.

Then there's the Martha Stewartization of America, in which we are meant to sculpt the carrots we put in our kids' lunches into the shape of peonies and build funhouses for them in the backyard; this has raised the bar to even more ridiculous levels than during the June Cleaver era. Most women know that there was a massive public relations campaign during World War II to get women into the workforce, and then one right after the war to get them to go back to the kitchen. But we haven't fully focused on the fact that another, more subtle, sometimes unintentional, more long-term propaganda campaign began in the 1980s to redomesticate the women of America through motherhood.[13] Why aren't all the mothers of America leaning out their windows yelling "I'm mad as hell and I'm not going to take it anymore"?

So the real question is how did the new momism—especially in the wake of the women's movement—become part of our national common sense? Why have mothers—who have entered the workforce in droves at exactly the same time that intensive mothering conquered notions of parenting—bought into it? Are there millions of us who conform to the ideals of the new momism on the outside, while also harboring powerful desires for rebellion that simply can't be satisfied by a ten-minute aromatherapy soak in the bathtub?

There are several reasons why the new momism—talk about the wrong idea for the wrong time—triumphed when it did. Baby boom women who, in the 1970s, sought to enter schools and jobs previously reserved for men knew they couldn't be just as good as the guys—they had to be better, in part to dispel the myths that women were too stupid, irrational, hysterical, weak, flighty, or unpredictable during "that time of the month" to manage a business, report the news, wear a stethoscope, or sell real estate. Being an overachiever simply went with the terrain of breaking down barriers, so it wouldn't be surprising to find these women bringing that same determination to motherhood. And some of us did get smacked around as kids, or had parents who crushed our confidence, and we did want to do a better job than that. One brick in the wall of the new momism.

Many women, who had started working in the 1970s and postponed having children, decided in the 1980s to have kids. Thus, this was a totally excellent time for the federal government to insist that it was way too expensive to support any programs for families and children (like maternity leave or subsidized, high-quality day care or even decent public schools) because then the U.S. couldn't afford that $320 billion appropriation to the Pentagon, which included money for those $1600 coffee makers and $600 toilet seats the military needed so badly in 1984.[14] (Imagine where we'd be today if the government had launched the equivalent of the G.I. bill for mothers in the 1980s!) Parents of baby boomers had seen money flow into America's schools because of the Sputnik scare that the Russkies were way ahead of the U.S. in science and technology; thus the sudden need to reacquaint American kids with a slide rule. Parents in the 1980s saw public schools hemorrhaging money. So the very institutions our mothers had been able to count on now needed massive CPR, while the prospect of any new ones was, we were told, out of the question. Guess who had to take up the slack? Another brick in the wall of the new momism.

The right wing of the Republican party—which controlled the White House from 1980 to 1992, crucial years in the evolution of motherhood—hated the women's movement and believed all women, with the possible exception of Phyllis Schlafly, should remain in the kitchen on their knees polishing their husband's shoes and golf clubs while teaching their kids that Darwin was a very bad man. (Unless the mothers were poor and black—those moms had to get back to work ASAP, because by staying home they were wrecking the country. But more on that later.) We saw, in the 1980s and beyond, the rise of what the historian Ruth Feldstein has called "mother-blaming," attacks on mothers for failing to raise physically and psychologically fit future citizens.[15] See, no one, not even Ronald Reagan, said explicitly to us, "The future and the destiny of the nation are in your hands, oh mothers of America. And you are screwing up." But that's what he meant. Because not only are mothers supposed to reproduce the nation biologically, we're also supposed to regenerate it culturally and morally. Even after the women's movement, mothers were still expected to be the primary socializers of children.[16] Not only were our individual kids' well-being our responsibility, but also the entire fate of the nation supposedly rested on our padded and milk-splotched shoulders. So women's own desires to be good parents, their realization that they now had to make up for collapsing institutions, and all that guilt-tripping about "family values" added many more bricks to the wall.

But we are especially interested in the role that the mass media played, often inadvertently, and often, mind you, in the name of *helping* mothers—in making the new momism a taken-for-granted, natural standard of how women should imagine their lives, conceive of fulfillment, arrange their priorities, and raise their kids. After all, the media have been and are the major dispenser of the ideals and norms surrounding motherhood: Millions of us have gone to the media for nuts-and-bolts child-rearing advice. Many of us, in fact, preferred media advice to the advice our mothers gave us. We didn't want to be like our mothers and many of us didn't want to raise our kids the way they raised us (although it turns out they did a pretty good job in the end).

Thus, beginning in the mid-1970s, working mothers became the most important thing you can become in the United States: a market. And they became a market just as niche marketing was exploding—the rise of cable channels, magazines like *Working Mother, Family Life, Child,* and *Twins,* all supported by advertisements geared specifically to the new, modern mother. Increased emphasis on child safety, from car seats to bicycle helmets, increased concerns about Johnny not being able to read, the recognition that mothers bought cars, watched the news, and maybe didn't want to tune into one TV show after the next about male detectives with a cockatoo or some other dumbass mascot saving hapless women—all contributed to new shows, ad campaigns, magazines, and TV news stories geared to mothers, especially affluent, upscale ones. Because of this sheer increase in output and target marketing, mothers were bombarded as never before by media constructions of the good mother. The good mother bought all this stuff to stimulate, protect, educate, and indulge her kids. She had to assemble it, install it, use it with her child, and protect her child from some of its features. As all this media fare sought to advise mothers, flatter them, warn them and, above all, sell to them, they collaborated in constructing, magnifying, and reinforcing the new momism.

Here's the rub about the new momism. It began to conquer our psyches just as mothers entered the workforce in record numbers, so those of us who work (and those of us who don't) are pulled between two rather powerful and contradictory cultural riptides: Be more doting and self-sacrificing at home than Bambi's mother, yet more achievement-oriented at work than Madeleine Albright.[17] The other set of values that took hold beginning in the 1980s was "free-market ideology": the notion that competition in "the marketplace" (which supposedly had the foresight and wisdom of Buddha) provided the best solutions to all social, political, and economic problems. So on the job we were—and are—supposed to be highly efficient, calculating, tough, judgmental and skeptical, competitive, and willing to do what it takes to promote ourselves, our organization, and beat out the other guys. Many work environments in the 1980s and '90s emphasized increased productivity and piled on more work, kids or no kids, because that's what "the market" demanded. Television shows offered us role models of the kind of tough broads who succeeded in this environment, from the unsmiling, take-no-prisoners DA Joyce Davenport on *Hill Street Blues* to Judge Judy and the no-nonsense police lieutenant Anita Van Buren on *Law & Order*. So the competitive go-getter at work had to walk through the door at the end of the day and, poof, turn into Carol Brady: selfless doormat at home. No wonder some of us feel like Sybil when we get home: We have to move between these riptides on a daily basis. And, in fact, many of us want to be both women: successful at work, successful as mothers.

Now, here's the real beauty of this contorting contradiction. Both working mothers *and* stay-at-home mothers get to be failures. The ethos of intensive mothering has lower status in our culture ("stay-at-home mothers are boring"), but occupies a higher moral ground ("working mothers are neglectful").[18] So, welcome to the latest media catfight: the supposed war between working mothers and stay-at-home mothers. Why analyze all the ways in which our country has failed to support families while inflating the work ethic to the size of the *Hindenburg* when you can, instead, project this paradox onto what the media have come to call, incessantly, "the mommy wars"[19] The "mommy wars" puts mothers into two, mutually exclusive categories—working mother versus stay-at-home mother, and never the twain shall meet. It goes without saying that they allegedly hate each other's guts. In real life, millions of mothers move between these two categories, have been one and then the other at various different times, creating a mosaic of work and child-rearing practices that bears no resemblance to the supposed ironclad roles suggested by the "mommy wars."[19] Not only does this media catfight pit mother against mother, but it suggests that all women be reduced to their one role—mother—or get cut out of the picture entirely.

At the same time that the new momism conquered the media outlets of

America, we also saw mothers who talked back. *Maude,* Ann Romano on *One Day at a Time,* Erma Bombeck, Peg Bundy, *Roseanne,* Brett Butler, Marge Simpson, and the mothers in *Malcolm in the Middle* and *Everybody Loves Raymond* have all given the new momism a big Bronx cheer. They have represented rebellious mothering: the notion that you can still love your kids and be a good mother without teaching them Origami, explaining factor analysis to them during bath time, playing softball with them at six A.M., or making sure they have a funny, loving note in their lunch box each and every day. Since 1970, because of money and politics, the new momism has conquered much of the media, and thus our own self-esteem. But it has not done so uncontested. The same media that sell and profit from the new momism have also given us permission—even encouraged us—to resist it. However, it is important to note that much of this rebellion has occurred in TV sitcoms which, with a few exceptions, offer primarily short-term catharsis, a brief respite from the norms in dramatic programming, the news, and advice columns that bully us so effectively.

Okay, so men and kids—well, some kids, anyway—benefit from the new momism. But what do mothers get out of it besides eyebags, exhaustion, and guilt? Well, because of how women have been socialized, a lot of us think the competitive, everything-has-a-price mindset of the workaday world is crass, impersonal, and callous. Many of us, then, want our homes to embody a rejection of a world that celebrates money and screwing over other people, in part because we know all too well how that world has screwed over women and children. So, it's not surprising that many women are seduced by ads, catalogs, and TV shows that urge us to turn our homes into softly lit, plug-in scented, flower-filled havens in a heartless world. The new momism keeps us down by demanding so much of us, but keeps us morally superior because through it we defy a society so driven by greed and self-interest.[20] Plus, many of us, having left a child home in the care of a man to return to find the kid eating Slim Jims and marshmallows for dinner, and the floor covered with spilled Coke, dirty socks, and guinea pig excrement, have concluded that men can't do it, so we shut them out and do it ourselves. We resent men for not helping us more, but also bask in the smugness that at least here, in this one role, we can claim superiority. So through the new momism women acquiesce to *and* resist good, old-fashioned sexist notions of how the world should work.

There are already bleacher loads of very good, even excellent books attacking the unattainable ideals surrounding motherhood, and we will rely on many of them here.[21] But while many of these books expose and rail against the cultural myths mothers have had to combat—putting your child in day care proves you are a selfish, careerist bitch, if you don't bond with your baby immediately after birth you'll have Ted Kaczynski on your hands, and so forth—they have not examined in detail, and over time, the enormous role the mass media have played in promulgating and exaggerating these myths.

We want to fill this gap, to examine how the images of motherhood in TV shows, movies, advertising, women's magazines, and the news have evolved since 1970, raising the bar, year by year, of the standards of good motherhood while singling out and condemning those we were supposed to see as dreadful mothers. We want to explore the struggle in the media between intensive mothering and rebellious mothering, and consider how it has helped make mothers today who we are. This imagery may have been fleeting, and it may have been banal, but it told common, interlocking stories that, over the years, evolved into a new "common sense" we were all supposed to share about motherhood, good and bad. This imagery has also provided us with a shared cultural history of becoming mothers in the United States, yet we may not appreciate the extent to which this common history has shaped our identities, our sense of success and failure as mothers, and the extent to which it ties us together through mutual collective memories. So instead of dismissing these media images as short-lived (and sometimes even stupid), let's review how they have laid down a thick, sedimented layer of guilt, fear, and anxiety as well as an increasingly powerful urge to talk back.

We've chosen to start roughly around 1970, for several reasons. This was when the women's movement burst onto the political scene as one of the biggest news stories of the year, and one of the central tenets of the movement was to critique how existing models of marriage and motherhood trapped millions of women in lives they found frustrating and in economic arrangements that were deeply unfair. At the same time, the soaring divorce rate was producing an unprecedented number of single-parent households, 90 percent of them headed by women. The "stagflation" of the 1970s—roaring inflation combined with rising unemployment (which Gerald Ford cleverly sought to combat by distributing "Whip Inflation Now" buttons to the citizenry)—also propelled millions of mothers into the workforce. In 1970, only 28.5 percent of children under age six had a mother working outside the home. By 1988, the figure had jumped to 51.5 percent. Nor was the idea of having children then as surrounded by the occluding, spun-sugar romance that encases it today. In a widely reported survey done by Ann Landers of fifty thousand parents in the mid-1970s, a rather mammoth 70 percent said that if given the choice to do it again, they would not have children; it wasn't worth it.[22]

In the 1970s and later, it was clear that the media would have to respond to this crisis in the 1950s common sense about motherhood. After all, some women (and men) welcomed these changes while others hated them. In fact, in the 1970s various TV shows, women's magazines, and movies incorporated the feminist challenge to motherhood in their wise-cracking mothers and tales of self-discovery. Yet by the 1980s, the media began to backtrack. The result? An ever-expanding, thundering media avalanche of anxiety about the state of motherhood in America.

To give you an idea, let's look briefly at the news, which has played a much more central role in policing the boundaries of motherhood than you might think. Few books have reviewed the enormously influential role the nightly news played in shaping national norms about motherhood—revisiting Good Housekeeping or The Cosby Show makes sense, but the news? Yet it is in the news that we can track especially well the trajectory of the new momism. Most people don't get (or want) to look at old news footage, but we looked at thirty years of stories relating to motherhood. In the 1970s, with the exception of various welfare reform proposals, there was almost nothing in the network news about motherhood, working mothers, or childcare. And when you go back and watch news footage from 1972, for example, all you see is John Chancellor at NBC in black and white reading the news with no illustrating graphics, or Walter Cronkite sitting in front of a map of the world that one of the Rugrats could have drawn—that's it.

But by the 1980s, the explosion in the number of working mothers, the desperate need for day care, sci-fi level reproductive technologies, the discovery of how widespread child abuse was—all this was newsworthy. At the same time, the network news shows were becoming more flashy and sensationalistic in their efforts to compete with tabloid TV offerings like A Current Affair and America's Most Wanted.[23] NBC, for example, introduced a story about day care centers in 1984 with a beat-up Raggedy Ann doll lying limp next to a chair with the huge words Child Abuse scrawled next to her in what appeared to be Charles Manson's handwriting. So stories that were titillating, that could be really tarted up, that were about children and sex, or children and violence—well, they just got more coverage than why Senator Rope-a-Dope refused to vote for decent day care. From the McMartin day-care scandal and missing children to Susan Smith and murdering nannies, the barrage of kids-in-jeopardy, "innocence corrupted" stories made mothers feel they had to guard their kids with the same intensity as the secret service guys watching POTUS.

Having discovered in the summer of 2001 that one missing Congressional intern and some shark attacks could fill the twenty-four-hour news hole, the cable channels the following year gave us the summer of abducted girls (rather than, say, in-depth probes of widespread corporate wrongdoing that robbed millions of people of millions of dollars). Even though FBI figures showed a *decline* in missing persons and child abductions, such stories were, as *Newsweek*'s Jonathan Alter put it, "inexpensive" and got "boffo ratings." [24] It goes without saying that such crimes are horrific and, understandably, bereft parents wanted to use the media to help locate their kidnapped children. But the incessant coverage of the abductions of Samantha Runnion (whose mother, the media repeatedly reminded us, was at work), Elizabeth Smart, Tamara Brooks, Jacqueline Marris, and Danielle van Dam terrified parents across the country all out of proportion to the risks their children faced. (To put things in perspective, in a country of nearly three hundred million people, estimates were that only 115 children were taken by strangers in ways that were dangerous to the child.) [25] Unlike mothers in the 1950s, then, we were never to let our children out of our sight at carnivals, shopping malls, or playgrounds, and it was up to us to protect them from failing schools, environmental pollution, molesters, drugs, priests, Alar, the Internet, amusement parks, air bags, jungle gyms, *South Park*, trampolines, rottweilers, gangs, and HBO specials about lap dancers and masturbation clubs. It's a wonder any women had children and, once they did, ever let them out of their sight.

Then there were the magazines. Beginning in the 1980s, and exploding with a vengeance in the '90s, celebrity journalism brought us a feature that spread like head lice through the women's magazines, as well as the more recent celebrity and "lifestyle" glossies: the celebrity mom profile. If any media form has played a central role in convincing young women without children that having a baby is akin to ascending to heaven and seeing God, it is the celebrity mom profile. "Happiness is having a baby," gushed Marie Osmond on a 1983 cover of *Good Housekeeping,* and Linda Evans, at the peak of her success in *Dynasty,* added in *Ladies Home Journal,* "All I want is a husband and baby." Barbara Mandrell proclaimed, "Now my children come first," Valerie Harper confessed, "I finally have a child to love," and Cybill Shepard announced, "I'll have a fourth baby or adopt!" [26] Assaulting us from every supermarket checkout line and doctor's and dentist's offices, celebrity moms like Kathie Lee Gifford, Joan Lunden, Jaclyn Smith, Kirstie Alley, and Christie Brinkley (to name just a few) beamed from the comfy serenity and perfection of their lives as they gave multiple interviews about their "miracle babies," how much they loved their kids, what an unadulterated joy motherhood was, and about all the things they did with their kids to ensure they would be perfectly normal Nobel laureates by the age of twelve. By the summer of 1999, one of *People*'s biggest summer stories, featuring the huge cover headlines "BOY, OH BOY," was the birth of Cindy Crawford's baby. The following summer, under the headline "PREGNANT AT LAST!" we had the pleasure of reading about the sperm motility rate of Celine Dion's husband, information that some of us, at least, could have lived without. In 2003 Angelina Jolie claimed that her adopted baby "saved my life." The media message was that celebrity moms work on the set for twelve hours a day, yet somehow manage to do somersaults with their kids in the park, read to them every day, take them out for ice cream whenever they wanted, get up with them at 3:00 A.M., and, of course, buy them toys, animals, and furniture previously reserved for the offspring of the Shah of Iran. These were supposed to be our new role models.

In the women's magazines in the early 1970s, advertising focused on the mother and her alleged needs—whether for hand cream, hair dye, toilet cleaners, or tampons. [27] Anacin, for example, announced "Mother of 5 Active Children Tells How She Relieves Her Nervous Tension Headaches." (Ditch the kids with a sitter and head for Cozumel with Denzel Washington?) Rarely were mothers and children pictured together as some beatific unit. Ads showed mom spraying the kitchen with Lysol, or smiling in a field of daisies because she'd just used a fabulous Clairol product. When babies were pictured, they appeared alone.

But by 1990, images of children were everywhere, and there was a direct address from the ad to you, the mom, exhorting you to foresee your child's each and every need and desire. No doubt copywriters had read Dr.

Spock's latest pronouncement that mothers had to "anticipate wishes which [the baby] can barely recognize let alone formulate."[28] "Giving your kids a well-balanced meal when you're busy is no fun and games. Until now," proclaimed Banquet, a maker of frozen meals for kids. The gleeful face of a cherubic child beamed out from the ad, which informed us that this new "kid cuisine" featured a special "FunPak" with "puzzles and games that help kids learn about history, space exploration, and all kinds of interesting things."[29] Or you could "Help your children get free 'Learning Tools for Schools' with Scott Paper purchases." By saving the special apple seal from Scott paper products, you, Mom, could help your child's school get microscopes, audio/visual equipment, "and more" to "help your children prepare for the environmental and educational challenges of the future."[30] "Put a song in their hearts!" urged Disney as it hawked its sing-along videos, telling moms to "give your kids the magic of music."[31] Mothers learned that "your child will travel in style" with the new carrying case loaded with Legos, which "makes every trip a journey into imagination."[32]

The new momism, then, was also promoted through the toys and myriad other products sold to us and our kids. Coonskin caps and silly putty were just not going to cut it anymore. The good mother got her kids toys that were educational, that advanced gross and fine motor skills, that gave them the spatial sensibilities and design aptitude of Frank Lloyd Wright, and that taught Johnny how to read James Joyce at age three. God forbid that one second should pass where your child was idle and that you were not doing everything you could to promote his or her emotional, cognitive, imaginative, quantitative, or muscular development. And now mothers and children in ads were pictured in poses that made the Virgin Mary in the pietà seem neglectful. Dazzling, toothy smiles about to burst into full throaty laughter defined the new, characteristic pose of the truly engaged, empathetic mom as she hugged, held, nursed, and played with her kids, always with joyful spontaneity. The classic image was of a new, beaming mother, holding her baby straight up in the air and over her face, and smiling into its little elevated eyes, cheerfully unaware of the rather common infant behavior such an angle might produce: projectile vomiting.

All these media suggest, by their endless celebrating of certain kinds of mothers and maternal behavior and their ceaseless advice, that there are agreed upon norms "out there." So even if you think they're preposterous, you assume you'll be judged harshly by not abiding by them. In this way media portrayals can substitute for and override community norms.[33] You know, when our kids say "all the other kids get to do it" we laugh in their faces. But when the magazines suggest, "All the other moms are doing this, are you?" we see ourselves being judged by the toughest critics out there: other mothers. Mothers who had thrown their TV sets out the window could still absorb all this through talks with friends, relatives, other mothers, and, most aggravating of all, their own kids.

At the heart of the new momism is the insistence that mothers inhabit what we in the academy would call the "subject positions" of our children as often as possible. (In the parlance of childcare experts, this means always climbing inside your child and seeing the world only and entirely through his or her eyes.) We like to think of ourselves as coherent and enduring selves, but we are just as much a composite of many, often contradictory identities or subject positions. The media, which bombard us with TV shows, movies, catalogs, ads, and magazines, serve as a kind of Home Depot of personas to draw from and put on, providing a rapid transit system among many identities.[34] "It's Sunday afternoon—shall I be Cindy Crawford or Joan Crawford?" (The kids pray for the former, and usually get the latter.) Surrounded by media morality tales in which we are meant to identify first with one type of woman and then another, women have gotten used to compartmentalizing ourselves into a host of subject positions, and this is especially true for mothers.

But to crawl inside our kids' own skin and heads, to anticipate and assume *their* subject positions, too, so we will know exactly how they will feel two hours from now and what they will need to make them feel loved, cherished, bolstered, stimulated—how did we get sucked into *this* one? And to do this we have to appreciate each and every more finely grained stage of child development so that we know exactly where in the kid's evolution to place ourselves. Yikes.

And have you noticed how we've all become "moms"? When we were kids, our mothers would say, "I have to call Christine's *mother*," not "I have to call Christine's mom." Our mothers would identify themselves to teachers as so-and-so's *mother*. Today, thanks in part to Dr. Laura ("I am my kid's mom") and Republican pollsters (who coined the term "soccer mom" in 1996), we hear about "the moms" getting together and we have become so-and-so's mom. "Mom"—a term previously used only by children—doesn't have the authority of "mother," because it addresses us from a child's-eye view. It assumes a familiarity, an approachability, to mothers that is, frankly, patronizing; reminiscent, in fact, of the difference between woman and girl. At the same time, "mom" means you're good and nurturing while "mother" means you're not (note the media uses of "celebrity mom" versus "welfare mother" and "stay-at-home mom" versus "working mother"). "Mom" sounds very user-friendly, but the rise of it, too, keeps us in our place, reminding us that we are defined by our relationships to kids, not to adults.

Because the media always serve up heroes and villains, there had to be the terrible mothers, the anti-Madonnas, the hideous counterexamples good mothers were meant to revile. We regret to report that nearly all of these women were African American and were disproportionately featured as failed mothers in news stories about "crack babies," single, teen mothers, and welfare mothers. One of the worst things about the new momism is that it is like a club, where women without kids, or women deemed "bad" mothers, like poor women and welfare mothers, don't belong. It is—with a few exceptions, like Clair Huxtable on *The Cosby Show*—a segregated club.

At the very same time that we witnessed the explosion of white celebrity moms, and the outpouring of advice to and surveillance of middle-class mothers, the welfare mother, trapped in a "cycle of dependency," became ubiquitous in our media landscape, and she came to represent everything wrong with America. She appeared not in the glossy pages of the women's magazines but rather as the subject of news stories about the "crisis" in the American family and the newly declared "war" on welfare mothers. Whatever ailed America—drugs, crime, loss of productivity—was supposedly her fault. She was portrayed as thumbing her nose at intensive mothering. Even worse, she was depicted as bringing her kids into the realm of market values, as putting a price on their heads, by allegedly calculating how much each additional child was worth and then getting pregnant to cash in on them. For middle-class white women in the media, by contrast, their kids were priceless.[35] These media depictions reinforced the divisions between "us" (minivan moms) and "them" (welfare mothers, working-class mothers, teenage mothers), and did so especially along the lines of race.

For example, one of the most common sentences used to characterize the welfare mother was, "Tanya, who has _____ children by _____ different men" (you fill in the blanks). Like zoo animals, their lives were reduced to the numbers of successful impregnations by multiple partners. So it's interesting to note that someone like Christie Brinkley, who has exactly the same reproductive MO, was never described this way. Just imagine reading a comparable sentence in *Redbook*. "Christie B., who has three children by three different men." But she does, you know.

At the same time that middle- and upper-middle-class mothers were urged to pipe Mozart into their wombs when they're pregnant so their kids would come out perfectly tuned, the government told poor mothers to get the hell out of the house and get to work—no more children's aid for them. Mothers like us—with health care, laptops, and Cuisinarts—are supposed to replicate the immaculate bedrooms we see in Pottery Barn Kids catalogs, with their designer sheets and quilts, one toy and one stuffed animal atop a gleaming white dresser, and a white rug on the floor that has never been exposed to the shavings from hamster cages, Magic Markers accidentally dropped with their caps off, or Welch's grape juice. At the same time, we've been encouraged to turn our backs on other mothers who pick their kids' clothes out of other people's trash and sometimes can't buy a can of beans to feed them. How has it come to seem perfectly reasonable—even justified—that one class of mother is supposed to sew her baby's diapers out of Egyptian cotton from that portion of the Nile blessed by the god Osiris while another class of mother can't afford a single baby aspirin?

So who the hell are we, the authors, and what biases might we bring to this tour down motherhood's recent memory lane? Well, we are of a certain vintage—let's just say that if we were bottled in the 1960s, we'd be about to go off right about now. So we have lived through the women's movement and its aftermath, and, between the two of us, have been raising kids from the 1970s to the present. That does not mean we are authorities on child rearing (just ask our kids), but rather that we've seen very different takes on motherhood put forward and fought over, different fads and standards come and go. While neither of our lives comes close to those of Cindy Crawford or Kathie Lee Gifford (no nannies, no personal assistants, no cooks, no trainers, no clothing line named after either one of us, no factories in Paraguay), we are nonetheless privileged women. We live near excellent daycare centers and schools, we have health insurance, and we benefit from the advantages that come automatically with being white and heterosexual. So we have not stood in the shoes of mothers who don't have live-in partners, health insurance, or decent day care, who live in dangerous neighborhoods and substandard housing, who have to work two crappy jobs so they can feed their kids, or who have faced custody battles simply because they're lesbians. We can hardly speak for all, or even most mothers.

We can, however, replay the dominant media imagery that has surrounded most of us, despite our differences, imagery that serves to divide us by age and race and "lifestyle choices," and seeks to tame us all by reinforcing one narrow, homogenized, upper-middle-class, corporately defined image of motherhood. We speak as mothers who succumb to and defy the new momism. And our main point is this: Media imagery that seems so natural, that seems to embody some common sense, while blaming some mothers, or all mothers, for children and a nation gone wrong, needs to have its veneer of supposed truth ripped away by us, mothers. For example, while there have been "zany" sitcoms about families with "two dads" or a working mom living with her mother and a male housekeeper, the white, upper-middle-class, married-with-children nuclear family remains as dominant as a Humvee, barreling through the media and forcing images of other, different, and just as legitimate family arrangements off to the side. We want to ridicule this ideal—or any other household formation—as *the* norm that should bully those who don't conform. After all, as any mother will point out, the correct ratio of adult-to-kid in any household should be at least three-to-one, a standard the nuclear family fails to meet.

The new momism involves more than just impossible ideals about child rearing. It redefines all women, first and foremost, through their relationships to children. Thus, being a citizen, a worker, a governor, an actress, a First Lady, all are supposed to take a backseat to motherhood. (Remember how people questioned whether Hillary Clinton was truly maternal because she had only one child?) By insisting that being a mother—and a perfect one at that—is the most important thing a woman can do, a prerequisite for being thought of as admirable and noble, the new momism insists that if you want to do anything else, you'd better prove first that you're a doting, totally involved mother before proceeding. This is not a requirement for men. The only recourse for women who want careers, or to do anything else besides stay home with the kids all day, is to prove that they can "do it all." As the feminist writer (and pioneer) Letty Cottin Pogrebin put it, "You can go be a CEO, and a good one, but if you're not making a themed birthday party, you're not a good mother," and, thus, you are a failure.[36]

The new momism has evolved over the past few decades, becoming more hostile to mothers who work, and more insistent that all mothers become ever more closely tethered to their kids. The mythology of the new momism now insinuates that, when all is said and done, the enlightened mother chooses to stay home with the kids. Back in the 1950s, mothers stayed home because they had no choice, so the thinking goes (even though by 1955 more mothers were working than ever before). Today, having been to the office, having tried a career, women supposedly have seen the inside of the male working world and found it to be the inferior choice to staying home, especially when their kids' future is at stake. It's not that mothers can't hack it (1950s thinking). It's that progressive mothers refuse to hack it. Inexperienced women thought they knew what they wanted, but they got experience and learned they were wrong. Now mothers have seen the error of their ways, and supposedly seen that the June Cleaver model, if taken as a *choice,* as opposed to a requirement, is the truly modern, fulfilling, forward-thinking version of motherhood.

In the 1960s, women, and especially young women, were surrounded by mixed messages, one set telling them that there was a new day dawning, they were now equal to men and could change the world, the other telling them they were destined to be housewives, were subservient to men, and could never achieve equality. Electrified by the civil rights and antiwar movements and their demands for freedom and participatory democracy, women could no longer stand being pulled in opposite directions, and opted for equality. Of course, the contradictions in our lives did not vanish—in the wake of the women's movement we were supposed to be autonomous, independent, accomplished, yet poreless, slim, nurturing, and deferential to men.[37] In the early twenty-first century, we see a mirror image of the 1960s, but without the proud ending: The same contradictions are there, but now the proposed resolution, like a mist in the culture, is for women to give up their autonomy and find peace and fulfillment in raising children.

In other words, ladies, the new momism seeks to contain and, where possible, eradicate, all of the social changes brought on by feminism. It is backlash in its most refined, pernicious form because it insinuates itself into women's psyches just where we have been rendered most vulnerable: in our love for our kids. The new momism, then, is deeply and powerfully political. The new momism is the result of the combustible intermixing of right-wing attacks on feminism and women, the media's increasingly finely tuned and incessant target marketing of mothers and children, the collapse of governmental institutions—public schools, child welfare programs—that served families in the past (imperfectly, to be sure), and mothers' own, very real desires to do the best job possible raising their kids in a culture that praises mothers in rhetoric and reviles them in public policy.

Plenty of mothers aren't buying this retro version of motherhood, although it works to make them feel very guilty and stressed. They want and need their own paychecks, they want and need adult interaction during the day, they want and need their own independence, and they believe—and rightly so—that women who work outside the home can be and are very good mothers to their kids. Other mothers don't want or need these things for the time being, or ever, and really would rather stay home. The question here is not which path women choose, or which one is "right." The question is why one reactionary, normative ideology, so out of sync with millions of women's lives, seems to be getting the upper hand.

The new momism has become the central, justifying ideology of what has come to be called "postfeminism." Ever since October 1982, when *The New York Times Magazine* featured an article titled "Voices from the Post-Feminist Generation," a term was coined, and the women of America have heard, ceaselessly, that we are, and will be forever more, in a postfeminist age.

What the hell is postfeminism, anyway?[37] You would think it would refer to a time when complete gender equality has been achieved (you know, like we'd already achieved a *feminist* state and now we're "post" that). That hasn't happened, of course, but we (and especially young women) are supposed to think it has. Postfeminism, as a term, suggests that women have made plenty of progress because of feminism, but that feminism is now irrelevant and even undesirable because it supposedly made millions of women unhappy, unfeminine, childless, hairy, lonely, bitter, and prompted them to fill their closets with combat boots and really bad India print skirts. Supposedly women have gotten all they could out of feminism, are now "equal," and so can, by choice, embrace things we used to see as sexist, like a TV show in which some self-satisfied lunk samples the wares of twenty-five women before rejecting twenty-four and keeping the one he likes best, or like the notion that mothers should have primary responsibility for raising the kids. Postfeminism means that you can now work outside the home even in jobs previously restricted to men, go to graduate school, pump iron, and pump your own gas, as long as you remain fashion conscious, slim, nurturing, deferential to men, and become a doting, selfless mother.

According to postfeminism, women now have a choice between feminism and antifeminism and they just naturally and happily choose the latter. And the most powerful way that postfeminism worked to try to redomesticate women was through the new momism. Here's the progression. Feminism won; you can have it all; of course you want children; mothers are better at raising children than fathers; of course your children come first; of course you come last; today's children need constant attention, cultivation, and adoration, or they'll become failures and hate you forever; you don't want to fail at that; it's easier for mothers to abandon their work and their dreams than for fathers; you don't want it all anymore (which is good because you can't have it all); who cares about equality, you're too tired; and whoops—here we are in 1954.

Each of us, of course, has her own individual history as a mother, her own demons and satisfactions, her own failures and goals. But motherhood is, in our culture, emphasized as such an individual achievement, something you and you alone excel at or screw up. So it's easy to forget that motherhood *is* a collective experience. We want to erase the amnesia about motherhood—we *do* have a common history, it does tie us together, and it has made us simultaneously guilt-ridden and ready for an uprising. Let's turn the surveillance cameras away from ourselves and instead turn them on the media that shaped us and that manufactured more of our beliefs and practices than we may appreciate, or want to admit.

Especially troubling about all this media fare is the rise of even more impossible standards of motherhood today than those that tyrannized us in the past. For women in their twenties and thirties, the hypernatalism of the media promotes impossibly idealized expectations about motherhood (and fatherhood!) that may prove depressingly disappointing once junior arrives and starts throwing mashed beets on the wall. Peggy Orenstein reported in her 2000 book *Flux* that by the 1990s, "motherhood supplanted marriage as the source of romantic daydreams" for childless, unmarried women in their twenties and early to mid-thirties. To put it another way, "Motherhood has become increasingly central to women's conception of femininity, far more so than marriage." The women she talked to "believed children would answer basic existential questions of meaning" and would "provide a kind of unconditional love that relationships with men did not." They over-idealized motherhood and bought into the norm of "the Perfect Mother—the woman for whom childbearing supersedes all other identities and satisfactions." [38] A new generation of young women, for whom the feminine mystique is ancient history, and who haven't experienced what it took for women to fight their way out of the kitchen, may be especially seduced by media profiles suggesting that if Reese Witherspoon can marry young and become an A-list actress while raising a three-year-old and expecting another child, then you can "do it all" too. Just as Naomi Wolf, Susan Faludi, and Camryn Manheim sought to get women to say "excuuuse me" to the size-zero ideal, we would like women to just say no to the new momism.

Finally, this book is a call to arms. With so many smart, hardworking, dedicated, tenacious, fed-up women out there, can't we all do a better job of talking back to the media that hector us all the time? As we get assaulted by "15 Ways to Stress Proof Your Child," "Boost Your Kid's Brainpower in Just 25 Minutes," "Discipline Makeover: Better Behavior in 21 Days," and "What It Really Takes to Make Your Baby Smarter," not to mention "The Sex Life You Always Wanted—How to Have it *Now*" (answer: put the kids up for adoption), let's develop, together, some really good comebacks. And let's also take a second look at these "wars" we're supposed to be involved with: the "war" against welfare mothers, the "war" between working versus stay-at-home mothers. While these wars do often benefit one set of mothers over another, what they do best is stage *all* mothers' struggles, in the face of the most pathetic public policies for women and children in the western world, as a catfight. Then the politicians who've failed to give us decent day care or maternity leave can go off and sip their sherry while mothers point fingers at each other. Our collective dilemmas as mothers are always translated into individual issues that each of us has to confront by herself, alone, with zero help. These media frameworks that celebrate the rugged individualism of mothers, then, justify and reinforce public policies (or lack thereof) that make it harder to be a mother in the United States than in any other industrialized society.

As mothers, we appreciate all too well how much time and attention children need and deserve, and how deeply committed we become to our kids. We can be made to cry at the drop of a hat by a Hallmark commercial or a homemade Mother's Day card. We get roped into the new momism because we do feel that our society is not providing our kids with what they need. But the problem with the new momism is that it insists that there is one and only one way the children of America will get what they need: if mom provides it. If dad "pitches in," well, that's just an extra bonus. The government? Forget it.

We fear that, today, we have a new common sense about motherhood that may be as bad, or worse, as the one that chained mothers to their Maytags in 1957. It wasn't always like this. There was a time in the now distant past when there was something called the Women's Liberation Movement. They are the folks who brought you "the personal is political." Enough lies have been told by Pat Robertson, Rush Limbaugh, and others about what feminists said about motherhood and children to fill a Brazilian landfill center. But when we exhume what feminists really hoped to change about motherhood, hopes buried under a slag heap of cultural amnesia and backlash, the rise of the new momism seems like the very last set of norms you would predict would conquer motherhood in America in the early twenty-first century. Let's go back to a time when many women felt free to tell the truth about motherhood—e.g., that at times they felt ambivalent about it because it was so hard and yet so undervalued—and when women sought to redefine how children were raised so that it wasn't only women who pushed strollers, played Uncle Wiggly, or quit their jobs once kids arrived. Of course these women loved their kids. But were they supposed to give up everything for them? Are we?

Anyhow, the next time you read about Sarah Jessica Parker's perfect marriage and motherhood, don't sigh and say, "Oh, I wish that was my life." Instead, say, "Give me a break." (Or, alternatively, "Give me a %$#$% break." Of course, most of you probably already say that.) Because, you know, if we all refuse to be whipsawed between these age-old madonna–whore poles of perfect and failed motherhood, designed to police us all, then we—all of us—get a break. And that, as you shall shortly see, was what feminists were asking for in the first place.

ONE

Revolt Against the MRS

Imagine it's Mother's Day, and you are being taken out to one of those god-awful brunches where you and hundreds of other mothers will be force-fed runny scrambled eggs and flaccid croissants by way of thanking you for the other 364 days, when instead of the brunch you get "Mom, you shrank my sweater in the dryer and I need a new one by tomorrow," or "All the *other* mothers will be at the hockey banquet," or, simply enough, "I hate you. You never listen to me! I wish you weren't my mother!" As you walk toward the restaurant, you notice broadsides posted on the telephone poles all over town. They begin, "Today, one day of the year, America is celebrating Motherhood, in home . . . church . . . restaurant . . . candy shop . . . flower store." Obvious enough. But then the tone changes. "The other 364 days she preserves the apple pie of family life and togetherness, and protects the sanctity of the male ego and profit. She lives through her husband and children." Now things get more radical. "She is sacrificed on the altar of reproduction. . . . she is damned to the dreary world of domesticity by day, and legal rape by night. . . . She is convinced that happiness and her lost identity can be recovered by buying—more and more and more and more."[1]

Or a bunch of women are handing out flyers. They are titled "Notice to All Governments" and then demand "Wages for Housework." (Yes!) They read: "We clean your homes and your factories. We raise the next generation of workers for you. Whatever else we may do, we are the housewives of the world. In return for our work, you have only asked us to work harder." As a result, "we are serving notice to you that we intend to be paid for the work we do. We want wages for every dirty toilet, every painful childbirth, every indecent assault, every cup of coffee, and every smile. And if we don't get what we want, then we will simply refuse to work any longer." The result? "Now you will rot in your own garbage." The broadside ends with "We want it in cash, retroactive and immediately. And we want all of it."[2] *Oooo-weee.* Don't you think this would make Mother's Day a lot more, well, interesting?

The poster described above actually appeared in Cleveland on Mother's Day, 1969, courtesy of The Women's International Conspiracy from Hell (WITCH, founded in 1968 with the express purpose of staging outrageous and often very funny profeminist actions). "Wages for Housework" was a feminist broadside as well, one of many that appeared in the late 1960s and early 1970s denouncing the fact that housewives and mothers were overworked, underpaid, and very much underappreciated.

Once upon a time, and not so very long ago, millions of women across the country, many of them mothers, stood up for themselves, and demanded to know why women, and housewives and mothers in particular, were second-class citizens, consigned to financial dependence on men, relegated to do housework that was necessary, endless, yet looked down upon, and why women were deemed to be the only gender who should give up everything in exchange for raising children. Young women started wondering why they should get married at twenty-one, let alone eighteen, if that meant getting chained to the diaper pail all the sooner. Simply put, motherhood became political.

Welcome to the Women's Liberation Movement, which was, for those involved, lots of hard work, scary, exhilarating, dangerous, exasperating, infuriating, and fun. "Fun?" you ask. "Weren't feminists these grim-faced, humorless, antifamily, karate-chopping ninjas who were bitter because they couldn't get a man?" Well, in fact the problem was that all too many of them *had* gotten a man, married him, had his kids, and then discovered that, as mothers, they were never supposed to have their own money, their own identity, their own aspirations, time to pee, or a brain. And yes, some women indeed became bad-tempered as a result. After all, no anger, no social change. But to see that you had common cause with other women, to fight for your rights, to believe that you could change the world, your very own future, and that of your kids—all this was bracing, invigorating. So we want to unearth from the graveyard of history the brazen, outrageous, passionate things that women dared to say about motherhood and child-rearing in the late 1960s and early 1970s so we can see how far mothers have and have not come since those heady, rebellious days.

As outlandish as the expectations are today surrounding intensive mothering, they are hardly the fault of feminists. Feminists never said, "Hey, great, mothers are working ninety hours a week as it is, let's add a forty-hour-a-week job on top and not ask Dad to do an iota more than he's already doing." Feminists were the ones who tried to make mother-hood less onerous, less lonely, less costly to women. Look at Gloria Steinem's hopes for the future, printed in *U.S. News and World Report* in 1975. She predicted, "Responsibility for children won't be exclusively the woman's anymore, but shared equally by men—and shared by the com-munity, too. That means that work patterns will change for both women and men, and women can enter all fields just as men can." [3] Well, we're not there yet, but if you are a mother and have your own salary, let alone a job you find remotely rewarding, a day care center near you, after-school programs, maternity leave (however stingy), a daughter who gets to play soccer or basketball, a partner who understands that making lunches, finding baby-sitters, and taking the kid out in the stroller are not entirely your responsibility, and if you stay at home and see this as a choice and not an edict, then your life as a mother has been revolutionized by feminism.

Nonetheless, one of the reasons so many women say "I'm not a femi-nist, but . . ." (and then put forward a feminist position), is that in addi-tion to being stereotyped as man-hating Amazons, feminists have also been cast as antifamily and antimotherhood. Since we are feminists and mothers (and married, too, to men we actually like), and in point of fact know lots of unabashedly doting mothers who are also feminists, a ques-tion persists: How, exactly, have these stereotypes been sustained?

Sometime in the 1980s, in what we imagine to be a deep, subterranean grotto filled with stalactites, bats, and guano, a coven of men and women came together with an apparent simple mission: to rewrite the history of the women's movement and distort what feminists said and did. We'll call this group the Committee for Retrograde Antifeminist Propaganda (CRAP). The high ministers of CRAP have included—but have hardly been restricted to—Rush Limbaugh, Dr. Laura, Christina Hoff Sommers, Phyllis Schlafly, Anita Bryant, Pat Robertson, John McLaughlin, and

George Will, to name a few. Because they were always invited to hold forth on political talk shows, or hosted their own (sponsored by GE, or cures for male-pattern baldness, or God), they got to rehearse the CRAP version of history on a regular basis, which is how you turn something that is false into something everyone starts to take for granted as true. The CRAP version of women's history was essential to the promotion of the new momism, because the alleged evils of feminism made the new momism seem all the more reasonable, natural, inevitable, and just plain right. Of course, millions of women see through the CRAP line and would rather leave the planet for a space station than inhabit a world designed by Pat Robertson (who, we remind you, blamed September 11, 2001, on feminists and other evildoers, like gays). But the CRAP line has nonetheless sustained major misconceptions about feminism.

Let's see how successful CRAP was, by administering the patented "Full o' CRAP" quiz. What was the very first thing feminists attacked in the late 1960s and early 1970s? If you answered "motherhood," that is the correct CRAP answer. (If, however, you said "patriarchy, the fact that women made fifty cents to a man's dollar, widespread discrimination against women in education and employment, and the assumption that the only things women's tiny little brains were capable of handling was scraping cradle cap off their kids' scalps," then maybe you were around in 1970 or have read some real history and know what actually happened.) Who did these feminists hate the most? The correct CRAP answer is "stay-at-home moms" followed closely by "children." (Now, don't go saying things like "Wait—I remember Gloria Steinem insisting that housewives were getting ripped off because they did so much invaluable work that was unpaid," because that does not fit into the official CRAP story.) This is the World According to CRAP, a view and a history that CRAP has sought—with considerable success, we might note—to super-glue to what passes for our national "common sense." CRAP put forth two versions of the antifamily feminist man-hater. The first—Limbaugh's feminazi—is the never-married, child-loathing battle-ax in steel-toed boots. The second is the overly ambitious careerist who may, indeed, have kids, but neglects them in favor of her work. At the core of both versions is their alleged hatred of kids and of "real" mothers.

Let's just briefly sample a typical CRAP offering. In 1999, CRAP sent forth one of its high ministers, Danielle Crittenden, queen bee of the notoriously antifeminist Independent Women's Forum, with her very own

CRAP history, *What Our Mothers Didn't Tell Us: Why Happiness Eludes the Modern Woman,* to much media fanfare. (Danielle should *never* be confused with the fabulous Ann Crittenden, whose 2001 book *The Price of Motherhood* is must reading for every parent, male or female, in the country, and for anyone who has a say in policies affecting parents and children.) The book is a primer on the importance of the new momism. The "us" in Danielle's title refers to twenty- and thirty-something women, and "our mothers" refers to women who in the 1960s and 1970s got "taken in" by feminism. Even though these fem-bots excoriated motherhood, they decided to have children anyway. ("Why?" remains one of the innumerable mysteries of the book.)

According to Crittenden, young women today are deeply unhappy and confused because they ignored the siren song of the new momism and instead followed the really bad advice of their feminist mothers, who allegedly told their girls to forget marriage and motherhood. Instead, feminist mothers supposedly insisted that happiness only comes to those who climb the corporate ladder by impaling men's balls on their Ferragamo heels. (We are both card-carrying members of the feminist axis of evil, and we know of no mothers of twenty- and thirty-something daughters who have said, "Honey, I definitely do not want grandchildren. I want you to get that promotion and work seventy hours a week instead of sixty.") Having heeded their feminist mothers' advice, these loser young women have "postponed marriage and childbirth to pursue their careers only to find themselves at thirty-five still single and baby-crazy, with no husband in sight." [4] (No mention of the fact that once you remove the 10 percent of guys who are gay, and the other 30 percent who are snorting wasabi till they puke because they saw it on *Jackass,* the pickings can be slim.)

How did Crittenden determine that most women in America are miserable because they have failed to embrace the new momism? Instead of talking to actual, real women, she scanned the previous thirty years of women's magazines like *Cosmo* and *Glamour,* and concluded that ". . . my contemporaries are even more miserable and insecure, more thwarted and obsessed with men, than the most depressed, Valium-popping, suburban reader of the 1950s." Not only that, but "the unhappiness expressed in the magazines' pages [is] the inevitable outcome of certain feminist beliefs." [5] If she checked out a less glitzy source, *Statistical Abstract of the United States,* she would have to confront the fact that 80 percent of women between the ages of thirty and thirty-four in the 1990s had married at least once, and that the figure rises to 86.5 percent for women aged thirty-five to thirty-nine. True, some of these women divorce and don't remarry immediately, but the specter of an entire generation of women with "no husband in sight" is not borne out by what scholars refer to as "numbers." (This is hardly statistically valid, but none of the college women we meet in our classes *ever* want to go back to 1957. It, like, scares them.)

So let's get back to the actual feminists, not those of the CRAP imagination, and remind ourselves why they might have, for example, handed out leaflets at the New York City Marriage License Bureau that asked, "Do You Know That, According to the United Nations, Marriage is a 'Slavery-Like Practice'"?[6] To review briefly, in the late 1960s, men got paid more than women (usually double) for doing the exact same job. Women could get credit cards in their husband's names but not their own, and many divorced, single, and separated women could not get cards at all. Women could not get mortgages on their own and if a couple applied for a mortgage, only the husband's income was considered. Women faced widespread and consistent discrimination in education, scholarship awards, and on the job. In most states the collective property of a marriage was legally the husband's, since the wife had allegedly not contributed to acquiring it. Women were largely kept out of a whole host of jobs—doctor, college professor, bus driver, business manager—that women today take for granted. They were knocked out in the delivery room, birth control options were limited, and abortion was illegal. Once women got pregnant they were either fired from their jobs or expected to quit. If they were women of color, it was worse on all fronts—work, education, health care. (And talk about slim pickings. African American men were being sent to prison and cut out of jobs by the millions.)

Most women today, having seen reruns of *The Brady Bunch* and *Father Knows Best,* and also having heard of Betty Friedan's *The Feminine Mystique,* the bestseller that attacked women's confinement to the home, are all too familiar with the idealized yet suffocating media images of happy, devoted housewives. In fact, most of us have learned to laugh at them, vacuuming in their stockings and heels, clueless about balancing a checkbook, asking dogs directions to the neighbor's. But we should not permit our ability to distance ourselves from these images to erase the fact that all women—and we mean *all* women—were, in the 1950s and '60s, supposed to internalize this ideal, to live it and believe it.

Friedan's pathbreaking book identified one of the most important things feminists would denounce in the 1970s: the subject position of the happy housewife. Today we acknowledge that women inhabit many identities throughout the day, and they can be in conflict with each other, so we are constantly negotiating among them. But what the feminine mystique exposed was that all women, each and every one of them, were supposed to inhabit one and only one seamless subject position: that of the selfless, never complaining, always happy wife and mother who cheerfully eradicated whatever other identities she might have had and instead put her husband, her children, and the cleanliness of her house first. Once you grew up, you were supposed to encase yourself in this subject position as if it were a wetsuit, and never take it off. This asphyxiating and disciplining subject position might best be called Moms "R" Us, or MRS, the wife/mother, made familiar to all of us in the tele-person of June Cleaver and Donna Reed. It is important that we remind ourselves of the tyranny of the role of the MRS, because it was what feminists attacked as utterly oppressive, and because, under the guise of the new momism, it has risen, phoenixlike, and burrowed its way once again into the media and into the hearts and minds of millions of mothers.

According to the feminine mystique, an MRS didn't work outside the home, she loved caring for all children because she had a wired-in maternal instinct, she was confused by and thus uninterested in current events, she loved to polish chair legs and darn socks, she didn't understand the difference between drive and reverse, and she lived to serve men because they were superior. The MRS also had to appreciate the importance of Buying and Having Things; so the MRS didn't just think about her kids and husband, she was to think about them in relation to consumer goods. Inside the brain of the MRS, according to this gender ideology, you would *not* find any thoughts about the meaning of life, world peace, finding a cure for polio, let alone feelings of resentment, anxiety, depression, boredom, envy, frustration, or anger at a husband who might, on occasion, spend half his salary on beer for the guys and a "friend" named Lola. This enforced masquerade of the MRS was meant to be so consuming that, just like Yul Brynner in *The King and I,* you could never get out of character, not till you died.

That was the ideology, anyway. In "real life," by 1955, there were more women with jobs than at any point in the nation's previous history, and an increasing number of these were women with young children. By 1960, 40 percent of women were in the work force. Many of these were white middle-class women, and almost half were mothers of school-age children. One out of five had children under the age of six.[7] The ranks of professional women grew by more than 40 percent during the 1950s, faster than any other category except clerical work.[8] The figures were even higher for African American women. Yet everywhere these women looked in the media, the only self they were meant to inhabit, the only one even acknowledged, was the white MRS. By naming the "problem that has no name," Friedan opened the floodgates to what would soon become a tsunami of increasingly focused resentment and anger, namely, the women's movement that began in earnest in the late 1960s. Women didn't just attack the practices and results of discrimination. Until they also named the subject position of the MRS, and the expectations around it, as despotic, women themselves would not be able to see what else might be possible. Women didn't just need more equitable treatment. They needed the scales to fall off their eyes. Enter consciousness raising, one of the most important innovations of the women's movement.

Recently a student of ours, not known for his historical acuity, began his term paper with the following claim: "Sometime around 1968, a lot of things were happening." The kid did have a gift for understatement. Lyndon Johnson's announcement that he would not seek reelection, Martin Luther King Jr., killed, Robert Kennedy killed, police riots at the Chicago convention, escalation of the Vietnam War, feminist demonstrations at the Miss America pageant, indeed added up to "a lot of things . . . happening." Few were more revolutionary than feminism. Previously forbidden questions now proliferated with a vengeance. Why were men automatically the "head" of the household, on everything from credit applications to the forms used by the U.S. Census? Why should housework and childcare be women's exclusive responsibility? Did having a uterus really mean you loved scrubbing toilet bowls, and having a scrotum meant you couldn't even see dirt? Why should women have to take their husband's names when they got married, thereby symbolically eradicating their previous identity? Why should men be the only wage-earners in a family, with the women utterly dependent on him for everything, having no money of her own? Since housewives put in something like ninety-hour work weeks, shouldn't they get some kind of compensation?[9] Feminists offered answers that today seem, by turns, fantastical, utopian, defiant, and right on.

The mass media's condescending treatment of the women's movement has been well documented, so no need to replay all the moronic commentary by Frank Reynolds on ABC and even Uncle Walter on CBS.[10] Howard K. Smith on ABC news—just to pull one edifying example out of the archive—denounced feminism on the air because it might bring an end to the miniskirt, "the biggest advance in urban beautification since Central Park was created in Manhattan." [11] *Time* complained—erroneously—that the movement "has not produced much humor" and noted that Kate Millet didn't wash her hair enough. You get the idea. And despite the fact that a host of feminist activists, including Betty Friedan, were wives and mothers, the media singled out as "leaders" those—Kate Millet, Germaine Greer, and especially the telegenic Gloria Steinem—who were either unmarried, childless, or both. So even with the movement's emphasis on a host of issues affecting mothers and housewives, the dominant image of the liberated woman was "independent, unmarried and . . . childless." [12]

Having said that, what is remarkable is how much of the feminist critique of traditional family and marriage arrangements quickly migrated from the smokin' mimeograph machines of women's groups to the pages of *Time, Glamour, Redbook,* and even *The Saturday Evening Post,* albeit often in watered-down form. Feminist attacks on Dr. Spock, on the enforced primacy of children in women's lives, and on the inequities of housework (why did Mr. Clean only accost mom when that was dad's egg yolk annealed to the stove?) were, at the time, close to scandalous; thus they were newsworthy. And millions of women—and even some men—formed a ready, eager audience. Because the women's movement did not occur in a vacuum, but in fact drew oxygen from the civil rights movement, the antiwar movement, and the counterculture, when challenging the "accepted" way of doing things was everywhere, many people, and even the media—especially women's magazines—were receptive to quite revolutionary challenges to an institution even as "sacred" as the family. And while studies show that, in the early twenty-first century, men are not, indeed, doing half the housework or half the childcare, there has been a revolution in fatherhood, launched by feminism.

To look at the documents generated during the height of the women's movement is, especially if you were alive back then, like waking up from a coma and remembering what made the women's movement so exhilarating and made so many women feel, well, so *alive.* Given the sexist dreck in the mainstream media, feminists felt they needed to produce their own alternative media to express their common outrage and, in fact, to help women see that they were part of a slightly different, but quite large, imagined community: that of fuming, livid women who had simply had enough. Highly recommended bedtime reading, for example, is *Dear Sisters: Dispatches from the Women's Liberation Movement.* Curl up with it after your child has told you at 9:00 P.M. that he volunteered to bring four dozen blueberry muffins to school the next morning and you have, for the seventeen billionth time, washed your husband's stubble-studded shaving cream drips out of the sink because, well, he just doesn't *see* them. Behold, for example, a "Mother's Day Incantation" offered by WITCH.

> *Your family wants to thank you*
> *For your martyrdom.*
> *After all, without you*
> *No real work would get done.*
>
> *While Hubby challenges the world*
> *His wonders to perform*
> *You cook his meals, clean his home*
> *And keep his bedside warm.*
>
> *Your children are your challenge,*
> *In them your dreams are sown.*
> *You've given up your own life*
> *And live for them alone.*
>
> *Now look upon your daughter*
> *Will she too be enslaved*
> *To a man, a home, a family*
> *Or can she still be saved?*
>
> *This is your real challenge—*
> *Renounce your martyrdom!*
> *Become a liberated mother*
> *A woman, not a "mom."* [13]

In "Women of the World Unite—We Have Nothing to Lose But Our Men!," the feminists Carol Hanish and Elizabeth Sutherland admitted, "Yeah, flirting is fun." Then they added, "A man opens a door for me, I thank him, he smiles—and electricity ripples through us both. A year later

I'm flushing out a diaper and he's opening other doors."[14] Many women back then hooted in delight over stuff like this. CRAP would like women today to think that the women's movement was some dreary, humorless, forced march of angry women with hairy legs and cold hearts. What they don't want women to remember, and want younger women in particular not to know, was that exposing patriarchy was, while certainly danger-ous, also—let's face it—a blast.

So what did women start to propose as alternatives to the MRS that altered the existing common sense about marriage and motherhood? There were two broad challenges to motherhood that swirled through the culture in the 1970s. The first was that parenthood and marriage had to be reformed and made much more equal, for the good of everyone. These ideas blew into the mainstream media with the ease of dandelion fluffs. The second was that motherhood had become such a prison for women that they had to break out and never go back to business as usual. These ideas were more radical, and while they were not, in the end, widely embraced, they did prompt millions of women to postpone having chil-dren until they felt they had at least begun to crawl out of the hole of inequality.

As underground critiques, position papers, poems, and broadsides cir-culated around the country, the Manhattan-based Women's Liberation Movement decided to strike at the heart of the media machine that gained its profits from the subject position of the MRS, *Ladies' Home Journal*. In what became one of the most famous actions of the early movement, several hundred feminists walked into the offices of the *Journal* on March 18, 1970, to make some suggestions for changes in it and all women's magazines. During what ended up being an eleven-hour sit-in, the women asserted that since *LHJ* was a magazine for wives and mothers, the maga-zine should actually take motherhood seriously and establish an on-site childcare center for its employees with preschool children. They suggested to the magazine's less-than-amused editor, John Mack Carter, that the magazine, since it was supposedly *for* women, be run entirely *by* women, and that "the magazine seek out nonwhite women for its staff in propor-tion to the population." In response to these and other demands (like a minimum wage and more worker participation in editorial decisions), Carter, who had been bristling under his necktie for pretty much the entire eleven hours, said he'd give the women an eight-page insert in the August issue of the magazine.

In between articles titled "How Good Is Your Marriage?," "The Midi—And How to Wear It," and "The Beauty Guide to Eyeglasses," and printed on crappier, less glossy paper, came ideas and sentiments no doubt quite new to many *Journal* readers.[15] One sidebar was titled "Housewives' Bill of Rights" and demanded (on behalf of the housewives feminists supposedly hated) paid maternity leave, paid vacations, free twenty-four-hour childcare centers, social security benefits for housewives' years of labor, and health insurance (none of which we yet have). One reason these feminists issued such demands was that they themselves actually *were* housewives and mothers, another point we're not supposed to remember. In "Help Wanted: Female. 99.6 Hours a Week. No Pay. Bed and Bored. Must be Good with Children," they wrote "We have no respite. Our only vacation comes when we're totally incapacitated, when we're in the hospital for an operation or having a baby." They made women consider the perpetuation of such inequities in the future. "Our sons could be businessmen, welders or astronauts, but our daughters will be housewives, the only workers who labor merely for bed and board." Adding insult to injury, "we are not only not paid for our work, but are considered less than human because we perform it. . . . We are granted the title of 'just housewife' and, if we try to dignify it a little bit by calling ourselves 'homemakers,' we sense that we are on shaky ground." They noted how all too many husbands came home and smirked, "What have you done all day?" They then added, in language that was a tad jarring next to "Clairol Brings You Happiness!," "We are domestic slaves. It's a fate that awaits us when we are born female."

They were slaves when they gave birth, too. In another *Journal* submission, "Babies Are Born, Not Delivered," a new mother documented the humiliations of going to a maternity ward in 1970. Remember, this was before women and their partners went to birthing classes, before partners were allowed anywhere near the delivery room. The woman described having her pubic hair shaved off (a common procedure back then that was utterly unnecessary for birth), being wheeled into a room all by herself, and being told by a resident exactly when she would actually have the baby. When she felt the baby coming, she was told she was mistaken and that she would have to wait for when the doctor could tend to her. Just when she was about to deliver, an anesthesiologist appeared and gave her a spinal, even though she protested, and the doctor then pulled the baby out with forceps. "Women are, as a group, capable of effecting change that would make the system responsive to us rather than continuing as victims of the system. But until the time comes when we do gain control over our bodies, remember this, my sister: they really couldn't do it without you." At the end of the insert was a guide on how to start a consciousness-raising group, with the addresses of women's groups from around the country.

Throughout all of these pieces, one thing is especially striking: the mode of address to the reader. Unlike the accusatory tone of some of the ads ("There's a good chance our douche cleanses and deodorizes better than yours") or the condescending you-don't-know-anything tone of the advice columns ("How to Say No to a Child Without Guilt"), all of which involved an I-you or us-you division between authority figure and dumb supplicant, this mode of address suggested power, collective power. The mode of address, beginning with "Hello to Our Sisters," rested on a collective "we," we who are unappreciated, we who are underpaid, we who have babies and raise them, we who will resist and fight together, we who will smash the MRS, we who will speak truth to power. The constant use of the imperial and empowering "we" throughout the essays made you feel strong as you read them, made you feel other women rising up and that if you wanted to, you could rise up with them. This collective "we" was active, it was fed up, and it exposed gender roles as social constructions that were not "natural" but had been made. This "we" was angry and wasn't gonna take it anymore. This "we" took the ideological straightjacket of the MRS and simply tore it to shreds. And as even this brief review shows, it was a "we" centrally concerned about the economic and cultural discrimination against housewives and mothers.

By 1972, a group of determined feminists had decided that mimeographed position papers, books, and one guest appearance in *Ladies' Home Journal* were not adequate to give expression to women's experiences in a male-dominated world: They needed a monthly magazine. If a young woman today, who had not been alive in 1972 and had simply taken at face value CRAP's version of women's history, discovered an old pile of *Ms.* magazines, she would be taken aback—shocked, probably—at how dedicated the magazine was to improving the lot of housewives, mothers, and children. We both remember turning first to the letters to the editor, where women of all ages and situations flooded the magazine with letters recounting their personal encounters with the daily grind of sexism. The magazine virtually exploded with passion. They described what Jane

O'Reilly famously called, in her instant classic "The Housewife's Moment of Truth," their "click" moments, the precise occasion in which a woman comes to see that her private anxieties, anger, and despair are not personal failings but are understandable responses to the off-the-wall expectations of patriarchy. A "click moment" was that instant when a woman realizes she's being treated like a doormat.[16]

> I thought that most of my clicks were behind me, but tonight, as I cleared the table, I had a new one. I was complimenting myself (since no one else had) on a meal I'd gone to some trouble to prepare. I began to wonder why so many of us wait trembling for "the verdict" at every meal; why my mother and so many others risk antagonizing their families by asking outright if everything is okay.
>
> I decided it's not just neurosis. We really know they're judging even when they don't say so. Housewifing is an occupation in which every single waking act is judged by the persons who mean the most to you in the world. Is the house clean? Is the food good? Are the children well-behaved?
>
> A thousand times a day our contracts come up for renewal. No wonder our nerves are shot.[17]

During its first several years of publication, *Ms.*, that supposed bastion of mother-hating, antifamily propaganda, featured articles in almost every issue dedicated to helping mothers and their kids. Sample articles include "Job Advice for 'Just a Housewife'" (November 1973), "New Help for Mothers Alone" (February 1974), "How the Economy Uses Housewives" (May 1974), "Surviving Widowhood" and "Must We Be Childless to be Free?" (October 1974), a special section called "Kids in the Office, and What-Else-Is-New with Child Care" (March 1975), "How Hospitals Complicate Childbirth" (May 1975), and a special section on mothers and daughters (June 1975). In addition, *Ms.* published "Stories for Free Children" every month that mothers could read to their kids. The magazine devoted its entire May 1973 issue to the topic "Up with Motherhood." Feminist writer Letty Cottin Pogrebin, for example, while acknowledging (but not dismissing) that there were a few feminists who saw children as the bane of women's existence, pointed out that "The rest of us, scores of feminists of every age, race, marital status, and sexual persuasion are talking seriously, thoughtfully, and candidly about motherhood." She insisted that "We care deeply about children whether we have our own or not. We work to improve educational curricula, child-care facilities, health services, and the childbirth experience. We are saying that men are parents, too; that fatherhood need be no less important or time-consuming than motherhood. . . . Truly, feminists are talking about choice: about *making* the decision to become pregnant and *choosing* a motherly role that is right for ourselves and our children." [18]

Feminist proposals to make marriage and child rearing more equitable, whether first appearing in mimeo sheets or *Ms.*, had a powerful impact on the 1950s and '60s versions of intensive mothering. In 1970, Alix Kates Shulman, a wife, mother, and writer who had joined the Women's Liberation Movement in New York, wrote a poignant account of how the initial equality and companionship of her marriage had deteriorated once she had children. "[N]ow I was restricted to the company of two demanding preschoolers and to the four walls of an apartment. It seemed unfair that while my husband's life had changed little when the children were born, domestic life had become the only life I had." His job became even more demanding, requiring late nights and travel out of town. Meanwhile, it was virtually impossible for her to work at home. "I had no time for myself; the children were always *there*."

Neither she nor her husband was happy with the situation, so they did something radical, which received considerable media coverage: They wrote up a marriage agreement, which was widely circulated in feminist circles. Read it and weep. In it they asserted that "each member of the family has an equal right to his/her own time, work, values, and choices. . . . The ability to earn more money is already a privilege which must not be compounded by enabling the larger earner to buy out of his/her duties and put the burden on the one who earns less, or on someone hired from outside." The agreement insisted that domestic jobs be shared fifty-fifty and, get this girls, "If one party works overtime in any domestic job, she/he must be compensated by equal extra work by the other."

The agreement then listed a complete job breakdown, which included, "Waking children; getting their clothes out, making their lunches, seeing they have notes, homework, money, passes, books, etc.," and "Getting babysitters, which sometimes takes an hour of phoning," and even "Calling doctors, checking out symptoms, getting prescriptions filled, remembering to give medicine, taking days off to stay home with sick child; providing special activities." In other words, the agreement acknowledged the physical *and* the emotional/mental work involved in parenting, and valued both. At the end of the article, Shulman noted how much happier she *and* her husband were as a result of the agreement. In the two years after its inception, Shulman wrote three children's books, a biography, and a novel. But listen, too, to what it meant to her husband, who was now actually seeing his children every day. After the agreement had been in effect for four months, "our daughter said one day to my husband, 'You know, Daddy, I used to love Mommy more than you, but now I love you both the same.' "[19]

To the delight of many wives (and the discomfiture of many husbands), the April 28, 1972, issue of *Life* (of all places!) featured a six-page cover story on the marriage agreement. Redbook published it under the editors' title "A Challenge to Every Marriage" and received more than two thousand letters in response, most of them supportive.[20] *U.S. News & World Report* printed a sample contract in 1973.[21] By 1975 *Time* reported that there were then at least fifteen hundred different versions of marriage contracts being used. "Husbands commonly waive their legal right to determine where the couple will live," noted the magazine without a hint of surprise and "agree to do half of the household chores."[22] (There wasn't much coverage of what we assume came to be massive male breach-of-contract violations in that department.) Nonetheless, newsmagazines described fathers learning to cook and doing most of the "routine cleaning, washing and shopping."[23] By 1978, *Glamour*—yes, *Glamour*—featured an article on how to write your own contract.[24] The sociologist Marvin Sussman, who studied the proliferation of marriage contracts in the mid-1970s, predicted that "in the next ten years" they would become so widespread that they would become "the form of marriage law."[25] (Ah, the seventies.) The marriage contract may seem quaint today, but imagine if most men actually signed them—and abided by the fifty-fifty childcare and housework provisions!

Also newsworthy, and presented as an outcome of feminism, was the rise of the househusband. He stayed home, watched the kids, and mopped the floors while his wife worked or went to school. Often these stories served to corroborate feminist critiques of the housewife's situation. "I can't wait to get out of the house and get back to work," one such husband told *Time* in 1974. "I love my son Adam, but I can see how taking care of a kid can drive a woman up the wall." This article also noted that such role reversals often strengthened marriages and a father's ties to his kids.[26] In "When Dad Becomes a 'House-Husband,'" we learned that "This father stayed home to take care of the kids, and the whole family flourished."[27]

Letty Cottin Pogrebin profiled five househusbands, one of whom was, believe it or not, Ted Koppel. He and his wife had four kids, she had moved nearly a dozen times because of his job, and now she wanted to return to law school. So Ted took nine months off and took care of the cleaning, shopping, cooking, and the kids, and reported how it made him reassess the housewife's work. "[O]ne day after I'd finished mopping the kitchen floor, [my wife] came home from school and walked all over it. I started yelling, 'Take off your shoes, you're tracking up my floor!'—a sentence I'd heard her yell a hundred times. A light went off in both our heads. . . . I realized how unfair it is to put the total burden of a house and kids on one person."[28] What often happened was not that the husband suddenly said, "Okay, dear, I'll wash the floor too" (although some did), but that both spousal units agreed that housework was a drag and that they'd both do as little as possible. (These were the notorious "dark years" for Mr. Clean.)

Childcare experts also took it in the chops. Jo Ann Hoit, in her stinging critique of Dr. Spock, noted how he might speak of the concerns of "parents," but when there was a problem it was always the mother's fault, and always her responsibility to fix. Spock's gesture toward suggesting that fathers might have some responsibilities too in raising their kids was this: "I don't mean that the father has to give just as many bottles or change just as many diapers as the mother. But it's fine for him to do these things occasionally. He might make the formula on Sunday." Hot damn! So, noted Hoit sarcastically, while Dad's duty was to hold down an eight-hour-a-day job, "motherhood remains a twenty-four-hour job with no nights or weekends off."[29]

The feminist pronouncement that often shook up men—and many women—the most was the assertion that the labor of housewives was worth a lot of money and they were getting screwed because they were paid nothing and thus building up no credit in Social Security. Gloria Steinem, in her lectures around the country, insisted that despite media stereotypes and misreporting, the movement was not just for working women, "as if that excluded housewives," she chided. She then added with emphasis, "In fact, housewives work harder than anyone." Steinem asserted that the housewife should be paid, and then cited Department of

Labor statistics that put the value of her work somewhere between $8000 to $9000 a year, because that's what it would cost her husband to pay for her services, "not including on and off prostitution," a famous quip that invariably produced nervous titters in the audience. These remarks weren't restricted to college students or women's groups—ABC aired them in January of 1972 on the nightly news, and she repeated them on late-night talk shows where, yes, feminists used to be invited to chat.[30]

Within two years, even the readers of *McCall's* saw a similar analysis. One article suggested that the next time you were at a party, you ask the wives what they thought they were worth "in dollars and cents" to their husbands. Then, ask the husbands the same thing. Despite how "offensive" such a question might be to "middle class sensibilities," the article reminded readers, "Marriage is a bargain in which a woman gives her domestic services in exchange for support by a man" and the entire economic base of marriage was "lopsided and wobbly." Citing a study actually done by economists at the Chase Manhattan Bank, *McCall's* noted that by the time you totted up what it would cost a man to hire a cook, laundress, nursemaid, chauffer, and gardener, he'd be shelling out about ten grand a year (or about $38,000 in 2003). The article then indignantly noted that a wife who devotes seventeen years to cooking, cleaning, and child rearing was not entitled to any Social Security but that nuns were.[31] Even *The Saturday Evening Post*, which was by 1977 a vestigial media organ, a throwback to maybe 1952 (if not 1932), featured an article by Clare Booth Luce, "Equality Begins at Home." Luce, prominent wife of publishing magnate Henry Luce, also argued that marriage was unequal, that in many states women legally had the status of "unpaid servant," that the work of housewives and mothers was now worth about $20,000 a year.[32] But since they weren't getting paid what they were worth—or anything, for that matter—many were now entering the workforce. When a feminist critique of marriage entered the pages of *The Saturday Evening Post*, it was safe to say that a new sensibility was afoot.

Ms. insisted that mothers and their children were political constituents who had the right and the duty to make feminist demands upon their government. "The American Child-Care Disgrace" (May 1973) suggested that there was something quite perverse about a country that poured billions of dollars into nuclear submarines but not a penny into a life raft for children of working mothers. Maureen Orth lambasted Richard Nixon for a nearly overnight abandonment of his commitment, announced in

1969, to "provide all American children an opportunity for healthy and stimulating development during the first five years of life." By 1971, Nixon claimed that there was no demonstrated need for a national child-development program, and worse yet, that such a program was anti-family.[33] It was no wonder then that working mothers were, as *Ms.* put it, ". . . reluctant to admit that they need help and reluctant to demand that some of their tax dollars go toward childcare. As long as the American mother has feelings of guilt and is unable to see childcare as more than a personal problem, the politicians will continue to ignore her and the basic rights of her children."[34] But Nixon aside, this thing called "childcare," unheard of to most women in the mid-1960s, also began to circulate as a crucially important innovation.

Not surprisingly, many women's liberation organizations around the country began fighting for day-care centers in their communities, which included establishing cooperative nurseries, pressuring employers to found on-site centers for working mothers, and lobbying city, state, and federal governments to provide more funding for day care. Some women staged "child-ins:" Together they brought their kids to work to dramatize their need for day care. Day care was not only about helping working mothers. Feminists wanted to help housewives, too, to give them a break from the 24/7 of motherhood. Many feminists also believed, especially given the al-ready proven success of the Head Start program, that quality day care, with its schedule of activities, curriculum, and exposure to preschool teachers and other children, would be for many children a welcome supplement to staying home with mom all the time. They attacked the notion that day care was somehow a "necessary evil," needed for those women who "had to work," instead of a great opportunity for early childhood education.

As Louise Gross and Phyllis Taube Greenleaf put it in "Why Day Care?" (1970), "We would like to assert that day-care centers in which children are raised in groups by men and women could be as important for the liberation of children as it would be for the liberation of women." They envisioned (sigh) centers with sexually integrated staffs who were paid decent salaries and who encouraged boys to play with stuffed ani-mals and dolls if they wanted and girls to play with toy saws and trucks.[35]

Some feminists, of course, went much further than demanding twenty-four-hour day-care centers and compensation for housework. There were radical feminists who insisted that women's reproductive biology was a principal source of their enslavement to men. Here was the charge: It was precisely because women had to bear babies for nine months and then nurse them that they could never ultimately enjoy equality with men. Only when everything—including childbirth—was equal, would women stand a chance. Their attacks on pregnancy, in the context of today's insistence that waddling around for over half a year encased in the equivalent of seven Michelin extra-wides is "sexy" and "energizing," will seem loony, even anti-woman to some. "Does anyone wish to try to hold that the blood-curdling screams that can be heard from delivery rooms are really cries of joy?"[36] asked Ti-Grace Atkinson with typical wryness. "Pregnancy is barbaric," asserted Shulamith Firestone.[37] (She actually got to say that on national television.)

It turns out that there were women who did not think Firestone was off the wall. In 1970 thousands of women found themselves reading Firestone's book *The Dialectic of Sex: The Case for Feminist Revolution*, in which she argued very persuasively that the inferior economic and social condition of women would persist unless they were freed "from the tyranny of their reproductive biology by every means available."[38] How would this be achieved? Firestone proposed that big research and development dollars be invested in the design of artificial wombs, the only way, she insisted, to truly liberate women. In the meantime, mothers should be compensated for their reproductive labor (which may sound nuts to Americans but actually happens in most European Union countries), and men should participate fully in the rearing of children. Firestone argued, audaciously, that children themselves would benefit by being cut loose from a notion of childhood that prolonged their own dependency, especially on parents who would very likely pass their own neuroses onto the vulnerable psyches of their kids. To top it all off, Firestone insisted that the nuclear family must be cast aside in favor of households that foster the liberation of women and children by de-emphasizing "blood ties" and having all the adults raise all the kids. You know, kind of like a kibbutz.

In other words, Firestone's work was filled with ideas that in the United States today would seem bizarre even on *Star Trek*. On the one hand, as we look back at this from the vantage point of the hypernatalist early twenty-first century, Firestone's vision of artificial wombs freeing all women from pregnancy seems really naïve and a denial of the importance of women's bodies. On the other hand, there is no doubt that she was right. If men could have babies too (and could nurse them!), or if all babies were gestated in artificial wombs, there would indeed be the basis for the still deferred revolution in gender roles and sexual equality in the country. Pregnancy is so romanticized in the early twenty-first century that many women may find the idea of an artificial womb chilling. But think about it—the fetus goes in a perfectly nourishing, unstressed, temperature controlled environment and you get to continue jogging, drinking coffee, drinking wine, eating what you want and maintaining your same clothing size while avoiding sciatica, vomiting, varicose veins, bloating that makes your ankles vanish, heartburn, and hemorrhoids the size of Texas. Isn't this just a tad tempting?

To many, especially to young women who, above all, hoped to escape the fate of their own mothers, motherhood seemed to be the ultimate trap. Unable yet to imagine how the mother/child relationship could exist outside the confines of man-dependent domesticity, the initial feminist resistance to motherhood was perfectly understandable. In the 1970s, many women began to defer having children until they were older, and many young feminists wondered whether they should have kids at all. As the writer Ellen Willis put it, many young feminists had decided not to have children, either ever or for the time being, "because we felt that motherhood, under the present conditions, was incompatible with our priorities." She added, "[O]ur system of child-rearing lays on mothers an enormous responsibility that by rights should be shared by fathers and the community at large. Just as many mothers resent this inequitable burden, I resent the fact that I can't have children unless I'm willing to assume it. . . . For me, as for the rebellious mother, the answer is political change." [39]

Not surprisingly, there *were* those who made the case, as Jeffner Allen put it in her quaintly titled essay, "Motherhood: the Annihilation of Women," that motherhood must be "evacuated" as one would evacuate a town in advance of an approaching army. Any concessions to motherhood, she argued, would inevitably put women right back under the thumbs of men. [40] To be sure, arguments like these are not without their difficulties, but they insisted that motherhood—valued in the text of Hallmark cards but no place else, exceedingly costly to women both financially and emotionally, while highly beneficial to men—had to be rejected in its 1950s form. Thus, such arguments, however extreme they might seem today, really did prompt many women, especially young women, to ask whether the price of motherhood was worth it. And it is true that there were feminists who, as a result, felt that having children was tantamount to acknowledging that you had succumbed to the brainwashing of a male-dominated society.

But there were also feminists like Jane Alpert, an unlikely candidate for mother-of-the-year given that she was wanted by the FBI on charges of conspiracy to bomb federal offices. Alpert requested, from her underground hideout, that *Ms.* publish her 1973 article "Mother Right," which argued that the family should be reshaped "according to the perceptions of women." "Mother Right" was closely read and controversial—it drew more reader reaction than any other piece the magazine had published to date. (The February 1974 issue devoted seven full pages to the letters that poured in.)[41] In direct opposition to Firestone, Alpert insisted that motherhood was the source of female power and should be harnessed in service of women's liberation. "[A]s we begin to define ourselves as women, the qualities coming to the fore are the same ones a mother projects in the best kind of nurturing relationship to a child: empathy, intuitiveness, adaptability, awareness of growth as a process rather than as goal-ended, inventiveness, protective feelings toward others, and a capacity to respond emotionally as well as rationally," she argued. Because motherhood "cuts across economic, class, race and sexual preference, a society in which women were powerful by virtue of being mothers would not be divided along any of these lines."[42]

The positive qualities associated with motherhood, then, should not be abandoned or dismissed; rather, they could change the world. Or to put it another way, Alpert argued that the very traits that have been essential to child rearing and housekeeping and that have kept women in their place are actually enormous strengths that give women the power (and the responsibility) to make society more caring and humane. So here was the central question she raised. Should women come to think of themselves as people, not all that dissimilar from men except in how they had been socialized, and thus reject their own socialization as passive, nurturing, and empathic and simply behave more like men and pursue male goals and occupations? Or, conversely, were women, precisely because they could and did bear children, naturally more inclined to be nurturing, pacifistic, empathic, and cooperative and thus should claim these traits as distinctly female and use them to try to change a male world that was too competitive, individualistic, and destructive? (This latter position would come to be called "essentialist.") This debate has hardly been resolved—it still surrounds us and informs debates about gender equity today.

The main point about all these articles, books, and broadsides is this: Far from dismissing motherhood as dull and old-fashioned, something to be cast aside on the road to self-fulfillment, the women's movement engaged the subject of motherhood with both passion and rigor. Feminists simultaneously embraced motherhood and condemned it, and motherhood itself surfaced as an object of real and legitimate ambivalence. Feminists insisted that motherhood actually be given its due, as the work of a fully formed, though highly constrained, individual human. They debated, in all sorts of forums, about the extent to which motherhood gave women a particular moral authority that they should use to assert more political and economic power, or whether motherhood, as currently institutionalized, always kept mothers disempowered, voiceless, oppressed.

Perhaps the most moving and inflammatory analysis of motherhood to appear during this period was Adrienne Rich's enormously influential *Of Woman Born: Motherhood as Experience and Institution* (1976), which won the National Book Award. When we were young women, we and everyone we knew read the book, and some of us gave it to our mothers, a gesture not always greeted with the same delight that flowers or bath oil evoked. "When we think of motherhood, we are supposed to think of Renoir's blooming women with rosy children at their knees, Raphael's ecstatic madonnas," Rich wrote. "We are not supposed to think of a woman lying in a Brooklyn hospital with ice packs on her aching breasts because she has been convinced she could not nurse a child . . . of a girl in her teens, pregnant by her father . . . of two women who love each other struggling to keep custody of their children against the hostility of exhusbands and courts. We are not supposed to think of a woman trying to conceal her pregnancy so she can go on working as long as possible, because when her condition is discovered she will be fired without disability insurance. . . . Men have spoken, often, in abstractions, of our 'joys and pains.' We have, in our long history, accepted the stresses of the institution as if they were a law of nature." But she saw motherhood as a patriarchal institution imposed on women "which aims at ensuring that . . . all women—shall remain under male control." [43]

Rich, who had been recognized as an important "woman poet" (for whatever *that* was worth at the time), recounted her own experience as the mother of three young boys. Instead of proposing, somewhat optimistically, that motherhood would be so much better if there were just marriage contracts and day-care centers, Rich cut to the everyday experiences of raising kids and said, simply, motherhood can be hell. The first chapter of the book begins:

> My children cause me the most exquisite suffering of which I have any experience. It is the suffering of ambivalence: the murderous alternation between bitter resentment and raw-edged nerves, and blissful gratification and tenderness. Sometimes I seem to myself, in my feelings toward these tiny guiltless beings, a monster of selfishness and intolerance. . . . I love them. But it's in the enormity and inevitability of this love that the sufferings lie.[44]

By exposing her own ambivalence—and the book was a brave and powerful act of exposure—Rich launched a scathing critique, not of mothers or of motherhood itself, but of the institution that it had become. Rich demanded that we acknowledge not only the hard labor that mothering required, but also its emotional, cognitive, and psychic demands as well. Instead of taking women's willingness to mother for granted by seeing it as nothing more than a hormonal inevitability, Rich made clear how utterly remarkable women are for persevering under oppressive conditions. "Motherhood has been penal servitude," she announced. "It need not be." Having begun the book with a wrenching confession, Rich ended with a utopian exhortation:

> We need to imagine a world in which every woman is the presiding genius of her own body. In such a world women will truly create new life, bringing forth not only children (if and as we choose) but the visions, and the thinking, necessary to sustain, console and alter human existence—a new relationship to the universe. . . . This is where we have to begin.[45]

Feminists didn't just take on motherhood; they took on child rearing, too, and sought to write stories and songs for kids, and develop new advice and guidelines for nonsexist parenting that would produce a whole new generation of liberated boys and girls. Today, with Barbie selling as briskly as ever and the World Wrestling Federation Smackdowns some of the most popular programming for adolescent boys, it seems impossible that anyone would be so wet behind the ears as to try to develop a project dedicated to eliminating sexism from child rearing. Imagine, for example, that Julia Roberts had a brainstorm and gathered together Jim Carrey, Jay Leno, Will Smith, Jennifer Lopez, Michael Jordan, Pink, JayZ, the Dave Matthews Band, and Raffi to produce a kids' album and TV show that celebrated gender equality and racial harmony. This seems so naïve today (and unnecessary, according to postfeminism). But their 1970s counterparts did just that.

In 1972, Marlo Thomas, star of the hit sitcom *That Girl*, put together *Free to Be You and Me*, a kids' collection of songs, stories, and poems designed to undermine what was popularly known as "sex-role stereotyping." The album sold five hundred thousand copies and was nominated for a "best album of the year" Grammy. (In 1972 Helen Reddy won a Grammy for her song "I Am Woman" in which she proclaimed, "I am strong, I am invincible." Three decades later we got Britney Spears singing, "Hit Me Baby, One More Time." But we digress.) The album featured performances by a range of stars, including Diana Ross, actor Alan Alda, Broadway star Carol Channing, comedian Mel Brooks, singer Harry Belafonte, and football star Rosey Grier, a three-hundred-pound defensive tackle for the New York Giants, who weighed in with "It's All Right to Cry," a song licensing boys to let the tears flow. The record became the basis for an ABC-TV special, and in 1974, McGraw-Hill published a book by the same name. All profits from sales of *Free to Be* went to the Ms. Foundation (and later to an off-shoot, the Free to Be Foundation) to fund projects that "help children grow up free." As an antidote to pop culture's girls-wear-pink, boys-shoot-bazookas address to the country's pint-sized consumer, the songs and stories invited kids and their parents to imagine a world in which the co-liberation of children and women opened doors, stirred the air, and freed the soul from insidious social constraints. The title song (in true American spirit) celebrated the convergence of individuality and togetherness. It urged children to come together and invited them to a place "Where the children are free . . . And you and me are free to be you and me." [46]

The songs' messages were unambiguous: Inside each and every one of us, there is a person chomping at the bit to throw off the shackles of gender and become, well, a person. In "William Wants a Doll," a boy is teased mercilessly by his peers for wanting a "doll to have and hold" so that he can grow up to be a good father. Though his own parents try to rid him of his perversity (his father gives him a bat and ball), his grandmother comes to the rescue. And it turns out that a kid can be good at baseball and have a doll at the same time. The poem "Housework" ridiculed advertisers' insistence that women increased their self-esteem by scrubbing toilets, and suggested that everyone (including Dad and Junior!) should pitch in at cleaning time. Perhaps even more subversive, it revealed that the happy housewife in the commercial was smiling because "she's an actress. And she's earning money for learning those speeches that mention those wonderful soaps and detergents." In the song "Parents Are People," kids could sing along with "some mommies are ranchers or poetry makers or doctors or teachers or cleaners or bakers. . . . Yes, mommies can be almost anything they want to be."

For the blink of an eye, we were permitted, even encouraged to think that the gendered rigidity of childhood was a thing of the past, that the current generation of children would initiate a new world order. Wearing their striped Oshkosh overalls, bowl cuts and Afros, girls and boys would march together into a land where dads changed diapers, moms changed tires, and nobody made bombs. The Emmy-winning TV special cemented *Free to Be*'s reputation as the holy grail of liberation. How could anyone have resisted the ingenue Michael Jackson, in his trademark Jackson Five outfit, singing that he didn't care what you looked like and, more to the point, he liked his looks just fine. It didn't matter if you were pretty or if you were tall. He reassured kids "We don't have to change at all." Ah Michael, see what happens to you when you drift away from feminism?

In a nutshell then, the women's movement in all its forms succeeded in shattering the assumption that all women had to, as it were, assume the position of the MRS. Consciousness-raising worked. But whatever constitutes a culture's common sense is never permanent: It is fought over, it evolves, re-forms, and, yes, it regresses. This is why the CRAP assault is so important to watch: Maybe if you tell another story, or try to get people to forget that certain things happened in the first place, people will think that those "other" people in the past—in this case feminists—were crazy, stupid, mean, selfish, or all of the above and that what they tried to achieve in the end makes zero sense at all. So think where we would be today if feminists had had some real policy victories—if the day care bill Nixon vetoed had instead been passed, if paid maternity and paternity leave became the national standard, if men accepted, as a given, that they were equally responsible (and we mean equally) for the raising of kids, if homemakers got some compensation for raising kids and keeping house. (Where you would be, probably, is Denmark.)

Feminism was—and remains—a revolutionary movement. Once feminists disrupted the common sense about motherhood and the family, the mainstream media had to respond. The feminine mystique was out—but what was in? From *One Day at a Time* to Dr. Spock, the media would struggle with this question. Meanwhile, intensive mothering, with a stake in its heart, lay dormant, waiting patiently for new soil and for the night to come.

TWO

Mouthing Off to Dr. Spock

The seventies: Just mention the decade and you're awash in kitsch. Platform shoes, the Fonz, pet rocks, shag haircuts, people snorting coke in Studio 54 while listening to The Village People, and drivers on their CB radios yelling "breaker, breaker." Then there were the body-convulsing therapy fads like "primal scream" (where you reenacted your birth by writhing on the floor like a stabbed snake while screaming). Recent movies about the 1970s focus on glittering disco balls and people trying out every possible kama sutra position available to the nongymnast. Mothers? There weren't mothers in the 1970s, were there?

It's not particularly easy to glamorize and idealize these times, the way Tom Brokaw, in his not-so-subtle slap at the baby boomers, idealized the "greatest generation" of the Depression and World War II. But far away from the Symbionese Liberation Army, *Laverne & Shirley,* and the Billy Beer brewery, a total revolution was taking place in American motherhood, and it too required a word rarely applied to mothers: heroism. By the end of the decade many people struggled to make ends meet in the face of a 9 percent unemployment rate, a 15 percent inflation rate, and 18 to 20 percent mortgage rates. Mothers knew how to whip inflation—they went to work. The most rapidly growing segment of the workforce was mothers with preschool children.[1]

The math alone tells the story of the impact of both the women's movement and the rotten economy on motherhood. In 1970, 40 percent of married mothers worked; in 1984, 59 percent of married mothers worked. In 1970, only 24 percent of mothers with a child one year old or younger worked; in 1984, 46.8 percent of mothers with a child under one worked.[2] Black married mothers were even more likely to be in the labor force than their white counterparts.[3] Single-parent households increased by a whopping 79 percent during the 1970s, and 90 percent of these were headed by women.[4] The years 1975 to 1980 witnessed an especially large surge: The participation of married mothers in the labor force grew faster then than in 1970–75 or 1980–85. And the most rapid increase between 1970 and 1985 was among mothers of very young children—participation rates of mothers of infants under one year of age doubled.[5]

Now, did our government officials, well aware of such figures, say to the mothers of America, "What can we do to ensure your success as a mother and a worker?" Unlike civilized countries—Denmark, France, or Italy—everything here was stacked against these women. Let's remember that when it came to family policy—and this is true today—the United States was still in the ooze of prehistory compared to Europe or Japan. There were very few day-care centers, and there was no maternity leave, paid or unpaid. There was no flex time. There were no after-school programs. There was not even the stingy Family Leave Act—if your kid got sick and you worked, you called in to say *you* were sick, so as not to make it seem like being a decent mother interfered with your job. And the two most important inventions for the working mother, the microwave and the VCR, were not yet widely available.

So, stand back, Mr. Brokaw. This generation of women, who are now approximately fifty years old and older, who raised kids in the 1970s and beyond—these are the ones who are great. It is because of them that companies even established day-care centers, that there are tax deductions for childcare expenses, that there is maternity and even paternity leave (however paltry), that there are now baby seats in supermarket carts. If you are one of these mothers, and your now grown children are even remotely functioning, stand up and take a bow.

What was the media environment that surrounded these mothers like? Of course there was much from the era of the MRS that clung to TV, films, and women's magazines like barnacles, the most tenacious being the magazine pediatricians, who remained cryogenically frozen in 1957. Ironically, the number of famous kid shrinks and celebrity pediatricians rose in the 1970s and beyond, in part because more research was being done on infants and toddlers for them to report about, and in part because young mothers, whether they were feminists or not, were looking for expert advice as they raised kids in circumstances very different from those their own mothers had faced. Unfortunately, turning to these guys was often like going into confession and finding that the Dark Lord was on the other side of the screen. At the same time, soothing, loving white mothers who never got angry and always reasoned calmly with their children—like Mrs. Brady or the one on Walton's mountain—showed the rest of us how to do it right. Intensive mothering remained a powerful ideology, and despite real feminist successes in opening up popular conceptions of marriage and motherhood, it gnawed at mothers through various media forms, especially child-rearing advice columns.

Yet one could also argue that the media were more progressive then than they are today, and that for a brief period of time, intensive mothering indeed went out of style. The feminist insistence that motherhood was political actually found its way, although in mutated forms, into the mass media. In the process we got the mouthy mother—Maude, Florida, Ann Romano, and Alice—the media's version of a feminist with kids, who hurled feminist-inspired barbs at her children, her building superintendent, and the cosmos. The rebellious mother's best weapon here was sarcasm, and while the mouthy mother gave millions of women permission to talk back to intensive mothering and patriarchy, she also suggested that bigger achievements were probably not possible. Meanwhile, advertisers' rendition of the liberated mother was the supermom, the high-powered attorney who was also a Girl Scout troop leader and built her own computers. On the one end of the media maternal spectrum was the MRS, still hanging on, and on the other end the supermom, with everyday women struggling, with and through the media, to renegotiate their stance toward intensive mothering in the face of feminism and tough times.

In the 1970s, then, mass-mediated critiques of the plight of the MRS that said the institutions of marriage and motherhood were a hopeless mess, warred with media reassurances that these institutions just needed a little tweaking, and also, not surprisingly, a few good men. And if we use two movies as bookends to the decade—*Diary of a Mad Housewife* at the beginning, *Kramer vs. Kramer* at the end, we see, by the 1980s, which images of motherhood and feminism were going to hold the day.

Hollywood, which was in 1970 pretty much an all-male shop, was, at first, mostly flummoxed by the women's movement. With films like *The*

Graduate, Midnight Cowboy, and *Five Easy Pieces,* for example, the industry that had just recently given Americans *That Touch of Mink* and 2000 B.C. discovered the psychic and box office benefits of social criticism, especially that directed at the banality and empty materialism of suburban life. Some version of the angry, mystified, and/or alienated young man— the young Dustin Hoffman, the young Jack Nicholson—was central to such films. But a feminist critique of society driving a film? Like, what was that? The notion that women might be, well, *people* was so imponderable to most Hollywood directors and producers in the early 1970s that they just decided not to feature women in films at all until, hopefully, the whole thing blew over. Enter the deluge of the male buddy film: *Butch Cassidy and the Sundance Kid, The Sting, M*A*S*H.*

There were a few exceptions, most notably *Diary of a Mad House-wife.* The director, Frank Perry, who had been nominated for an Oscar for his first film, *David and Lisa,* may have fallen into an estrogen vat as a child, because he made two films in short succession about neglected, put-upon women married to self-centered prigs: *Diary* (1970), based on a popular novel by Sue Kaufman, and *Play It As It Lays* (1972), based on Joan Didion's bestseller. *Diary* took nearly every example of female oppression itemized in *The Feminine Mystique*—wives' economic dependence on their husbands, the mindlessness of housework, the way women are supposed to give up everything for their families and, most of all, the misogyny of men—and dramatized them in excruciating vividness on the large screen.

Tina Balser, a Smith-educated housewife played by Carrie Snodgress (who was nominated for a Best Actress Oscar for her performance), suffered from a truly severe case of "the problem that has no name." Except that in this case, it did: Jonathan Balser. Her loathsome husband, played to the hilt of smarminess by Richard Benjamin, was a preening, condescending reptile, an up-and-coming lawyer utterly convinced of his own superiority and right to be treated like Little Lord Fauntleroy. He liked his ice cracked, not in cubes (and we know who was supposed to crack it); insisted "I'm in charge of financial matters around here"; dictated what Tina was supposed to cook for Thanksgiving dinner; ate only Damson Plum preserves on his toast. This was the face of patriarchy, and it wasn't pretty.

Within the first minutes of the film we saw her horrible, suffocating lot in life, despite her wealth: to listen patiently as Jonathan complained adenoidally and relentlessly about Tina's failure to do anything right while she served as his personal doormat. (He told his two daughters sarcastically at breakfast, "Your mother made Phi Beta Kappa at Smith but I don't think she can make a four-minute egg.") We knew we had an hour and a half left of this movie and already we wanted to jump into the frame, stab Jonathan in the heart, grab Tina's hand and drag her to a consciousness-raising group. (By the way, we wanted to kill the ingrate kids, too, who said things to her like, "Mom, you'd bloody well better clean up that mess before Daddy gets home.") A few scenes later, after his incessant belittlement, he then shifted into high-pitched baby talk and asked her repulsively for "a little roll in the hay." By now we wanted to tie a dry-cleaning bag on his head and drag her to a gay bar where she could meet some decent women.

Jonathan later wondered whether he should have gone to law school right out of Harvard. "I shouldn't have blocked my creative potential the way I did," he sighed. The irony that he was whining about his lost potential to a Phi Beta Kappa from Smith who was doomed to spend her life polishing the silver and cleaning dog excrement off of the rug for one simple reason—she had a uterus—was hardly lost on audience members who had by now heard of the Equal Rights Amendment. As Jonathan made a Caesar salad, he told Tina—whom he called "teen"—"I'll never be happy doing just one thing. I have to express myself in many different ways. That's the kind of man I am." Line after line like this drove home the entrapment of so many women and their husbands' utter blindness to their wives' lot.

Most remarkable for a Hollywood "women's film" of any era, the female lead did not finally find solace in the arms of a man, as she would just a few years later in *Alice Doesn't Live Here Anymore* and *An Unmarried Woman*. Indeed, though Tina enjoyed some really good sex with George, the sultry, sexy writer (played by Frank Langella) with whom she had an affair, he was such a self-absorbed, misogynistic creep, there was no way he could turn out to be Prince Charming. (Would you want to continue having an affair with a man who pointed out that you have a pimple on your ass?) Thus the movie was emphatic on one point: Men are hopeless jerks, demeaning, arrogant, self-centered, tyrannical, sexist. Nor were children the adorable, constantly loving kids we'd soon get to see in *Kramer vs. Kramer* and the *Beethoven* movies, the kind of Hollywood kids who make reproduction seem desirable. Instead, the Balsers' two daughters were ungrateful, demanding, whining brats who criticized Tina's clothes and spit out Thanksgiving dinner onto their plates because they hated it. They personified the feminist case for the toxicity of the *Father Knows Best* family.

Then there was *Up the Sandbox* (1972), which contained the immortal line delivered by one mother to another, "I've read all the child psych books. To be a good mother you gotta learn to eat shit." Based on the novel by feminist writer Anne Roiphe, the movie explored the ambivalence about feminism that many young mothers were feeling in the early and mid-1970s. Margaret (Barbra Streisand) adored her two small children; the movie opened with the sight of splashing water running down an infant's back in a scene that captured the joyful sensuality of bathing your baby. At the same time, though, Margaret had feminist friends, some of whom criticized how all their lives were defined solely by their husbands' work and achievements. Margaret moved between the details of her life—feeding the kids, doing the laundry—and wild fantasies (most of them bizarre) about debating publicly with Fidel Castro over the status of women or blowing up the Statue of Liberty with black militants. (Don't ask—we don't know why it was in the movie either.)

But the film captured the confusion of the early 1970s for young mothers raised to see family life as the end-all and be-all and now coming to a new consciousness of new possibilities in the age of feminism. Like other media forms at the time—especially women's magazines—the film validated the absolute importance of preserving a nurturing style of motherhood during such difficult political times (especially since, as Margaret told Fidel, men "have brought the planet to the point of extinction.") At the same time, she gave voice to the feminist criticism that mothers worked like dogs with zero acknowledgment of the value of their labor. After going to a party where young busty women fell all over her husband because he was so interesting, and then being told by her husband about the female Ph.D. candidate who intended to have one kid, "check off the woman thing," and go back to work, she lost it. "A woman like me works twice as hard, and for what? Stretch marks and varicose veins. You've got one job, I've got ninety-seven. Maybe I should be on the cover of *Time*— dust mop of the year, queen of the laundry room." She said she couldn't live up to any of these standards: She wasn't accomplished like his colleagues, yet couldn't even keep the house as clean as her mother did. "I'm a zero, a nothing." Her husband cluelessly offered that maybe she'd be happy if she did more. "Did more? I cook. I sew. I squeegee. I spend hours waiting in line for a sale on baby sandals just to save a few pennies. . . . I'm an errand boy, a cook, a dishwasher, a cockroach catcher, and *you* say I'd be happy if I did more." At the end of the film, she made her husband watch the kids while she took the day off. What would happen to this young mother? Would she eventually take advantage of the new possibilities now opening up because of the women's movement? Like *Diary, Up the Sandbox* offered a critique of how confining middle-class motherhood was for women, but stopped short (this was Hollywood, after all) of exploring the alternatives real-life women would be pioneering in just a few short years.

If these two Tinseltown offerings acknowledged, however tentatively, that feminists did, after all, have a point, women's magazines faced a more daunting task. How, exactly, were you going to accommodate yourself to sentiments ranging from "equal rights now" and "wages for housework" to "marriage is slavery" and "pregnancy is barbaric" if you were a traditional women's magazine that for decades had proffered advice about how to conquer diaper rash, crochet pastel-colored covers for your toilet seats, and produce a birthday cake that looked just like Snoopy?

Although the readers of *Redbook, Good Housekeeping, Ladies' Home Journal,* and *McCall's* were not usually the same women who were out hexing Playboy clubs, polls showed that they, too, became powerfully influenced by the women's movement. By 1973, a *Redbook* poll indicated that nine out of ten respondents knew women earned less than men for the same work, three-quarters thought that media imagery degraded women, and "a vast majority" believed that women were second-class citizens. Two-thirds of them (yes!) supported the women's movement.[6] Increasing numbers of them, by desire and necessity, were joining the workforce, even when their children were small. More and more of them were divorcing. They were scrambling for child care. They were scrambling to pay the bills. They wanted a break.

They didn't get one, at least not from the nation's child experts. It was in the various advice columns of the women's magazines—often avidly read because they were about raising kids, had a user-friendly format, and allowed you to compare your behaviors against others'—that intensive mothering was most vehemently defended. (This was also true in the 1980s and '90s, and it's true today.) You think you want to or need to work? You think sheer common sense can guide you with your children? Fine, whatever. But the kid shrink experts of America fortified intensive mothering against the feminist onslaught.

Here were the rules. The last thing a mother should be is overprotective, but you had to be protective enough. You couldn't be over-attentive or "over-invested" in your kids' lives, but you had to make them feel totally loved and that everything they said and did was wonderful. You had to help them be independent, but not let them feel that their needs were neglected. You shouldn't be too strict, but not too permissive either; after all, permissiveness had produced nothing but spoiled hippies. Despite all this relentless, fine calibrating of your precise, exact behavior on an hourly basis, you also had to be lighthearted, as "a parent's spontaneity is the most wholesome gift that can be offered to a child." All of it was on you, the mom, and any imperfection in the child was due to your misguided failings. In the monumentally mistitled "Guilt-Free Motherhood: A Psychiatrist's Guide" (1974), just to select one example, we learned that "Mommies find themselves abused, neglected and put upon because of their own actions—or should I say, over-actions. So look to yourselves, mothers!"[7]

Feminists sick of all this had, in the early 1970s, singled out Dr. Spock because his advice dominated the women's magazines in the 1950s and '60s; his book, originally published in 1946, had sold more than any other in history, with the exception of the Bible.[8] Spock had warned against women working outside the home then, and now feminists were going to make him pay for the guilt that he had so successfully propagated. (In response to the women's movement, Spock was compelled to face the reality of working mothers, and revised subsequent editions of the book accordingly.) The feminist attacks made him really defensive, his columns now sounding like a Reagan-era press conference after one of the president's various off-the-cuff remarks: "What I meant to say" now peppered his pieces. "I never meant to tell parents that they *must* wean their babies by the time they were a year old," was a typical response to his apparently bulging bag of hate mail.[9] "I never said," he wrote (falsely) in *Redbook* in 1970, "that women should stay at home rather than go to work." But, he lectured, "babies and young children have needs and rights too, and some adults have no idea what they are." That's why we needed him. "One of the jobs of professional people in the children's field is to spell them out," he huffed.

Well, spell them out he did, and he had help from the other magazine kid shrinks. The one thing you could never do is just relax and trust your common sense, or forgive yourself for those inevitable errors in judgment. Reading these advice columns, thirty years later, feels like being in London during the blitz, but with no Underground or bomb shelters. What was there to protect mothers from the repeated ideological strafing from these privileged white men, none of whom had been mothers, let alone working mothers?

Here, according to Spock in 1970, was what the good mother did, women's movement or no women's movement. "Psychoanalytic studies" (i.e., the Tablets on the Mount) showed that those individuals who become "extraordinarily productive or creative in their fields" got their inspiration "from a particularly strong relationship with a mother who had especially high aspirations for her children." (Forget all those stories about famous authors, artists, and actors whose mothers were nightmares.) As "instinctive expressions of an intense emotional relationship," the good mother "tries instinctively to get a smile out of her baby," and "teaches him pat-a-cake and peek-a-boo. She plays his favorite records and points out the pictures in his books. . . . She uses baby talk to teach him the names for his family and foods."

While these abilities were hard-wired into mothers, a "mother substitute" (e.g., childcare provider) could do these things too, admitted Spock. But here was the rub. The child could develop a "real dependence" on the substitute. Then, if the substitute left, "the deprivation will be as great as the average child would feel if his mother had died [!!!] and will have long-lasting effects" such as "a deep reluctance to love anyone else again." (This 1970 article was titled, believe it or not, "Working Mothers: Some Possible Child Care Solutions.") Anyone who really loves her child "can't talk casually about turning him over to a nursery or a commune or an individual for most of his waking hours during his first three years to allow his mother to work full-time." If mothers of children under three have to work, they should work two to three hours a day. Once the kid was in school, mother should still make sure to be home by 3:30 or 4:00 at the latest.[10] So, Dr. Spock thought it was fine for mothers to work, as long as you didn't really care about the psychological well-being of your child. At the end of the column we learned that "Dr. Spock regrets that he is not able to answer letters personally." We can only imagine what kinds of comments were starting to fill his mailbox.

Spock was one of the first to bring the now totally discredited notion of bonding to a large female audience.[11] In 1976, he told *Redbook* readers that two pediatrician friends of his, John Kennel and Marshall Klaus, had found that if babies were brought to their mothers within one hour of birth, their mothers showed "an inborn instinct" (there it is again) to touch and fondle their babies all over. This touching "instinct" was manifested in one and *only* one uniform, predictable, and correct pattern, starting with the arms and legs, then the face and fingertips, then the chest, abdomen and back, "which they feel with their palms." Subsequent "studies" showed that one month and one year later, the mothers who had "bonded" with their kids in this crucial first hour (and it could *only* really happen then) were more caring, and their kids were "better nourished and had fewer infections." The other, bond-aversive ice mothers, when near their kids, just "looked elsewhere and let their babies cry." Spock wrote, "You can see why the psychology-minded obstetricians, pediatricians, psychologists, and nurses" who knew of the bonding studies had "pushed for natural childbirth and rooming-in." So Spock got women two ways. He guilt-tripped them by foisting the notion of bonding on them and then, on top of it, rewrote recent history. Most doctors did everything they could to *resist* the natural childbirth movement not only because it challenged their dominion over the labor room, but also because it wreaked havoc with their golf schedules. It was ordinary, defiant women who wrought the revolution in childbirth.

When in doubt, male experts have always found ways to use examples from the animal kingdom to keep women in their place. Naturally enough, the bonding research reminded Spock of studies done on baby monkeys which, when "isolated in infancy and then placed with others at puberty show very abnormal behavior." They beat and attacked other monkeys, were uninterested in sex, and the females grew up to be "quite inadequate mothers." Wither goest the monkey moms, so go we. (Please note that for Spock there was apparently no difference between bonding with your baby during the first hour, and *only* the first hour after birth, and separating a baby monkey from its mother for years until it was nearly grown.) These monkey studies also provided fodder for the fear that if you failed to bond properly, you'd raise someone who buried bodies in the backyard. "A psychologist named James Prescott has speculated as to whether the high rate of violent crimes in our society may be related in part to the infrequency of close contact between babies and mothers."

Now, what if you had already had your kid and had failed to bond in the first hour? Well, "it doesn't mean that your baby has been seriously or permanently deprived," but you'd still better "try to make up for lost opportunities." Buy a baby sling immediately so that the baby would be regularly strapped to your chest and back—this was now essential during the first three months of life. If your child was too old for this, well, see you in juvey court. "Isn't it amazing," Spock asked, "that one hour's early contact could make this much difference in mothers' behavior toward their babies?" [12] Why yes, it was quite amazing, now that you mention it. Barely credible, as it later turned out. A load of guano.

In his efforts to seem empathetic, Spock could produce the most inflated, alarmist commentaries on motherhood. Get this passage about how mothers felt when they stopped breastfeeding. "The disappointment and pain are comparable to what one feels on being retired, being relieved of a job in which one felt indispensable, or being jilted by a lover." Spock actually claimed that a "majority of mothers" had told him that when they weaned, "they felt hurt by the casual attitudes of their babies." [13] Was there no one, not one mother who said, "That was nice, did my duty, but thank God it's over. No more cracked nipples, breast milk squirting down my blouse at all hours, and being the only one who can do the three A.M. feeding"?

Spock's specialty was noting some highly unusual behavior and then suggesting that it might be more frequent than you thought, that it could happen to you if you weren't careful. He often used just one anecdote to suggest that an epidemic of chronic maternal malfeasance was in the works. He knew of "a couple of cases" in which the mother picked the baby up every time it "whimpered." Result? "The baby eventually became a disagreeable tyrant." Let your two-year-old climb into bed with you one night because of a bad dream? Why, Spock knew of such children "who were still going into their parents' beds and absolutely refusing to budge at ten years of age." Wipe your toddler's butt when he's being potty trained? Spock knew six-year-olds who were "still calling for their parents to wipe them after bowel movements." [14]

Bruno Bettelheim, another in the holy pantheon of know-it-alls, in his monthly column "Dialogue with Mothers" in Ladies' Home Journal, set himself up as the Yahweh of child rearing with the poor, stupid, semi-addled mothers sitting at his feet. (Let's not forget that this was the guy who wrote the definitive book about children on a kibbutz without speaking one word of Hebrew.)[15] The column followed the same rough setup. He was allegedly sitting around with a group of mothers, chatting about a particular issue, like how to help your child deal with a bully at school or how to help a child through divorce. (Whether he actually held these chats, or made the whole thing up, including what the mothers said, is a suspicion that nags at the reader. For example, when he reported that one mother thought that the best way to help an older child deal with the arrival of a new baby was to give him a picture of the new baby to throw darts at, one wonders how far away the bong really was from Bruno's typewriter.)

At first, in the beginning of the "dialogue," the mothers were set up to seem pretty reasonable, thoughtful, sure of the values they wanted to teach their children and how best to do it. But it turned out that they were never quite right. Guess who was? Bettelheim, the wise, omniscient, ever fair-minded sage, patiently showed the dumbo moms how they were only partially right or, more often, dead wrong. A typical sentence, after we heard from the mothers, began, "I felt that these mothers were off base," or "There is another problem here that the mother did not see." [16] In a discussion about how to deal with sibling rivalry, Bruno suggested that the mothers think about how to help the older child not feel jealous of a new baby. "The mothers found themselves stumped about how this could be done." [17]

Bettelheim was especially condescending when he damned with faint praise, to wit: "I thought this mother had made a good beginning by being willing to talk things over with her child, but that is *only* the beginning." [18] Bettelheim's moms *thought* they knew what to do in various situations, but their instincts actually blinded them to the real, enlightened, Bruno-approved course of action. Once Bruno began to dispense his wisdom, however—and this happened invariably about halfway through the column—some of the mothers objected to his advice, or failed to see his point. They were obstinate, thick as a plank, really. It was here, especially, that we got to see the ever-patient Dr. Bruno explain things once again until, finally, the moms got it. By 1973, there was no more "Dialogue with Mothers" in *Ladies' Home Journal,* the victim, one hopes, of mothers who vowed to hunt him down and pull out his tongue with pliers.

The magazine gurus—Bettelheim, Joyce Brothers (*Good Housekeeping*), and especially Lee Salk (*McCall's*)—insisted on the importance of calm rationality in mothers. The persona the mother was supposed to inhabit was that of—guess what—a therapist. She was supposed to adopt the rhetorical style and dispassionate stance of the professional clinical psychologist. True to this genre, Salk told a mother whose three-year-old son had developed a fascination with toy guns to make her displeasure known, but not to overreact "to such an extent that the forbidden gun-play becomes even more desirable." [19] Mothers should never be harsh, but communicate with "warmth, frankness and openness," always displaying their understanding of their children. [20] The worst, most destructive thing Mom could do was lose her cool, as this would scar the kid for life—"permanent psychological damage" was the preferred mantra. At the same time that she was supposed to act like a shrink, she should beware, Salk warned, of "over-psychologizing" and of "jumping to psychological conclusions and ignoring other possible explanations." [21] While any unusual trait that could be cast as an abnormality was the mother's fault, the father's role was hardly ever discussed, let alone criticized. Repeatedly, as if they were getting kickbacks from the American Psychiatric Association, the magazine shrinks urged that letter writers get "professional help" from a therapist, the underlying assumption being that she had the time and the money to do so and that therapy always works. (Look what untold hours of it did for Woody Allen and Mia Farrow.)

Salk, author of "You and Your Family," which premiered in 1972, was posed every month in *McCall's* like the bust of "The Thinker." The format here was more snappy: Mothers wrote in questions and he answered. For him, too, there were still few problems that weren't Mom's fault. How's this advice to a mother whose kids liked to squirt each other with toothpaste? "Before becoming critical of your children it is important to examine your own behavior." [22]

Noting that the working mother's child had a "self-esteem clearly in jeopardy," he opined in 1972 that "I think that children who have working mothers may possibly feel that their mothers' work is more important than they are." Children whose mothers were too busy to join the PTA, be homeroom mothers, and so forth, could become defiant. "They are not problem children—they have, in a sense, problem parents who ignore the emotional needs of their children until the children develop problems of their own. . . . It is clear that when the working mother cannot participate in school activities, the situation may lead to a child's underachievement." [23]

A child who began reverting to baby talk (gee, no normal kid has ever done that!) "indicates some unfulfilled need. Your daughter obviously feels that being a five-year-old does not provide her with the kind of emotional gratification she needs," so "you should make special efforts to give your child some individual and undivided attention." [24] One mother wrote that her three-year-old son cried whenever she tried to leave him with a sitter. It is our observation that every child ever left with a sitter or at a day-care center cries at some point when the parent leaves—bawls his or her eyes out hysterically, actually—and within two minutes of the parent's departure is happily sticking peas up the nose of some hapless guinea pig. Not so, chided Salk. Clearly "he has had some unpleasant experiences involving separation from you. . . . You may need to seek professional help to gain insight into your specific situation," Salk advised. [25] A teenager caught cheating on a math test at school may be angry at his parents and have "some underlying resentment toward you," and thus "you may be forcing him to do something even more horrendous as a means of expressing anger toward you." [26] How about he hadn't studied his geometry, everyone else was cheating, and he should be grounded?

Now Salk's special "demean the mom" strategy was to look for or suggest a problem over and above what the reader actually asked, to really put the fear of God in her. For example, a mother of an eight-month-old wrote, "My husband and I really need a vacation" (amen), so would it be okay if they went away for a week and left their child with the grandma, whom the baby already knows well? The correct answer is yes, call Nana immediately. Not so fast, warned Salk. The dividing line for being away is just under a week, but not a week or more. After that, here's what would happen to your kid. Children will "turn away" from their parents and "become very attached to their 'caretakers.' . . . In some instances, children of this age become depressed while the parents are gone and may even stop eating. In many cases, children also develop sleep problems, which may persist after the parents return. Nor is it surprising for little children to have temper tantrums and indulge in destructive behavior." [27] Still want to go on that vacation, hon?

What Salk would do is take a simple question or concern and then blow it up a bit to dramatize what would happen if the problem was just a little worse. And at that point, the child would need "professional help" of the kind he offered. (By now Salk has built a four-thousand-square-foot addition on his house.) One mother noted that her four-year-old seemed quite happy playing by himself, and asked whether this was okay, or whether he needed to be more "social." Correct answer—he's fine, and count yourself amazingly lucky that he isn't calling you every two seconds asking, "Mommy, will you play with me and my Duplos?" Hold your horses, warned Salk. "If your child is *always* in his own world [note, *not* what the mother said] and seems unable to *ever* interact socially, this may reflect an emotional problem that"—you guessed it—"requires professional help."[28] (A summer house for Salk.) Another mother asked whether it was normal for her twelve-year-old daughter to still be playing with dolls. Well, answered Salk, it was okay for now (which was what the mother was asking about, *now*), but if she continued to do so after "pubescent physical development" then the mother would know that there was "an underlying emotional problem" which would require "competent psychological help."[29] (A Mercedes LS 3700 for Salk.) It would be quite gratifying to dismiss Salk and his ilk as the sort of pompous airbags women of today no longer have to endure, except that thirty years later mothers are stuck with that throwback Dr. William "attachment parenting" Sears, who insists that mothers who don't lash their babies to their chests for five years or so are cold-hearted banshees. But more on him later.

At the same time that Spock was telling women that if they didn't march to the tune of even more intensive mothering than that of the 1950s, their kids would end up like crazed monkeys, and Salk was herding them off to the shrinks of America, the women's magazines had to address their readers' newfound concerns, ambitions, and anxieties—and their newfound feminism, however modest. So within the very same magazine, some features—the kid advice column—upped the ante of intensive mothering, while other features—roundtable discussions among mothers, or articles written by readers—gave voice to the struggles mothers faced, especially newly working or single mothers. And here was where the women's magazines incorporated feminism into their pages, and where the edicts of intensive mothering were questioned and sometimes jettisoned. The women's magazines were never going to consider, for one second, radical feminists' attacks on the gender inequalities structured into the institutions of marriage and motherhood. As one *Redbook* article put it in 1974, "a great many feminists had absolutely no conception of the real joys of motherhood. A loud minority showed unconcealed contempt for full-time mothers and talked about the nuclear family as though it were an incurable disease." [30] *Ladies' Home Journal* echoed this a year later: While it was great that mothers now saw through the "Victorian sentimentality" that had put motherhood on a pedestal, there was a new danger that people were now simply going to "put down" motherhood. "We cannot let a new mythology tyrannize us out of being mothers," the magazine insisted, carving off reasonable from unreasonable feminism. [31]

But these magazines did start to acknowledge, for example, that mothers who didn't work were not economically independent, and they began taking up Gloria Steinem's assertion that the work performed by housewives actually had a market value. This was the era when multiple magazine articles urged mothers who felt they had no marketable skills to convert things like running bake sales and getting Susie to stop pulling Tommy's hair into "fund raising" and "human resources management" on their new resumes. The women's magazines also frequently gave voice to the now permissible complaint that many stay-at-home mothers felt "trapped, lonely, and out of touch with people." Speaking for millions, one mother wrote "all of my self-confidence had vanished." [32] The women's magazines took this call for help to heart.

One of their first steps was to publish articles that encouraged housewives to find work outside the home, even if they hadn't worked for years (or ever). In 1972 *McCall's* featured a piece by Felice Schwartz (who would, twenty years later, get into heap big trouble over her "mommy track" proposal) and others titled "How to Go to Work When Your Husband Is Against It, Your Children Aren't Old Enough, and There's Nothing You Can Do Anyhow." Housewives had to see the worth of their work in market terms, to understand that what their husbands and kids took for granted actually had great value. "You have run a home, which requires the combined skills of purchasing agent, time-study expert, dietitian, interior decorator, and personnel manager," advised Schwartz and her coauthors. "You've also learned how to . . . [coax] the best out of the plumber, the butcher, and the baby-sitter. This sort of experience might be translated into personnel work, sales, administration, or any other job that involves dealing with clients or the public." [33]

Whatever the kid shrinks were warning about the dire consequences of working, other articles assured mothers that it was just fine. In 1971, the *Ladies' Home Journal* started a column by feminist writer Letty Cottin Pogrebin titled "The Working Woman," and the first one gave women twelve symptoms to look for to ascertain if they were ready to go to work.

"Forget about 'society's' idea of a woman's place," advised Pogrebin. If you're sick of housework, are tired of being introduced as so-and-so's wife, and want your own identity, go for it. At the end of the column, Pogrebin provided information about the first women to take on high-powered new positions and where to get more information about job discrimination.[34] In her August 1974 column, Pogrebin, possibly with the kid shrinks in her mental crosshairs, featured interviews with kids of working mothers and concluded, "None of the children said they resent their mothers' jobs, and none feel envious of kids whose mothers are at home."[35] In 1979, she quoted psychologists who asserted, "There is no evidence of any negative effects traceable to maternal employment."[36] Some kids claimed that learning to help run the house "was fun" and that they liked their newfound independence. Various kids in other articles said they admired their working mothers, and the daughters insisted that when they grew up, they'd be working mothers, too.[37] "I never once remember feeling ignored or slighted because of her work" went a typical comment.[38] (Of course, talk about getting the bends: In a 1978 McCall's article "How Children Feel About Their Working Mothers," kids said "I get mad when my mother comes home late, and then we fight, my sister cries," or "I'd like my mom to play Monopoly or badminton or games out in the yard with me, but she gets too exhausted all the time," and "mothers who didn't work were always home to answer questions.")[39]

Pogrebin's column, which ran for ten years, was revolutionary for the Ladies' Home Journal. "I sought to carry the feminist epiphanies of the time through an acceptable vehicle" to women who would never read Ms. Readers wrote to her in gratitude, many claming that they had shown her column to their husbands by way of initiating changes in their lives. If it was in Ladies' Home Journal, after all, it must be okay. "In each house a mini-revolution was being fought out," Pogrebin noted, and her columns and the other articles about women and work gave readers what they saw as the intellectual, fact-based ammunition to proceed.[40]

By offering first-person accounts by working mothers, some of them individual, some of them in the form of panel discussions, the magazines clearly wanted to be seen as clearinghouses, switchboards, really, that connected working mothers to each other, and enabled them to share advice and support through the magazine's pages. Such articles sought to simulate that most brilliant of feminist inventions, the consciousness-raising group. While the word "sisterhood" was as rare as a snail darter in these publications, that was nonetheless the concept they were responding to and seeking to promote. Here's what jumped off the pages in this corner of the media: Mothers were in it together, and they needed to work together to help each other out and to promote policy changes, like a national day-care system, that would help all mothers.

In "Double Jeopardy: The Working Motherhood Trap," two working mothers talked about how important it had been to them to compare notes, learn from each other's mistakes, and devise "ways of balancing home and career that no books ever taught." They wanted to share what they had learned with "*Redbook* readers who are considering the same course." This was not some rose-colored view of working motherhood, but a frank discussion of all the double-binds working mothers faced. Employers thought that if you put your kids before your job, you were disloyal, but if you put your job before your kids, you were unnatural. A baby-sitter who will "stimulate, love, and care for the children . . . is a rarity" and working mothers had "a series of baby-sitter horror stories." They didn't have enough time and "the problem of guilt remains a difficult one." Someday, they wrote wistfully in 1974, "part-time work for both mothers and fathers, longer maternity leaves, equal pay for women, and quality day care will be facts, not just glimmers in a feminist's eye." [41] Articles like these looked outward—to employers and the government— as sources of mothers' problems and solutions, not only inward, to the mother herself.

In "Someday I'd Like to Walk Slowly," *Redbook* brought together twelve young working mothers to talk and compare notes with Bess Myerson. The women worked because they didn't want to be financially or emotionally vulnerable: Several said that if you worked you enjoyed more equality within your home. They talked about the Herculean efforts required to get husbands to help with the housework and, this being the pre–Martha Stewart era, their tendency to let the housework go. "[F]ew . . . felt that their children had suffered because their mothers had jobs." [42] Here other working mothers, who had overflowing laundry baskets on the living room sofa and didn't feel guilty because they worked, knew they were not alone.

Several articles insisted that going back to work had made the women better mothers. One formerly stay-at-home mother of two confessed that she had "gained seventy pounds and . . . was watching eight to ten hours of television every day." Her problem was simple: "When I quit work, I dedicated myself to my family and forgot about my own needs. This self-sacrifice was unhealthy and unnecessary." She realized that to be a more patient mother, "I needed to spend some time away from my children."[43] Taken together, these articles suggested that working outside the home could make you a happier mother, that your kids would become more self-reliant and independent, and that your husband, of necessity, would become more involved in the housework and in raising the kids.[44]

By 1978 McCall's was offering $1000 for "Working Woman" stories "that reflect the special problems, conflicts, and opportunities that confront women who have jobs outside the home." Instead of the emphasis on the enterprising individual that characterized portraits of motherhood in the 1950s (and would do so again in the 1980s and beyond), here we saw 1970s-style collective action. In "New Ways of Taking Turns," Jane Adams reported on groups of mothers in different cities who had gotten together to pool their resources. One group set up a grocery shopping collective, another an errands collective. Others combined car pooling to Little League with overlapping dentist and doctor appointments so one mom took several kids at the same time to get their teeth cleaned or get their shots.[45] McCall's also introduced us to four single mothers, all of whom were looking for a place to live but could barely afford an apartment, let alone a house, because their salaries were so paltry. They also needed childcare and companionship. One recent divorcée advertised for a roommate in the paper, and by the time the dust settled, had found three women to share a large house, which also allowed them to pool their resources to hire one sitter for all their kids and to share in food preparation and in baby-sitting.[46]

What is so striking about these various articles is how they gave voice to the experiences and concerns of everyday mothers, and provided the reader with a range of different attitudes and reactions to identify with. Here we heard mothers wrestle, explicitly, with the norms of intensive mothering, regarding many of them as unnecessary and overly demanding, yet getting pulled into their riptides through the specter of the hurt, lonely, damaged child. Some mothers cried when they left their children at day care for the first time; others didn't cry at all and, in fact, couldn't wait to drop the kid off. Some felt guilty about working; others believed it made them better mothers. We saw mothers going through their own thought processes and sometimes reaching dead ends: solutions that simply weren't going to work. So they tried again, and found another solution. Because these magazines so actively invited mothers to submit pieces about their own experiences, there were also articles by older working women whose kids had grown up just fine, putting the lie to the work-equals-ax-murderer equation spouted by Spock, Salk, and others.[47] There was no one, all-commanding opinion of the expert, no "I'm-the-best-mom-in-the-world-and-you're-not" pap from some actress. So, for a brief time in the media, there were multiple personas for mothers to connect to, try on, reject. And, in these features, mothers were doing things, trying things: active agents in search of solutions. They forged ahead, together.

Meanwhile, because feminists had given women permission to say that the rosy myths of marriage and motherhood weren't what they were cracked up to be, we began to see the rise of the mouthy mother, sometimes deadly serious, most often making a joke of her predicament. For example, in 1976 "A Bill of Rights for the Mother Person" conceded that there had been, until recently, a "taboo" against discussing "our negative reactions to mothering." The most taboo of these reactions was anger, yet "anger is inevitable" and "completely normal," the authors insisted. Mothers in this article admitted to losing it: "When Sarah bit me yesterday, I kicked her and said, 'You dirty little animal.'" (Imagine Kathie Lee admitting this.) They talked about the "shrieking, demanding, enervating noise of living with children, the "mental fatigue," the guilt, the loss of sense of self. They concluded, "Either mothers are individual women with the same constitutional and personal rights to freedom and self-development as any other human being or they are less than fully autonomous beings, mere adjuncts to children and others."[48] Lynn Caine, author of the bestseller *Widow*, wrote about the "black months when I thought I was destined to go through life giving up everything for my children, when I felt chained to and enslaved by their needs." She urged single mothers to do whatever it took to get out of the house on their own. She railed against the discrimination that existed against single-parent families, who were rarely invited to join outings with two-parent families and whose kids were referred to as coming from a "broken home."[49]

Maternal humor pieces, in which the writer assumed the persona of a sarcastic, jaundiced mom, admitted that raising children was not always a spiritually elevating experience but was, rather, often a pain in the ass. The astringency of these pieces was clearly a self-conscious antidote to the treacle offered on *The Waltons*. In "Confessions of a Wicked Step-mother," Georgia Lee Cox, who had no children of her own but had recently married a man with four, admitted, "I was always afraid of children. Now I know why. Children are as bad as I thought they were." There were jokes about swatting the kids and stuffing pillows in their mouths, after which a much-needed martini was called for. One sibling got into a fight with his sister, and announced to his stepmother, " 'I'll die before I'll play with her.' 'Prepare to die then,' I said, and went back for another Martini." [50] Judith Viorst offered "The Confessions of a Mean Mommy," in which she proposed that one way to get a kid to clean up his act was to warn him, "you are inches from death." [51] Not only was June Cleaver never supposed to say such stuff, imagine *InStyle* telling us that Cindy Crawford gets her kids to pick up their Lincoln Logs by warning them that they are "inches from death"?

As scholars like Andrea Press point out, there was no "feminist moment" on TV, no shows that for even one second captured women's collective experience of being discriminated against based on gender. [52] But there were efforts, Hollywood style, to address and, yes, take advantage of the women's movement. Television, especially, distilled feminist critiques of marriage and motherhood into the exemplar of the mouthy mother. The first was *Maude* (1972), the Amazonian matriarch with the deep booming voice whose tongue was laced with curare. But Maude was married (if, indeed, for the fourth time) and well-to-do; she even had a maid. And while she was an enormously cathartic character to watch (*ooo-wee*, the stuff she got to say to men!), she was also a caricature of the feminist as strident battle-ax. [53] She offered few points of identification for the working or single mother.

By 1975, TV executives appreciated that there really was a transformation in motherhood afoot, and one that would attract female viewers. So in December of that year, CBS unrolled *One Day at a Time*, a sitcom about Ann Romano (Bonnie Franklin), who had divorced her husband of seventeen years and moved to Indianapolis with her two teenage daughters. The show became an immediate hit: It lasted for nine seasons, regularly ranked among the top twenty shows, and was often in the top ten. [54] Ann struggled with a low-paying job, power struggles with her ex, outbursts from her constantly feuding daughters, and the incessant come-ons of the building superintendent, the oily, narcissistic Schneider with the pack of smokes rolled up in his T-shirt sleeve.

With the divorce rate and the number of female-headed households soaring, millions of women responded powerfully to a character who was, by turns, certain that what she was doing was right, yet filled with self-doubt about her success as a mother, about aging, about remarrying, about money. The upbeat theme song, "This is it! This is the one life you get, so go and have a ball," which accompanied scenes of Ann and the kids throwing their suitcases in the car and Ann jumping for joy as she made tracks, was almost an ad for dumping the old man and starting over.

What is so striking about viewing *One Day* over twenty-five years after it premiered is the ease with which feminist language and assumptions about marriage and the family imbued the show. After her divorce, she reclaimed her maiden name and went by Ms., "Annie Romano, liberated woman, master of her fate," as she proclaimed. In the premiere, Ann came home and lay on the floor to stretch out her back. She looked heavenward and addressed the great almighty. "God, a lot of people think you're a woman. If you are, how about rooting for the home team." The general audio level was loud, and, like Maude, Ann's feminism was marked by her ability to joust verbally with men and especially to deflate the working-class macho pretensions of Schneider. In one exchange he assumed that because she was divorced, she was sexually desperate. "You're a woman of the divorced persuasion. And here I am. Use me." "I'd like to recycle you," she shot back. "I love my wife very much," he implored. "But I have so much love I have to spread it around." "Well, go spread it on the lawn," she sneered, to the delighted howls of the studio audience. Later he knocked on the front door, and when she opened it he leered, "I see you're alone." "That's right. And so are you," she retorted as she slammed the door in his face while the audience applauded again. The feminist mother here was marked by her verbal aggression, something you didn't see in, say, *Family Ties*, just a few years later.

Her boyfriend wanted her to get married but she wanted a taste of independence because, "For the first seventeen years of my life my father made the decisions; for the next seventeen years my husband made the decisions." As media scholar Bonnie Dow puts it, the show made eminently clear that Ann's life "as a traditional woman has handicapped her." [55] Having said that, however, it was her boyfriend to whom she turned for advice about one of her daughters in the series' premiere, and it was he who came up with the solution, even though he was eight years younger than she and had zero kids. Mothers still needed men, and men often still knew best.

Ann bore strong similarities to Alice (Ellen Burstyn, who won an

Oscar for her performance) in *Alice Doesn't Live Here Anymore* (1974). (Burstyn was also a single mother in *The Exorcist,* and look what that got her.) Alice's abusive bastard of a husband got killed in a car wreck, and suddenly Alice had to fend for herself. She decided to drive out west, heading for Monterey, to resume her abandoned career as a singer. With Alice's mouth, we were safely in Erma Bombeck country, and happy for it. When Alice and her eleven-year-old son Tommy were driving out west, he kept bugging her with the classic "are we there yet" whining. She said, "If you ask me that one more time I'm going to beat you to death." He complained that he was bored; she yelled, "Well, so am I. What do you want from me, card tricks?" She was not afraid to yell at him, show her impatience or, God forbid, to leave him alone in the motel watching TV while she went job hunting. Of course, she was a single mother and this was a Hollywood film, so the neglected Tommy indeed hooked up with the androgynous Audrey (Jodi Foster), a very bad influence. Alice also made major mom mistakes, like forcing Tommy to get out of the car and walk home because she was pissed at him, only to have to collect Tommy later at the local police station. But in talking back to Tommy, she talked back to sugary conceits about motherhood that ignored the realities of being stuck someplace with no contacts at all and needing desperately to support your kid. And despite these not insignificant maternal screw-ups, the movie presented her as a good and loving mother. The movie led to the TV show *Alice,* which premiered in 1976 and was also a major hit. In it Alice (Linda Lavin) and the mouthy "kiss my grits" Flo (Polly Holliday) insulted their boss, Mel, and challenged his male chauvinism both directly and manipulatively, behind his back.

Mouthy was good; we liked mouthy. And mothers did indeed have to have a sense of humor about their predicament. But to confine feminist takes on motherhood to sassy one-liners helped to trivialize them and also to suggest that now that these concerns were out in the open and being joked about, why, they were nearly resolved. Also, look at who got to take the rap for patriarchy: Schneider, the working-class super, and Mel, the working-class diner manager. If this was the headquarters of patriarchy—absurdly macho but ineffectual working-class guys—then it couldn't really be all that powerful, now could it?

And speaking of mouthy, what about African American mothers on the tube? Invisible for decades, black women—especially in the form of the verbally aggressive, threatening matriarch—now made it onto sit-

coms, especially those produced by Norman Lear. Designed to raise socially relevant issues about race and racism—which they did—these
shows, and *Good Times* in particular, offered a sympathetic portrait of
the poor, African American mother at the same time that it trafficked in
the usual stereotypes suggesting that all black mothers were rolling-pin-
wielding viragos. Esther Rolle, as the mother, Florida, brought great range
to the role, so in between her deflating one-liners to her husband and kids
there were scenes that reminded white viewers that black mothers were
just as fiercely devoted to their kids as Donna Reed. But, as many critics
have noted with regret, the show degenerated into a minstrel showcase for
J.J. to do his "Dy-no-mite" shtick, and the struggles of a mother trying to
raise her family in the projects too often devolved into jokes about the
Ghet-Toe.

  Alice, and the other major "suddenly single" film *An Unmarried
Woman* (1978), brought single motherhood out of the media closet and
focused on the horrors of dating and the everyday forms of sexism that
these women encountered. But we started to see a shift here from *Diary of
a Mad Housewife.* While all these films acknowledged implicitly that
there may be a social and economic system one could call patriarchy, in
Alice and *An Unmarried Woman* the real issue was that there were
"good" men who responded positively to the women's movement (or
were never pigs in the first place), and those throwbacks who remained
unreconstructed male chauvinists. While our heroines had to learn to get
by on their own, they also met really hunky men with soft beards and
mustaches who tried to do almost anything to make them happy. Alice got
derailed on her trip to California and ended up waitressing in Arizona.
Here she met David (Kris Kristofferson), who fell in love with her *and* her
kid; she nonetheless kept insisting on getting to Monterey. "Go ahead,
pack your bags, I'll take you to Monterey. I don't give a damn about that
ranch," David told her. "That ranch" was the huge spread we saw him
lovingly tend to, and thus it was hard to believe he would give it up so easily. But here, it was the gesture that counted: as soon as David made such
a feminist-friendly pledge, Alice understood how much he was willing to
give up for her, so of course she decided that she and her son should stay
right where they were with David. Likewise, in *Unmarried Woman,*
whom should Erica (Jill Clayburgh) meet shortly after her weasely husband left her and her teenage daughter but the fabulously successful abstract expressionist painter Saul, played by an irresistible Alan Bates,

English accent and all. He adored her, was good to her, offered to support her, and asked her to come with him to Vermont for the summer, which she refused to do because she didn't want to resume dependency on a man. He called her stubborn and independent as he stroked her leg and looked at her admiringly. In other words, he got it, would put up with it, and still loved her, independence and all.

With guys like Alan Bates out there, there couldn't really be an entire system called patriarchy holding women down, could there? Indeed, by the time we got to *The Turning Point* (1977), the feminist insistence on the liberation from patriarchy had begun its slide into the morass of "lifestyle choices." Emma (Anne Bancroft) chose a career as a ballerina while Dee Dee (Shirley MacLaine), Emma's friend, chose marriage and motherhood. There was no patriarchy, or even bad men: just women's choices, which they make and then must live with. Dee Dee smoldered with envy over Emma's fame and success, but the film had two messages: Dee Dee was happier and had the richer life as a housewife and mother, and her daughter, an aspiring ballerina, wouldn't have to make the same stark choices and might be able to have it all. You would outgrow and lose a career because of age, but you never outgrow or lose motherhood. "What I'm doing offstage is just waiting to get back on," Emma confessed pathetically to Dee Dee. In the Hollywood films of the 1970s, then, feminism got a toe in the door and exposed marriage and the family as traps for women, but over time suggested that being a wife and mother now could be different, better, liberated, if you just found the right guy, with the requisite facial hair.

If TV and some movies gave us the mouthy moms in response to feminism, advertising gave us the supermom, the one who had and could do it all, had the energy and the resources—except for the one thing that the advertiser was hawking—to make everyone, even herself, happy. The infamous commercial for Enjolie perfume, in which the new modern mom shimmied onto the screen singing, "I can bring home the bacon, fry it up in a pan, and never, ever let you forget you're a man" was one of the more classic exemplars of Madison Avenue's new, imagined, multitasking mama. The magazine features in which various mothers spoke honestly about maternal anger, postpartum depression, guilt, stress, bratty kids, and husbands who didn't get it, were also defying, whether they knew it or not, the bread and butter of the magazines, the advertisers who relied on the promise of happiness to sell their products. In order to maintain the connection between contentment and consumerism, advertisers tapped into fantasies born of exhaustion, namely that a vitamin pill, a new flavor of Hamburger Helper, or a bathroom cleaner might provide mom with brand new psychic invigoration during the "second shift." One-a-Day vitamins, for example, quickly glamorized the new working mother. She wasn't harried or tired: "She's always on the go." With One-a-Day vitamins, "She handles them all . . . husband, family, great job, too." In one photo she and her family were joyously riding bicycles; in the other she was working at her desk, responding pensively to a question.[56] Stress? What stress?

An ad for Oil of Olay asked in a bold headline, "Planning to Go Back to Work?" "Good for you," the ad congratulated. "You've updated your resume and have a flattering new haircut. Your wardrobe looks perfect for a working woman. And you know in your secret heart that someone like you . . . who has run a household, done community work, entertained business and personal friends, and made the whole thing look easy . . . has the efficiency and organization that the business world is dying for." That last part was a bit of a stretch on the flattery front, but that's what advertisers do—say you're great, but still not good enough without their product. So here came the "but" part. "Yet you still find it a little scary competing with all those fresh-faced young girls just out of college." Time for Oil of Olay. "If the lovely possibility of looking younger would give your confidence a boost when job-hunting, wouldn't it be a good idea for you and Oil of Olay to go to work together?" Also, once you had landed that great job, when you came home from work, "while the children are helping cook [!!], freshen up before dinner with Oil of Olay."[57]

Was motherhood political, as some of the magazine features suggested, requiring new public policies for women and children to help make family structures more equitable? Or was the new motherhood simply an individual "lifestyle" choice, calling for new skin cream and witty repartee? Out of the conflict between intensive mothering and the women's movement, a new "common sense" about motherhood began to emerge, although it too was not without major contradictions. Now it was okay, often necessary, for mothers to work. Many women needed the money, and many needed to put their talents to other uses besides canning beets. It was even starting to be okay to go back to work while your children were toddlers or even infants, although this was, of course, highly contested. It was, as a result, okay to let the housework go if you had to. It was okay to get divorced if you were unhappy, even if you had children. It was okay to say you didn't want to have children at all.

But there were new risks to children as a result of all this, and part of this emerging common sense, which would really come to the fore in the 1980s as the new momism began to take root, was that mom would pay for her new independence—if that's what it was—by having to be more vigilant than ever when it came to the whereabouts and activities of her kids. What was not okay was for a mother to be so involved with her work that she failed to put her children first, always.

At the beginning of the decade, between the women's movement and the counterculture, there was a strong emphasis on women seeking out and finding collective solutions to the challenges of raising children. By the end of the decade, with runaway inflation, the Soviet invasion of Afghanistan, and the Iranian hostage crisis dominating the news, the feminist insistence on childcare, family leave, flex time, and equal pay had fallen on the deaf ears of policy makers. If women wanted to work, they were just going to have to add it on to their other endless responsibilities. If they couldn't hack it, well, too bad for them.

If we see *Diary of a Mad Housewife* as an exemplar of feminist criticism, however class-bound, finding expression in media culture—a bookend marking the beginning of the decade—then we should probably look at *Kramer vs. Kramer* (1979) as the other bookend, marking the repudiation of feminism on the big screen at the end of the decade. The film, which won Oscars for best picture, best director, best actor, best screenplay, and best supporting actress, received multiple kudos for its thoughtful, sensitive treatment of divorce. The acting is great. So it is especially important to see how under the guise of seriousness, sensitivity, and art, the backlash against the feminist critique of motherhood got expressed, and justified. Antifeminism is no more acceptable if it's in a beautifully produced package with actors you admire.

In *Kramer,* Tina Balser has been transformed into Joanna Kramer (Meryl Streep), wife of Ted (Dustin Hoffman), and mother of seven-year-old Billy (and unlike Tina's brats, the cutest little boy in America). Joanna is drained to the point of lifelessness. The Kramer family lived in upscale New York City and Ted (Dustin Hoffman), like Jonathan Balser, was completely preoccupied with his own corporate ambitions. But then, practically the first words we heard out of Joanna's mouth were, "Ted, I'm leaving you." But what was really shocking, even by 1970s standards, was the next part of the sentence: "and I'm not taking Billy."

Why was Joanna leaving? We weren't sure, because, as a variety of feminist film critics have noted, this was Ted's story, not Joanna's.[58] We never saw the seven years of getting up at 1:35 A.M. to deal with night terrors while Ted slept, the endless hours of playing Candyland until she was bored out of her mind while Ted exchanged ideas with adults, the weeks and months of isolation, self-doubt, and exasperation that some mothers actually feel when they are alone with children for most of the day. Because we didn't see or hear about any of this, we couldn't imagine why she was abandoning her adorable child in whom she had invested so much. Thus it was almost impossible to have any sympathy for her.

Instead, the movie suggested that the real reason she was leaving was because she let feminism—which cons women into abandoning their children in the name of fulfillment—get the better of her. Just as importantly, the movie powerfully redefined fathers not as tyrannical or uninvolved oppressors of women and children, but rather as deeply caring, self-sacrificing nurturers who could mother children just as well, or even better, than mom, especially a mom contaminated by feminism. Ted became such a great mom that even his career ambitions were put on the back burner because he had to take Billy to the doctor and attend events at school. (To the film's credit, it showed how antifamily the corporate world was, and how any single parent, male or female, had to constantly choose between their children and work. It just seemed so much more unfair— and poignant—when that worker was a man.)

The film represented Ted's transformation in a series of visual sequences showing his evolving ability to cook. Right after Joanna deserted them at the beginning of the movie, we were treated to a scene in which Ted's attempt to make French toast left the kitchen looking like Pompeii after Vesuvius blew. By the end of the movie, Ted and Billy turned out perfectly rendered slices of French toast in an immaculate kitchen. This achievement—which would be utterly banal for a woman—was presented as comparable to conquering open heart surgery. Kids were better off with dads like this than with moms who had read too much Germaine Greer and *Ms.* magazine.

After her feminist vacation, which led to a new job, Joanna returned to claim custody of Billy, which took the Kramers to court. Here we started to get her story, but it was too late—the audience was already on Dad's side. Confessing that she had thought Billy would be better off without her because she had such low self-esteem, she wanted Billy back now that her self-worth had been restored. But then Ted posed the pivotal question, "What law is it that says that a woman is a better parent simply by virtue of her sex? . . . I don't know where it's written that a woman has a corner on that market." Good point. But the movie made clear that a man *is* the better parent by virtue of his sex if the mother has committed the cardinal sin of motherhood: putting herself, however temporarily, before her child.

The judge eventually ruled in Joanna's favor (he "went for motherhood right down the line," observed Ted's slimy attorney), but it was clear who *should* have won. Ted's earnest embrace of the traits essential to intensive mothering ("constancy, patience, listening, pretending to listen," as he puts it in his testimony) make it clear that he was the one who deserved Billy. He gave up his masculine prerogatives, and hence his standing in the world of men, while his wife wanted to have it both ways—the rights previously reserved for men to work (and to leave if they want) and the rights automatically granted to mothers that children are their sole province. The film insisted that we cannot let her have it both ways.

Despite the judge's ruling (and because this is a Hollywood film), Joanna recognized that she had lost her moral claim to Billy and ceded him to the now warm and fuzzy Ted. The feminist scales fell from her eyes. In order to uphold the ideal of Motherhood with a capital M, Joanna had to sacrifice her child; she had to give him up to reaffirm how central self-sacrifice is to true motherhood.[59] Only then could she be redeemed as a mother.

Tearjerker movies, mouthy moms on sitcoms, kid advice columns all exerted their pull on mothers, showing them how to thumb their noses at intensive mothering while reminding them that rejecting intensive mothering meant their kids would be screwed up forever—and would blame them for it. But there were two camps, especially in the early 1970s, and feminists had pointed out that putting intensive mothering all on the mother prevented female equality with men. The kid shrinks said that mothers who failed to read and study everything—especially the shrinks' own columns and books—were in danger of producing a future generation of permanently scarred psychos or deeply pathetic, unloved wretches. Advertisers, often paving the way, had a solution: be a supermom. Embrace feminism *and* intensive mothering. This was not quite what feminists had in mind. But this was exactly the fusion—between two ethics impossible to reconcile—that the media, and millions of mothers, began to go with as the Gipper took the helm.

THREE

Threats from Without: Satanism, Abduction, and Other Media Panics

Razor blades in Halloween apples. Day-care centers staffed by child molesters. Pajamas that catch on fire. Improperly installed car seats. Satanism. Bottle-cavity syndrome. Child pornography rings. Toys that choke your kids. Alar in apple juice. Peanuts trapped in a toddler's windpipe. Stalkers. Rapists. Radiation from television sets. Child murders in Atlanta. Dust mites in stuffed animals. Kidnappers. Fetal Alcohol Syndrome. Gangs. Car hijackings. Liver damage from Tylenol. More Satanism. Missing children on all the milk cartons of America.

Everything led to "permanent damage": letting the baby fall asleep with a bottle (cavities), not putting enough Gore-Tex on your kid (frostbite), not having his/her eyes tested regularly (poor classroom performance due to vision problems), not curing ear infections quickly enough (deafness, learning disabilities), not identifying knee injuries quickly enough (limping; uneven leg growth), not putting enough 48 SPF sunscreen on the kid (skin cancer). Mothers needed to be the equivalent of physicians' assistants, pharmacists, child product safety testers, nutritionists, crafts people, and district attorneys.

Welcome to the new, risk-saturated world of motherhood in the early and mid-1980s in which childhood danger became a national fixation.[1]

An obsession with the Threats From Without was the first phase in the formation of what would become the new momism. In addition to pressures like finding reasonable day care or getting a dinner on the table that was, just for once, not pizza, now mothers had a Greek chorus of dire, terrifying warnings surging into their ears all the time. Of course there had been serious worries for mothers in the 1950s and 1960s, polio being one of the scariest. If our mothers were any indication, they worried when you didn't call home and worried when you did (answering the phone with "What's wrong?" instead of hello). They, too, fretted about you eating the right foods, falling out of a tree house, or talking to strangers.

But full-blown panics about children at risk take flight when women go off to work. In the 1940s, when women entered the workforce in record numbers to help win the war, they were surrounded by moral panics about juvenile delinquency and latchkey kids burning down the house. And now their daughters and granddaughters could enjoy the same fear, but at an even more heightened level. More mothers were working than ever before, and more media outlets, increasingly addicted to tabloid journalism, could bombard them with sensationalized terror. Working mothers reached a record number in 1984, with 19.5 million, or six out of ten women with children under eighteen, working outside the home.[2] Studies indicated that while nonparents worked about fifty-six hours per week, mothers, what with their duties at work and at home, put in an eighty-four-hour work week.[3]

By 1984, the most rapidly growing segment of the workforce was mothers with preschool children; the number of mothers with infants under one year of age in the workforce *doubled* between 1970 and 1985.[4] The rates for African American women with infant children (one year or under) was fifteen percentage points higher than the rate for whites, in part because the unemployment rate for black fathers with preschool children was 10.2 percent, as compared with 5 percent for white fathers.[5] In 1984, Catalyst, a nonprofit organization dedicated to expanding opportunities for women in business, reported that 68 percent of working mothers returned to work in four months or less of a baby's birth.[6]

And these women were not making what Demi Moore, Joan Collins, or the fictitious Clair Huxtable did. "Most women do not earn enough money to support themselves and their families," reported the *Labor Law Journal* in 1984. Or, to put it another way, 80 percent of all women still held low-paying, traditionally female jobs in retail sales, clerical, service, or factory work, and they earned, on average, for full-time work, mind you, just over $12,000 a year, while men earned $20,500 a year.[7] (Three million full-time female clerical workers actually earned less than the poverty threshold, $9,000!)[8] Almost half of the families headed by a mother alone had incomes below the official poverty level.[9] If a mother was lucky enough to live near a day-care center, the workers to whom she entrusted her kids earned less than liquor-store clerks.[10] This kind of economic vulnerability only heightened fears about your own kid's defenselessness. When mothers opened a magazine or turned on the TV, they read that indeed they could "have it all" and, at the same time, saw that their kids were in constant mortal peril.

In 1984 in particular we see a turning point in the media representations of American motherhood. Two major media events exemplified the cultural contradictions in which working mothers were caught: On one end of the spectrum, the McMartin day-care child-molestation scandal (followed by a barrage of other, similar scandals), and on the other end of the spectrum, the premiere and runaway success of *The Cosby Show*. The former served as the direst warning of what happens when mothers go to work and entrust their children to others. The latter suggested that you could work at a demanding job, express frequent exasperation with your kids and jokingly threaten to murder them on a regular basis, and yet have a loving husband and children and be a terrific mother. Thus, one persona you were supposed to inhabit was a one-woman paranoiac, FBI agent, and vigilante. Another persona you were *also* supposed to inhabit was that of a carefree, wisecracking, spontaneous mom with a light touch, an elegant refinement of the 1970s mouthy mother. You were thus supposed to have inside you a perfectly calibrated gyroscope that moved you between these different identities at a moment's notice. In 1984, the media simultaneously acknowledged that, why yes, of course mothers worked and that was completely natural, and yet warned that, oh no, this is a catastrophe for children and the nation at large. In the ongoing battle over intensive mothering, the media panics in the news insisted that it was precisely because mothers were working that they had to be more obsessive than ever, while *The Cosby Show* suggested it was high time for mothers to lighten up and relax.

The possibilities and anxieties opened up by the revolution in family life reached a cultural boiling point as the sun rose in Reagan's "new morning in America." By 1984, there were two hugely important maternal markets complete with monikers, working "mothers" and stay-at-home "moms," and often they needed and wanted the very same things. Mothers mattered and needed to be flattered, as consumers and as voters. At the same time, the Reagan presidency and the rise of the religious right led to a well-funded and often vehement backlash against feminism, most frequently expressed as "family values," which meant Dad should be the boss again and Mom should make family heirlooms out of the lint from the clothes dryer. The ongoing battles over motherhood, and the enormous changes in how families operated, in how children were raised, especially with so little institutional support of any kind, together constituted a seismic societal shift that generated deep cultural anxieties about the fragility and future of the family.

These anxieties got expressed and amplified in a variety of media panics most sensationally manifested in the news, women's magazines, and made-for-TV movies. The image of the lost or sexually defiled child became the dominant metaphor for the risks and costs of the feminist-inspired new motherhood. The favorite journalistic word in the 1980s about the family was "epidemic," as in the epidemics of child molestation, child abuse, runaway teens, and teen pregnancy.

Media panics identify a person or a group, an event or a condition, as a profound, deeply destructive threat to society. The person or group is then represented in a highly sensationalized and stereotypical fashion, and certain authorities, including reporters, assume the role of moral police, expressing outrage and demanding swift punishment and a massive dragnet of all other potential threats. The media thus become central to providing information to the public about "the shapes the Devil can assume." (You know, quiet guy, kinda weird, keeps to himself.) [11] The panic becomes a powerful news peg on which other stories that would not get reported under different circumstances get hung and connected, so the media can then escalate the coverage until the threat seems nearly out of control.[12] Thus, a media panic can last months, even years. Those charged with the heinous wrongdoing are assumed guilty (even if they are later found innocent). Media panics most often stem from powerful fears about a newly perceived vulnerability of the nation. Although media panics rarely begin as a conscious effort to bolster the power of governmental authority, they often inadvertently reinforce conservative political stances and policies not shared by the majority of the population, but now deemed necessary because of the panic. The television networks, for ex-

ample, hardly intended, in their coverage of the day-care scandals, to endorse the government's refusal to fund day-care centers for the millions of
kids who needed them. But that was one of the results of their coverage.

To appreciate why the endangered or despoiled child became such a
ubiquitous figure in the media at this time, it is crucial to understand the
economic and psychic changes wrought by Reaganism. An entire industry
has emerged to burnish Ronald Reagan's reputation, to have every public
building and airport named or renamed after him, and to cultivate public
amnesia about the true consequences of his presidency, especially on
mothers and children. So let's be clear—Ronald Reagan's administration,
its policies interlarded with antifeminist suet from the religious right, was
dedicated to re-establishing women's dependence on the patriarchal family.[13] Reagan's promise of economic renewal rested on cutting as many
government programs as possible, especially those that did not benefit
corporate America or the military-industrial complex. Programs that
helped women and children, especially poor ones, were just, well, too expensive.[14] And they weren't needed, anyway, because all the wealth from
rich folks would now "trickle down" to everyone, including those single
moms earning nine grand a year. Thus, it was quite clear that government-
sponsored programs that would have thrown to mothers the kind of life
preservers that Congress offered to the Chrysler Corporation or, later,
to the savings and loan industry, would not be forthcoming. The point
was clear: Children are the individual responsibility of the family, not
the collective responsibility of the country. Under Reagan, funding for
day-care centers was cut by tens of millions of dollars.[15] The WIC program (Women, Infants and Children) was cut, and infant mortality rates,
which had declined in the 1970s, especially for women of color, began to
climb again.[16] Maternity leave? Take it to court, sister. Day care? We don't
need no stinkin' day care. Family leave? Pu-leez.

Meanwhile, the vulnerable, helpless child was also irresistible to a
news media increasingly infested by the voyeuristic sensibilities of tabloid
journalism. Media panics about missing, abducted, or molested children
exploited people's worst fears; but they also had a creepy, prurient edge as
they asked viewers to imagine a child being sodomized or fondled. They
rested on voyeurism masquerading as modesty. The violated child evoked
a combination of titillation and outrage that was designed to keep people
tuning in.

In the media sources where mothers sought out information—

women's magazines and the news—risks of the new motherhood lay everywhere. You want day care? Go ahead. Your child will be sick all the time, exposed to diseases and infections unknown at home. (Of course, your kid *is* more likely to get head lice or chicken pox at day care. But that's also true if he joins Pee Wee League T-Ball or, for that matter, attends first grade.) *Parents* warned in 1982 that day-care kids were "more easily frustrated, less cooperative with adults . . . more destructive and less task-oriented." [17] In other words, future hoodlums. (Unlike the sorry truth about the head lice, this was rubbish, as later studies would prove.) Babies who spent more than twenty hours a week in a center would eventually reject their mothers, *Parents* warned. By the late 1980s, working mothers could open *Parents* magazine and read that the children of two-career families felt "neglected" and were susceptible to "delinquency, sexual promiscuity, running away, substance abuse, and other problems." [18] Some of the warnings provided welcome, previously unheeded precautions, like the need to wear bicycle helmets and to strap your toddlers into car seats. The heightened awareness around child safety was a natural outgrowth of the consumer rights movement that had started with Corvairs and Pintos, and had now moved to the chewability of eyes on Teddy Bears. But with uncertain government protection, mothers now had to adopt the tactics of a HazMat crew.

The sensationalizing of childhood perils did not really reach its peak until the mid-1980s and beyond, but we see its roots earlier. In February of 1975, *Ladies' Home Journal,* having dispatched the blowhole Bettelheim, introduced a new column by Geraldine Carro called "Mothering." This was pitched as offering "the latest news, ideas, and information every mother needs to know about child-rearing." And it was *by* a mother *for* mothers, "who must after all be counted among the experts on children." (Take that, Bruno.) In her opening column, Carro noted how liberating it was to finally admit—without guilt—"that as a condition, motherhood rates mixed reviews." The column, she promised, would "offer but not impose opinions. For too long, we've been living by other people's books." [19]

The column featured three or four short pieces on topics like "How to Pick a Pediatrician" or teaching your kids how to cook. Within three months, any regular follower of this column would have been terror-stricken. In the first one, we learned that mothers had to maintain "a constant and crucial watch on small objects" that a child might put into his or her mouth, because these could cause choking or lung damage. "Your safe bet is to think ahead." And then we got the list: no toys with "tiny eyes, buttons, and other potentially detachable small parts," no marbles or tiny plastic toys, no buttons, pills, screws, beads, no opened safety pins (duh!), no peanuts.[20] If you had bought a car seat for your child, look out—this is "confusing business." "Many seats now sold have been proved unsafe." There *were* safe ones. "But even the best seat," warned an expert, "is no better than a rocking chair unless a parent installs it correctly." [21] With car accidents being the number-one cause of death for children under five, this, of course, was important information. But the constant tone of warning, that whatever you were doing might still not be enough, or may be wrong, meant you could never be at peace. And the assumption underlying much of this advice was that mothers had absolutely no common sense and if they had instincts about their children's care, those instincts were wrong, dead wrong.

In "How Safe Is Your Child's Summer Camp?" (1975), readers learned that in 1974, "close to 100 deaths and 250,000 accidents occurred in the country's nearly 10,000 children's camps." To prevent such a tragedy from happening to your child, mothers were given fourteen steps to follow. They should investigate whether the camp is accredited, get the camper-counselor ratio, establish whether there were enough life preservers for each child in each of the camp's boats, determine that all state health, sanitary, and fire codes were met, ascertain whether all the waterfront counselors had Red Cross training, and make sure that all the counselors were experienced. Jeez—our mothers just put labels in our clothes and sent us off. Now mom had to add being a one-woman Ralph Nader to her other maternal requirements.[22]

Parents who stupidly tossed their babies in the air were risking whiplash "and consequent hemorrhaging of the blood vessels that feed into the child's brain." [23] Okay, fair enough. But parents also shouldn't introduce their baby to a new baby-sitter and a new crib on the same day, lest this lethal combo make the child freak out. In the adjacent column we learned that "Each year . . . 12,000 children are poisoned, some fatally, by eating plants and flowers." [24] By 1975, children's sleepwear had to be flame retardant, but unless the mother washed them just right, using only warm water, a high-phosphate laundry detergent (great for the environment), and no soap, bleach, or fabric softener, they stopped being flame retardant. (Now who oversaw *that* legislation?)

You should teach your child how to swim by eight months. No, wait, you should not teach her until age three. If you wait, your kid will drown (she won't know how to survive in water), but if you do she'll drown too (you'll become complacent and think she's safer near a pool than she really is).[25] Even Santa was dangerous, because some children were "frightened by the idea that Santa will come down the chimney and prowl around the house when they are asleep." And you should never tell your kids that Santa is real, because "we're teaching them that it's all right to lie." When shopping for Christmas presents, make sure the toys are neither too simple nor too complex. "Look for a well-informed salesperson," presumably like the ones at Toys "Я" Us. And especially buy sturdy, good-quality toys. If you don't, noted a Rutgers psychologist, and the toy breaks, your child will feel not just disappointed but guilty, too.[26]

Halloween was now a nightmare. All costumes should be flame retardant. Mothers had to put reflective tape strips on all costumes and trick-or-treat bags. No child should go out without a flashlight, although it was preferable to restrict trick-or-treating to the daylight hours. Children shouldn't wear masks anymore—they prevent kids from seeing oncoming cars and "other hazards." And finally, "Examine thoroughly all edibles children bring into the house. Cut open candy and fruits to inspect for foreign objects."[27]

"How do you protect your kids from danger without making them overly fearful?" Carro asked in 1977. There was a new catalog available that mothers could study called Safety Now that listed the safest equipment for kids.[28] Carro reported that one out of four children was afraid to go out and play, and two-thirds worried that someone would break into their homes and hurt them.[29] (No wonder—if their moms talked out loud about any two of these columns, what kid wouldn't be petrified to leave the bedroom?) Time and again it was the individual mother who had to make up for inadequate government regulations and protections, the mother who must do the investigating, protecting, sorting out of conflicting information.

By the early 1980s there was the seemingly new and horrid phenomenon of the missing child. As soon as you let your kid out of your sight, he or she was in danger of being abducted. The first notorious case occurred in May of 1979, when Etan Patz, six, was kidnapped in downtown New York just before getting on his bus for school. Despite a frantic, highly publicized search, involving television pleas from his mother, flyers posted all over the city, and the work of hundreds of police, Etan was never found.[30] The case was the basis for Beth Gutcheon's 1981 bestseller, *Still Missing*. Then another six-year-old, Adam Walsh, was kidnapped from the toy department of a department store in Florida, also vanishing without a trace. His story was memorialized in the made-for-TV movie *Adam*, first broadcast in October of 1983 with huge ratings and starring Daniel J. Travante as Adam's father, John Walsh, of *America's Most Wanted* fame. In March of 1984, ten-year-old Kevin Collins, missing for more than a month, was on the cover of *Newsweek* next to the bold headline STOLEN CHILDREN.[31]

These cases were, of course, horrific, and not to be trivialized. But the media exploited them—to draw attention to a possible new problem—and they universalized them, to draw in viewers. If this could happen to Adam, it could happen to any child, to your child, anytime, anywhere, so keep tuning in, to see if it's still going on and what you can do about it. Missing children became an important news peg, reminding parents on a regular basis that this was now something they had to think about constantly and regard as a daily threat. This lucrative news frame for the 1980s—the endangered, vulnerable child—was sensationalized, magnified, and exaggerated until few mothers were comfortable letting their kids play on the front lawn without a leash. Wildly exaggerated figures—that as many as two million kids disappeared each year and that five thousand a year were abducted and killed—circulated in the media.[32] Revised figures in 1988 suggested that, in fact, somewhere between two and three hundred kids nationally were abducted by strangers for any length of time, and of those, somewhere between 43 and 147 died as a result. A small number of tragic cases became a blanket of terror thrown over us all.

Note, for example, the highly dramatic tones of this NBC report on March 28, 1984. Under the logo *Parent's Fear*, Tom Brokaw reported, "The fear is thick around Denver these days. A number of kidnappings have made everyone nervous—parents, children, and police." People were alarmed by "a rash of child kidnappings, sexual assaults, and attempts by people to pick up school-age children." In Denver, there had reportedly been eleven such cases in the last eight school days. "The children are frightened. And so are their parents." NBC reported that many parents were not letting their kids take the bus but instead were driving their kids to school and waiting until they saw their kids walk inside the building (a little advice about what you should be doing).[33] Such stories did not then explore what kind of collective, social commitment the country might make to improve child welfare. No—this was about your kids, about the danger posed to your particular child, about what you and you alone should do.

At the very same time, also in the spring of 1984, a huge comet of a story, with appalling accounts of child rape, sodomy, and animal butchery swirling in its tail, hurtled into the living rooms of America. Let's say you were there, and in your mid-thirties. And let's say that your husband, forty, had just announced that he needed to "find himself," and intended to do this with the help of Misty, twenty-two. He moves across the country, leaving you with your two kids, ages one-and-a-half and four, and never sends you a dime or a forwarding address. Your mother lives five states away and you have no family in town. You can either go on welfare or go to work. You go to work, but must find childcare for the kids. After desperate searching—remember, this is when six million kids need day care and there are only one million slots, and nearly half of all mothers with kids under the age of one are working—you find a neighborhood place that takes about eight kids and is run by a grandmother and her daughter-in-law. They seem really nice; the house is clean and full of toys; they have room; you can afford it. You go for it.

Two weeks later, in late March 1984, screaming headlines expose a "Nightmare Nursery" in Manhattan Beach, California. "In what may become one of the biggest child molesting cases ever on record," announced Tom Brokaw, seven nursery school teachers at the McMartin Preschool had been arraigned on over one hundred counts of child molestation. "It's a parent's nightmare," he continued. "The person entrusted to guard and keep their child suspected of betraying that trust."[34] According to the charges, grandmotherly Virginia McMartin, seventy-six, who wore Snoopy earrings and was confined to a wheelchair, presided over a day-care center in which she and her family members allegedly drugged, fondled, raped, and sodomized at least 125 children, some as young as two, over a ten-year period. "The adults took pictures, sometimes movies," the press reported. To dissuade the children from tattling, the teachers allegedly cut off the ears of live rabbits and smashed baby turtles in front of the kids. In case this didn't drive the point home, the teachers supposedly beat a horse to death with a baseball bat, also in front of the kids. All of this was reported in the press with a straight face, and by quoting the prosecutors, news outlets like NBC, KABC, and others did not have to use the word *allegedly*. With coverage like this, it is not surprising that in the absence of any evidence—and re-member, none of the defendants in the McMartin case was willing to testify against any of the others in exchange for leniency—a whopping 90 percent of Los Angeles residents surveyed in 1986 believed Ray Buckey and his grandmother Virginia to be guilty.[35]

At this place, parents didn't take their kids to day care; as *Newsweek* put it, they "delivered their children to an outlet for child pornography and prostitution."[36] Kee MacFarlane, one of the therapists hired to get the children to discuss the abuse, told ABC News, "I've heard more detailed descriptions of things than I ever wanted to hear in my life . . . and that I'm going to have a hard time forgetting . . . adult nudity and children being exposed, all the way to forcible rape and sodomy."[37] Outraged parents naturally denounced the childcare providers as the scum of the earth. "I want them out of society forever," said one mother. "They should never even be allowed to be with other children or anybody else for that matter."[38]

In the late 1970s and early 1980s, there had been minimal news cover-age of day care in America, except for occasional stories that documented the huge gap between the millions of kids who needed it and the all-too-few centers that could provide it. And then this. All of a sudden, media panics about molestation, abuse, and satanic rituals involving children were everywhere. This was the 1980s version of McCarthyism, but in-stead of a Red Scare, it was a Kid Scare. And it was big. In *The New York Times,* for example, there were approximately 50 stories about day care in 1980, most of them innocuous and emphasizing the undersupply. In 1984 the number had soared to 240, many of them about the scandals.[39] These stories terrified working mothers right down to their bone marrow and helped demonize day care for years and years to come, legitimating the government's refusal to establish a national day-care system. And if you don't think self-interest and profits were involved, get this: KABC in Los Angeles chose to break the story in February 1984, during the ratings sweeps weeks.[40]

Some of the child-molestation accusations were serious and true—but most of them, it turned out, particularly the most publicized ones about the day-care centers like McMartin, were not. Some of the charges were actually fabricated by overeager, unlicensed "therapists" who used pup-pets and relentless prodding to get the kids to agree to previously made-up stories. (The kids at McMartin, for example, denied any abuse until relentless badgering by therapists who used leading questions and threats to get the kids to talk.)[41] Other charges were fabricated by jailhouse snitches who traded perjured testimony for reduced sentences, and then were blown completely out of proportion by overeager prosecutors.[42] After McMartin, over one hundred additional cases of satanic child abuse in day-care settings were brought to trial.[43] In 1989 to 1990, California received over 440,000 reports of child abuse; 84 percent were deemed to be unfounded. Of the remaining, 8,448 of the cases were defined as sexual abuse. While this is indeed an infuriating number, the fact that there were *fifty-two times* as many allegations as there were cases documents many people's charges that estranged spouses, angry coworkers, and others were using such charges to get back at people, and that the heightened news coverage may have prompted some people to see a modern-day form of witchcraft where none existed.[44]

Most of the media treated the accused as guilty until proven innocent, and milked every sensationalistic drop they could out of the lurid accusations. As *Ladies' Home Journal* warned mothers in the fall of 1984, "Nobody knows how many habitual child molesters work as teachers, bus drivers, Little League coaches, camp counselors, or scouting troop leaders. But there is no doubt that these are the jobs of choice for many abusers." The magazine then cited a study that asserted that "more than half of the pedophiles studied used legitimate child-care positions to seduce vulnerable children," and warned that "about a half-million children nationwide . . . will be molested this year."[45]

In the wake of the McMartin charges in 1984, the sexual and physical abuse of children, especially at day-care centers, became a staple of the nightly news. On April 6, Terry Drinkwater on CBS reported that nationally over a million children were in day-care centers and nursery schools, "enrolled, in most cases, because their mothers must work." While the "vast majority" were properly cared for, "elsewhere, in alarming numbers, preschoolers have been exploited, *sexually.*" What had happened at McMartin "is just the latest."[46] The founder of the Children's Theater Company in Minneapolis, John Clark Donahue, was forced to resign after allegations that he had molested three boys. "It's the latest in what seems to be an epidemic of child abuse in this country," intoned Brokaw on April 19.[47] Another center, Little Rascals Day Care in North Carolina, also became notorious when its owner and cook were charged with molestation. (The owner's conviction was eventually overturned.)[48] On May

2, Brokaw, flanked by a graphic featuring the words *Child Molesters* written in chalk across a blackboard with a Raggedy Ann doll drooping against a block, announced, "Nearly every week, this year, we've heard another story of sex abuse of children." Now there was another problem: "fathers who abuse their children during weekend visits." In this story viewers heard from a mother of two little girls, ages three and four, who charged that their father sexually abused them on their weekend custody visits.

On and on it went. On May 21, we met a Los Angeles teacher brought into court on charges of child molestation at an elementary school.[49] Ten days later, ABC and CBS reported that "at a church-run boarding school for boys" in Walterboro, South Carolina, the boys were beaten and abused. The school "was more like a chamber of horrors," according to ABC, which showed handcuffs, pipes, and sticks used for beating the boys, and a metal-grated door leading into a solitary jail cell that looked like something right out of *Papillon*.[50] Three weeks after this, in late June, CBS and ABC told Americans about a fundamentalist commune in Island Pond, Vermont, that was raided—taking more than a hundred kids from their homes—because it was alleged that church elders and their own parents had abused them. One former commune member told ABC that something called "scourging" went on where kids were stripped naked and beaten with a rod from the soles of their feet to the top of their heads.[51] Church members did not dispute that they used corporal punishment to discipline the children and, in the end, the children were released and the case was dropped. "Suddenly it seems that the problem of child abuse has become a national epidemic," Brokaw warned again.[52] We then met a mother, her face in the shadows so we couldn't see her, who said her five-year-old was sexually abused in a day-care center in the Bronx. "His case is not an isolated incident," noted the reporter; "reports of day-care abuse are frequent."

Over on ABC, viewers were taken to a Senate hearing where testimony linked child abuse to child pornography "rings." One FBI expert said that hundreds of thousands of Americans sexually abuse children and that pornography is often involved. According to the feds, a book called *How to Have Sex with Kids* circulated among child molesters and instructed them on how to locate and seduce children, which included trying to get baby-sitting jobs.[53] Two days after that, Mark Potter of ABC reported, "Once again there have been charges today that young children have been sexually abused," this time in South Dade County, Florida, also at a day-care center. Like McMartin, which had been a much-admired center prior to the accusations, Country Walk Baby Sitting Service was "in a fashionable house in a well-to-do Miami suburban neighborhood."

The subtext of all these stories was clear by now: No place was safe, class privilege guaranteed nothing, and you can't judge a center by its location, appearance, or previous reputation—you just never, never know. The Dade County day-care center was not licensed by the state and, worse, its owner, it turned out, had previously faced manslaughter charges, as well as charges of lewd and lascivious behavior.[54] On August 16, 1984, Dan Rather reported that a San Diego grand jury brought charges against the operator of a small foster home for the handicapped who was accused of sexually abusing two young girls, both of whom were confined to wheelchairs and unable to care for themselves. By September 5, 1984, Tom Brokaw, in a special segment on the national need for day care, was able to say "it is an explosive subject these days" because a number of day-care centers "have been involved in outrageous child molestation cases." Again, he did not feel the need to use the word *allegedly*.[55]

Physical abuse could be equally shocking. In April 1985, CBS announced that six children at a church day-care center in Kansas City "suffered the kind of broken bones usually linked to violence." The children, the oldest of whom was only seventeen months, were diagnosed with having a total of eleven broken arms and legs. The reporter emphasized that the day-care center was not licensed, because Missouri exempts church-run day-care centers from licensing. (Ah, the merits of "faith-based" institutions.) There were no suspects.[56]

Everywhere, children were in danger: in big cities and in small towns, where everyone thought they knew everyone else and could trust them. Even if your kids *weren't* in day care, they still weren't safe. And molestation cases were especially newsworthy if they happened in places supposedly far removed from the corruptions of big cities. One of the biggest stories of the year, which broke in late August of 1984, focused on Jordan, Minnesota, where the most extensive case of sexual abuse in Minnesota's history supposedly came to light, putting the lie to the theory "that 'it can't happen here,' " as Peter Jennings reminded us. A shot of a white church spire (with church bells ringing) signified that we were indeed in small-town, pastoral, Christian America. *Time* described the town as "Rockwellian . . . idyllic . . . a model American community."[57]

Twenty-four defendants, which included "factory workers, house-wives, and a grandmother," were all said to be part of a "sex ring" and were charged with more than four hundred counts of sexually abusing dozens of children, including their own. ABC reported that the children were allegedly forced to play "a perverted game of hide and seek—during which kids were forced to have sex with adults, each other, and even ani-mals." *Time* said that "one young girl reported being forced to eat a cat and a pet gerbil, 'fur and all.' " [58] (How, exactly, do you get a kid to eat a gerbil, "fur and all"?) The prosecutor, Kathleen Morris, insisted that child molesters "look just like you or I do . . . they have good jobs," so you never know one when you see one. [59] All those who were charged had their kids taken away from them and put into foster care. In a special report on child molestation, ABC in November of 1984 featured a pediatrician from Columbia Presbyterian Hospital in New York who said, "We are seeing so much of it that it's just mind boggling. It's coming in all the time . . . coming in every day, almost." At the end of the story, ABC previewed the next day's follow-up: "Tomorrow, the children. Do they ever forget?" [60]

A centrally important theme in the media coverage of these stories was the failure of government agencies to oversee day-care centers and to catch the molestation in time. The failings of government regulation, espe-cially when linked to a major scandal, are almost always newsworthy. But during the Reagan years, such supposed lapses resonated with the admin-istration's daily mantra that government agencies were unnecessary in part because they were ineffective and thus wasteful. Hence, such stories helped undermine the notion that the government might itself fund and operate day-care centers. Some of the centers weren't licensed; others were but weren't inspected; others were inspected but still contained abuse. Were you really going to trust your kids' care to anything the gov-ernment oversaw?

By 1985, *Newsweek* recounted the tale of a ten-year-old who reported that he and twenty-five kids were taken to a satanic ritual where adults threw knives at a baby, dismembered him, and forced the kids to drink his blood. [61] Satanism was another very hot story. Geraldo Rivera—are we surprised?—did a typically sensationalistic show on Satanism and the sa-tanic "ritual abuse" of children. A voiceover intoned that over a thousand children were still suffering "from the horror they experienced at the McMartin Preschool." The show described McMartin's locale as "the molestation capital of the world." [62]

Around the country, priests were outed as having molested altar boys and other young men with whom they came in contact. For example, the news reported in 1985 on a Roman Catholic priest in rural Henry, Louisiana, who admitted he sexually abused at least thirty-five boys and was sentenced to twenty years' hard labor.[63] (Of course, in 2002, we saw how seriously the Catholic Church had taken such cases. They were too busy telling mothers to shut up, never use birth control, and accept their fate rather than investigating their own.) In August of 1985, NBC and CBS reported on a poll published in *The Los Angeles Times* indicating that child sexual abuse was "more widespread in this country than previously believed." Twenty-two percent of adults said they were victims of sexual abuse when they were children; many never told anyone, and seven out of ten who did tell said no action was ever taken against the abusers.[64]

What were you supposed to think of that kindly grandma's day care where your kids spent their days now? Virginia McMartin, a grandma for Pete's sake, was about the last person one would connect to the word *pedophile*. But the stories kept emphasizing that looks were deceiving; there was no one you could trust. According to dozens of news stories, America was now in the grips of a "child-abuse epidemic." [65] Less well publicized were the follow-up stories about these cases documenting that day-care centers were not, in fact, dens of child porn and molestation.

For example, it later turned out that the kid who started the accusations at McMartin, which focused especially on McMartin's grandson Raymond Buckey, had only been in the center fourteen days and had not been in Buckey's class; plus Buckey's defense attorney found two doctors willing to testify that the child told them that it was his own father who had "poked him" in his anus.[66] The boy's mother, Judy Johnson, who circulated the initial charges against McMartin and brought them to the police, was known to be mentally ill (diagnosed as an acute paranoid schizophrenic), and especially had trouble distinguishing between fantasy and reality. For example, she also accused a Los Angeles school board member of molesting her son, and claimed her kid had been injured by an elephant and forced to drink baby's blood while in the McMartins' care.[67]

All the children initially denied any abuse—something conveniently left out of *People* magazine, *Newsweek,* and all the network news coverage. Instead, the puppet "therapist" Kee MacFarlane was quoted as saying she had never seen kids so scared in her life. She was probably right—by the time she and the other "therapists" had gotten done with the kids, they had named gas station attendants, community leaders, and store clerks as molesters.[68] It was MacFarlane, not the kids, who came up with the name "naked movie star" for a game the teachers allegedly made the kids play. The videotapes of the interviews revealed that the children at first had no idea what she was talking about; but she kept badgering them, saying things like, "You want to be smart like the other kids who told, don't you?" or, once she got them to agree to her story, "You must not be a dummy after all." When she asked a kid about being "poked" (i.e., sodomized), he said he remembered the story and said that Ray poked someone with a chair. Wrong answer, kid. "How about when he poked him with himself?" prompted the therapist. "Oh yeah," said the kid, and then identified the body part, "his foot." Wrong again. "Remember when we talked about his penis?" On it went like this, in a questioning technique that was soon to become infamous.[69]

Jurors who had viewed the tapes of her interviews with the children were appalled at how directly MacFarlane led their answers. During the trial the children constantly changed their stories or answered "I don't remember" when asked about the abuse. The prosecutor visited the kids before they testified to coach them on their stories. Nonetheless, several denied, on the witness stand, that any abuse had ever occurred.

As if the leading questions weren't bad enough, it turned out that MacFarlane, the naked puppet lady, had had an affair during the early months of the case with Wayne Satz, the television reporter for KABC who broke the McMartin story and won two "Golden Mike" awards for his coverage, which included interviews with MacFarlane.[70] Hardly a high moment for what used to be called journalistic ethics. After nearly six years and a whopping $15 million—the longest and most expensive criminal trial in American history—Ray Buckey and his mother were found not guilty.[71] There was a hung jury on some of the counts, so the state retried them. They were still found not guilty.

But at the time, what with Ray Buckey instantly characterized by *People* as "a loner" who "didn't have friends," who had a "bent for wearing shorts with no underwear" and was "viewed by some as a dim mama's boy,"[72] it was almost impossible to suggest he might be innocent. Who needs actual evidence when you've got this kind of dirt? In their account of the McMartin trials, *The Abuse of Innocence,* Paul and Shirley Eberle report that *The Los Angeles Times* reported the prosecutor's take on the case over the defense's by a ratio of approximately fourteen to one.[73] (Virginia McMartin died in 1995. Peggy McMartin Buckey, who in 1990 noted bitterly, "I've gone through hell, and now we've lost everything," died in 2000. Ray Buckey, who was incarcerated for five years while the trials dragged on, later went to law school.)[74]

As early as the fall of 1984, the Jordan, Minnesota, cases started falling apart. One couple was acquitted of abusing their six-year-old son and four other children, and they vowed to regain custody of their three sons taken from them nine months earlier. Then the more than four hundred sexual abuse charges against twenty-two people were withdrawn. Forty children had been taken away from their parents as part of the witch hunt.[75] By November 28, 1984, Peter Jennings was able to report that the only person who pled guilty in the Jordan case, James Rud, now said he lied when he implicated others. The same highly aggressive questioning style of the children deployed in the McMartin case had been used here, too, by the prosecution—one nine-year-old was reportedly questioned twenty separate times by the authorities. In a subsequent investigation into the prosecution's handling of the case, one child admitted that he based his story on a TV show and lied to please the prosecutor.[76]

Besides the childcare providers, of course, whose fault was all this? Why, Mom's, of course. In a special series on "The Molested Child," ABC interviewed a mother, her face hidden in the shadows, who said her three-year-old daughter was being raped while in day care. The reporter asked about guilt, and of course she felt terrible guilt, because every day she was pushing her toddler into a room where she was being raped. "And I never knew it and I feel as though I neglected her, I feel as though I should have known. . . . I don't know how I could have known but you're still responsible for your children."[77] *Ladies' Home Journal* warned mothers that certain "high-risk" kids were targeted by molesters: "a child who comes from a broken home" (e.g., raised by a single mom), a child who is "craving attention," or a child "whose father travels a lot."[78] After McMartin, day-care centers for a while became synonymous with sexual abuse. *Good Housekeeping* got to the point in 1984 with its article "When Child Care Becomes Child Molesting." *McCall's* advised its readers in 1987, "The vast majority of children who are sexually molested are victimized not by strangers, but by someone they know and trust: a friend, a neighbor, a teacher, a relative or, as newspaper headlines too often remind us, by a caregiver at a preschool or day-care center."[79] *Ladies' Home Journal* admitted that now "we can never put the issue of child abuse out of our heads entirely." [80] As Susan Faludi would later reveal in *Backlash*, a three-year study showed that kids were twice as likely to be abused at home as they were in day care.[81] But media panics tend to develop an immunity to counterevidence, and so this study was not reported on by the women's magazines.[82]

At the same time, the women's magazines also reassured mothers that day care was fine, that your kid would never love a childcare provider more than he or she loved you, that kids learned skills in day care they didn't at home, and that a ten-year-old could very well handle being home alone for a few hours after school. As Kathryn Keller, in her study of mothers and work in popular magazines put it, "Each negative image of day care and the implication behind it that women should not be working but should be at home with their children was countered by a positive image." [83] So mothers were surrounded by mixed messages that warned them that they should stay at home to protect their kids but assured them the kids would be safe if mothers also go out to work.

The day-care and sex-abuse panics all created a climate of terror and paranoia for mothers that lingers to this day. On the one hand, issues closeted for years, like the sexual and physical abuse of children (most often by members of their own family), got the exposure they deserved. On the other hand, in the face of a dramatic shift in how family life was organized—more divorces, more mothers working outside the home, more families headed by single women, more kids in some form of day care—the media availed itself of the selling power of child sensationalism. It was true, of course, that many in the media sought to further protect children by exposing child molestation and abuse. But there was also little doubt that such stories increased ratings and sales, and thus made it quite profitable for the media to terrify mothers all out of proportion to the real risks their kids actually faced.

If the network news in the mid-1980s issued near daily warnings about the dangers for children of mothers working outside the home, entertainment programming offered the fantasy that women had already finessed the work-family tug-of-war. Clair Huxtable (Phylicia Ayers-Allen, later Rashad) was gorgeous, had a loving husband, five kids, and a career as an attorney. Clair's life—except for the occasional moment when Rudy wouldn't eat her brussels sprouts—ran as smoothly as Ban roll-on. *The Cosby Show*, as everyone knows, was *the* hit sitcom of the 1980s—

number one in the Nielsens from 1985 to 1990—and by the end of its first season it ranked as the top program for women viewers between eighteen and forty-nine.[84]

What was so appealing about this show to women—and particularly to mothers—since it was a 1950s sitcom throwback about the patriarchal nuclear family that one critic labeled "Cosby Knows Best?"[85] Most important, the show acknowledged and joked about the relentless exasperation of raising children. Just as Alice cracked wise to her kid in *Alice Doesn't Live Here Anymore*, pelting him with mockery when she'd simply had enough, so too did the Huxtable parents, including Clair, threaten to kill their kids, leave them out in the cold, and send them to Siberia. But their obvious loving indulgences made clear that humorous, even sarcastic hyperbole was an essential tool in the parental survival kit. In the first episode, Clair served Theo sunnyside-up eggs and he complained that he wanted them scrambled. So she took her spatula and broke the eggs up on his plate: voila, scrambled. She later looked in the mirror and sighed, "I was a beautiful woman once, before the children came." As they went to sleep, Cliff said, "I just hope they get out of the house before we die." In another first-season episode, after the usual screaming from upstairs, Cliff looked at Clair and asked, "Do you want me to destroy them now?"

What is also especially striking about the first season's shows was how messy the house was—the coffee table was cluttered with papers, clothes and toys were strewn around the living room, Theo's room looked like a bomb went off in a thrift shop, and the bathroom was littered with discarded towels and clothes. Clair and Cliff made mistakes, too—overreacting to Rudy's goldfish dying, being tough one minute and indulgent the next. What mother wouldn't want to see a parent say to a kid, "Unless you're planning on eating that basketball, get it off the table," or, upon seeing Theo's disaster of a room, deadpan, "Hard to get good help, isn't it?" (Interestingly, the house was already much neater by the second season, with much less clutter in the living room, and by the fifth season there was only one magazine strategically placed on the coffee table and no clothes or toys anywhere.)

The sensibilities of the show—that parents love their kids but that kids will drive you absolutely nuts—resonated with Erma Bombeck's writing. Bombeck began writing her columns "At Wit's End" and "Up the Wall" in the mid- and late 1960s, and lampooned the endless demands placed on mothers in bestsellers like *The Grass Is Always Greener Over the Septic*

Tank (1972) and *I Lost Everything in the Post-Natal Depression* (1974). In 1983 and '84 she had another bestselling book, *Motherhood, The Second Oldest Profession.* In it she joked about how immediately after childbirth, "every new mother drags from her bed and awkwardly pulls herself up on the pedestal provided for her. . . . Some can't stand the heights and jump off, never to be seen again." [86] She made fun of the supermom type who "painted the inside of her garbage cans with enamel . . . color-coordinated the children's clothes and put them in labeled drawers . . . and delivered her son's paper route when it rained." But on a more serious note—and why readers loved her so—she spoke the truth: "No mother is all good or bad, all laughing or all serious, all loving or all angry. Ambivalence runs through their veins." [87] In 1984 you could still say these things. By the mid-1990s (unless you were Roseanne) you couldn't.

Feminist media scholars have taken *The Cosby Show* to task for its erasure of the stressful, everyday struggles working mothers really faced, and for its seemingly genial, good-humored reassertion of patriarchy.[88] It's true that we rarely, if ever, saw Clair at work, nor was she the one constantly trying to lie down on the couch because she was exhausted. She remained the "toughy" in the kids' eyes. Nonetheless, there were episodes when, confronted by a disciplinary problem, Clair basically fell back on the "wait till your father gets home" routine. In the end, the show was more about him since he was the seasoned stand-up comedian with the comic riffs and long, slow takes.

But while we women will always take in media fare that is somewhat bad for us, most women don't embrace media fare that is all bad for us. One of the pleasures of *The Cosby Show* was, in fact, watching Cliff both succeed and fail at asserting his paternal authority. He demanded of his kids "Come here now!" and sometimes they did and sometimes they didn't. Clair was often tougher, or more sensible, than he was, giving the kids advice they could really use and act on, forbidding Vanessa from going to a party hosted by college kids while Cliff, totally conned by Vanessa, says, Sure, go ahead. And let's not forget what else was crucial about this show: that Clair Huxtable was probably the first African American mother on television, with the possible exception of Diahann Carroll on *Julia,* with whom white women identified and whom many wanted to emulate.

In "real life," major shifts were beginning to occur in fatherhood, but dads were still stonewalling in 1984. One study in 1986 showed that fathers spent, on average, about twenty minutes a day with their children.[89] *McCall's* reported in 1987 that a study of 160 sets of parents with children in kindergarten or fourth grade revealed that of eleven different child-related tasks, such as buying them clothes, supervising baths, and so forth, 70 percent of fathers did not assume *one single responsibility,* 22 percent assumed one, and only 8 percent assumed two or, at the very most, three.[90] And in her highly influential and deeply depressing book, *The Second Shift,* Arlie Hochschild also documented that after a forty-hour (or often longer) workweek, it was Mom who scrubbed the toilets, cleaned out the moldy leftovers from the fridge, did everyone's laundry, and chauffeured kids to their soccer matches while Dad lay on the couch watching the NBA finals (which seemed to be on from March through July) or, perhaps, reading Bill Cosby's *Fatherhood* (1987) or Bob Greene's *Good Morning, Merry Sunshine* (1984), paeans to the joys of fatherhood. The women's magazines favored the image of the new, enlightened, participatory dad, but in reality he remained mostly clueless about the difference between 6X and 32AA and between Downy and Easy Off.[91]

So, when watching *Cosby,* you could enter a cozy world in which Dad *did* talk to and discipline the kids, was deeply connected to them, but also did not always know best and often needed guidance and reinforcement from Mom. This was a kinder, gentler patriarchy in which Dad was often, well, more like a woman. And, of course, in between the many jokes and setups about the ceaseless frustrations of parenthood were strong normative messages about how to raise kids. There was discipline, there were firm rules, but you always had to listen to your kids and assume a therapeutic stance with them.[92] Clair and Cliff occasionally raised their voices, but they never really yelled, never totally lost their tempers like real parents, and never pulled out the vodka after reading a kid's report card. So while the show indeed gave mothers permission to express their exasperation with motherhood, its proposed remedy for the trials and tribulations of motherhood was to remain calm and to look at everything with a sense of humor.

With the possibilities of the new motherhood personified by Clair Huxtable on the one end of the maternal spectrum, and the perils of the new motherhood embodied by the child-endangerment stories on the other end, it's not surprising that motherhood began to be depicted as a "war" between stay-at-home mothers and working mothers, with most of us, whether we worked or not, caught in between. Despite the women's movement, a woman's need or desire to work was constantly pitted against the safety and healthy development of her kids.[93] Let's not forget that this was the era of the catfight, as exemplified by Krystle and Alexis's mud fights and hair-pulling wrestling matches in water-lily ponds on *Dynasty*. The motif of the catfight had framed the news media's coverage of the battle for the Equal Rights Amendment, and now it framed the coverage of motherhood and child rearing.[94]

The subtext of the media panics of 1983–84 and beyond was that working mothers' most unforgivable sin was exposing their children too soon to the "outside" world, a place full of overly commercialized relationships and self-interested predators. They had brought their kids into the marketplace to be cared for rather than keeping them in the home, the one place allegedly free from and even at odds with marketplace values, a place where kids were priceless and sacred. Maybe, these panics suggested, it wasn't worth it: Equality for women was too expensive for kids. The legacy of these panics has been deep and lasting, making mothers worry, often excessively, about whether their kids can walk to school safely, ride their bikes around the neighborhood, or let go of Mom's hand for even a second at the local fair. But they also fueled an incipient backlash against working mothers that rested, crucially, on pitting them against mothers who did not work outside the home.

While letters to the editor and articles written by readers for the women's magazines indeed indicated that some stay-at-home mothers resented or felt threatened by mothers who worked, and vice versa, the women's magazines also seem to have inflamed and exaggerated this tension.[95] While the women's magazines in the mid- and late 1970s sought to cultivate their role as switchboards between struggling working mothers, they also drew from news media conventions that emphasized conflict. *Versus* was an important headliner word. With a catfight between working and nonworking mothers, you had conflict, which always sold, and you addressed both sides of your readership. Thus you could get a flashy title like "Women vs. Women: The New Cold War Between Housewives and Working Mothers" by Nancy Rubin in *Ladies' Home Journal*, which purported to document a battle between working and nonworking mothers, with resentment and condescension on both sides.[96]

Women who stayed at home were no longer housewives; they were *homemakers*. You weren't just passively married to an inanimate object—

a house; you were actively making a home, something that had enormous value and took talent, creating an emotional sanctuary from the world of work and school. *Homemaker* connoted a woman who had actively chosen the task and considered it on a par with other specialized professions.[97] In many of the women's magazines, the term *homemaker* began to give way to *full-time mother*. Her role in her child's development—not the laundry, or dinner, or cleaning out refrigerator bins—was the central, crucial justification for her choice and her work. Articles like "The Myth of Quality Time" in a 1984 *Ladies' Home Journal* insisted that unless you were home all day with your kids, they would feel deserted and be deprived because you and only you should be the one to deal with all of their needs immediately when they occurred.[98] So now the "war" was quality versus quantity, when this was, of course, a false dichotomy.

The rhetoric of choice—adopted straight from the women's movement—became central to descriptions of stay-at-home moms. These were not the trapped, unfulfilled, Valium-guzzling housewives of *The Feminine Mystique*. These women loved staying home and raising their kids, and insisted it was much more fulfilling and important than any stinky old job.[99] As *Parents* put it, these "new traditionalists" had "carefully weighed the pros and cons of paid employment" and then opted "to be the primary caregiver, pursuing volunteer activities that are compatible with her family needs. She doesn't mourn the path not taken but functions contentedly with a marriage based on financial and political equality." Most important, as *Ladies' Home Journal* reported in 1984, "it is in their relationship with their children that the new stay-at-home mothers find the most significant dividends.[100] Of course this was true for millions of women, and many feminists had wanted the role of housewife to be a choice (and a compensated choice, we might add) rather than an edict. But this choice, in the face of the media panics, could now be used to vilify the "choices"— or, more usually, the exigencies—that brought millions of other mothers into the workplace.

Gone, magically, were the 1970s concerns about financial dependence and emotional isolation. Gone also were the concerns about trying to reenter the workforce after, say, an eight-year absence to raise the kids.[101] In "Don't Call Me Supermom" (1984), Jean Marzollo urged women to rediscover the joys of acquiescence to men, and of scrubbing the porcelain facilities. "Isn't there something repulsive about the image of a man cleaning a toilet bowl?" she asked. "Any woman who makes her husband do such a job is, well not quite a woman." [102] (And any man who refuses to do such a job deserves a subpoena.) By the mid-1980s, if the working mother was stressed out, if she was a "superwoman," it was her own pathetic syndrome, and one she had to cure by herself.[103]

Two crucial elements of the new momism—the need for constant vigilance, and the importance of being easygoing and fun-loving—had now been poured into its foundation. If this wasn't already an impossibly contradictory set of messages to juggle, the media gave us more. Because the 1980s also witnessed the rise of that now inescapable model of motherhood, the always gorgeous, always sexy, always devoted celebrity mom. The biggest kahuna of them all was Princess Diana. In the vision of the celebrity mom, the conflict between intensive mothering and working, between the stay-at-home mother and the working mother, was beautifully and romantically resolved. In the process, the new momism got fitted with rocket launchers. So let's go back to 1981, and check in with Debby Boone.

FOUR

Attack of the Celebrity Moms

It was January 1981, the month when Ronald Reagan was inaugurated president of the United States. On the cover of *Good Housekeeping*, a beaming Debby Boone, who had in 1978 won a Grammy for best new artist, displayed her three-month-old baby under the headline HE LIGHTS UP MY LIFE, lyrics that had referred to the Great Almighty, but now wittily referred to her son.[1] Just as her father, in the 1950s, had succeeded in oozing his own sticky brand of self-serving wholesomeness over various sectors of rock 'n' roll, Debby Boone, in the early 1980s, helped inaugurate another enduring piece of cultural treacle, the celebrity mom profile.

Inside, we learn that "little Jordan . . . eats heartily and sleeps soundly eight hours a night." Why is he such a good, easy, healthy baby? "Jordan's splendid disposition and health are due, his mother believes, to the good care she took of herself during her pregnancy." You see, "Debby has been a student of nutrition and has eaten only foods that are good for her." Debby added, "I exercised. I swam every day." The night before Jordan was born, Debby dined at a health-food restaurant where she had "avocado, cheese and sprouts, and a protein drink." Debby gained twenty-six pounds during her pregnancy, and lost them instantaneously. In fact, three days after Jordan's birth, "I weighed a pound less than I did before I was pregnant." Many readers no doubt had shared this experience of the have-a-baby weight-loss program.

Debby and her husband, Gabri, were apparently a bit unclear about the birds and the bees (we can only imagine what Pat told her), because

"God arranged Jordan's arrival ... she and her husband certainly didn't." But even though her pregnancy came as a surprise (the news no doubt delivered by the angel Gabriel), "It doesn't take long at all to start wanting and loving your child," noted Debby. The interviewer effused that "Mother and child exchange looks of pure love and joy." One reason is that "he seldom cries." He also likes music, not because all three-month-old babies love music, but because "he probably inherited this taste from his grandparents and great-grandfather ... the legendary country singer Red Foley."

Jump ahead to February 1994 and Kirstie Alley, the star of *Cheers* and the *Look Who's Talking* movies, is the cover girl for *InStyle*, a magazine that pays fawning tribute to the charming idiosyncrasies and "lifestyle" choices of our nation's celebrities. Among Kirstie's recent lifestyle choices is the purchase of her fourth house. *InStyle* advises us respectfully that, "As with all of her houses, Kirstie paid cash." On a tour of her new Bangor, Maine, island retreat (whose renovation was paid for by a quick voice-over job she did for Subaru), we discover that both Kirstie and her house are "at once down-to-earth and whimsical."

Kirstie must be down to earth, of course, because now, at long last, she is a mother. Her "playful sense of style" is made evident by the decoupage grapes that grace her son True's highchair. "It was painted and cracked to make it look old," *InStyle* informs us with a straight face. (Why not simply rely on natural toddler effluvia to give the chair that petroglyph look?) Though True is only one year old, his whimsical highchair faces an equally whimsical ceramic pig holding a blackboard on which a new word appears each day to encourage True's reading.

In our journalistic tour through Kirstie's hideaway, we encounter an entourage of decorators, a nanny, a cook, and various personal assistants. Kirstie spends True's two-hour (!) naptime working out with her personal trainer and then being served a healthful, fat-free lunch by the cook. Lounging in her livingroom (painted to "echo" the surrounding firs and elms), reflecting on the challenges of motherhood, Kirstie gushes, "... being a mother has given me a whole new purpose. Every day when I wake up it's like Christmas morning to me, and seeing life through True's eyes gives me a whole new way of looking at the world." Perfect house. Perfect husband. Perfect child. Perfect career. Perfect life. Kirstie is a perfect mother. *InStyle* invites you to curl up on the sofa with Kirstie, but then makes it quite clear that you'd probably just spill your tea on it.

Forward ahead to 1997. There's Kirstie again, now star of *Veronica's Closet*, beaming at us once more from *InStyle*. "A new man, a new show, a brand new life," proclaims the cover. Since 1994, her island mansion has "become a place to play." Each of the fifteen bedrooms (!!) is decorated with Kirstie's "eclectic and playful eye." Now most people, according to *InStyle*, would have found decorating this sixteen-thousand-square-foot house daunting, but not Kirstie. She explains, "I'm very fast. . . . I don't shop. I just point: boom, boom, boom." Having outgrown his high chair, True now has his own miniature lobster boat. In addition, he and his new sister, Lillie, can frolic in their personal nursery-rhyme garden, complete with Mother Goose figures especially commissioned by "fun-loving" Kirstie because, as she puts it, "I hope I give my children a spirit of play."

Kirstie swears by the facial treatment she receives every morning on her terrace as the fog burns off Penobscot Bay. It involves "blasting her face with oxygen and enzymes . . . through a plastic hose hooked up to two pressurized tanks." Though her life was perfect in 1994, she has since set aside her husband Parker Stevenson in favor of her "soulmate" James Wilder (ten years her junior), who is a "cross between Houdini, Errol Flynn and Marlon Brando." Apparently Kirstie uses the same technique for choosing her lovers as she does for choosing sofa fabrics. With James, "it was like comet to comet. Boom . . ."

Meanwhile, back in California (from which Kirstie retreated because the people in Maine are "more real"), in the home she refers to as "Casa de Mayhem," Annie Potts watches serenely as her new nanny attempts to corral sixteen-month-old Jake to avoid his collision with Potts's personal assistant. The star of *Love & War* shows off for *InStyle* the "do-it-yourself decorating style" of her new wing, built in anticipation of Jake's arrival. The wing includes a darkroom for her husband, a bedroom for her assistant, and an office for her. Jake's stake in the wing, despite his role in having it erected, remains unclear. Potts also added a pool. "If I don't swim," explains Potts, "then I'm like the Tin Man. I'll just rust up." Despite the "ruined villa look" Potts cultivates in "Casa de Mayhem," the photographs of the snow-white upholstered furniture, crystal lamps and vases, perfectly plumped needlepoint pillows, and immaculate floors, free of partially gnawed teething biscuits and petrified Play-Doh, suggest the effacement of human life—especially human life under the age of twenty-five.

But don't let these images of regal grandeur intimidate you, insists *In-*

Style: Potts is still one of us. After all, in her spare time, she made all the curtains in the house. As Potts puts it, "The things that you can make—unless you're dropping a grand a window—are so much more interesting than what you can buy." In between photos of Potts frolicking joyfully with Jake on her veranda, she reveals that Jake may well be the reincarnation of her dead cat Gus, whose ashes she keeps in a vegetable bin in the kitchen. The reincarnation insight came to her from the psychic she met in the waiting room of the holistic vet she patronizes. Unlike Alley, Potts allows as how children can strain one's decorating strategies. So she covered the chairs in her breakfast room with Holstein cow–print vinyl.

Welcome to the celebrity mom profile, a media genre that snowballed as the 1980s progressed and became a dominant fixture of women's and entertainment magazines by the 1990s. The celebrity mom profile was probably the most influential media form to sell the new momism, and where its key features were refined, reinforced, and romanticized. Here the celebrity had to be photographed displaying a broad toothy grin, her child in her lap or lifted with outstretched arms above her head, an accessory who made her look especially good on her sofa or balcony. Celebrity mothers are invariably surrounded by pastels and suffused in white light; the rooms we often see them in feature white or pastel furniture. Often they are backlit or simply shot against a white backdrop for a nice halo effect. The mother herself was almost always white and, it goes without saying, insistently heterosexual (although by the late 1990s Rosie O'Donnell and Jodie Foster—whose sexual orientation has been guarded as if it were Fort Knox—snuck in).

Rising out of the ashes of feminism, and repudiating its critique of the narrow confines of middle-class motherhood, the celebrity mom profile was an absolutely crucial tool in the media construction of maternal guilt and insecurity, as well as the romanticizing of motherhood, in the 1980s and beyond. The celebrity mom profile, while presenting images of working mothers who had allegedly found a balance between work and family, was a powerful Trojan horse, reinforcing all of the tenets of the new momism, and particularly intensive mothering, at a time when mothers were working harder than ever. And most important, the message of the celebrity mom profile has evolved from "how I do it all" to "it's really much more fun and rewarding to quit my job and stay home with the kids."

It's high time to dissect the celebrity mom profile, to trace its lineage (which, as we'll see, has royal bloodlines), to lay out the guidelines that govern it, and to see how, despite our best defenses, it often gets under our skin. We can make fun of celebrity mom profiles all we want, but the fact of the matter is that they worked—they hooked readers, served the celebrities well, and sold mountains of magazines. In addition to offering us delectable fantasies, these profiles read like instruction manuals, suggesting how we could do it better if we just did it like Kirstie. We were always the understudies, the ones not yet ready, the ones not as big and accomplished as the savvy grown-ups in the story. Often, the goal of the profile was to get us to feel commonality: "She's like me." At the same time, however, depending on the story and the star, we could also feel superior, say to ourselves, "Thank God that's not me," or "Isn't she a complete ass?" as we resisted the undertow of envy and inferiority pulling at our psyches.

We don't mean to single out Boone, Alley, and Potts for ridicule—although such self-serving bilge makes it irresistible. Sadly enough, we could have chosen Kathie Lee Gifford, Kelly Ripa, Gloria Estefan, Meg Ryan, Kelly Preston, Cindy Crawford, Vanna White, Angelina Jolie, Reese Witherspoon—the list goes on and on—to make the same point. We assume that most (but not all) of these celebrity moms were not trying to gloat, or to rub our noses in our own poor lifestyle choices (which invariably include the failure to choose being thin, white, gorgeous, famous, and rich). And of course they love their children. We've all said mushy things about how much our kids mean to us, especially in the immediate aftermath of birth, before the months of sleep deprivation and projectile vomiting produce a slightly more jaundiced view of the joys of motherhood.

But really, we ask you, what *are* the regular mothers of America to make of such journalistic hogslop? Few of us have mansions with fifteen bedrooms, a SWAT team of nannies, or the option of replacing our snoring husbands with newer, fart-free models. And in the real world, adorable toddlers have a way of growing up into sullen teenagers; celebrity mom profiles never focus on the star when her kid is sixteen and in rehab. The only older kids we see in these profiles are the ones who have grown up into mom's "best friend." The celebrity mom, in addition to being cushioned by beauty, wealth, and fame, is further protected by a spin-doctor publicist, and thus her mistakes are shielded from exposure in a way that our calling our thirteen-year-old an asshole in front of three of his friends is not. One could dismiss *InStyle,* and its reduction of motherhood to just another decorating challenge, as an especially flagrant example of the whorishness and banality of celebrity journalism, and leave it at that.

But that's the problem: *InStyle* was not an exception. Similar portraits of the celebrity supermom as the serene, supremely contented woman who found motherhood the most ecstatic experience of her entire life colonized the magazines, book racks, and talk shows of America. Just consider the barrage of one inane, melodramatic magazine cover headline after the next: FROM DESPAIR TO PRAYER: CONNIE SELLECA TALKS ABOUT THE MIRACLE OF MARRIAGE AND MOTHERHOOD; MICHELLE PFEIFFER'S BABY LOVE: THE LONGING SHE HAD TO SATISFY (EVEN *BEFORE* THE WEDDING); HOLLYWOOD'S LATEST BABY BOOM MOM-O-RAMA; and THE NEW SEXY MOMS![2] Of the four magazines geared especially to wives and mothers—*Redbook, Ladies' Home Journal, McCall's,* and *Good Housekeeping*—only one of their covers in 1976 featured a celebrity mom, in which Princess Grace and Caroline were on the cover of *Good Housekeeping* under the headline PRINCESS GRACE: THE PROBLEMS OF BEING A MOTHER. Other more typical nonmaternal cover titles included BARBARA WALTERS INTERVIEWS HERSELF (now *that* must have been rich), GOLDIE HAWN IS HAPPY IN LOVE, and OLIVIA NEWTON-JOHN MODELS OUR EXCLUSIVE DO-IT-YOURSELF SCARF CLOTHES. (Oh, dear.) In 1977 there were no celebrity mom covers, and in 1978 and '79 there was only one out of forty-eight for each year. The Boone cover in 1981 marked a turning point: That year, celebrity moms appeared on five covers, with Debby Boone taking two of them. (The second one, also on *Good Housekeeping,* featured an excerpt from the twenty-five-year-old chanteuse's autobiography *My Life So Far.*) By the late 1980s and early 1990s, between one fifth and one fourth of the covers of these magazines featured celebrity moms, often pictured with their gleaming, cherubic children. By April 1988, for example, the harried regular mother waited for her turn in the supermarket checkout line with kids screaming in the cart as the cover of *Ladies' Home Journal* announced AN EXCLUSIVE AT-HOME INTERVIEW with Cybill Shepherd and her twins; *McCall's* showed us Priscilla Presley, who TALKS ABOUT HER BABY AND LISA MARIE; and Barbara Mandrell announced on the cover of *Redbook,* NOW MY CHILDREN COME FIRST.

Aside from the fact that these profiles seem designed to make the rest of us feel that our own lives are, as the great seventeenth-century philosopher Thomas Hobbes put it, miserable, brutish, and short, why should we care about something so banal as the celebrity-mom juggernaut? One answer is that it bulldozed through so much of American popular culture just as motherhood and maternal practices became a national obsession in the 1980s and 1990s, reinforcing the norms of intensive mothering while providing a powerful counterpoint to the other dominant media maternal icon in the late 1980s, the welfare mother. Profiles of celebrities, from Joan Lunden to Celine Dion, equated motherhood with winning the Nobel Prize, climbing Mount Everest, and experiencing a transforming religious experience, all at once. (How celebrity X "does it all" became a chiding refrain of such profiles.) In these profiles, once you get pregnant and have a child, some special, previously untapped feminine *eau de mama* gets released throughout your entire body and mind and changes your relationship to children, domesticity, and the family of humans forever. It also energizes you! If *you* don't feel like motherhood has transformed every day into a festival of lights, you must have an attitude problem.

Feminists and women humorists like Erma Bombeck and Judith Viorst said in the 1970s and '80s what June Cleaver never could or would: that having children made your stomach and ass fall down to your knees, and that sometimes all you wanted to do was murder the kids and bury them near the septic tank (that, of course, was vintage Bombeck). The celebrity mom profile banished all such negativity: No ambivalence, not even a mouse-squeak of it, was permitted. Celebrity moms loved their kids unconditionally all the time; they loved being mothers all the time; they yearned for babies if they didn't have them and yearned for more if they did. They had everything under control and their children were perfect because the celebrity moms always did everything right. The celebrity mom profile, then, offered a symbolic, fantasy response to the very real deficiencies mothers experienced in everyday life. Most real mothers were often exhausted; the celebrity mom profile offered the fantasy of endless energy. Most mothers had to budget to make ends meet; the celebrity profile offered the fantasy of abundance—money, toys, houses, personal assistants. Most mothers had repetitive, even dreary jobs; the celebrity mom seemed to live a life of intensity, her work filled with glamour and excitement.[3]

Why did we begin to see, in the early and mid-1980s, this explosion in celebrity mom profiles? The Reagan administration, with its dogma of trickle-down economics and unembarrassed celebration of wealth, created a climate in which becoming rich and famous was the ultimate personal achievement. Reagan's message was simple—the outlandish accumulation of wealth by the few is the basis of a strong economy. *Dallas,* which worshipped *and* excoriated the rich, was an international phenomenon, and *Dynasty* and *Falcon Crest* quickly followed. Glossy ads by Ralph Lauren and others, showcasing English country estates and Italian villas, made inequality seem noble and hierarchies thrilling.[4]

Meanwhile, celebrity journalism—something so common now we can barely imagine when it was more marginal—increasingly colonized a host of magazines and even the nightly news. The use of children and PR-produced images of the happy, loving family to burnish the images of celebrities was hardly new in 1981. Since at least the 1920s, with the success of first movie and then radio fan magazines, certain stars—or their agents or studios—offered fans stories about their family life to make them seem like nice, decent, normal people and to boost box office revenues. The publication of *Mommie Dearest* revealed the extent to which Joan Crawford used her adopted children to paint herself in the press as a doting mother, and she was hardly alone. But celebrity journalism—despite newspaper gossip columns and celebrity profiles—remained until the 1970s somewhat apart from the mainstream news, women's magazines, and the tabloids.

Then, in 1974, after market researchers for *Time* reported that nearly every reader went to its "People" section first before reading any other part of the magazine, Time-Life launched *People. Us* quickly followed. *The National Enquirer,* which had previously specialized in stories like "Woman Gives Birth to Frog," also shifted to celebrity journalism and to color photography, as did its competitor *The National Star.* Even *The Globe,* for whom "Woman Gives Birth to Frog" would have been Pulitzer material, eventually took up the celebrity beat. Local TV newsmagazines like *Evening,* which aired in the 1970s after the network news, gave way to *Entertainment Tonight,* a half-hour of nakedly blatant press releases from the culture industries urging us to buy their movies, magazines, and TV shows. Pretty soon we were hearing Dan Rather tell us about Mike Tyson and Robin Givens's marital disputes on *The CBS Evening News.* It began to seem like no society had ever had as many celebrities as ours or had revered them as intensely.[5]

There was, simultaneously, a dramatic rise in the number of women who worked outside the home and raised small children at the same time. Pulled between established wisdom—if you worked outside the home before your child entered kindergarten you were bound to raise a sociopath—and the economic and psychic need to work, many of these mothers were searching for guidance and reassurance. Experts like Dr. Spock didn't seem as infallible as they used to. Besides, had *he* juggled parenting and work?

No, this was the era of the role model—we were supposed to have role models and be role models. But since many women didn't have such mentors in real life, they looked to the media. Celebrity moms were women who *had* combined demanding careers with motherhood, and magazine editors figured they could use celebrities to sell magazines *and* to serve as role models for their readers. And the celebrity mom also suggested something that many of us wanted to believe: that becoming a mother didn't automatically mean you were now an unattractive, asexual has-been of a woman.

As the number of women's magazines proliferated in the 1980s, competition among them intensified. Since showcasing celebrities had worked so well for *People*, increasing those crucial newsstand sales, why not put them on the cover of *Redbook*? According to a women's magazine editor who wishes to keep her job and thus remains nameless, *Redbook*, to pick just one example, constantly conducted focus groups to see which celebrity would sell best, and at any one time there was a circle of about ten of them that the magazine would especially feature. So one year Kathie Lee was everywhere, and then a few years later Meg Ryan was everywhere. If the story about them and their kids included "a tragedy, a triumph, and a secret," you had a cover.

Celebrity moms were perfect, then, for this era and beyond. They epitomized two ideals that sat in uneasy but fruitful alliance with one another. On the one hand, they exemplified the unbridled materialism and elitism of the Reagan era. On the other, they represented the feminist dream of women being able to have a family and a job outside the home without being branded traitors to true womanhood. Beneficiaries of wealth, fame, and craven publicists, they could be what no ordinary mother, even a supermom, could be: a highly successful professional with often grueling hours who also excelled at intensive mothering.

We are not suggesting that the editors of *Good Housekeeping* et al. sat around their conference tables and wondered, snidely, how they could make their readers feel like losers. In fact, their intentions were no doubt just the opposite: to show that if a busy celebrity can have children and be a good mother, then anyone can. Celebrity mom profiles, however preposterous, offered a vision of the future self you could become, a future self that would be happier and less stressed out. Nor are we suggesting that Debby Boone, and the countless other celebrity moms who followed in her footsteps, were calculating cynics who would use anything, including (and even especially) their children, to advance their careers (although we reserve judgment on Kathie Lee). One-hit wonders like Boone, or stars whose once top-rated TV series (remember *Hotel?*) had been cancelled, sought, with the prodding of their agents and publicists, to get such cover stories to keep their names in the public's minds and hearts. To do so, they often had to—or chose to—use their kids.

But the point here is not intention, it is effect. How is the reader supposed to feel, *really,* when the mother she is reading about has perfectly coiffed hair, is beaming ecstatically, has a hunky, rich husband allegedly fully involved in child rearing, an infant who sleeps through the night and never cries, and who actually weighs less after childbirth than she did before getting pregnant, all because she ate bean sprouts, exercised, and prayed? *She* made smart choices, *she* exercised control, *she* has that phony fantasy of bliss, beauty, and unconditional love after childbirth that you, sputum-covered, exhausted slob in your bathrobe, do not. You ate Mueslix, prunes, carrot sticks, and skim-milk yogurt during your pregnancy too, but *your* kid screams from 4:00 P.M. until 9:12 P.M., and then is up every hour-and-a-half during the night with diarrhea, night terrors, and a missing blankie. Since the celebrity profile insists that this is all under the mother's control, you must have done or be doing something very, very wrong. Or maybe you're just a bad person. The "you *can* have it all" ethos of these pieces made the rest of us feel like failures while dramatizing that we could do it all if we just had the right attitude.

The publication of *Mommie Dearest* (and the 1981 high camp movie of the same name), revealing the highly abusive child-rearing practices behind Joan Crawford's veneer of the perfect mom, may have prompted Hollywood publicists in general and certain stars in particular to insist that all Hollywood mothers were not like that and, in fact, could be and were truly devoted to their children. But in the very early celebrity mom profiles, such as the one of Cheryl Ladd in the March 1979 *Ladies' Home Journal,* under the intimidating banner WIFE, MOTHER & ACTRESS—HOW SHE DOES IT ALL, we see that the form was still inchoate, intermixing enviable references to conspicuous consumption with admissions that it was often stressful trying to juggle work and childcare, even for celebrities. So while we read about Cheryl Ladd's "two maids in white uniforms" and "black Mercedes," we also read that "jumping back and forth" between work and motherhood "takes its toll," especially since Cheryl works twelve hours a day. Nonetheless, as with all celebrity mothers to come, Cheryl "embraced motherhood with the same drive and enthusiasm that has fueled all her ventures." Because "from the moment" her daughter was born, Cheryl bathed her, massaged her, and talked to her, now " 'she has the vocabulary of a nine year old and she's only four,' " Cheryl bragged. Her marriage, "one of the best show business marriages around," was so close and fabulous that her husband " 'even shared the pregnancy with me. He had psychosomatic labor pains.' "[6] Goldie Hawn, too, admitted in a 1979 profile, " 'I'm a working mother and it's not easy,' " although it had to help that she had a nanny, a secretary, and "the girl who comes twice a week to clean."[7]

By the late 1980s the "it's not easy" admission was gone; now motherhood was eternally joyous, relaxing, and, of course, sexy. Jaclyn Smith was everywhere, in features like "Superstar Moms" or "How to Have a Baby Without Losing Your Figure" (answer: adopt) or she and her daughter would model "21 Fabulous New Do's."[8] Marie Osmond, Cristina Ferrare, Loni Anderson (when she and Burt felt "blessed"), Priscilla Presley, Kim Alexis, Fergie ("Will Her Second Baby Change Her?"), Candace Bergen, Connie Selleca, Mel Harris, Michelle Pfeiffer, Ann Jillian, Kirstie Alley, on and on they came, month after month, on the covers of the women's magazines.

Celebrity mom profiles were almost all alike and haven't changed much in twenty years, except that the houses and toys became more lavish as the 1990s progressed. As we can see from a cursory glance at the life trajectories of so many celebrity moms, their embrace of motherhood after years of sweating under the klieg lights brought them in touch with their true, essential, feminine natures. Most importantly, motherhood is a powerfully transforming experience; it always changes these women, and always for the better. "Neither fame nor fortune, nor a truckload of awards and thousands of adoring fans can compare to the incredible feeling, the state of being, the satisfaction that comes from the art that is motherhood," opined *Ebony* in its profile of Whitney Houston. "I've never found anything more fulfilling than being a mother," confessed the singer.[9] "I feel more enriched and compassionate toward others since having my son," said Elle McPherson.[10] According to Vanna White, "Motherhood has changed my whole attitude about a career. Now I'd be very happy living at home with my child for the rest of my life. Being a mother is the most important thing."[11] (Why she was still flipping letters on *Wheel of Fortune,* was not, however, addressed.) Christie Brinkley did multiple covers about wanting babies ("Why She wants a Baby So Fast" in February 1997, followed two months later by "Stops Baby Rumors") and then, of course, about having them.[12] Of her second child, from her third marriage, which lasted only a few months, Christie rhapsodized: "It's like I went to hell and came back with this angel."[13] *Ladies' Home Journal* told us that Christie Brinkley's third child, her daughter Sailor (so named because her father is a descendant of Captain Cook), "Barely tipping the scale at eight pounds . . . has become Brinkley's anchor, a midlife miracle well worth waiting for."[14] (These quotes must have made her first child feel really special.) No impolite chiding here, à la the welfare mother, about three kids by three different men. Instead, Christie got to announce her satisfaction with her latest family formation on the cover of *McCall's,* "I finally got it right."[15]

The celebrity mom profile is predicated on the interview, in which we hear extensively from the mother herself about how much she loves her kids and what she does to enrich their lives. Unlike news stories, for example, this is a media form designed to showcase the mother's subjective processes and inner life and, thus, to celebrate her distinctive individuality. The interview emphasizes when she laughs, or when her eyes well up with tears. We're meant to hang on her every word, no matter how banal. The myth of the determined individual, fully capable of vaulting over all sort of economic, political, and social barriers, is beautifully burnished in these profiles. It's all up to you, if only you'll try, and try, try again. There are no such things, in this gauzy world, as structural inequalities, institutional sexism, racism, or class privilege. Nor are there tired, pissed-off partners or kids who've just yelled, "I hate you! I wish you were dead!"

The celebrity mom profile allowed little deviation: It became a sturdily ossified genre, and those who chose to contribute to it had to embody and emphasize certain traits. As our informant editor told us, "She never questioned the myth of motherhood. She always told you motherhood was great. The stories were, in fact, interchangeable." She was everything that you, harried, every-day-is-a-bad-hair-day, over-budget slob, were not:

serene, resourceful, contented, transformed, perky, fun-loving, talented, nurturing, selfless, organized, spontaneous, thin, fit, poreless, well-rested, well-manicured, on-the-go, sexy, and rich. She had absolutely no ambivalence about motherhood, would prefer to spend all her time with her kids if only she just could, and found that when she came home from a draining day her children recharged her as if they were Energizers. She was never furious, hysterical, or uncertain. She was *never* a bitch. She was June Cleaver with cleavage and a successful career. She always took her kids to the zoo and museums, read to them every day, and taught them how to bake tarte tatin. Often she struggled over something, but emerged triumphant. In a 1997 cover story titled "The Sexy New Moms," *People* told us, "Postpartum depression isn't an option for such celebrity moms as Whitney Houston, Madonna, and supermodel Niki Taylor." Unlike you, being subjected to sleep deprivation and raging hormones was a choice for these women, and they just said no.

Celebrity children don't wreak havoc with work: Why, they enhance it and even fortify your bargaining position with the boss. Donna Mills brought her daughter to work and insisted "she's a big hit on the set." Added actress Gigi Rice, "Now, basically, if they want you to do a job, you say, 'Well, my baby comes with me.' What are they going to say— no?"[16] In addition, *People* told us, "Contractually mandated star perks typically include first-class airfare for the entire entourage; a separate trailer for the kiddies and a 24-hour limousine on standby to ferry them wherever they want to go; paid hotel accommodations for the nanny; even a nanny allowance."[17] It's just like your workplace, *n'est-ce pas?*

For those mothers who can't bring the child to the set every day, they make it quite clear that their children are nonetheless their top priority. For example, *Redbook* in January of 2000 told us all about Meg Ryan's "devotion to her two 'boys'" (meaning her son and her husband) and "the silly ways she and Dennis [Quaid] stay close." Ryan asked that her shooting schedule for *Hanging Up,* which was being filmed in New York, be arranged so that she could return to Los Angeles every weekend to see her son. "She spent a lot of time on the plane, flying home Fridays after grueling weeks of 12- to 14-hour workdays." Someone suggested that she bring her seven-year-old son to New York, "but she was firm about keeping his life stable. *She* would do the traveling."[18] (We're not supposed to notice that six months later this ideal wife and mother had split with her husband and was dating Russell Crowe and that those "silly ways" between Meg and Dennis seem to have evaporated into the smog that en-shrouds L.A.)[19] Here, intensive mothering is heroic, noble, and utterly taken for granted.

Celebrity mom profiles are carefully packaged fantasies, but they ask readers to approach them as if they were real.[20] In fact, they deliberately blur the lines between reality and daydreams: The lives they show aren't really authentic, but they aren't completely counterfeit either.[21] Taking you, oh special, privileged reader, behind the scenes, behind what you know is the carefully constructed public artifice of "the star," "inside" the celebrity's "real life" which is supposedly spontaneous and not con-structed, is a ploy as old as entertainment publicity itself. Being "at home" with the celebrity mom, seeing her real, true self, who is always a caring, doting, fun-loving, selfless mother, you see why you and so many others made her a star in the first place—you rightly sensed that in addition to being pretty, thin, and maybe talented, she's also got a great personality and is a good, deserving person.[22] Often, in the profile, the celebrity mom has triumphed over various heartbreaks and challenges, and the very structure of the story is designed to get us to root for her. In addition, in the interview, the celebrity both notes how she is above the herd but is also so much like you, especially because she is a mother. Retaining their success is essential for celebrities, and the more you want to identify with them, the better their chances of staying in the limelight. So it is vital that the celebrity interview walks the tightrope just right, confirming your envy of the goddess, but reaffirming that she's also just regular folks, someone you could talk to about toilet training, someone confiding in *you* about her baby's highchair.

Features like those in *InStyle*—"Jane Seymour relaxes with her twins on Barbados"—appeal to our emotions, urge us to escape from the rules and facts of the "real world" (where the words "relaxation" and "infant twins" cannot be uttered in the same breath), want us to suspend all dis-belief, to be cognitively passive, and to feel pleasure. But just because that's what the publication offers us, doesn't mean that we all comply, or that we comply completely. For sometimes, just as we are sinking into this warm bubble bath of a media text, our brains don't shut down. We might actively search for information ("How *does* Jane manage to smile and have her hair combed now that she has twins?"). We measure our lives, our relationships with our children, how we interact with them and what we do for and with them, against the make-believe reality before us. So these profiles aren't pure escape because women *do* bring lessons, ideas, and anxieties back to real life, to their own roles and behaviors as mothers. Because motherhood is such a high-stakes undertaking and because the rules of the game are at once compelling and capricious, we're always working, even when we're relaxing or daydreaming.

At the very same time, we may also be talking back to the maternal mirage before us. But even as mothers resist this bilge, saying to themselves things like, "Well, yeah, you princess, *you* can be ecstatic about motherhood twenty-four hours a day, *you* have a live-in nanny, a maid, a private secretary, and a personal masseur," powerful norms nonetheless slink in past the epithets. So there are three broad categories of readers of these celebrity profiles. On the one end is the totally accepting uncritical fan, on the other end is the cynical hip mama who don't believe none of it, and in the middle—where most women are—are the negotiators who work and play with what they know to be the blurriness between fact and fantasy.[23] But even as mothers resist the soppy slop about Cindy Crawford's "miracle baby" and her perfect life—and letters to the editors of *People* confirm that many mothers actively talk back to this stuff—most are not invincible. Their armor is not complete.

When the genre began, there were very few African American (or Latino or Asian American or Native American) celebrity moms. Writers and editors at the white women's magazines maintained that white women don't want to read about black women. But by the 1990s, some women of color—Whitney Houston, Gloria Estefan—appeared in these profiles. By 2001, *Ebony* featured a cover story titled "The New Motherhood" with Jasmine Guy, Tammy Franklin, Yolanda Adams, and Tracey Edmonds on the cover. Inside, there was a story on "The Joys of Being a Stay-at-Home Mom," in which we learned that "Many highly educated, highly employable Black women have tossed their careers to the wind, opting to stay home and wholeheartedly depend on their men to support them."[24] (As is typical with such "career woman leaves it all for hearth and home" stories, no actual statistics are given to document how many "many" is.) A few pages later, we got to the celebrity moms who "take pregnancy in stride" and continued "their active lives without missing a beat." "From the first to the third trimester of pregnancy, with nursing infants, toddlers, preschoolers and kindergarteners, the stars attend galas and movie premieres, award shows and fund-raisers with their little ones often in matching Gucci attire." Although these celebrity moms work, and take very good care of themselves, as with the white celebrity mom profile, "I'm a mom first" and a performer second. With determination, these women show that "the modern mother can have it all." [25]

Now, should African American women be gratified that *finally* their roles as mothers are celebrated and they are being depicted in such glamorized ways instead of only as welfare mothers? Or should African American women be concerned that the same kind of postfeminist sculch being directed at white women is now being turned on them too, urging them to shut up, work harder than ever, and be more dependent on men? For women of color, this kind of media visibility around motherhood is indeed a double-edged sword.

Few celebrity mothers were more closely watched, or managed to inspire more points of identification among everyday women during the 1980s and '90s, than the Princess of Wales. The endless profiles of her became the template that would crystallize into the celebrity mom profile. It was also in 1981—July 29 to be exact—that millions of Americans (an estimated 750 million worldwide) got up at the crack of dawn to watch the "storybook" wedding of the century: the marriage of Charles and Diana. Having been certified by Her Royal Highness's gynecologist as unspoilt and fertile, the royal family and the public hoped for princelings soon, and they were not to be disappointed. In June of 1982, Prince William arrived to worldwide acclaim and jubilation, and two-and-a-half years later Harry appeared. And more so than any other woman, Diana became the iconic celebrity mom of the 1980s and 1990s.

When Diana emerged as the chosen one in 1981, she was not just any celebrity, but a real princess, out of one of the oldest, most durable narratives we know, the fairy tale. The future King of England plucked her out of the sea of all the possible women in the land (well, all the possible aristocrat Protestant white virgins in the land). As *McCall's* put it, "Little more than a year ago she was an obscure kindergarten teacher's aide. Now she is about to give birth to the heir to the throne of England." [26] Although she was born to aristocracy, we commoners (and Yanks, to boot!) got let into her hopes and insecurities so we could feel we had things in common with her. The magazines told us that she had pinned a picture of Charles to her wall when she was sixteen, dreaming of the impossible. So she too had fantasized about distant, seemingly unattainable, famous men. She was shy. She was unsophisticated: The vultures in the press had tricked her into posing for them with the light behind her, so that the contours of her legs could be seen through her skirt. We wouldn't have known any better either. But despite all this—or, as fantasies go, maybe because of all this—she had won the heart of the future King of England.

The media's eagerness to embrace and embellish this "fairy tale" hooey from the start, in a totally uncritical fashion, was in keeping with much of the media's slavish, lapdog coverage of elites in the 1980s.[27] Given what we now know about Charles's fantasy of becoming one of Camilla Parker-Bowles's feminine hygiene products, the press accounts of Charles's adoration of his wife seem especially ludicrous. But they were a central part of the narrative frame so often imposed on stories about the royal couple during those early years, that of the romance novel. In this telling, Diana was a shy but beautiful and headstrong woman determined to land—and tame—the initially disinterested, womanizing future King of England. One of the ways she cemented his love for her and transformed him into a sensitive, caring man was, of course, to have his babies.

According to one James Whitaker, one of the various royal-watching blowhards who couldn't wait to tell *McCall's* readers that "I spent many hours at [Diana's] west end apartment learning what made her tick," Diana played Charles "like a salmon, and, when he was hooked, there was no one more delighted than Charles himself."[28] Diana De Dubovay, also letting it be known that she was "part of a carefully screened coterie of reporters . . . granted permission by Buckingham Palace to observe Diana and Charles up close," gave us the verbatim inside scoop: "Slowly but surely, she's twisting him around her little finger."[29] "Since learning of her pregnancy, the Prince, always attentive, has blossomed into an even more attentive father-to-be."[30] Charles "has taken to family life with remarkable ease, and no doubt Diana is responsible for his 'domestication,'" admired *Ladies' Home Journal*.[31] Rule one about the celebrity mom profile: The mom is gorgeous, in clear control of her destiny, and her husband loves her even more once she becomes pregnant and the baby is born.

Because she was young, beautiful, utterly feminine, was widely reported not to have been much of a student, worked with little kids, did not have a "threatening" career, and seemed utterly untouched by the women's movement, it was a given that she would be the ideal mother. "As everyone knows," *Ladies' Home Journal* confided, "Diana is a natural for motherhood; her love of children was as apparent in her choice of a job as a preschool teacher, as it is now in the evident joy she receives from greeting children on her official duties. Diana is happiest when surrounded by hordes of adoring youngsters." [32] One wonders whether such characterizations would have been as forthcoming had Diana been, say, a corporate attorney prior to her marriage. Throughout her marriage and public career, even in the very early years, Diana got bad press—about shopping too much, or sacking Charles's longtime aides, poking people in the butt at Ascot with her bumbershoot, or wearing hats that looked like UFOs. But never, ever were her credentials as an ideal mother challenged. "Her devotion to her children is unquestioned," asserted *Ladies' Home Journal*.[33]

From what any of us can tell from outside the palace ramparts and across the Atlantic (and remember, all we know is what we read and saw in the press and tell-all books), it certainly seems the case that Diana adored her children and worked hard to raise them so that they would not spend their lives with a ramrod up their sphincters like, say, Prince Philip. So we are not suggesting that, when it came to her children, Diana was only performing for the cameras. But she was part of a carefully coordinated public-relations campaign by the Windsors to promote the royal family as the ideal family and to cover up the fact that, behind the scenes, she was throwing herself down the royal staircases while her husband was on his cell phone with his mistress. What readers got was a highly prescriptive image of the perfect mother. And with article titles like "Princess Diana: Royal Role Model" or "The Princess Who Loves Children," it was clear that we should emulate her, and it was clear why: She embraced and embodied intensive mothering.

Diana, herself, seems to have been very savvy about ensuring that she was photographed frequently with her children, both in highly flattering staged shoots in, say, the nursery at Highgrove, and in paparazzi shots of her taking them out for hamburgers, to the movies, for go-cart rides, or letting them bury her in sand at the beach. After she and Charles had split, and were locked in a public-relations war over whose side people should take, even *People* sniped that her highly publicized outings with her kids—like when she took them to Disney World—seemed designed, in part, "to demonstrate that she—and not Prince Charles—was the boys' more dedicated parent." On another occasion, she took the boys to a go-cart course. "In full view of photographers, she made a point of cuddling them every time they came off the track, huffed *People*." [34]

Diana clearly became a student of the press and public relations, learning from her successes and mistakes. Diana appreciated that downplaying her royal status, and insisting that her boys had experiences that "normal" children did (while ensuring that she was photographed supervising these experiences), elevated her standing as "the people's princess." She also knew it was crucial to look joyful at these moments with her children. As she reportedly told a friend, "I've got what my mother has. However bloody you are feeling, you can put on the most amazing show of happiness." [35] Rule number two about celebrity moms: They are always radiantly happy when they are with their kids.

It goes without saying that while pregnant, "Diana's special glow is brighter than usual." [36] Not one to miss this cliché, *People* also reported, "she was said to be positively glowing after the news was made public" that she was expecting a second child.[37] When pregnant with Harry, *Good Housekeeping* gushed, "Diana looked so elegant and slim it hardly seemed possible that she was five months pregnant." [38] Of course she "exercises regularly," eats health food, "a light lunch," and "a dinner of fish or meat," and "has never looked better." [39] Diana made a point of continuing to work right up until shortly before her children were due, adding to the acceptability—even the glamour—of pregnant women remaining in highly public jobs. According to those truly in the know at *Ladies' Home Journal*, Diana timed her pregnancies as if she were Eisenhower planning D-Day. "Diana purposely did not get pregnant again immediately after William's birth. She wanted 'Wills' . . . to have two years of his parents' total attention without having to share with a brother or sister." [40] Rule number three of the celebrity mom profile: They always look and feel fabulous—better than ever—while pregnant, because they are nutrition experts and eat exactly what they should and have the discipline to exercise regularly. No varicose veins, no dreaded "mask of pregnancy," no total exhaustion, no unflattering comparisons to Weber barbecue kettles or Chris Farley. And they time their babies perfectly. Control, control, control.

Press accounts of Diana's performance as a mother repeatedly emphasized her "common touch," her insistence that her children not be subject to arbitrary (and seemingly impersonal) royal protocol, and the word used most frequently to describe her feelings toward her children was "devoted." She was widely credited with insisting on more nurturing (even permissive) child-rearing practices, and with ensuring that her incredibly privileged children mingled with "normal" kids and learned how they lived. She "insisted on having her baby in a public hospital," *McCall's* reminded us in 1986, and "refused to leave her son behind" when she and Charles went on a royal visit to Australia in 1983. Diana "would never turn [her children] over completely to a nanny." (This, of course, was false, even according to Diana. She told Andrew Morton that she was prepared to leave Prince William behind for four weeks while she and Charles went to Australia, but brought him after the Australian Prime Minister invited her to do so. As it was, she barely saw him during the trip.) As the boys grew up, much admiring coverage was given to the fact that Diana tried to "inject a semblance of ordinariness" into her children's lives. They were the first royal heirs "to go to a nursery school away from home where they could mix with other, nonroyal, children." [41] Diana got great press during the 1987 Christmas holidays because, as *People* informed us, "although she could have easily jumped the queue, Di stood with her two sons for 15 minutes at Selfridges, a London department store, waiting to visit with Santa." What the women's magazines—and many of us, apparently—wanted to believe was that Diana thought a more middle-class approach to motherhood was superior to an aristocratic one, and was determined to import it into the palace nurseries. Her method required that she not take royal protocol—which would have relieved her of a great deal of parenting chores—for granted.

Diana was also a working mother, and while this term was used only rarely to describe her (the words *work* and *royalty* seem oxymoronic when put side by side), the articles in the women's magazines constantly emphasized the public demands on her and the challenges she faced to save enough time for her kids. Although "Charles and Diana . . . have to be away from time to time like a lot of working couples," advised *McCall's*, "they are both very involved with their children." In fact, despite Diana's "increasingly heavy workload . . . the family is paramount." As a result, Diana "tries to organize her work around her two children," not starting her public engagements until after 10 A.M. and trying to be home by 4:00 or so. (This, presumably, is "royal flex-time.") [42] However, "nannies . . . are inevitable, as they are for many working parents," suggesting, laughably, that just like Diana, most of us had an au pair stashed in the guest room. [43] Nonetheless, "She gives William his breakfast each morning and often takes him to his play school. She makes an effort to have lunch with both children whenever possible, and she tries to plan her schedule so she can be with them at bath time and bedtime. She loves to read them bedtime stories."[44]

Right away, despite her royal standing, American women could relate to this young woman who was reportedly defying the stuffy, outdated, aristocratic—and thus emotionally sterile—rules about child rearing supposedly imposed by the Queen and royal tradition. Rule number four of the celebrity profile: Whatever your schedule, whatever institutional constraints you confront that keep you away from or less involved with your kids, it must be clear that they are your number-one priority, no matter what. These reported struggles of Diana's—to make royal tradition and schedules more kid friendly—resonated with working mothers in the mid-1980s, who often faced unyielding rules at the workplace that made it hard for them, indeed, to make *their* kids the number-one priority all the time. Yet she seemed to have succeeded—this persistent individual—where we had still failed.

Some of these articles about Diana made clear that because she was a mother she had the same struggles and pressures that we did, possibly even worse ones. Just like any mother, royal or not, Diana would have to manage sibling rivalry. Hilariously, several pieces asked child psychologists to give advice to Diana about child rearing, thus bringing her down a few pegs to our level—subject, just like us, to the relentless advice of distant, unknown experts. (None of these experts was asked to give advice to the person who was with the royal offspring most of the time, the nanny.) For example, Dr. Lawrence Balter, "professor of educational psychology at New York University," suggested that Diana didn't time things quite perfectly with her second child. " 'Nursery school age, around age three, is considered the "ideal" age to add a second child,' Dr. Balter explains." But William would only be two-and-a-half when the new baby arrived. " 'It wouldn't be at all surprising if a two-and-a-half-year-old voices some significant objections when a new baby arrives,' " Dr. Balter warned the Princess vicariously. (Hello—as most mothers can tell you, unless they're twelve or older when a new baby arrives, they "voice significant objections" to sibling competition no matter what the spacing is like.)

Even Diana did not escape the surveillance of the media mother police. "According to child-care experts," Charles and Diana would also have to make sure that the younger child didn't envy the eldest too much, especially since he would get to be the King of England and all. *McCall's* called on Penelope (never let your child cry for more than three seconds without picking her up) Leach to advise the couple on the sibling rivalry they were sure to encounter. Later on, once the marriage fell apart, *McCall's* offered advice on how to help the boys through the separation, under the subheading "Parenting do's and don'ts for Diana." Although "most family-therapy professionals are staunchly behind the way Princess Diana is handling things," the magazine warned, "some feel she is in danger of smothering William and Harry with too much affection." [45] In addition, reports had it that her kids were as bad as our kids—maybe even worse. Countless stories about Wills, whom Diana dubbed "my mini tornado," described his penchant for flushing things, including his father's "handmade Italian shoes," down the toilet; for throwing food at parties; for breaking everything he touched; and for hitting his playmates at school. [46]

Here is rule number five of the profile: There must be some human frailties, some family tragedies, some struggles or foibles that bring the celeb down a peg, make her seem a bit more like us and allow some of us to identify with her. Diana's own biography—the daughter of divorce, blindly in love with Charles, and then, later, victim of depression and bulimia, and prisoner in a loveless marriage—brought empathy from millions of women. When it all fell apart, Diana reassured the herd once again: Being a princess wasn't all it was cracked up to be; it was lonely; it was relentless; there was no privacy; there was no love. She hadn't escaped after all.

Sometimes, in sidebars to such stories, we'd also learn about Princess Caroline of Monaco, who had three children between the ages of seven months and three-and-a-half by 1988. "I hope nobody thinks that I leave the raising of my children to others," *People* reported her saying, insisting that she, too, subscribed to intensive mothering. Although she had "two nannies, a full-time secretary, a daily maid and a security guard," Caroline "regularly bathes and dresses her kids and often cooks meals herself. . . . Caroline makes up bedtime stories for the children, but there's a telling difference: Her stories are almost always about ordinary boys and girls instead of princes and princesses." [47] So *these* working mothers, who didn't have to rush and juggle as frantically as the rest of us because they always had kid coverage, nonetheless chose to do so, because they naturally liked it. What didn't get foregrounded was that behavior regarded as criminal in regular working mothers—like leaving your toddler for three weeks to go on a business trip—was perfectly normal for royalty. What regular women had to do every day, like it or not, tired or not, was showcased as a special, delicious treat for these moms.

Once it was no longer possible for the press to sustain the fairy-tale motif—by early 1991, when the Windsors were spending only about nine visibly miserable minutes together a year—Charles started taking it in the chops in the press, while Diana, in no small part because she had cemented her image as a "devoted mother," got credit for being a "surrogate father" as well while he allegedly moped around the moors of Balmoral talking to small ferns.[48] *People* went so far as to refer to his long absences from his sons as "parental malfeasance" and featured a photo of Diana and the boys with the caption, "Where *is* Dad?—a most maternal Diana posed with Wills and Harry at Highgrove." *Ladies' Home Journal* advised that what both boys "need desperately now [is] a father who puts them first," because the boys are "clearly starved for paternal attention."[49] In his most egregious gaffe, Prince Charles left the hospital to go to the opera while Prince William was being operated on for a fractured skull.[50] Diana, by contrast, reportedly spent two nights on a cot at her son's bedside.[51] Charles's side of the family lavishes "affection on dogs and horses rather than children," sniggered *People*. Unlike earlier portraits, which painted him as a very involved father, especially for a royal, now we heard about Charles's "hands-off approach to fatherhood," in which he "plays the part of a remote, aristocratic parent." "Not so Diana: She is the boys' favorite nurse when they are sick, their entertainer when they have parties, their playmate after school, their confidante at night. If they have bad dreams, it is her side of the bed they will creep into."[52]

Putting aside, for a moment, the question of how in the hell *Ladies' Home Journal* knew this, consider this list of idealized maternal qualities: nurse, entertainer, playmate, best friend, and protector. The famous photographs of Diana taking her kids on roller-coaster rides, or giving Harry a piggy-back ride while they both wore Mickey Mouse sweatshirts, laughing and cheering at Wimbledon, or running toward them, arms open wide to hug them after a separation, showed us her spontaneity, her eagerness to display her love and affection. Rule number six: The celebrity mom is fun-loving, eager to jump up and play with the kids at a moment's notice. She's always in the mood. She never says, "Not now, honey. I don't feel like it. Mummy's tired. Mummy's too lazy. Roller-coasters make Mummy barf."

Rule number seven of the celebrity profile insists that truly good, devoted mothering requires lavishing as many material goods on your kids as possible. This wasn't hard in writing about Diana, given that she was the future Queen of England. "The garden is a paradise for the children," we learned of Highgrove, the country estate that we later learned Diana loathed. "They have a pet rabbit that lives by the swimming pool, two ponies stabled in the yard next to the main house, a jungle gym, a swing, a playhouse, and acres of land (350 in all) to play in." [53] Here we see the beginnings of the central connection that emerged in the 1980s between being an enviable mother and being able to live as if you were Tsar Nicholas.

The central message of Diana's life, as staged in the press, up to the white card reading "Mummy" on her casket, was that if you failed at motherhood, you failed as a woman. Had Diana been the kind of mother Queen Elizabeth had been—gone so often and so remote that her four-year-old son Charles, when meeting her train, ran up to and hugged the wrong woman—she would have never attained her status as "saint." Diana foregrounded, in the royal family and in the pages of the press, the absolute centrality of being a doting, "hands-on" mother to the final assessment of a woman's worth. Diana was, then, a contradictory icon: While seeming modern and iconoclastic, which she was by "royal" standards, her public image reinforced powerful, prefeminist standards about what made women truly worthwhile: their relationship to children.

By the turn of the twenty-first century, celebrity mom profiles were completely out of hand. Who wouldn't want to have a baby, and believe that doing so would make you feel ecstatic 24/7, after sucking in this journalistic sugar water? In July 2000, *InStyle* featured profiles of seven, count 'em, seven, "Hollywood Moms—and Their Babies." For Josie Bissett, formerly of *Melrose Place,* pregnancy was fantabulous. "The bigger I got, the better it got." Really? No swollen ankles in the eighth month? No needing a crane to help you roll over in bed at night? Of course, she was writing a book on child-rearing tips. Jasmine Guy said that when you become pregnant "you join this secret league of women who tell you things." (Is this, uh, like the Masons?) She was now "happier and more focused. . . . there is always the wonderful feeling of knowing that you will never be alone again." Which is true—when you try to have a conversation with your partner, go grocery shopping, or pee, you will indeed never be alone again. Julie Moran, cohost of *Entertainment Tonight,* said that with a baby, "I'm just a little more relaxed about everything. You have to learn to go with the flow. . . . It's a wonderful release." [54]

Then we got the full media blitz from the Travolta-Preston family. In the summer of 2000 it was impossible to pick up a women's magazine without having them and their children, Jett and Ella Bleu, wallpapered over your eyes. Possibly this was to erase the memory of the most embarrassing box-office bomb of 2000, *Battleship Earth. Shameless* is the word that most immediately comes to mind when witnessing how these people used their kids, including Ella Bleu in utero, to promote their image as the most perfect couple in America.

" 'I *loooove* being pregnant,' " went the first line of *InStyle*'s profile of the expectant Kelly Preston. " 'I feel sexy. Johnny thinks I'm sexy too. . . . I actually feel prettier naked than dressed.' " Preston stayed in shape by doing yoga twice a week and walking several miles every day. " 'When you're pregnant, you feel special,' " she added, " 'you're so much more in tune with everything.' " To wit, she "talked to Ella in the womb all the time—and played classical music." To prepare the house for the new baby " 'we renovated the whole house and made it toxin free.' " Using a king-size (!) daybed, she created a "princess and the pea" bed for her new baby.[55] Shifting venues once the baby arrived, Preston posed nude in a close-up with the benighted Ella Bleu on the cover of *Redbook,* and announced, " 'the greatest moment in my life was right after Ella was born.' "

The trajectory of these articles over time has moved toward suggesting that once the celebrity mom discovers motherhood, she sees the pursuit of a career as a much lower priority. In almost every article in the early 2000s, you got some version of the following question, here asked by none other than Emma Thompson: " 'When I'm on my deathbed, will I regret not having taken this or that job? It's very rare that the answer is "Yes." ' " Adrienne Barbeau, former star of *Maude,* at fifty-six was the mother of five-year-old twins. " 'If I walk in the door, and one of them comes running and says, "Mommy, you're home!" everything else pales in comparison.' " Kim Basinger has also "reprioritized" since having a child. " 'She realizes there's more to life than having a career,' " her father told *People.*[56]

InStyle's paeans to intensive mothering started colonizing prime-time TV with the April 2001 Cindy Crawford–hosted show *InStyle Celebrity Moms.* Crawford opened by itemizing her achievements as a model, spokesperson, and TV personality. "But there's a new role I'm playing these days that's more exhilarating and more challenging than anything else I've ever done—it's being a mom." Here we heard more about how very, very sexy pregnancy is, how easy it was to go right back to work after having a baby, and how the stars would give up the money and fame for their kids in a heartbeat, if they had to. For Kelly Ripa, the most important thing is being a parent, "and if that meant I had to give up my jobs tomorrow, I would." Easy for her to say. (And we assume that if and when these celebs split from their perfect husbands, they are actually happy they didn't quit their day job.) Ming-Na of *ER* was back working on the set three weeks after giving birth to her daughter, in part because she could bring her baby to a totally toy- and nanny-stocked trailer on the set.

Various celebrity mothers dressed their babies in designer clothes because, as Crawford noted, "It's never too early to start looking good." We saw infants in Gucci leather jackets and suede fedoras with matching booties and a sterling silver rattle. Over-the-top decorating was crucial, too, to the message that you really, really cared. Lisa Rinna and Harry Hamlin showcased their forthcoming baby's new nursery, whose theme was "The Secret Garden," replete with an artist-commissioned hand-painted wall mural. "Your room is so special to you," explained Lisa, "it's your first home, and I just want this baby to love her room." Kimora Lee and Russell Simmons also opted for the wall mural, "creating a magical forest" for their daughter that *InStyle* told us took a year for the artist to paint. In this world, no expenditure was too excessive, no consumption too conspicuous when it came to demonstrating how precious your baby was.

By the twenty-first century, the celebrity mom profile steamed ahead full force, and now with the message that putting kids first means setting yourself aside, that motherhood really is the best avocation in the world and women's place is, first and foremost, in the home. In its April 2002 cover story with the blood-red headline PUTTING FAMILY FIRST, *People* added, "Finding more joy in being mom than playing movie star, many celebs are making parenting—not Hollywood—their top priority." The cover showcased Jodie Foster ("tries to make just one movie every two years"), Celine Dion ("took two years off"), Demi Moore ("hunkered down in Idaho"), and Sissy Spacek ("quit L.A. for Virginia"). (Note that Tom Cruise, Jude Law, James Gandolfini, or Pierce Brosnan isn't shown as feeling the same compulsion.) Inside was an homage to abandoning your work, no matter how good you are at it, and putting the kids first all the time.

This article would have been right at home during the postwar redomestication program of the late 1940s and early 1950s, when mothers who wanted to work outside the home were deemed neurotic. Celebrity after celebrity was reportedly "just as happy staying home as working . . . happier, even."[57] Jodie Foster was quoted as saying that raising her sons was "so much more interesting than anything else I do." The story tells us that "an increasingly long list of the biggest names in show biz" are either giving up working altogether or working intermittently or part-time. Photos of the celebrities are accompanied by a caption that lists their children and then their "Maternal Move": e.g., "turned her back on showbiz to be, for now, a full-time mom" (Demi Moore). Former soap star Emma Samms left the business to raise her kids and said, "There was no agonizing. If I was going to have children, I was going to raise them myself. It's just a matter of priorities." Country music star Martina McBride decided to tour only during school breaks with her kids in tow rather than leave them behind, "Because I'm the mommy." And Celine Dion resumed working after building a home near Caesar's Palace in Vegas so she could sign a three-year, $100-million-dollar deal and still "be able to put her boy to bed before going to work five nights a week, and be asleep early enough to be rested for patty-cake the next day." (Of course, the story didn't mention that this arrangement also allowed her manager/husband to indulge his penchant for high-stakes gambling.) If celebrity moms do bring their kids with them to the set, they are a source of unadulterated joy. During a break from shooting *American Beauty,* according to the movie's screenwriter, Annette Bening " 'took off her high heels, put on her tennis shoes and played tag with them. She was having so much fun. . . . I thought, "Gee, I wish my mom had done this." ' "[58]

While the text of the article indeed acknowledges that showbiz is a dicey business—one year you're a star, the next a has-been—and that pursuing a career in film or TV is a bit more time and labor intensive than some other jobs, so juggling acting with mothering can be a challenge, the dominant message of the article is about how laudatory it is to put your kids first. It's about the nobility of the Mommy Track and the new momism. Here the new momism just makes sense, and it's righteous, too.

This is powerful stuff. If women who have been at the top of their careers—"A-List" actresses—with whopping salaries, professional success, and international recognition, and the envy of millions, if *they* say working isn't worth it compared to playing Chutes and Ladders, then how are you—waitress, bank teller, real estate agent, mid-level manager, teacher—supposed to set your priorities? For millions of other working mothers out there who are also devoted to their kids, there actually are aspects of work that are tons more gratifying than trying to get your kid to clean her room, going to the park yet again, or surviving temper tantrums. There really are days when someone at work saying "Great presentation" or "You handled that really well" feels a lot better than "Mom, I got my homework wrong and it's all your fault." But increasingly, the celebrity mom profile shuts down that kind of talk.

Because celebrity journalism focuses, by definition, on the individual celebrity, it shoulders out stories about larger groups of mothers and children and what they, as a group, might need from the government and business to make family life less stressful. *People*'s "Putting Family First" cover story reminds us that being able to scale back at work because you have children is a luxury, a privilege only some women have. Having on-site day care—in the form of a toy-packed trailer staffed by a nanny— is a perk only for the rich and famous. Some mothers, it seems, deserve this autonomy, these support systems, and others just don't. And those of us who "chose" to work full-time (and even overtime) because we have to, want to, or both, are, in this Hollywood-dictated family album, selfish mothers with absolutely wrong priorities.

In fact, if you are a celebrity, you are entitled to have children whenever and however you want them, no matter how many you already have or how old you are. If you can't have them yourself, you buy them. Joan Lunden, age fifty-two and already mother of three, simply would not tolerate the fact that she could not give her new forty-two-year-old husband some babies. For a mere $65,000 (which includes legal and medical fees), "the blonde dynamo" hired a surrogate who became pregnant with twins. Now, don't get all huffy about the ethical implications of paying a woman to serve as your incubator because your own equipment is outdated. "'I'm choosing a lifestyle where I will have a couple of little ankle biters chasing me around for the next ten years,'" Lunden told *People*. "'I want it!'" So there. Besides, "'I'm not the typical fiftysomething,'" she bragged condescendingly.[59] True enough—most fiftysomething women are delighted to take a break from installing childproofing hooks on the kitchen cabinets and scraping ossified oatmeal off of high chairs. They also lack the huge disposable income and the even larger sense of entitlement that permit Lunden to promote the notion that no marriage is complete without your own biological children. Locked in a joyful, sisterly embrace, Lunden posed with her big-bellied surrogate for the cover of *People* because, selflessly, she and her husband saw it as "an opportunity to see if we can help others who struggle." Other celebrity millionaires, you mean?

Celebrity mom portraits resurrect so many of the stereotypes about women we hoped to deep-six thirty years ago: that women are, by genetic composition, nurturing and maternal, love all children, and prefer motherhood to anything, especially work, so should be the main ones responsible for raising the kids. More perniciously, they exemplify what motherhood has become in our intensified consumer culture: a competition. They rekindle habits of mind pitting women against women that the women's movement sought to end, leaving the notion of sisterhood in the dust. Why do Kirstie and Vanna and Whitney love being mothers in some unequivocal way that you do not? Because they're successful mothers and you're not.

Sure, many of us resent and ridicule these preposterous portraits of celebrity momdom, and gloated when the monumentally self-righteous "I-read-the-Bible-to-Cody" Kathie Lee got her various comeuppances. (For example, "Kathie Lee Sweatshop Is Killing My Kids!" screamed the ever–socially conscious *Enquirer* in October of 1999.) But the standards set by celebrity motherhood in the 1980s and beyond, with their powerful emphasis on individual will, choice, and responsibility, did more than make the rest of us feel like incompetent and inadequately energetic underachievers. They encouraged self-loathing in those of us financially comfortable enough not to have to worry about where our kids' next meals are coming from. But they also played a subtle but important role in persuading so many of us to think about motherhood as an individual achievement and a test of individual will and self-discipline.

Celebrity mom profiles haven't been just harmless dreck that helps sell magazines. The rise of the celebrity mom profile coincided, in the late 1980s, with the "war" on welfare mothers, which also played out in the media, and with several ongoing real-life melodramas in the news about motherhood gone bad. While this was hardly their intent, celebrity mom profiles and their emphasis on pulling yourself up by your bootstraps may have severely undercut sympathy for poor mothers and their children who were depicted as just the opposite of determined and enterprising.

So the next time you're in the checkout line, looking at the various celebrity mothers smiling beatifically from the covers of women's magazines, *People,* and *InStyle,* under headlines about their miracle babies, and how motherhood is always better than working outside the home, say something sarcastic, and say it loud. Because these stories suggest that we, too, can make it to the summit if we just get up earlier, laugh more, are more self-sacrificing, and buy the right products. They promote standards of child rearing impossible to achieve—even for them!

The parade of successful, beautiful, rich, admired women who embodied the new momism, who swore by it, who were made ecstatic by it, confirmed that this new momism came entirely from women themselves, and that it was the opposite of the feminine-mystique version of motherhood—after all, these mothers had agents and worked. Thus, the new momism could never be in the service of what we used to call patriarchy. To the ordinary mothers of America, those of us lacking the staff of a French château, and the joyful outlook that goes with it, these ceaseless profiles of celebrity moms with their perfect children and perfect lives are a rebuke, a snub, and a warning. Fail to get with the program and your kids will not make the grade, your husband won't look at you the way he used to, and, worst of all, other mothers will see you for what you are: an unworthy loser, a bad mother. Paying lip service to a Botox-injected feminism, celebrity momism trivialized the struggles and hopes of real women, and kissed off sisterhood as hopelessly out of style. This kiss was especially lethal when blown toward other mothers not showcased in the glossy magazines, but displayed in mug shots on the nightly news.

FIVE

Threats from Within: Maternal Delinquents

From Beechnut baby food containing pebbles, to car seats whose buckles tended to pop open while you were doing sixty on the freeway, to satanic childcare centers featuring blood-stained carcasses of small woodland animals, in the early and mid-1980s the media were filled with threats to mothers and children scary enough to frighten Freddie Kruger. Even when you turned on the tube to veg out after deep-sixing the kids, you had to see Val, of *Knots Landing,* have her newborn twin babies stolen from the hospital and sold on the black market. But by the late 1980s, these threats from without had been supplemented by a danger even scarier: the threat from within, the threat to children from mom herself.

At the same time that rich, white, air-brushed celebrity mothers schooled us in how to do it right, a parade of mothers gone bad—very bad—marched through our living rooms on the nightly news in a series of sensationalized media events that attracted enormous attention. Unlike the mothers of the 1940s, those women guilty of "momism" who allegedly ruined their children by coddling and overprotecting them, these mothers weren't protective enough. In fact, they were deadly. Beginning in the late 1980s, the new respect for, even glamorization of mothers who worked so hard inside and outside the home was punctuated by minidramas in which mother bashing, and the spectacle of maternal failure—and corruption—became an ongoing news peg. Surveying the lineup, we were invited to ask: Do you recognize yourself among the criminals?

TV news, appropriating the shocked tones and lurid images of the recent tabloid TV successes *A Current Affair* and *America's Most Wanted*, brought us a rotogravure of motherhood gone wrong, perverted, rotted from within. This reprehensible lineup included all manner of maternal depravity—crack mothers, abusive mothers, neglectful mothers, and murdering mothers. Lowest of the low, of course, was Susan Smith, who drowned her toddler sons by strapping them into their car seats and letting the car roll into a lake. These were not just news events: they were melodramas, big ones. Some of these stories were more legitimately newsworthy than others. However different all these supposedly repellent mothers were from one another, their stories, as they piled up and assaulted our psyches, had a common warning: mothers, police thyselves. Turn the searchlights within.

Just at the time when the new momism was upping the ante for mothers—hip, savvy, doting ones worked outside the home, yet chaperoned school trips, made sweetbreads *en croute* for dinner, and attended youth basketball, hockey, and soccer matches all weekend, often at the same time but at opposite ends of town, while smiling—what were we to make of mothers who just said no, who were out beyond the pale? What about mothers who seemed to love their kids too much or, worse, not at all?

In the fall of 1986, two stories broke that riveted national attention to the dangers posed by the deviant mother. The Baby M case and the "epidemic" of the "crack baby" dominated the news between 1987 and 1989. Both stories have been written about separately elsewhere, but we aim to put them together, and to connect them to the 1994–95 Susan Smith murder story. Why? All of these stories were sensational, but we want to reconsider why they commanded so much attention and why these mothers, all of them powerless and victimized in a variety of ways, were portrayed as freaks of maternal nature, their actions utterly incomprehensible. And in retrospect, we see how these cautionary tales added many building blocks to the ideology of the new momism. For a new set of rules about proper behavior to take hold, warnings about what will happen if you break the rules also need to circulate through the culture. And let's remember that the media are about creating drama—that's what they do. To create drama, you need heroes and villains. The nightly news relies just as much on this basic Hollywood narrative structure as the entertainment media. The heroes have wonderful qualities we're supposed to envy; the villains, repugnant traits we're meant to disdain or despise.[1]

It is a commonplace that serious deviance is newsworthy, as are a range of stories that focus on moral disorder, like crimes or political scandals.[2] That the deviance of mothers became such a major news peg in the late 1980s and 1990s is testimony to the revolutionary changes in family life and motherhood affecting millions of Americans, and to the resulting tensions between the aspirations of feminism on the one hand and, on the other, a nostalgia for some allegedly simpler, safer time when mom stayed home with the kids. Millions of women now led lives completely different from their mothers', yet social institutions and most men had not kept pace with these changes, and there was genuine anxiety about the consequences of this gap. But the news media's obsession with maternal delinquents is also testimony to the success of the New Right and its "mercenary intellectuals" in making sexism respectable again and getting their views a wide hearing on television.[3] So the question, explicitly pushed by some, and often more symbolically—and often even unconsciously—dramatized in the media was this: How far would feminism take motherhood? Would mothers come to pursue self-fulfillment or money or their own guilty pleasures so much that the kids of America would be veritable orphans? Wasn't it true, these media dramas seemed to suggest, that if taken to its logical conclusion, feminism was dangerous to children?

The evening soap operas of the early and mid-1980s, especially *Dynasty* and *Falcon Crest,* featured big, tough, ruthless, black-widow spider moms with padded shoulders who would just as soon betray their kids (or, in Alexis's case, seduce them) as look at them. Behind a veneer of oily, oozing, big-eyelashed faux concern lay the heart of a serpent. (Of course these women had been corrupted by too much power at work.) But what's striking about the media during this period is how much the news began to resemble such soaps. The news media now took the feminist assertion that "the personal is political" to heart, but hardly in the way feminists meant. Rather, the personal lives of the delinquent mothers were open to the most merciless inspection, and in the process intensive mothering got bolstered as a universal norm while judgments about who was inherently, inescapably a bad mother—African American and working-class white women—got cemented. The Baby M saga, the exposés about crack babies, the Susan Smith case, were maternal morality plays that lasted months or years. Their lead characters were conniving villains and their innocent victims were their own kids, and their plot lines out-twisted those of *Days of Our Lives* and *General Hospital*. We—the "viewing public"—were invited to join the production as judge, jury, and live studio audience, any member of which might be called onto the set to pay for her own maternal failings. These mothers had gone over the edge, stepped over the limits, not because they were pushed there, but because of some defect within themselves. As mothers, they were newsworthy because their internal maternal gyroscopes—the ones supposedly wired into all who give birth—had spun out of control, or just fallen over, dead.

Mary Beth Whitehead, crack mothers, and later, Susan Smith, allegedly shared another trait that no decent mother could ever have: narcissism. Because they were too self-centered, they were deviant, and dangerous, not only to their children but to the American way of life. Even the celebrity, whose job is to be the center of attention, to be self-promoting and self-absorbed, could not be an unadulterated narcissist once she had kids. To finesse the tension between such narcissism and the nurturing required for motherhood, the celebrity mom profile portrayed its subjects as narcissistic on *behalf of their kids*. The indulgence in expensive, highly personalized products, the ongoing attention to your looks, the pampering, this was not self-indulgent if it looked like it was providing your little miracles with what they were entitled to and deserved. But if you were a plain regular mother, and you made the mistake of having a couple of your own needs and desires, ones that actually had nothing at all to do with your children, then you were a threat to your own children and to the institution of motherhood itself.

With so many mothers working, with reproductive technologies expanding the ways that babies were made, with so many single mothers and recombinant families, were mothers losing their moral bearings? And if so, what was the right path to take? One of the stories that made this question a central part of the national agenda was the ubiquitous story of Baby M, which got its cloak of legitimacy from the fact that reproductive "technology," and resultant questions about medical ethics, were allegedly at its center. But it was not the technical aspects or potential ethical repercussions of artificial insemination that got news producers salivating, or prompted them, often, to abandon any pretense of distinguishing their product from *Soap Opera Digest*. The battle between one kind of mother and one kind of father, between one kind of mother and another kind of mother, between a father's rights and a mother's rights, as well as a contest to determine what kind of mother was the most desirable, the most worthy, those were the issues that kept the newsprint flowing and the klieg lights glowing. It didn't hurt that Baby M herself was a chubby-cheeked little cutie complete with blond curls and a winning smile.

The scene was suburban New Jersey, 1985. Dr. and Mr. Stern wanted to have a baby. Dr. Stern was in her late thirties, suffering from a mild form of multiple sclerosis. Her biological clock was ticking. She may not have suffered from the newly discovered "epidemic of heartbreaking infertility" (as it was generally referred to in the media and resulting, it was implied, because feminists told women to work first, have babies later). But she did fear the health risks of a pregnancy. Rather than adopt a baby, a process that was in many cases long and arduous, the Sterns decided to investigate the option of seeking a surrogate. They went to the New York Infertility Institute, an agency run by Noel Keane, who had been a vocal advocate of surrogacy arrangements. After qualifying as prospective parents, Mr. Stern, a biochemist, was introduced to Mrs. Whitehead (aka Mary Beth), a mother of two, married to a sanitation worker. Based on her separated-at-birth likeness to Dr. Stern, and the fact that Mary Beth had already had two successful pregnancies, the Sterns decided that she was the one. As she herself would say on the witness stand two years later, "I don't have an education. I don't have a skill. The only skill I know I do well is being a mother." The parties signed a contract in which the Sterns agreed to pay Mary Beth Whitehead $10,000 upon receipt of a baby, the result of her impregnation with William Stern's sperm. In addition, the Sterns agreed to pay her medical expenses and a $7,500 finder's fee to the Institute.

On March 27, 1986, Mary Beth Whitehead gave birth to a baby, whom she named Sara. Everything looked just fine, except for one thing: After having the baby, Mary Beth changed her mind. She said, effectively, you keep your money; I'll keep my baby. The Sterns decided to hold her to her contract. She pleaded with them to let her keep the baby for a week, so that she could say good-bye to her. At the end of the week, Mary Beth Whitehead still refused to give the baby to the Sterns. The Sterns went to court. The judge awarded temporary custody of the baby to the Sterns, whom they named Melissa. And thus, Baby M was born.

The drama then began in earnest. When Mr. Stern came to pick up the baby from the Whiteheads' house, Mary Beth handed the baby to her husband through a back window. They fled to Florida, where Mary Beth's parents lived. They left their two older children with their grandparents and began a fugitive existence, "staying in no less than 15 hotels, motels and as well with an assortment of relatives and friends."[4] Three months later, a private detective hired by the Sterns found them. After relinquishing the baby to the detective, Mary Beth Whitehead returned to New Jersey where she initiated a suit for custody.

Surrogate motherhood had received some media attention prior to the Baby M case, but it was largely confined to the confessional pages of the women's magazines and *People*. Stories about surrogacy implied that childlessness was heartbreaking and intolerable, and that women with children had a stake in ensuring that all women have kids. Surrogate mothers, like Elizabeth Kane in 1980, were supposed to deliver "her gift of love" and then "kiss her baby good-bye."[5] (Ironically enough, Elizabeth Kane would later became a staunch opponent of surrogacy, eventually testifying on behalf of Mary Beth Whitehead.) Not surprisingly, these stories celebrated women doing what women do best: having babies and making sacrifices for others, especially other family members. For the love of motherhood, properly equipped women showed the true meaning of the feminist slogan "Sisterhood is powerful." Poignant stories like "To My Sister With Love," "I Gave Birth to My Sister's Baby," and "I Had My Sister's Baby" recounted the experiences of robust, procreative women giving up babies to their infertile sisters, a gift that any really loving sister would willingly give.[6] Another dramatization of female altruism in the name of motherhood occurred in *The Big Chill* (1983), when the monumentally noble Sarah (Glenn Close) gave her husband, Harold (Kevin Kline), to her best friend, Meg (Mary Kay Place), for the night so that Meg, unmarried, could have a baby of her own. (Maybe we're unnaturally possessive, or inadequately selfless, but asking one's husband to have sex with one's best friend was not a solution that would have come immediately to mind under these circumstances.) Nonetheless, in media texts like these, the institution of motherhood itself was replenished by individual mothers sacrificing their babies to other women who would otherwise fail to experience maternal fulfillment. The other side of the story, from the recipient's end, which also bolstered the notion that a woman wasn't really a woman if she didn't have children, included the shame of a woman who could not produce the child that her husband deserved and that she craved (e.g., "I Had to Pay Another Woman to Have My Baby").[7]

Once Mary Beth Whitehead changed her mind, and the case moved to the courts, the news media discovered surrogacy. The case received the kind of exhaustive and wide-ranging coverage usually reserved for full-scale military incursions or high political malfeasance. *The New York Times,* for example, kept its readers focused by offering not only daily reports on the progress of the seven-week trial, but also columns entitled, "Key Dates in the Case," a timeline of significant events, and a full-page opinion sampler in "The Week in Review" in which the likes of Al Gore, Betty Friedan, and Rabbi William Feldman commented on the case and unburdened themselves over who should get custody.[8] Between November 1986 and the summer of 1992, the networks collectively carried at least forty-four stories about the Whitehead case and other surrogacy controversies. After 1992, the story fell off the planet. When the women's movement coined the slogan "the personal is political," few anticipated that the media would embrace the sentiment so avidly and parlay a tug of war over a baby into a prolonged exemplar of voyeuristic infotainment.

As Tom Brokaw told us in November of 1986, there had been, by then, about five hundred babies born, with no media fanfare, to surrogate mothers. NBC showed us some of these good surrogates (the ones who didn't change their minds), like the mother of two who wanted to help someone else know the joys of parenthood. But Mary Beth reneged. Once she had her baby she couldn't give her up. Was her contract with the Sterns valid, given that this commercial enterprise was entirely unregulated? Was she selling her baby or renting her womb? Although the networks emphasized that surrogacy was a "creation of modern medicine,"[9] the true media contest was this: Who deserved the baby more, the woman from whose egg it came and who carried the baby for nine months, but was lower middle class and married to a garbage man? Or the man who had contributed the sperm and the money, but who was upper middle class and married to a doctor?

The trial in the New Jersey Superior Court began on January 5, 1987, and in short order the case became an indictment of Whitehead as, womb or no womb, pregnancy or no pregnancy, an inherently unfit mother. (Increasingly, the case came to resemble rape cases in which the victims, not the perpetrators, were put on trial.) Whitehead seemed to be resurrecting two misogynistic stereotypes about women: that they can never make up their minds, and that they are hysterical. At the time, the battle appeared to be between Mary Beth Whitehead and Bill Stern. While not to let the man Whitehead referred to as "Mr. Sperm" off the hook, it was his attorney, Gary N. Skoloff, who pursued a scorched-earth policy on White-head's qualifications as a mother. On February 2, NBC reported that the Sterns' attorney listed thirty-five reasons why Whitehead should not get Baby M, alleging that she was "a liar," "unstable," and in an "unhappy marriage to an alcoholic." But the big bombshell that turned much of the country against her aired two nights later. When Mary Beth had fled to Florida with the baby, she and Bill Stern spoke on the phone in July of 1986. She begged Stern to abandon the contract and let her keep the baby, who was three-and-half months old by then. Mr. Stern had the presence of mind to record the conversation without Whitehead's knowledge and pass it along to his attorney, who played it in court, thus making it available to the news media and the public.

In the conversation, Whitehead was frantic. In addition to wanting to keep her baby, Mary Beth had discovered that the Sterns had gotten a judge to freeze all of the Whiteheads' assets, including their home, the fur-nishings inside, their car, and their bank accounts, a detail about daddy dearest reported in *The New York Times,* but not on the networks.[10] So she was at the end of her rope and took desperate measures. On television, we heard the recording and, lest we missed any of it, saw a text version run across the screen like subtitles. "I'd rather see me and her dead before you get her," Mary Beth threatened. "I'm going to do it, Bill. . . . I'm going to do it; you've pushed me to it. . . . I gave her life. I can take her life away."[11] All three networks aired portions of the recording and *The New York Times* printed the entire transcript. As Bob Schieffer of NBC noted, "the mother's death threats" on the tape gave him a chill. Played in public, for the benefit of television viewers, the threats indeed made Whitehead seem crazy, a danger to herself and the child. The networks had taken the sensational bait and used the tapes exactly the way the Sterns' lawyer wanted them to: as *prima facie* evidence of Mary Beth's unfitness, as evi-dence that being uneducated and working class are risk factors associated with irrational, unhinged, overly attached mothers.

What didn't come across, probably couldn't come across, but is clear from the phone transcript is Whitehead's overwhelming sense of power-lessness against the financial and legal resources of a well-connected pro-fessional man. He had frozen her assets, gotten a court order to take the child away, and was using a detective agency to hunt her down. Now, threatening to kill your baby Medea-style does suggest that you are com-ing unglued. But it is also true that desperation can cause people to say things they don't really mean. Imagine if your worst argument found its way on to national television. How sane would you look? When the Sterns' attorney played the tape in court, Whitehead broke down, acknowledging later what was all too obvious: "I gave birth to that baby. There's no way I would hurt her or allow anybody else to hurt her." But by then, the damage to her case was done. Notably, what the networks did not air from the tapes were heart-wrenching passages like these: "I've been breastfeeding her for four months. Don't you think she's bonded to me? Bill, I sleep in the same bed with her. She won't even sleep by herself . . . she knows my smell, she knows who I am—don't I count for anything?" [12] Instead, on March 12, when the attorneys for both sides delivered their closing arguments, Tom Brokaw asked, "When should a mother be forced to give up a child?" and, as if to answer his own question, aired—yet again—the infamous telephone death threats. [13]

As the case proceeded Mary Beth and her family were torn apart for public scrutiny, and in the process some quite bizarre measurements for assessing good motherhood got added to the maternal scales. On the stand she admitted that, yes, her husband had been an alcoholic, they had separated for a while and she had gone on welfare, her son had had problems in school, and her daughter, Tuesday, had gotten frostbite one night when the furnace in their house broke down. Then the Sterns' lawyer, who kept Whitehead on the stand for as long as five hours, got her to admit that she had once worked as a "barroom dancer." [14]

Okay, this was not sounding so good. But once the mental-health experts in the case weighed in, Mary Beth was held to stratospheric standards of maternal perfection. One expert testified that Mary Beth should not get custody because she didn't play patty-cake correctly with the baby and—get this gaffe—gave Baby M a stuffed panda to play with (wrong!) instead of pots and pans (right!). Even worse, Whitehead dyed her prematurely gray hair brown, was thus narcissistic, and was therefore not an ideal mother. (Apparently Cybill Shepherd and Heather Locklear, who were "worth it," got a pass.) Appalled by these preposterous standards, a group of 124 women, including Meryl Streep, Gloria Steinem, Carly Simon, and the novelist Lois Gould, issued a statement of solidarity, which read, "By these standards, we are all unfit mothers." [15]

Because the story often seemed to take the form of a game show (*Family Feud*?) about "two women fighting for one baby," the two female contestants, Dr. Stern and Mary Beth, had to be represented as miles apart:

doctor vs. housewife; barren womb vs. procreatrix; repressed vs. hysterical; educated vs. ignorant; "career woman" vs. "homemaker"; Ann Taylor vs. Dress Barn. So Dr. Stern did not come across all that great either. She was the opposite of Mary Beth, which so far was good, but she had to soften up, to show that in spite of her self-contained self-satisfaction, she had the right hormones for motherhood and was thinking only of what would be best for the baby. On television she was no more than a cipher; the principal drama was staged between her husband and Mary Beth. She committed maternal gaffes too, but for her, professional woman that she was (and consort to the rightful father), the networks never took the gloves off.

When Dr. Stern took the stand on February 2, the networks covered the attacks on Whitehead, not Dr. Stern's testimony. In it, according to *The New York Times,* she said she was going to cut back on her work because "I didn't realize how much time is required to raise a child." (Imagine if this clueless comment had been replayed over and over on the networks with accompanying text.) Elizabeth Stern claimed that she was the baby's true mother because she was her "psychological mother." (Say what?) The Sterns' lawyer insisted that she contradict her husband's previous testimony that they would put the child in full-time day care at age four; instead, she testified, the child would only go to day care part-time, even at that age.[16] Her reported activities with the child included "pulling at the clothes in Bloomingdale's." Worst of all, Dr. Stern spilled the beans on the conditional, "if I can't have it my way, then I don't want to play at all" terms of her attachment to the baby. "During cross-examination, Dr. Stern said that she did not want to see the child if Mrs. Whitehead were awarded custody."[17] (So much for "psychological motherhood.") In part because these kinds of comments did not get on the network news, and because Whitehead was repeatedly cast as "emotional" (which she was, since she was about to lose her baby), few took Whitehead's side. A *USA Today* poll revealed that 58 percent of respondents said the Sterns should get custody because "a deal is a deal." Only 20 percent of those polled supported Whitehead.[18]

As for Mr. Stern, no one seemed quite sure what to make of him. Maybe if he had the commanding machismo of Blake Carrington or J. R. Ewing, his efforts to do whatever it took to assert the power of the patriarch might have come in for more criticism. But his nerd glasses and Columbo trench coat, and his tearful insistence that "fathers have feelings, too," muted the fact that he was an upper-middle-class man whose lawyer savagely exposed, in public, every imperfection in Mary Beth Whitehead's life so that the rights of the man would prevail over the rights of the woman.

On April 1 (in what turned out to be a fitting date), the judge, Harvey Sorkow, announced his decision. He took there to be two issues in the case: first, the legitimacy of the initial surrogate contract; and second, the determination of custody, which is based on what the judge perceives to be the best interests of the child. He held the contract to be valid; in addition, he awarded custody of the baby to Mr. Stern, on the grounds that he and his wife would provide better care for the child than would Mary Beth Whitehead. Most shocking to nearly all observers, Sorkow denied Mary Beth any visitation rights whatsoever. NBC reported that 75 percent of the public supported the judge's decision.[19] Shortly after the ruling, Judge Sorkow signed the documents enabling Dr. Stern to adopt the baby, thereby terminating all of Whitehead's parental rights, and changed the baby's legal name to Melissa, the name given to her by the Sterns. On April 10, Mary Beth regained brief visitation rights. That summer she and her husband split up and she remarried. She also became pregnant. In the midst of her court battle to gain expanded visitation rights to Baby M, the Sterns' lawyer charged that her latest pregnancy was "further proof of her personality problems."[20] But by the following April, the appeals court threw out Sorkow's ruling on the grounds that, among other things, it condoned baby selling. Dr. Stern's adoption was invalidated and Whitehead's maternal standing was restored. Though the Sterns' retained physical custody of Melissa, Mary Beth was awarded significant visitation rights. This rather radical reversal received cursory media attention. The story evaporated.

As millions of mothers—most of them not surrogates, not doctors, and no longer full-time homemakers—found themselves surrounded by this drama, many found it difficult to identify with either Mary Beth Whitehead or Elizabeth Stern. Each seemed a caricature, one a throwback to the 1950s, a woman too caught up in the love of her baby, the other a craven careerist who seemed to see children as nothing more than an essential accessory item, and who exuded the warmth of a frozen potpie. The media drama cast both women, ironically, as too self-centered. So the story, aside from its high drama tug-of-war over the heart of a child and dumbfounding new reproductive arrangements, got so much attention because, as staged, it enacted another tug-of-war, between the feminine mystique millions of women were determined to get rid of, and a masculinized careerism, with children relegated to the sidelines, that women did not want to embrace either. Mary Beth failed to conform to the new norm of "savvy" motherhood in the media, especially as exemplified by the celebrity mom, of the educated, authoritative, highly organized woman who read every childcare book published, fed her kids tofu and "all natural" Cheerios, carefully calibrated the balance between emotion and intellect, and juggled work and family.

In the yuppified mid-1980s, the women's magazines had recast motherhood as a "career" (not a job) that could only be done properly by middle- and upper-middle-class women deploying professional-level skills. Mary Beth was nowhere close to the briefcase-toting moms in FedEx commercials, let alone the moms on Who's the Boss or Family Matters. She was one of those bad old "smothering" mothers who would be, in the end, bad for her child. That she was consistently referred to as a "surrogate mother" undercut the fact that she had indeed given birth to the baby, which at the very least secures the title of birth mother. In the media's eyes, "surrogate" became at best a synonym for "substitute."[21] What lingered, then, was the spectacle of the unfit mother, the one who had failed to be upwardly mobile, the one who couldn't control her emotions, the one who had already produced a child with learning disabilities, who probably hadn't played Mozart to him in the womb, the one who insisted that biological ties and gestation were enough. But they weren't anymore. Worst of all, Mary Beth didn't get it that her baby would be better off with all the *stuff* that the Sterns had to offer.

But if Whitehead came across as a throwback, Elizabeth Stern evoked the brave new world feminism allegedly promoted, in which women didn't even have their own babies but bought them on the open market, and had the maternal sensibilities of a turnip. Stern, with her advanced degrees, appeared to be one of those women who would stock the nursery with flash cards, read aloud from the Children's Book of Virtues, and take Baby M to The Plaza for tea in one of those outfits from Bloomingdale's. She stirred up stereotypes about rich, frigid mothers who gave their children everything but love and pretended to be focused on them but were really worrying about whether to take the prospective client to the Tavern on the Green or Nobu for lunch.

The question the Baby M case raised wasn't whether or not Mom should work outside the home. The question was whether or not she understood the obligations of her true profession: motherhood. The line to walk was not the one laid down by Mary Beth or Elizabeth: It was somewhere in between, and mothers better figure out exactly where. The contribution the case made to the new momism at this stage of its evolution was to insist that mothers perfectly regulate their behavior, that they never become *over*invested in their kids but never seem *under*invested, either. And the greatest sin they could commit was being too self-centered, either in their roles as mothers or in their careers. The media drama indicated that it might just be time to crack down on mothers who thought they could play by their own rules.

As a result of the public-relations campaign that Gary N. Skoloff, the Sterns' attorney, organized inside and outside the courtroom, he successfully turned Mary Beth Whitehead into the antimother, the one no right-minded woman should be similar to, let alone emulate. There's no doubt that as Skoloff's campaign plowed along, Whitehead indeed appeared to be unstable to millions of people, and who knows, maybe she was.

The attacks on her, and the version of motherhood represented by Elizabeth Stern, confirmed that both were outside the boundaries of acceptable motherhood, which tightened the noose for us all. Of course mothers kept dying their hair, giving their kids stuffed animals to play with, and crying in public when they weren't supposed to. But in the wake of the Baby M case, scrutinizing mothers, including the tiniest details of the toys they bought or how they played with their kids, just seemed more acceptable, even necessary. The Baby M case, in unspoken, subtle ways, simply made it more legitimate to dissect and judge every aspect of maternal behavior.

Mary Beth Whitehead may have failed to bring out the pots and pans at the right moment, but at least she had produced a healthy, chubby white baby. There were mothers who had screwed up even worse, and the news media jumped at the chance to introduce them to us. Probably the most distressing and graphic images of motherhood gone very, very wrong were the parade of coffee-colored, peanut-sized, writhing "crack babies" that first appeared on the network news in the fall of 1985 and reached their peak in 1988 and 1989. Like the other media panics about mothers and children, the newly discovered "epidemic" of crack babies "overwhelming" the maternity wards of America turned out later to have been highly exaggerated and sensationalized.[22] The medical researchers, in particular, on whose studies the "crack baby" stories were based, were appalled to see how their work was distorted.[23] Ira Chasnoff, whose initial research on cocaine use during pregnancy sparked the media frenzy, bemoaned the press's misuse of medical research in the service of "selling newspapers" and said "poverty is the worst thing that can happen to a child," not cocaine. (He has since given interviews and published articles denouncing the concept and the term "crack baby," which he never used.)[24] As Janine Jackson of the media watchdog organization FAIR put it, the mainstream media indulged in "an astonishing spree of sloppy, alarmist reporting and racial and economic scapegoating that still echoes today."[25]

The shocking images of "crack babies" could have been used, for example, to illustrate the desperate consequences of Reagan's cuts in prenatal care for poor women. (While pushing for a Human Life Bill that would "protect the unborn," Reagan simultaneously sought to rip everything away from poor kids once they left the womb.) Under Reagan, funding for his "war on drugs" quadrupled between 1981 and 1989, while in one year, 1981, more than one million poor women and their children lost medical benefits.[26] As Susan Faludi reported, in California alone, the number of babies born to parents with no health insurance rose by 45 percent between 1982 and 1986, and they were 30 percent more likely to be sickly or to die. By 1985, one out of two African American women had inadequate prenatal care. A Florida study concluded, "[I]t is safer for a baby to be born to a drug-abusing, anemic, or diabetic mother who visits the doctor throughout her pregnancy than to be born to a normal woman who does not."[27] But this was not the news frame we got. Instead, crack babies served as the most powerful metaphor for motherhood poisoned by the excesses of the 1970s and '80s, like drugs, self-indulgence, and female self-actualization run amok. They were "the littlest victims."[28] These babies—teeny, twitching, barely able to hold on to life—had been contaminated by women so selfish, so promiscuous, so insensitive to human life itself that they served as a powerful warning of where children—and the nation itself—would end up if mothers really "just said no" to their maternal instincts.

"Crack babies" served as proof that poor, black, inner-city mothers were "she-devils," the grotesque opposite of caring, white, middle-class mothers.[29] Mothers who had missed the first half of the school play, or smacked their kid on the behind that morning, or left their toddler with someone who watched The Price Is Right and All My Children all day, could breath a sigh of relief after comparing themselves to these maternal monstrosities. At the same time, however, that "crack babies" served to divide mothers into "us" and "them," almost exclusively along racial lines, they were also a powerful, controlling symbol of the potential deterioration of The Family writ large, a warning to all mothers about the utter fragility of motherhood itself. Repeatedly the stories about crack babies became stories about the future of America, a future that was bleak, handicapped, poised on the brink of self-destruction. And all because these mothers could not, or would not, control themselves.

In October 1982, Ronald Reagan announced his "war on drugs," the centerpiece of which was the Just Say No campaign. Nancy Reagan took up the cause in part to counteract her image as a cold, uncaring mannequin who preferred shopping for Adolfo suits to spending time with any of her children. Then, in 1985, the news media discovered crack, and when the athletes Len Bias and Don Rogers both died from cocaine overdoses in 1986, and Reagan announced an intensified war on drugs, a drug hysteria swept the media and much of the nation.[30] It is important to emphasize the media's role in hyping this hysteria. Use of illegal drugs had been declining in the 1980s since its peak in 1979–80. In an April 1986 poll, only 2 percent of respondents picked drugs as the nation's most important problem. But during the spring and summer of 1986, there was a huge jump in the number of stories in the press and on TV about drugs, and especially crack: 406 stories about cocaine between March 30 and December 31 alone. *Newsweek* featured three drug-abuse cover stories in five months, and Dan Rather hosted a much-hyped CBS Special in September 1986 called "48 Hours on Crack Street." It is not surprising, then, that by September—just four months after the April poll—respondents listed drugs as the nation's most important problem.[31]

At first, the connection to motherhood focused on the need to protect older kids from crack and crack dealers. But this was also the era of increased warnings about the dangers that careless pregnant women pose to their fetuses. In April 1984, for example, Peter Jennings warned hyperbolically, "Doctors now say that a woman in the last three months of pregnancy who goes out for just a single evening of cocktails and after dinner drinks could risk brain damage to her baby."[32] So it was not surprising when Susan Spencer, reporting for CBS News in September 1985, covered a *New England Journal of Medicine* study claiming that cocaine had just

as devastating an effect on pregnancy as heroin, that it caused spontaneous abortions, and that babies born to mothers who used coke went
through withdrawal. It was, as one of the authors noted, a limited but important study designed to raise questions and concerns about using cocaine while pregnant.[33] A white mother who had used cocaine then
described her baby's symptoms and confessed "it was awful, such a feeling of guilt, like I did this to her." Spencer ended the report with a direct
address to viewers: "The message is clear, if you are pregnant and use cocaine, stop." As the media scholars Jimmie Reeves and Richard Campbell
have pointed out, Spencer did not focus on the culpability of the white
mother, but rather on the health warnings to be heeded by all. The story
was not structured as an us/them account of decent folk versus abusers.
But that quickly changed.[34]

Just six months later, NBC connected teen pregnancy with drug abuse,
and reported that in Los Angeles alone, the number of addicted babies had
risen by 500 percent since 1981. All the babies we saw in the story were
black or Latino. "There is no indication that the number of babies born
addicted will decrease any time soon," cautioned reporter Noah Nelson.
"They are becoming a new generation whose future is doubtful."[35] Such
gloomy and inflated prognostications became de rigueur in covering the
"crack baby" epidemic. By November of 1986, CBS, citing no studies and
zero data, reported that "some physicians" estimated that the number of
pregnancies involving cocaine abuse "could be as high as one in every
ten," on its face a preposterously high figure. Later in the report we heard
that "no one knows how many babies have been damaged by drug
abuse," again suggesting that the number was too high to count.[36] By
1989, CBS cited estimates that 15 percent of all babies born had mothers
who abused drugs. They reported that a woman could use coke only once
during her pregnancy and still see "very dire consequences" in her baby.[37]

"As cocaine spreads like a cancer through this society," Tom Brokaw
intoned, so does the "population explosion of crack babies." To document the epidemic, the networks, after showing the requisite preemie in a
neonatal ICU, then routinely showed dozens of bassinettes lined up side
by side in maternity wards, all of which allegedly contained "crack babies." All kinds of estimates were thrown out—that anywhere from three
to five hundred thousand crack babies would be born that year alone, that
15 percent of babies born were crack babies, that five years hence the

schools would be overrun by "a tidal wave" of crack kids who would be handicapped in all kinds of ways.[38] Crack babies, CBS reported, were destined to have short attention spans, learning handicaps, to be impulsive and undisciplined, and to have poor social interaction skills.[39] Their "only inheritance," as ABC put it, "is addiction to cocaine."[40] *The Washington Post* warned of "A Time Bomb in Cocaine Babies" in the fall of 1989, while the *St. Louis Post-Dispatch* the following year declared, "Disaster in Making: Crack Babies Start to Grow Up."[41] "The schools of this country better start to prepare," warned CBS in January 1989.[42] ABC put a price tag of $5 billion a year on the problem, confirming its estimate by showing a baby born eight weeks premature and suffering from a host of problems, including cerebral palsy: "His mother's drug abuse has condemned him to a lifetime of medical and emotional problems."[43] Only one week later, ABC had upped the estimated cost to $20 billion a year![44] The networks also showcased the most sensational cases—a baby born weighing only fifteen ounces, for example—to dramatize how extreme the situation was. NBC warned in the fall of 1988, "No one is even guessing at how widespread the epidemic of crack babies will be," but experts say "the price will be enormous." We then heard from a white congressman who said they would be "the most expensive babies ever born in America and are going to overwhelm every social service delivery system." Added a white judge, "they'll grow up to be tomorrow's delinquents." These figures and predictions were highly alarmist. Later they proved to be almost entirely false.

But at the time, the spewing of crack facts created its own momentum. Reporter Michelle Gillen predicted "there are tens of thousands more crack babies on the way" as the camera showed us three black babies, "a generation that may pose an even greater risk"—a claim illustrated, in the final shot, by a black baby peering into the camera.[45] Images of black babies, cast as "genetic deviants," personified this bleak future.[46] Crack babies, of course, were "permanently damaged" because their crack-induced afflictions "could last a lifetime." They were, as CBS reminded us, "different from other children."[47] For those of you who remember seeing them, they were heartbreaking little things—wrists like straws, tubes everywhere, shaking involuntarily, either screaming their hearts out or, worse, too weak to cry at all. Because the networks always went to the neonatal ICUs to illustrate this story, because there was already a media panic about a national crack epidemic, and because we were bombarded with so many bloated figures about the enormity of the problem while we watched these walnut-sized babies struggle for life, it was hard to feel anything but shock and outrage.

Conservative columnists like Charles Krauthammer had a field day, and foretold the end in 1989. "The inner-city crack epidemic is now giving birth to the newest horror: a bio-underclass, a generation of physically damaged cocaine babies whose biological inferiority is stamped at birth." Drawing from commentary by the right-wing American Enterprise Institute, Krauthammer continued, "This is not stuff that Head Start can fix. This is permanent brain damage. Whether it is 5 percent or 15 percent of the black community, it is there." Krauthammer likened crack babies to "a race of (sub)human drones" described in Huxley's Brave New World, and warned that their "future is closed to them from day one. Theirs will be a life of certain suffering, of probable deviance, of permanent inferiority. At best, a medical life of severe deprivations." In his opinion, "the dead babies may be the lucky ones." [48]

Thus, "crack babies" contributed to a new common sense about the fruitlessness of trying to rescue children from bad or impoverished circumstances. The story coincided with new scientific findings about how early in infancy babies seem to respond to language and how important early stimulation was to their development. Studies were also suggesting that some children might never be able to compensate for or overcome early abuse and neglect. The "permanent damage" aspect of the "crack baby" stories implied that poor, black children were already a lost cause, even before they were born. So why devote any resources to them after they were born? It would all just go down the rat hole anyway.

After all, just look at their mothers—nearly all of them black—who were the perpetrators of this unconscionable blight. As a Washington Post headline put it, CRACK BABIES: THE WORST THREAT IS MOM HERSELF.[49] In October 1988, for example, in a "Spotlight Story," NBC introduced us to "Stephanie," one of those mothers who "frequently vanish back into the streets and crack houses" after leaving their crack-addicted babies behind for the hospitals and foster-care system to deal with. Stephanie, wearing a distinctly menacing hooded sweatshirt (read: homie girl to some gang member) had already had two crack babies, we were told. She claimed to want her children but couldn't raise them, she told the reporter, "with no financial help or nothing." We then learned that "Stephanie is back on the streets, back on crack and pregnant again." Stephanie had no story, no history, absolutely nothing to evoke sympathy or understanding: On the contrary, she was meant to evoke disgust.[50] She cranked out one permanently damaged baby after the next and left them on America's doorstep.

She wasn't alone. The story moved to Hale House in Harlem, where we saw a little boy whose mother had left him there and then called and said, "I don't want him."[51] A March 1989 CBS story about addicted babies being abandoned by their mothers told us that the typical crack mother "leaves the kids; she doesn't come home until she finds drugs." Over an image of a black woman holding a baby in a rocking chair, we were reminded that these mothers were "unable or unwilling to take care of their kids."[52] As a Los Angeles Times headline put it succinctly, aping Reagan's slogan: PARENTS WHO CAN'T SAY "NO" ARE CREATING A GENERATION OF MISERY.[53] Repeatedly journalists emphasized that crack mothers lost, or never had, basic maternal instincts and "had utter disregard for their children"; crack severed "that deepest and most sacred of bonds: that between a mother and child."[54]

Another news media archetype that emerged was the criminal crack mother, again, almost always black, indicted for child abuse and distributing drugs to a minor because she took drugs while pregnant. In the absence of a drug panic such mothers might not be newsworthy, but they frequently made the nightly news in 1989. Pamela Ray Stewart—who was a white, married mother of two—was convicted of a misdemeanor for taking speed while she was pregnant, which allegedly resulted in her baby's death. Of all the misdemeanor cases—let alone felony trials—before courts throughout the land, that this one should merit national news coverage speaks to the power of this new news peg: the drug-abusing mother.

But once she was a black crack user, the defamation intensified. "What would you do," asked the honey-voiced golden girl Diane Sawyer, looking meaningfully into the camera as only she can, "to mothers who use drugs while pregnant and pass those drugs on to their babies?" Before you could answer, Sawyer advised, "You should know" that some think it's time to prosecute. She then showed a crack mother, "the victim—her own baby."[55]

We were introduced to a host of mothers so bad that they got a jump-start on child abuse by harming their kids before they were even born. In 1989, we met Toni Hudson, indicted for administering illegal drugs to a minor because she used coke while pregnant and her baby was allegedly born addicted.[56] NBC showed us three black women all up on charges of child abuse for doing coke while they were pregnant. One district attorney cast these women as "wanton" because they did "irreversible, fatal harm" to their babies and, as if to confirm how unrestrained such women were, one black woman admitted on camera, "I could not help myself." Several networks covered the case of Jennifer Johnson, charged with delivering drugs to a minor. Johnson admitted that she was an addict, but said she had no intention of hurting her baby. In fact, she told doctors she used cocaine in the hopes of getting treatment. Instead, she was arrested and became the first woman convicted of using drugs while pregnant.[57] The news showed us a black woman who had been up on manslaughter charges in Illinois because she allegedly used crack and her baby died, even though we then learned that the charges had been dropped. ABC News, at least, seemed to endorse such arrests. As Peter Jennings noted in September 1991, this was "a new approach, it's tough, it seems to work." [58]

Such stories fueled support for arresting crack mothers: Since 1985, more than two hundred U.S. women have been prosecuted on charges that their use of the drug while pregnant constituted a crime against the fetus.[59] Even though there are similar levels of illegal drug use among white women and black and Latina women, the women of color account for 80 percent of those women prosecuted for taking drugs while pregnant.[60] In the early 1990s in South Carolina, of twenty-three prosecutions, twenty-two were of African American women; the lone white woman was married to a black man.[61] When the news media trotted out mothers who had been addicts and were trying to get clean, however, it was white women who were given center stage.[62] No comparable arrests were made, at country clubs, say, of mothers who took Valium, smoked, or drank excessively.

Now, here's what we did not see—a "crack mother" who cared about her kids. We did not see a "crack mother" snuggling her child or taking her to the playground. Yet Marsha Rosenbaum, a researcher affiliated with the The Lindesmith Center in San Francisco who studied crack mothers, emphasized that unlike their vilification in the news, these women felt a strong responsibility for their children, as well as deep pride. They nurtured their kids and wanted to be good role models. Many tried to quit (with very few drug rehabilitation programs available to them in the wake of government cuts) but also found that crack helped them escape temporarily from the pressures of parenthood in an often brutally impoverished setting. Claire Sterk, in her acclaimed 1999 study of women on crack, drove home how many of these mothers were victims of physical and sexual abuse, neighborhood violence, racism, and sexism, and often turned to crack out of desperation. Nonetheless, they viewed motherhood as their most important role, some working overtime to provide for their kids and struggling to get off the drug. Sterk added that for some of these women, the discovery that they were pregnant was a turning point in kicking drugs.[63] But we didn't see them on the networks, either.

Was there an epidemic of underweight babies damaged for life, destined to become a menace to society because their mothers were smoking crack? No. Or, to put it another way, crack babies were a media creation, a hyping and misrepresentation of medical studies, some solid and some not, that indicated that women should not do coke while pregnant.[64] It turned out that there was no convincing evidence that use of crack actually caused abnormal babies, even though the media insisted this was so. The effects of cocaine on fetuses was greatly exaggerated, and the negative effects on babies attributed to crack were often caused by other factors.

It turns out that the symptoms the news media attributed to crack use as often as not were the effects of alcohol, tobacco and, most importantly, poverty and lack of prenatal care. (There is an actual syndrome, fetal alcohol syndrome, that indeed produces damage in a child, often for life. Yet there was no media panic about "alcohol babies.") Most poor women had, not surprisingly, very poor diets, and many did not appreciate— because Reagan had cut prenatal care for them—how important diet was. Studies found no consistent relationship between a mother's cocaine use while pregnant and long-term deficiencies in the child; those motor-skill problems associated with crack disappeared by seven months. Studies showed that mothers using cocaine who had medical care throughout their pregnancies (with or without drug treatment) had significantly healthier babies than women who didn't have such care.[65]

As one study put it, "Cocaine does not produce physical dependence, and babies exposed to it prenatally do not exhibit symptoms of drug withdrawal. Other symptoms of drug dependence—such as 'craving' and 'compulsion'—cannot be detected in babies. In fact, without knowing that cocaine was used by their mothers, clinicians cannot distinguish so-called crack-addicted babies from babies born to comparable mothers who had never used cocaine or crack." [66] The studies that did claim that cocaine use caused irremediable damage used biased samples and have been criticized by a variety of researchers. Just to give one example, early studies that claimed there was a "fetal cocaine withdrawal syndrome" were nonblind, meaning the observers were told which infants had been exposed to cocaine. So, you know, they were kind of looking to find something in those babies. In later studies, in which the observers did not know which infants had been exposed to what, they were unable to detect "fetal cocaine withdrawal." [67] But these subsequent studies correcting the myth of the crack baby got virtually zero coverage. In fact, even in the academy (like we're really pure and immune to trends) the hysteria found a home. One 1989 study in *The Lancet*, a highly respected medical journal, found that "scientific results describing harmful effects of cocaine use during pregnancy were more likely to be accepted for conference presentation and publication than studies of equal or superior methodology showing few or no effects." [68]

Media coverage of "crack babies" served as a powerful cautionary tale about the inherent fitness of poor or lower-class African American women to be mothers at all. In addition, crack babies, while dividing mothers and children up between "us"—decent, responsible, caring, disciplined white people—and "them"—promiscuous, irresponsible, out-of-control, wanton black women—was also a normalizing story for *all* mothers. It raised the question that would come to haunt the next decades. As a mother, were you being sufficiently vigilant, were you, at every turn, resisting the selfish, stupid choice in favor of the selfless, smart one? What were you eating/smoking/drinking/popping while you were pregnant? Crack babies reminded us how crucial it was for all of us to be on guard, or else.

Serving as the ongoing backbeat for this sensational news frame of endangered children and maternal delinquents was the rise in stories about child abuse. One of the most revolting—and visually shocking—was the Lisa Steinberg case (1987–88), in which a six-year-old was tortured to death by her adoptive father, Joel Steinberg, while her mother, Hedda Nussbaum, also horribly abused by Steinberg, looked on. The news media's coverage of child abuse, which increased dramatically during this same period in the late 1980s and early 1990s, was crucial to raising national awareness of the problem. On September 4, 1992, Oprah Winfrey hosted an hour-long show on child abuse, "Scared Silent," broadcast simultaneously on NBC, ABC, and PBS, and it was reportedly seen in 13 million homes. When hot-line numbers appeared on screen, "the response was dramatic," reported NBC, with some hot-lines getting four thousand calls an hour.[69] So the media's public-service role here was admirable and indisputable. But the Steinberg case aside (and ditto for the much publicized "home alone" case in which a white couple left their four-year-old and nine-year-old alone for a week while they went on vacation), most of the individual stories about abuse focused on black or Latino women. Stories about child abuse also attacked child welfare services that were, indeed, underfunded and understaffed, without also attacking the government officials and agencies that refused to provide these agencies with the support they needed. Rarely did the stories emphasize the connection between structural problems like unemployment and poverty and child abuse and neglect. It was hard not to develop a sense of fatalism watching such reports, that nothing could be done collectively, that it was up to individuals themselves.

The ultimate maternal delinquent was the murdering mom (always much more shocking, and thus more newsworthy, than murdering dads). One of the first murdering mothers to make it to the nightly news was Christina LoCasto, who gave birth in an airplane in Newark airport, and then stuffed the baby in the plane's waste bin and covered her with paper towels. She was charged with attempted murder, but the story did not last beyond the initial incident.[70]

The Susan Smith case was, of course, another matter. On October 24, 1994, in a story wrenchingly titled "Where Are My Children?" and introduced as "a mother's nightmare," NBC reported that a carjacker with a gun highjacked twenty-three-year-old Susan Smith's Mazda with her fourteen-month and three-year-old sons still strapped inside as they drove in rural Union, South Carolina. The network showed us the crude police sketch of the suspect based on Smith's description, a black man in a ski hat with rather large white lips, perfect for a minstrel show.[71] A "nationwide alert" began for the man, and on the twenty-seventh Smith and her husband went on national television to plead for the childrens' safe return.[72] It was to be one of many nationally broadcast appeals.

From the start, Smith seemed to be unusually composed when she was on TV begging for the return of her kids. Her husband was a basket case, usually on the verge of tears or crying right out, but not Smith.[73] The next day viewers learned that Smith and her husband had, in fact, filed for divorce. After eight days, Connie Chung described yet another "emotional appeal from brokenhearted parents." Smith now acted tearful (although you couldn't see any actual tears), addressing "my babies" and telling them "Momma loves you so much, your daddy loves you so much." She said that she felt in her heart that they were okay, but again addressing them directly, she told them they had to take care of each other.[74] As some began to speculate that either she or her husband might have been involved, the two of them appeared on *Today*, saying it hurt to be accused of harming their kids and that it was very painful to think that anyone would accuse them of having anything to do with the abduction.

So the networks were hardly amused when, "just hours after another tearful, grieving appearance on national television," as Tom Brokaw put it, Smith confessed to the FBI on November 3. This, too, was "nightmarish news."[75] Smith had, in fact, driven her car into Lake John D. Long with her kids strapped in the backseat and jumped out before the car went under. Her actions appeared to be premeditated, to say nothing of ruthless and depraved, since this was hardly an instant death. When the sheriff announced the arrest, the crowd gathered around him gasped in horror. ABC also showed Smith's appearance just that morning on NBC's *Today* when she said it was hard not knowing how her kids were. "Turns out she knew all along," Peter Jennings noted grimly.[76]

Smith's arrest and trial, the funeral of her children, and the effects on Union, South Carolina, were huge stories, and they often played back-to-back with stories about the O. J. Simpson trial. Every network had a reporter posted in Union, and the story received ongoing, regular coverage from November 1994 until late July 1995, when Smith was sentenced. The story served briefly as a peg for other murdering moms—Pauline Zile in Florida, who claimed her daughter had been abducted from a flea market and also went on TV to appeal for her return, but was really covering up for the stepfather who had beaten the child to death; and a woman who strangled her five-month-old.[77] But none of these had the traction of the Smith case. The fact that Smith had killed her kids was bad enough. The fact that she had been so calculating as to dupe the media—and the nation—seemed even worse.

When Smith was brought to the courthouse for arraignment, network cameras captured Union townspeople lined up and down the streets, screaming "baby killer" at her. "Grief and suspicion turned to rage," Brokaw reported. Then we learned that Smith had been dating a wealthy young man, Tom Findlay, who had broken up with her in part because he did not want to get involved with a woman with small children. She seemed willing to eliminate her kids because they proved inconvenient to her love life.

The overwhelming response was incredulity and a complete inability to fathom how a mother could have murdered her own kids. By 1994, with the rise of the romanticized new momism in celebrity profiles and elsewhere, which rendered ambivalence about having children—let alone the desire to escape from them—inconceivable, Smith was totally outside the new common sense that had elevated motherhood to a state of ecstasy and all toddlers to sainthood. Thus, despite her own history of depression and abuse, she was beyond our understanding. HOW COULD SHE DO IT? demanded *Time*, its cover saturated with a close-up of Smith's anguished face, the fuzziness of the image offset by a hyperfocused studio portrait of the two little boys smiling compliantly for the occasion. How indeed? Some people dealt with their disbelief by making a shrine to the boys on the bank of the lake, and mothers went there, clutching their children, asking tearfully, "how a mother could do that to her children?"[78] Some focused less on the tragedy and more on the villainy: One African American woman, also holding a toddler, was hardly sympathetic. Mimicking Smith, she noted sarcastically, "She couldn't eat 'cause they were hungry, she couldn't sleep 'cause they were cold." She paused and, giving a mocking look of disbelief, added, "I guess she couldn't take a bath 'cause she thought they was drowning."[79]

The fact that Smith seemed to have masterminded the scenario so well and carefully and then had appeared on national television playing a role (bereft mother) that was the exact opposite of what she really was (cold-blooded murderer) truly stunned people. The role of grieving mother was simply not one you were allowed to fake. Even worse, her husband, David, in interviews with NBC, ABC, and CBS, insisted that she had been a dedicated mother. The maternal instinct is supposed to be so wired into mothers that motherhood is not some role they perform; they just *are* mothers. Mother love was not something you were supposed to be able to cast aside once something better, like a rich boyfriend, came along.

But Smith had shown that you could convince people you were a devoted mother, and then convince them you were a heartbroken, grieving mother, while being, throughout the performance, a conniving, selfish chippy and then a brutal, vicious killer. Susan Smith demonstrated that motherhood was a façade, something you put on, like eyeliner, to impress the outside world. Beneath that façade might lurk the darkest of evils. The internal, emotional landscape of mothers—soft, safe, forgiving, and filled with unconditional love, embodied in the dreamy face of the new mother in the Pampers ad—was really a snake pit. The inner life of the mother, or at least this mother, suddenly loomed as a scary, unpredictable place of secrets, deceptions, and unspeakable instincts.

This was not how any of us wanted to think about motherhood, especially white, small-town motherhood. Children threatened from forces outside the family was one thing, but one reason the Smith case attracted such enormous attention—aside from the shocking nature of the crime—was that it was a disturbing metaphor for American families, even white ones, doing in their own kids, throwing them away. The Smith case raised a more general and troubling possibility: that far from harboring children in the protective embrace of family values, Americans have come to see their children as akin to commodities—fungible, expendable, and often more trouble than those Pampers ads would have us believe.

Perhaps to ensure that we unleash the full arsenal of condemnation on Smith, the fiend who had the nerve to sucker the caring and supportive media, subsequent news coverage emphasized that the children had been alive when they went in the water.[80] The child's-eye-view account had the added advantage of establishing that the media would stand up for children even if their mothers wouldn't. Smith's lawyer was compelled to deny a *Newsweek* story that claimed that while one of the kids "was struggling in absolute terror for his life" she "watched and did nothing." (*Newsweek* printed her lawyer's absolute denial of the story, which allowed them to repeat the grisly rumor, too.)[81] The sheriff's office re-created the crime with cameras strapped in a car so people could see and feel exactly what it was like for the boys to go slowly under, and the networks, of course, aired the footage, so we could share the terrifying experience.[82] By the late 1980s, mothers had been schooled by ads and women's magazines to put themselves in their kids' shoes; mothers, especially in Union, did just that, repeatedly imagining the boys' deaths. "It was cold and dark and they had to be out there by themselves, drowning," cried an African American woman. (Interestingly, the Smith story was one of the very few in which black women appeared as good mothers, devoted to their kids, and outraged by such behavior.) In the same story, a white woman who said she had nightmares about the kids "crying from their watery grave," lamented, "I was unable to do anything to help them."[83]

Of course people did feel real anguish that the kids were alone, help-less, with no one—no mother—there to help. The media had been quick to raise the question of how she could do it, but they seemed unable to an-swer it. Later in the broadcast, NBC did feature a brief story of the stresses faced by millions of young mothers because of economic and psy-chological problems, and isolation. But such a take was unusual. This was not a story about the ravages of chronic depression, the effects of repeated sexual abuse, or the enormous, usually unacknowledged pressures of rais-ing small children. This was a story about one individual, Susan Smith, a mother we couldn't understand because the crime she committed was, ac-cording to the romance of the new momism, totally incomprehensible. There could only be one answer: She was poisoned from within.

It is hard to know how the subsequent revelations that her father com-mitted suicide when she was six and that her stepfather—a member of the Christian Coalition—had been sexually molesting her since she was six-teen, and was, according to his own testimony, *still* having sex with her, affected people's reactions to her crime.[84] (One social worker told NBC that she had tried to press charges, but the sheriff told her the case was closed and the records sealed—"its file disappeared.")[85] We learned that Smith had attempted suicide herself in her teens. Because Smith had con-fessed to the crime, the only issue at the trial was whether she would get the death penalty or life. David Smith, in tearful, wrenching testimony during the penalty phase of the trial, showed snapshots of his kids to the jurors, many of whom openly wept. "I don't know what I'm supposed to do without my kids," he cried. "Everything I planned to teach them: ride a bike, fishing, their first day at school, watch them grow up, all that has been ripped from me."[86] On July 28, 1995, the jury decided against the death penalty and sentenced Smith to life in prison. A *Newsweek* poll re-ported that 63 percent of those surveyed felt Smith should be executed.[87]

The incomprehensibility of the crime continued to dominate the cov-erage. As one grandmother who had made a pilgrimage to the lake put it, "How could you look down that ramp . . . how could you, how could you?" "The trial did not answer that," noted NBC reporter Bob Dotson.[88] Smith, as a mother, should have imagined quite vividly—as if it were hap-pening to herself—what her kids would go through in the sinking car. But apparently she didn't. The trial had revealed that cute little towns like Union—which Tom Brokaw reminded us had 130 churches—could be a hotbed of incest, molestation, and murder. "And in every small town in

America tonight," Brokaw continued, "residents comfortable in the sanctuary of their familiar surroundings are wondering, What's going on here that we don't know about?" [89]

The news media never really entertained the possibility that the "how could she?" question required an honest assessment of the conditions under which so many women mother in the United States. Those conditions were actually worse for millions of mothers because the new momism's ideology of joy—indeed, resurrection—through motherhood made it all the more difficult to admit you were unhappy, struggling, drowning, desperate. The idea that we might learn something from this tragedy about motherhood as an institution simply did not fit with the 1990s common sense that motherhood was a demonstration of rugged individualism, female-style, in which you showed your character by succeeding or failing. (By 2001, as we'll show later with reaction to the Andrea Yates case, criticism of how motherhood, as an institution, can drive some mothers over the edge had increased dramatically.) Instead, we got more hype, and a new syndrome to be wary of: the Medea Syndrome, in honor of the ancient Greek character who killed her children to spite their philandering father. In an article entitled "The Medea Syndrome: Women Who Murder Their Young," *Cosmopolitan* framed its relatively sympathetic treatment with the warning that the threat was greater than anyone had thought: "Although nobody knows exactly how many children are killed by their mothers every year in this country, the most frequently quoted stat was, until recently, between twelve hundred and fourteen hundred, but an increasing number of researchers now say that estimate is too conservative." By combing "the law-enforcement data" for "overlooked killings," experts have discovered "hundreds of other murders . . . passed off as accidental fatalities." According to one such expert, "'You have to read between the lines.'" [90]

In the aftermath of the Smith verdict, the news media treated us to a smorgasbord of maternal depravity. All failed to put their children first, to protect their children from the risks of adulthood, to don the habit of the new momism. We are hardly arguing that these were admirable mothers. Rather, we ask why these anomalies of motherhood remained so steadfastly newsworthy throughout the 1990s. In April 1996, we met the mother of seven-year-old Jessica Dubroff. In a publicity stunt that grabbed the news media's (and tabloids') attention, Jessica, a "miniature Sally Ride" as *The San Francisco Chronicle* put it on the morning of her departure from Half Moon Bay near San Francisco, attempted piloting a plane across the country.[91] The plane crashed, killing Jessica, her father, Lloyd, and a flying teacher. Lloyd came in for criticism for pushing a kid to risk it all to grab her fifteen minutes of fame ("I figure Jessica will do more for civil aviation than Amelia Earhart," he announced with morbid prescience[92]), but it was the mother, Lisa Hathaway, who was portrayed as the true monster.

Nearly every story about the tragedy featured at least one outraged mother who damned the mother's permissiveness. "'Not a chance he would ever, ever be flying a plane, even with dual controls,'" said Irene Graff, the San Leandro "mom" of Chuck. "'At age 7, he has no sense of judgment. His idea of personal freedom is being able to walk to a friend's house without an adult.'"[93] Not only had Hathaway allowed Jessica to fly, she seemed curiously unrepentant, and that just pushed reporters over the edge. Despite her child's death, "a mother was not about to apologize," reported Bob Faw for NBC. "Oh, I'd have her do it again in a second," the mom told the cameras without a tear in her eye. "You have no idea what this meant to Jess." But Faw countered, "Around the country, lots of mothers could only shake their heads," and one mother told Faw, "I would never let my daughter do something like that." The story then evolved into a warning about "the pushy parent," who included Wanda Holloway (the mother who hired someone to kill the cheerleader who aced out her daughter), Brooke Shields's mother, Jennifer Capriati's parents, Macaulay Culkin's father, and Steffi Graf's father. At the end of the piece, Hathaway appeared one last time and said, "I'm so grateful she was happy," and Faw quoted the mother as saying, "What more could I have asked?" When the camera cut back to the newsroom, Brokaw looked at the viewing audience with disgust.[94]

Various reports emphasized that Hathaway was a New Age, California-type granola-feminist, and that only such a woman could have said, "My daughter died in a moment of joy." Now, neither of us would let any of our kids fly a plane at age seven—letting them use a hand mixer at that age is risky enough. So what we find noteworthy here is not the condemnation of this particular child-rearing choice, but the ease with which the news media now commented on and policed motherhood, and focused on the sins of the mother rather than those of the father. After all, it was the dad who took her up in the plane, the dad who craved the limelight, the dad who Hathaway might have expected would step in if things went wrong. And there was only one prescribed way for a mother to grieve—bawl her eyes out and flagellate herself on camera. There are all kinds of things, some of them pretty crazy-sounding, that a mother who had just lost her child might say to get through the day. But if her comments didn't follow the script of the new momism, the mother was unfit.[95]

In the aftermath of the Susan Smith melodrama, the news peg about murdering mothers retained its magnetic pull. Infanticide by teens who disposed of their newborns with the same ease and speed with which you would take out the garbage further raised the specter of a new generation of young women immune to the new momism. In November 1996 the media moved on to Amy Grossberg, a New Jersey teenager who gave birth at the Comfort Inn, "swaddled the newborn boy in a gray plastic bag and dumped him in a trash bin."[96] This was a "deeply unsettling story," as Dan Rather put it, because, according to Jacqueline Adam's subsequent report, "It wasn't supposed to happen to *these* kids, college kids from wealthy New Jersey communities." But *"it happens more often than you think."* In case you wanted to know just how often, forget it. "There are no hard numbers, but more and more teens, no matter what their racial or economic status, are panicking in the face of childbirth."[97] Seven months later, Melissa Drexler, dubbed "The Prom Mom" by the media, gave birth in the girls' room at her high school prom, left the baby in the toilet, and went right back to the dance floor. In spite of interviewing a demographer who reported that there are far fewer infanticides by teenagers now than there were before the legalization of abortion in 1973, *Newsweek,* in a story entitled "Cradles to Coffins," devoted several pages to what appeared to be an epidemic of Melissas and her kind.[98] After a while, the questions, "How could she do it?" and "How does it happen?" themselves became disposable.

After the usual hand-wringing over the tragedy, these stories focused on the fact that kids like Melissa think that having a baby "interferes with a teenager's plans," casting them as selfish and depraved. The lurid, tabloid-journalism tone simply could not encompass an exploration, for example, of the schizoid messages teenagers get from a culture that is both prudish and pornographic, that uses sex to sell everything but tells them to just say no. Nor did such stories make any connection to the fact that in this country, with massive squeamishness about sex education, many teens have no one over the age of seventeen to provide advice or help about sexuality. Why didn't these stories ask, point blank, why disposing of a baby in a Dumpster seemed the only viable option? Instead, "How could she do it?" raised to grab our attention and then dropped, left us with a pervasive sense of impending doom in which the entire institution of motherhood, and thus we, as mothers, were somehow implicated.

Looking back, we see that these supposedly self-absorbed, out-of-control, deadly mothers were hardly the monsters they appeared to be at the time. Whitehead, whatever her emotional profile, got raked over the coals and held up to a standard of perfection no mother could match. The "crack baby" was a media myth; there was no "epidemic" nor are we seeing today, as predicted, schools overrun by hyperactive, inattentive, delinquent crack children. Most "crack mothers," nearly all of them beset by grinding poverty and zero health care, were not the fiends we saw on the news. Susan Smith, until near the end of her trial, got virtually no sympathy for suffering from chronic, debilitating depression, nor for being a victim of sexual abuse. Nor was there an "epidemic" of infanticide by heartless teens.

The spectacle of the deadly mother may have reassured "us" that, whatever our failings, at least we were nothing like "them." For a few moments we could believe that, despite the increasingly high standards of perfection emanating from the new momism, we were, indeed, good mothers. We could believe that we were the ones who had made the right "choices," that we had successfully resisted the darker impulses of motherhood. But in reality, these stories justified putting all mothers under increased surveillance.

Though we may have thought that these stories were about "other mothers," they contributed significantly to a vigilante culture in which mothers had to be carefully policed because they are, potentially, their own children's worst enemy. While this was hardly the intent of the news media, the parade of maternal delinquents reinforced an increasingly narrow norm of acceptable behavior that helped, as much as celebrity mom profiles did, to standardize the rules of the new momism.

The big, national news stories focused increasingly on a mother's private, subjective terrain. The three-hundred-pound gorilla of fear lurking in these stories, the one never spoken but always there, was this: Were feminists right, that women did not have some built-in maternal instinct? If so, what did that mean for the future of the society? If women were not born with one then they had better acquire one ASAP by seeing the horrors of a world in which maternal devotion was not part of women's genetic makeup.

What mothers were thinking deep inside, and whether in their hearts they were totally, 100 percent absorbed in their children—but in the proper way, of course—were henceforth up for public inspection. To fail to inhabit your children's subject positions, beginning when they are in the womb, lay at the core of maternal corruption. To fail to be utterly self-sacrificing all the time was deviant. To put on the façade of the new momism without truly living and breathing it was duplicitous and dangerous. If feminism—at least the media's version—went too far, mothers would become too self-indulgent, and children—and the nation—would suffer unspeakable pain. Just as celebrity mom profiles provided the primer on what good mothers must strive for, these tales of maternal delinquents were like warnings from some Head Warden of Motherhood. They notified us all that we were already inmates in the House of Maternal Corrections.

Stories about mothers gone wrong affected how all of us were looked at and judged. News stories about maternal delinquents reminded viewers that women's movement or no women's movement, there were boundaries of good motherhood that not even a "modern," "liberated" mother dared cross. Out beyond those boundaries, in the wilds, were those mothers who had crossed over, who refused to convert to the new momism, the mothers who made up their own rules or, worst of all, had murder, not unconditional love, in their hearts. The public vilification of moms who had gone to the other side kept us on our toes, alert to the possibility that we could, at any moment, with any slip, be judged inadequate or unfit. Their condemnation in the media helped construct a maternal panopticon, akin to the ideal prison envisioned by the nineteenth-century political philosopher Jeremy Bentham. A panopticon is the perfect prison: the cells are arrayed around a central watchtower. The surveillance potential of a single guard is magnified as each individual inmate lives with the knowledge that, at any moment, he could be in the guard's line of vision. By internalizing the virtually omniscient guard, each inmate becomes his own best watchdog. You can never, ever let down your guard. Isn't this how so many of us feel these days in both our public and private moments with our children? Will we be caught letting our attention stray when listening to a child retell the plot of a movie in real time? Will the warden notice when we linger, with obvious envy, over an ad picturing a childless couple lying on the beach in Tahiti? Will he hear us screaming invectives at a glowering teenager who can spend the day rollerblading but is too tired to fold her laundry?

Because both white and African American mothers have been open to mother bashing, it might seem that the media's metaphorical taming of mothers had adhered to an equal opportunity policy. But, in fact, an aggressive program of affirmative action has awarded much more air time to the maternal failings of African American women. These were not just certain unfit individuals, but an entire race of women, who, it seemed, should not be permitted to have kids. Not only were they destroying their children, they were threatening the future of the nation. But nowhere was this saga of the black mother gone bad more powerful than in the gathering "war" on welfare mothers.

SIX

The War Against
Welfare Mothers

Allow us to introduce you to Carmen Santana. Now don't get excited—
she is no relation to Carlos or any other famous musician or celebrity. (In
fact, we eventually learn that this is not her real name.) Carmen is "lazy"
and "jolly"; she has "no interest in national or international events." She
spends most of her time watching soap operas on television. She "curses
in Spanish," and when her children irritate her, she "gives them a good
cuffing." She and her children, who couldn't be bothered walking to the
nearest Dumpster, instead "throw their trash and garbage out their windows." There are "dirty dishes all over the kitchen." Her philosophy of
life is "what will be, will be" and "she makes little real effort to dominate
circumstances"; oh, she makes plans from time to time, but "they are
soon forgotten," as she "has never given much thought to the future."
Her conversation with the man "she took up with" is "merry and sala-
cious." She "avoids all physical exercise. She sits even while she is cooking." Her children's bedroom is "decorated . . . with graffiti, many of
which are obscene." She "does not keep a clean house." Carmen Santana
is, as the title of this 1975 *New Yorker* profile puts it simply enough, "A
Welfare Mother." [1] The word they left out, that you, the morally impecca-
ble reader, should supply, is *typical*.

The most important thing about Carmen, besides the number of children she has had by different men, is her weight. In the first three para-

graphs alone of this profile, there are eight references to her "obesity." We read about her "broad back," her "big breasts, her big belly, and her enormous thighs," and that she is so fat that "she is unable to take off her fashionable platform shoes unaided." A few paragraphs later things get more specific: She wears a size twenty and weighs more than two hundred pounds. If someone is eating that well, how could she possibly need welfare? In the United States, where, as Gloria Vanderbilt put it, you can never be too rich or too thin, an overweight woman's body is automatic, visible evidence that she must be lazy, undisciplined, and out of control. So we can get a better mental image of Carmen, who is Puerto Rican, the author describes, several times, her "wide nose, mulatto complexion, curly black hair, thick lips." [2] Not only is she lazy and porcine, she suffers from an additional character flaw: She is not white.

That she is also promiscuous goes without saying: Having had her first child at the age of fifteen, Carmen went on to have eight additional children by three different men, all of whom she regarded as husbands, but since the last two were common law husbands, the author puts the word in quotation marks, as if to wink at us knowingly. We superior white people know they weren't *really* "husbands." By the way, Carmen's mother had "three children by three different men," and now her eldest daughter is also on welfare. An endless cycle, reproduced from one generation to the next, of dependency, promiscuity, irresponsibility, and corpulence.

Carmen received, from the state of New York and from the feds, AFDC (Aid to Families with Dependent Children), money and food stamps. What did she spend it on? Her dresser was "cluttered with a multitude of lipsticks, perfumes, hair sprays, and other cosmetics." She also loved furniture and had recently bought a couch and two armchairs. She shops at the local bodega (where prices can be 20 percent higher) instead of at the local supermarket, and one of her children's "main activities" is "charging snacks (potato chips, cupcakes, soda, ice cream)." Is she a welfare cheat? Of course she's a welfare cheat. As Carmen herself admits, "Almost everyone she knows cheats on the welfare." Carmen cheats, in part, by living with a man without reporting it, and by playing the numbers. On those few occasions when she has won, the money has gone for "jewelry, beer and liquor for parties" and "trips to Puerto Rico."

The problem with this article was not that it was "factually" inaccurate in the usual sense. After all, *The New Yorker* is notorious for its anal-retentive fact checking. Certainly there were, in New York and elsewhere, welfare mothers who had had more children than they could afford, who quickly figured out how to supplement their puny welfare checks, and who weighed more than Cindy Crawford. Of course there were women and men on welfare who did not subscribe to middle-class mores about hard work, thrift, sexual restraint, and home decorating. And, yes, there were also mothers on welfare who neglected or abused their kids.

Rather, articles like this were pernicious because they trafficked in stereotypes; they exploited the fact that their readership was largely clueless about the real lives of their impoverished fellow citizens. However factual in detail, such portraits were not a window on some alleged reality. They were constructions. Absent any other sources of information, especially the voices of poor women themselves, Carmen, and other women like her, served as the Über Woman of the media sagas about welfare, and of the terrible consequences of failing to embrace the new momism.

Johnnie Tillmon, who was the first chairwoman of the 1960s activist group the National Welfare Rights Organization, saw welfare, and the stereotypes about welfare mothers, as a feminist issue. "I'm a woman. I'm a black woman. I'm a poor woman. I'm a fat woman. I'm a middle-aged woman. And I'm on welfare. In this country, if you're any one of those things—poor, black, fat, female, middle-aged, on welfare—you count less as a human being." She then reminded people about the interplay between bad luck and entrenched discrimination. "Welfare's like a traffic accident. It can happen to anybody, but especially it happens to women. And that's why welfare is a woman's issue. . . . There are a lot of lies that male society tells about welfare mothers; that AFDC mothers are immoral, that AFDC mothers are lazy, misuse their welfare checks, spend it all on booze and are stupid and incompetent. If people are willing to believe these lies, it's partly because they're just special versions of the lies that society tells about all women."[3] But Tillmon's version of welfare, for all the reasons she gave, would not be the one to prevail. During the late 1980s and the 1990s, politicians and the news media would cast welfare not as something that happened to women often because of circumstances beyond their control, but rather as a way of life certain women actively—even avidly—chose.

If someone were to blurt out the words "welfare mother" right now, most Americans would immediately, without even thinking, picture an

African American woman in some urban ghetto with six kids by six different men. This stereotype is so accessible, just waiting on the very surface of our minds to be evoked, because over the years, the newsmagazines and TV news have increasingly relied on images of black people and, more and more, black mothers with more than two kids to illustrate stories about welfare.[4] It actually *takes work* to fight the stereotype.[5] This was not some conspiracy on the part of those in the news media—in addition to following the lead of politicians, their cameras and reporters were a lot closer to Camden, New Jersey (a favorite, inner-city location for welfare stories), than they were to rural Nebraska (in the late twentieth century, one of the poorest places in the country) or Maine, where there were plenty of indigent white folks hundreds of miles from anything resembling a decent job. So simple news routines, as well as unconscious institutional racism, also contributed to highly racist portrayals.

As media obsessions about the status of the family and the state of motherhood dominated the national stage in the 1980s and '90s, African American mothers and other women of color became the scapegoats onto whom white culture projected its own fears about mothers "abandoning" the home, losing their "maternal instinct," and neglecting their kids. As the network news in the 1980s and '90s became flashier, and deployed a growing array of images and graphics in their newscasts, they used personification, more and more, to symbolize events and trends. Welfare—a vast, complicated bureaucracy—became personified through the welfare mother. And portraits like the one of Carmen, endlessly repeated in various forms in the news media over three decades, of the overweight, lazy, immoral, dark-hued baby machine with an attitude, her hand outstretched demanding her "entitlements," became the exemplar for all welfare mothers, whatever their circumstances, their skin color, their dreams, and their not inconsiderable hardships.[6] As such stereotypes of welfare mothers increased in the news media in the 1980s and 1990s, they played a central role in justifying a major shift in public policy away from declaring a war on poverty in America to declaring a war on welfare, and then, more specifically, on welfare mothers and their kids.[7]

Here's what profiles of women like Carmen incite us to feel: "Why should I get up at 6:30, make sure there are carrots in my kid's lunch, and drag my weary carcass to my stupid job where I'm stuck all day while Carmen gets to have sex and drink booze at noon in her living room with *my* tax dollars?" In other words, "Why should I buy into momism and all its stresses when Carmen gets off scot-free?" As the new momism grew deeper roots in the late 1980s and '90s, welfare mothers were cast as getting away with something that working mothers weren't, so they needed to be identified, blamed, and punished. In the 1970s, a typical headline for an article or news report about welfare was "The Welfare Mess," referring to a sprawling and dysfunctional bureaucracy. By 1994 *Time*'s cover announced, simply enough, THE WAR ON WELFARE MOTHERS, *U.S. News and World Report* announced the WAR ON WELFARE DEPENDENCY, and CBS's *48 Hours* aired a show that sounded like it could be hosted by Jesse Ventura, "The Rage Against Welfare."[8] The news frame had changed: The target was no longer the system, it was the mothers themselves.

Although it may have been hard to recognize at the time, the war against welfare mothers was indeed part of the broader war against all mothers. For momism to work as a new norm, there had to be delinquents who dramatized what happened to those who failed to comply, delinquents other mothers could feel comfortable about putting in detention.

The media myth that most welfare mothers were inner-city, unmarried black teens—who came from a family chain of welfare recipients longer than the Ming Dynasty and deliberately had more kids solely so they could increase their benefits—calls for a brief reality check before we proceed. The average welfare family in 1994, at the height of the antiwelfare frenzy, had three members—a mother and two kids. Thirty-nine percent were white, and 37 percent were black.[9] Now, it's true: African Americans were about 12 percent of the population but were about 35 to 37 percent of the welfare population. But, as Barbara Ehrenreich reminds us, welfare was for poor people, and African Americans were three times as likely as whites to live below the poverty level.[10] Only 10 percent of AFDC mothers had four or more children; 80 percent had one or two kids. Figures in 1993 showed that 75 percent of adults left welfare within two years.[11] Researchers studying welfare found no evidence that AFDC mothers had children either to get on the dole in the first place or to increase their benefits. Studies also showed that one-half of single mothers worked while on welfare, and that at any given point in time, about one-third of them were working to supplement their scrawny allotment and to try to get off the dole.[12]

The news media, however, focused excessively on families in which two or more generations were on welfare—even though this represented a tiny fraction of welfare families. The media were also obsessed with unwed teen welfare moms because they were shocking and titillating, when teenagers constituted only 1.2 percent of all mothers receiving public assistance.[13] Only 1 percent of welfare mothers were 17 or younger.[14] But these were the mothers, and the stories, that were newsworthy, precisely because they were sensational, and because these were the mothers all too many wealthy, white politicians repeatedly suggested were not the exception, but the rule. Meanwhile, African American working mothers, who were much less likely than white women to take a few years off from the job because they couldn't afford it, and thus could counteract any stereotypes about "laziness," remained invisible.[15] The "Welfare Reform" poster mother, then, as she emerged by the late 1980s, was a tad different from Christie Brinkley or Annette Bening. She only had a first name, she lived in the urban decay of New York, Chicago, or Detroit, she was a teenager, black, not married, had a pile of kids each with a different absent father, and she spent her day painting her nails, smoking cigarettes, and feeding Pepsi to her baby. Mostly, she was censored, in both senses of the term, damned by the coverage, not permitted to speak for herself. Thus, we met Letitia C., a high school dropout and "fourth generation teen-age mother" who had three children by three fathers.[16] In *Newsweek* you could meet Valerie, twenty-seven, and "the three children she has by different absentee fathers." She used to live with her mother, "who, at forty-two, has six grandchildren." But now Valerie lived amongst other families, all of whom "live side by side with trash-filled open apartments."

Another typical mid-1990s portrait of a welfare mother was that of Denise B., one of the "True Faces of Welfare," age twenty-seven with five daughters ages one to thirteen, brought to us courtesy of *Reader's Digest*. "All, after the first, were conceived on welfare—conceived perhaps deliberately," *Reader's Digest* grumbled, conjuring up the highly plausible image of Denise doing some quick math calculations, saying to herself, "Oh boy, an extra sixty bucks a month," and then running out to find someone to get her pregnant.[17] The other thing we learned about Denise was that she's a leech, and loves it. Why not get a job, even though she has toddlers? Because she's lazy. "To get a good job, she would first have to go to school, then earn her way up to a high salary," *Reader's Digest* reminded us, and then let the ingrate Denise speak for herself. "'That's going to take time,' she says, 'It's a lot of work and I ain't guaranteed to get nothing.'" What we learn of Denise's inner life is that she's a calculating cynic. Her kids don't make her feel like every day is Christmas; she uses *her* kids to get something for nothing. And God forbid that for Denise, motherhood is sexy!

Such depictions were so incessant and convincing that it was hard not to accept them as representative of all welfare mothers. By the time welfare "reform" passed in 1996, it was part of the national common sense that welfare mothers embodied the exact opposite of the new momism: they refused work because they were lazy; they willfully or thoughtlessly cranked out baby after baby; they were careless, even neglectful mothers; they never anticipated their children's needs or put them first; and welfare had to be eliminated because it encouraged twelve-year-olds to have six babies by the age of twenty instead of finish high school. In the early 1970s, newscasters often used the term "poor people" to describe welfare recipients. By the early 1990s, the word "poor," which does tend to provoke sympathy, was hardly ever used to describe these mothers. In 1983 and 1984, there were only, by our count, three major network news stories about welfare each year. By 1994, the number had jumped to thirty-eight, many of them long, in-depth "packages" focusing on individual welfare mothers, their failures, their attitude problems, and their need to get a job.

The news may not succeed in telling us what to think, but it does succeed in telling us what to think about: This is called agenda setting.[18] When the news does a lot of stories about celebrity overdoses and drive-by shootings, for example, people list drugs as a major problem, even if drug use is actually down. Coverage of welfare increased during the Reagan and Bush I administrations, when there were various workfare or welfare "reform" bills before Congress (as there were in 1988 and again between 1994 and 1996) and soared once Bill Clinton, a Democrat, hijacked the welfare issue from Republicans and declared he would "end welfare as we know it." And the news media, with exceptions here and there, gave us the same negative, monochromatic depiction of the welfare mother because they followed, often much too closely and uncritically, the agenda set by the conservative politicians then in power (and on this issue, Clinton was just as opportunistic in using welfare mothers for his own political gain as the Republicans). Since government officials are the major source of news for the networks, it's hardly surprising when the networks follow the lead of prominent politicians when constructing their newscasts.

And here's who we heard from in the "debate" about welfare reform.

Nearly 60 percent of the sources on the news were government officials; 9 percent were from think tanks or advocacy groups; and a whopping 71 percent were male. Only 10 percent were welfare recipients themselves.[19] At the same time, conservative (largely) male politicians and pundits on talk shows like *The McLaughlin Group* repeatedly identified the single mother, and especially the poor, single, African American welfare mother, as the cause of everything bad, from the "epidemic" of drug use to the national debt to rising crime rates. Through her, conservatives kept the coals of misogyny warm without offending the politically prized "soccer mom." And they succeeded. The poor mother no longer represented the failings of American society to take care of its own. She represented the failure of individual women to take their maternal responsibilities as seriously as possible. Thus, it wasn't just that conservative politicians and the news media sought to tell Americans that welfare mattered; they told Americans how to conceive of and personify the issue.

Even though there were more whites than blacks on welfare, which reporters occasionally noted, the networks time after time used graphic images of blacks to illustrate undesirable trends and "explosions" in the rolls. In a 1990 NBC story about people—most of whom were white— allegedly moving to Wisconsin because its welfare payments were higher than those of neighboring states, the network superimposed the face of an eighteen-year-old black mother over a map of the United States to illustrate the migration of this maternal kudzu to a state near you.[20] Whenever a reporter talked about "hard-core, long-term welfare families," the camera invariably cut to a black mother and child.[21] In an NBC story about the successive generations of families living on welfare, the final shot was a freeze frame of a black girl.[22] When New Jersey decided, in 1992, to stop giving additional benefits to mothers who had additional children while on welfare, the story title, "Setting Limits," was superimposed over a shot of a black woman and her baby.[23] ABC reported in 1995 that most welfare recipients were not black but, amazingly, actually used a shot of a black woman to illustrate the point.[24] When a CBS reporter asked an African American woman in 1994 why she was not in the workforce she drawled, "Bein' lazy." But now she was trying to become a nurse's aide. "I want to better my life, I don't want to sit around . . . getting fat and getting pregnant and watching the soap operas."[25] This was another network specialty—using black women themselves to confirm racist stereotypes.

In our collective history of motherhood in the media, then, the welfare mother had a central, starring role. In the late 1980s and 1990s, she became an omnipresent icon of motherhood gone wrong, a nationally recognized media villain, playing her part, against her will, as the other half of the media drama about motherhood.[26] This was what happened, the news stories warned, to children, to motherhood, and to the country if mothers failed to pick up the torch of the new momism. The welfare mother, then, inhabited the other side of the maternal media diptych, opposite the celebrity mom, and stood in stark contrast to the likes of Debby Boone, Joan Lunden, and Princess Diana. The former was a "mother" and the latter was definitely a "mom." Celebrity moms personified the joys of intensive mothering; welfare mothers embodied the social and individual catastrophes that resulted from the willful disregard of intensive mothering. Let's remember that the media, whether entertainment or nonfiction, are about creating drama—that's what they do. To create drama, you need heroes and villains. The heroes have wonderful qualities we're supposed to envy; the villains, repugnant traits we're meant to despise. Although we're not supposed to notice it, this basic Hollywood narrative structure shapes the news just as much as it shapes movies and dramatic TV. Such constructions may not be deliberate or even conscious, but they have real consequences.

As the push "to end welfare as we know it" gained momentum, the canonized celebrity mom and the demonized welfare mother emerged in the media and worked in powerful opposition to each other. We rarely read about these very different mothers in the same publication, or even considered them as members of the same species. So it is especially important to put these portrayals side by side and compare how these mothers were represented and what they were made to stand for. Celebrity moms graced the covers of magazines designed for self-realization and escape; welfare mothers were the object of endless morality tales in newspapers, newsmagazines, and the nightly news that focused on public policy.

Unlike celebrity moms, welfare mothers have not been the subject of honey-hued profiles in glossy magazines. In many of the news articles about welfare, we didn't hear from the mothers at all, but instead from academic experts who studied them, and not always sympathetically. They were not the subjects of their own lives, but objects of journalistic scrutiny. We didn't hear about these women's maternal practices—what they did with their kids to nurture them, educate them, soothe them, protect them, or keep them happy. Such portraits were the complete opposite of the celebrity mom profile. It was simply assumed that these women didn't have inner lives. Emotions were not ascribed to them; we didn't hear *them* laugh or see their eyes well up with tears when they talked about how much they loved their kids. It was simply assumed that they were clueless about, or hostile to, the new momism.

The iconography of the welfare mother was completely different, too, from that of the celebrity mom—she was not photographed beaming, holding her child up in the air, whizzing him about. In fact, she was rarely, if ever, shown smiling at all. In photographs of her and her kids, they weren't smiling, either. There was no backlighting, forming a halo around her head. Instead, we saw darkly lit, scowling families intermixed with the shirt-and-tied experts who knew best. There was never a *Redbook* or *McCall's* cover with a black welfare mom, her face and hair done up, her kids made up too, with that beautiful soft-focus lighting and a headline like FUN THINGS WE DO WITHOUT MONEY, or NEW YORK ON TEN DOLLARS A DAY! or GAMES TO PLAY WHILE WAITING IN LINE FOR A HOUSING VOUCHER. Such images are unimaginable.

At the same time that Jodie Foster, Rosie O'Donnell, Goldie Hawn, Farrah Fawcett, or even Madonna, to name just a few of Hollywood's unmarried mothers, were profiled approvingly in the glossies, a major article in *Newsweek* in August 1993, titled "The Endangered Family," warned us disapprovingly that "for many African Americans marriage and childbearing do not go together." If you were really rich, famous, beautiful, and white, being an unmarried mom was way cool. If you were poor and black, it was degenerate, the epitome of irresponsibility. If you were white and middle-class, it was expected that you would naturally have the same "baby lust" as Michelle Pfeiffer and act on it. If you were black and poor, you were not supposed to want babies at all, and you sure as hell didn't deserve to actually have them.

In other words, the very media forms in which welfare mothers appeared provided very few points of identification with them. The celebrity mom interview humanized the star, and invited us inside her subjective thoughts and feelings. The news piece on the welfare mother often dehumanized her—she was an exemplar of a trend, rarely an individual—and suggested that her inner life was devoid of thoughts, except where to score

Back to the Future? As these chilling mesomorph babies suggest, the new momism insists that mothers once again become totally subservient to their children, except that unlike the 1950s, the performance standards for mom today are much higher. Plus, babies are a way cool accessory that make you look great in haute couture.

A feminist send-up of Pete Seeger's then-popular rendition of the folk song "There Was an Old Woman Who Swallowed a Fly," the verses by Meredith Tax, a member of the Bread and Roses feminist collective, tell the story of a woman's gradual entrapment within the feminine mystique. After a liberating feminist purging, she is cleansed of the fluff and lies that threatened to do her in.

A HUD for Child Care

The federal daycare busybodies' plan for child care is (according to *The Wall Street Journal*) "a program right out of the 1960s that would do for children what HUD has done for housing."

It was obvious by 1972, when the Pruitt-Igoe federal housing project had to be dynamited in St. Louis (see picture below), that nobody wants to live in public housing. But the entrenched bureaucracy kept growing. Now we know that big easy money went to the bureaucrats, the consultants, and the people in the good ol' boy network who knew how to work the system for private gain.

That's exactly what proposed federal daycare bills would do:

- *finance government-regulated, secular daycare institutions where eligible parents will be forced to put their children or forfeit assistance, and*
- *enrich the bureaucrats, the consultants, the network of tax-salaried lobbyists in every state, and the favored daycare providers who know how to milk the system.*

Meanwhile, the big majority of parents would get nothing. The public housing scenario shows exactly what will happen if the daycare busybodies get their hands on a river of federal money.

Pruitt-Igoe public housing dynamited in 1972.

Any legislation that sets up a system of grants, certificates or vouchers will require an army of tax-salaried daycare busybodies who will:

- *discriminate against mothers who stay at home,*
- *discriminate against religious daycare,*
- *discriminate against all unlicensed and informal babysitting by relatives and neighbors,*
- *lobby for fatal licensing control and a $100 billion babysitting bureaucracy.*

This legislation is truly **"Catastrophic Child Care"** and will prove just as unpopular, unfair, costly, and worthless as the Catastrophic Health Act Tax.

You can protect your family from these threats by demanding what President George Bush promised: a $1,000 tax credit for every preschool child "without discriminating against mothers who stay at home."

Write or call President Bush and your Congressman and tell them to stand firm on this promise. Tell them you don't want another HUD for your babies — you want tax relief so you can choose your own child care.

Read the definitive book on the public policy issue of child care — $14.95
Eagle Forum
Alton, Illinois 62002

The federal daycare busybodies are after *YOUR* Child

They know that the hand that rocks the cradle rules the world!

In *Who Will Rock the Cradle?*, Phyllis Schlafly asserted that any government support for day care, however stingy, was like handing your baby over to alien baby snatchers. The New Right repeatedly stereotyped feminists as women who hated housewives and kids even though, as mothers themselves, they lobbied ceaselessly for quality day care for all children.

Television responded to the enormous changes in family life in the 1970s by finally featuring a divorced, single mother on *One Day at a Time* whose life was transformed for the better by—believe it or not—feminism.

Hollywood discovered the single mother in the 1970s films *Alice Doesn't Live Here Anymore* and *An Unmarried Woman*. But these single mothers managed, quite quickly, to find hunky guys with soft beards who had no aversion to kids, commitment or, amazingly, feminism.

Clair Huxtable on *The Cosby Show* was our fantasy: a gorgeous woman whose work and family obligations never clashed, and whose kids and husband adored her despite her regular threats to murder them.

Forget that it was Dad who accompanied Jessica Dubroff, age seven, on her ill-fated cross country flight. When the plane crashed, killing them both, it was Mom's fault.

Celebrity mom profiles colonized the women's magazines beginning in the 1980s. Here babies made life ecstatic. They never wreaked havoc with work or one's love life, and never even drooled on mom's fancy outfit or perfectly coiffed hair.

Welfare mothers, however, were supposed to stop having kids immediately. As *Time* made clear, the war on poverty had given way to a "war" on welfare mothers, who were almost always shown to be sullen African American women.

In the hands of the media, Princess Diana was idealized as endlessly energetic and fun-loving, two traits regular mothers often had trouble mustering on a daily basis. But if they followed Martha Stewart, mothers could make their homes more regal if they just got to work with their glue guns and Strip-eze.

Once advertisers discovered the new, working mother, the image of the superwoman who could "have it all" was everywhere. But the backlash came quickly.

With its "New Traditionalist" campaign, *Good Housekeeping* lobbied for the new momism by suggesting that truly good mothers were fleeing feminism for the "timeless, enduring values" of family. This particular ad targeted white mothers' anxiety by suggesting that their Asian counterparts were raising kids who scored 800 on their math SATs.

THE NEW TRADITIONALIST.

WHO SAYS YOU HAVE TO DISCARD YOUR OLD VALUES
TO BE A MODERN AMERICAN MOTHER?

Kwisoon Lee believes that "traditions are as important as your bloodstream."

Today she is bringing up a typical American family, and feeling the same pressures and stresses of contemporary life that we all do. But she will never compromise her values, or the quality of life she wants for her family.

"We are in a transition period of modernization," she explains, "but we are still hanging on to our values. Without them, you lose your identity."

Kwisoon Lee thinks of herself as "very old fashioned," but in truth she embodies the newest social movement in America.

More and more women have come to realize that having a contemporary lifestyle doesn't mean that you have to abandon the things that make life worth living – family, home, community, the timeless, enduring values.

That is why more and more marketers are discovering the power of Good Housekeeping Magazine.

We have always represented that traditional quality of life that contemporary women are seeking today.

Today's woman is looking for something to believe in. And more than ever, she trusts Good Housekeeping – the Magazine, the Institute, the Seal.

AMERICA IS COMING HOME TO GOOD HOUSEKEEPING

SEPTEMBER 1996 $1.95

Good Housekeep

OUR FAVORITE
20-MINUTE MEALS

THE GOOD NEWS ABOUT BAD FOODS

SAVE BIG!
Secrets from America's Top Penny-Pinchers

END DEPRESSION
The Best New Pills

6 SKIN SAVERS
Look Years Younger, Fast

When It's Right to Hold a Grudge

KATHIE LEE
Betrayed, attacked, and now fighting back, she faces the biggest challenge of her life

KIDS' HEALTH ALERT
Doctors' Advice About the New Viruses, Medicine Mistakes, and More

Few celebrities lorded their perfect motherhood over the rest of us in the 1990s more thoroughly than Kathie Lee Gifford, even in the face of scandals about employing child labor.

THE 100+ MOST INFLUENTIAL BLACKS

EBONY

MAY 2001 USA $2.75
CANADA $3.99

'HOT SHOT':
SHAGGY STAGES SUPER COMEBACK

Babyface & Tracey Edmonds

Tammy Franklin & Caziah

The New Motherhood

WHAT ARE THE 10 BIGGEST LIES ABOUT BLACK HISTORY?

A JOHNSON PUBLICATION

Yolanda Adams & Taylor

Jasmine Guy & Imani

www.ebony.com

It's about time black women appeared as doting and beautiful mothers, but now they too can be subjected to the same preposterous standards of perfection that the new momism has been foisting on white women.

In the "Baby M" case, the courts and the media subjected motherhood to a new high stakes achievement test. Mary Beth Whitehead was deemed unfit by one "expert" because she dyed her hair and gave her baby a stuffed panda—instead of pots and pans—to play with.

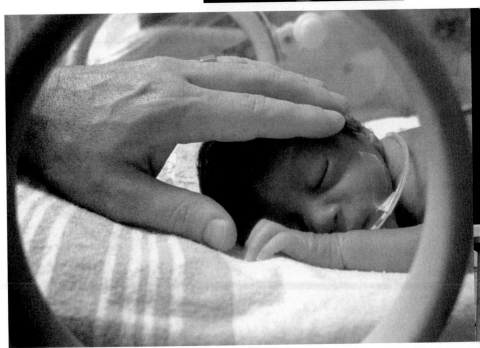

In the late 1980s, the news media created a panic about "crack babies"—a syndrome, it turned out, that did not exist. But the media hype further stereotyped black mothers as bad mothers.

In 1971, Richard Nixon vetoed—in language written by Pat Buchanan—a widely supported, bipartisan bill that would have provided child care to millions of families. Despite this and many subsequent setbacks, Marian Wright Edelman, head of the Children's Defense Fund, continued to lobby for decent day care for America's kids. Possibly because we had no such thing, murdering nannies transfixed the media in the 1990s. In *The Hand That Rocks the Cradle,* the nanny Peyton made Norman Bates seem mentally stable.

thirtysomething celebrated intensive mothering at every turn. The moms in this show loved nothing more than crawling under tables with their kids, and Hope nearly had a nervous breakdown when she stopped breastfeeding.

On *Married with Children*, Peg Bundy gave the new momism a large Bronx cheer.

Roseanne offered a much-welcome antidote to TV's insistence that mothers never yell, always put themselves last, and fit into a size four after having three kids.

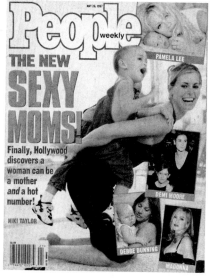

In the late 1990s, the new hypernatalism was inescapable and motherhood was proclaimed—lord help us—"sexy." By 2002, celebrity role models supposedly declared that it was much more rewarding raising children than being a rich and critically acclaimed A list actor.

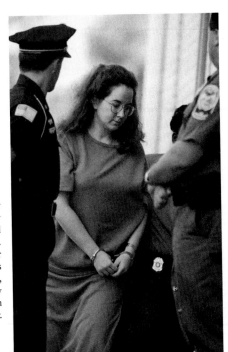

When Susan Smith killed her two children, she was widely vilified, and became a symbol of motherhood in peril. Smith got little sympathy for suffering from mental illness or for having been, for years, a victim of sexual abuse by her Christian Coalition stepfather.

When Andrea Yates, a stay-at-home, fundamentalist Christian, home-schooling mother with five small children, drowned them all in 2001, much was made of the dangers of post-partum depression and psychosis. But many mothers also saw the tragedy as a warning sign about the tyranny of the new momism.

Welcome to the hot new media cat fight for the 21st century: the "mommy wars" between women who supposedly had no common ground and thus hated each other's guts.

Dr. Laura, the Mussolini of the new momism, built a career and a fortune by telling other mothers they are neglectful if they aren't full-time stay-at-home "moms." She is shown here in her place of employment.

In the 21st century, babies can't play with their toes any more or lie around chewing on books. Now mothers have to teach them to read beginning at six months, when they customarily find their nose for one reason—to pick it.

Products unknown to mothers in the early 1990s now warn that the grim reaper lurks everywhere unless mothers disinfect their homes with a thoroughness usually reserved for isolation chambers at the Centers for Disease Control. This is the latest weapon of mass germ destruction mom is supposed to buy.

her next hit of crack or how to dupe her landlord out of a month's rent. Millions of us, as we read magazines and watched TV, were whipsawed between these two extremes of motherhood.

Journalists and politicians have hated welfare, with varying degrees of intensity, since at least the mid-1960s. In *Why Americans Hate Welfare,* the political scientist Martin Gilens found that when the "War on Poverty" began in the early 1960s, coverage focused on the desperately poor rural white folks in Appalachia and elsewhere, people left behind when mines or factories closed and no other employers came to replace them. These white faces of poverty were all too similar to those in *The Grapes of Wrath* or *Life* magazine photos of the Dustbowl, and thus deeply sympathetic. Especially in the wake of Michael Harrington's *How the Other Half Lives,* public support for a war on poverty was quite strong. But beginning in the mid to late 1960s, after the urban uprisings in Watts, Newark, Detroit, and elsewhere, and the rise in the welfare rolls, the news media began to rely almost exclusively on pictures of African Americans to illustrate stories about welfare, thus reinforcing the stereotype that most welfare recipients are black. What Gilens found was that as coverage of welfare became more negative, the color of the people used to illustrate the stories got darker. During 1972–73, for example, 75 percent of magazine pictures about welfare featured African Americans, while they were only 43 percent of welfare recipients at the time.[27] (Interestingly, during the Reagan recession of 1981–82, when many white people lost their jobs, coverage of welfare was more sympathetic and the faces illustrating the stories became lighter until the economic recovery.) The notion that welfare was a government program primarily for black folks who refused to work fanned white resentment against public assistance for the poor.[28]

But our concern here is how welfare came to get a *female* black face. Among broadcasters in the early 1970s there was indeed barely concealed disgust for the rise in the welfare rolls, but they did not single out or demonize welfare mothers. Relying heavily on the words "explosion" and "exploding," they regularly reported—once, even twice a month—the latest government figures for how many people were on welfare, and this became a mantra of exasperation. "Welfare costs are way up again," at an all-time high, Walter Cronkite reported in September 1971. He reminded viewers that this represented a one-year increase of 27 percent, "a record." A year later, David Brinkley complained, "In ten years the welfare load has risen 300 percent and it's still rising, and so is the high cost . . . There are many families now in their third generation on welfare, and to them it has become the normal way of life."[29] "Americans agree that the welfare system is no good and has to be changed," reported Howard K. Smith in 1971, citing no polls or evidence to back this up, but simply confirming it as common sense.[30] Over and over, the news media repeatedly reminded viewers that welfare expenditures were soaring, intolerable, and had to be contained. No context was provided to explain the rise: the deindustrialization and subsequent job loss in many northern cities, the collapse of many agricultural jobs in the south, the fact that black women, barred from welfare since the 1930s because of discriminatory practices, were now deemed eligible, the absence of decent day care for these women.[31]

Nonetheless, in these early stories, the imagined welfare recipient was usually faceless or a man. Stories about "welfare chiselers," and those who were supposedly so rich from welfare that they bought Cadillacs with the money, used the pronoun *he* and envisioned able-bodied men refusing to work. Richard Nixon, rarely missing an opportunity to pander to the "silent majority," noted in a national television address: "The thing that is demeaning is for a man to refuse work and then ask someone else who works to pay taxes to keep him on welfare. Nixon was so unabashed in his contempt for those on relief that he asked Johnny Cash to perform, at a formal White House event, the song "Welfare Cadillac," which made fun of welfare recipients and suggested they were all cheats. The request quickly became notorious and Cash refused.[32]

There *were* images in the press of "welfare queens" cranking out illegitimate babies in the 1960s. For example, journalistic exposés with titles like "The Shocking Truth About the Aid to Dependent Children Welfare Program," published in *Reader's Digest,* or "Welfare: Has It Become a Scandal?" in *Look,* both in 1961, warned readers about a mother of seven in Washington, D.C., who sent her kids out to beg while she and her boyfriend ate steaks, or another mother in New York who spent all her AFDC money on narcotics (she hid her needle in her bra so it would always be handy), or yet another in Newark who supposedly collected $61,500 a year because she had fourteen illegitimate kids. In a pattern that would persist right up to the 1990s, journalists singled out some utterly appalling cases of behavior and abuse, and made them personify all welfare recipients and all welfare cases. But in the 1960s and '70s, such sensationalized resentment-breeders circulated with the equally if not more infuriating image of "able-bodied men" collecting welfare checks instead of working, and with notions of bureaucratic ineptitude making the welfare mess worse. In fact, when some politicians proposed forcing welfare mothers to work, news anchors also reported this with a tone of mild shock.[33] Even David Brinkley, in a stinging 1972 rant about a "welfare mess" that "nobody likes," acknowledged, "About 85 percent of those on welfare are women with children and no husbands. There is talk of making them work. But if they work, what happens to their children? Day care centers to take care of them would cost more than paying their mothers to stay home." [34]

It was Ronald Reagan, the king of the "welfare queen" anecdotes, who was the politician most responsible for promoting the gendering of welfare in the popular imagination, and beginning in the 1970s his fractured fairy tales got a great deal of media play. He specialized in the exaggerated, outrageous tale that was almost always unsubstantiated, usually false, yet so sensational that it merited repeated recounting. "We just don't know," he sputtered in 1971, "how many are getting four or five or even more checks under different names." [35] And because his "examples" of welfare queens drew on existing stereotypes of welfare cheats and resonated with news stories about welfare fraud, they did indeed gain real traction. Note the directness and certainty of the story, as if it were about a specific woman he knew personally, this one used during his campaign for president in 1976. And note that unlike Nixon, Reagan had changed the pronouns. "She has eighty names, thirty addresses, twelve Social Security cards, and is collecting veterans' benefits on four deceased husbands. . . . She's collecting Social Security on her cards. She's got Medicaid, getting food stamps, and she is collecting welfare under each of her names. Her tax-free cash alone is over $150,000." [36] (If this were typical, of course, Watts and Newark would have been graced with the same starter castles dotting the hills around Reagan's ranch.)

Such apocryphal stories gained credence when real-life "welfare queens" got busted. Despite the alleged proliferation of such queens, the networks only found two of them, whose stories they nonetheless played to the hilt. In a June 1978 report, Walter Cronkite noted that Illinois had found two women who may have collected as much as $150,000 each in fraudulent welfare claims. "One of them was dubbed the 'welfare queen,'" Cronkite reported, "but she may have to surrender that title to a woman in California." One Barbara Jean Thompson, a black woman, was charged with eighteen counts of welfare fraud. She had allegedly collected nearly $290,000 in welfare checks, food stamps, and medical benefits over the past six years, "probably, say officials, the biggest case of welfare fraud in history." A computer check revealed she only had four kids, not thirty or forty as she had allegedly claimed. She reportedly got checks at eight different addresses by using false IDs, and a search of her $119,000 house revealed duplicating equipment and three cars, a Cadillac, a Porsche, and a Mustang.[37] ABC reported that she had claimed to have forty-seven children. The press kept inflating these numbers. By November, when she was convicted, CBS nearly doubled the figure, reporting that she had claimed to have as many as seventy dependent children.[38] Another female cheat appeared in 1983, when NBC reported that Dorothy Woods "set a new record in the annals of welfare fraud." She had reportedly collected $377,000 in welfare funds by claiming that she had forty-nine children and establishing twelve welfare cases under assumed names. "In the ten years she operated the swindle, Mrs. Woods acquired seven homes and six cars, including a Rolls-Royce." The networks failed to report that Mrs. Woods's husband had bought her a six-bedroom house and several cars before she ever went on welfare.[39]

Here we did not learn Mrs. Woods's race, but the stereotype of the welfare queen, which became part of the common sense about welfare in the mid-1970s, was a crucial first step in resenting, vilifying, and punishing all welfare mothers. (In 1994, possibly unable to find that palace full of all those welfare queens, ABC had to turn, once again, to Woods as an exemplar, now rehabilitated after serving an eight-year sentence, and here we did see that she was African American.)[40] Polls showed that Americans, in part because of the sensationalized "welfare cheat" stories in the press, vastly overestimated how much welfare fraud actually existed. In some polls, Americans guessed that 40 percent of those on the dole cheated, while Health and Human Services estimated that less than 4 percent of recipients actually lied about their financial situation.[41]

As the economy soured in the 1970s, conservative assaults on "entitlements" had often devastating consequences for poor women and their children. Proposition 13 in California, which put a limit on property taxes, inaugurated various tax revolts that sought to limit government spending. The religious right pushed its "family values" campaign. And when Ronald Reagan became president, a full-bore assault on welfare took center stage, and the image in the crosshairs was that of an African American mother. (Let's not forget that in the 1960s, affable ole Ronnie had opposed the Civil Rights Act of 1964, the Voting Rights Act of 1965, fair-housing legislation in California, and legislation to declare Martin Luther King Jr.'s birthday a national holiday.[42] Sounds kind of like Trent Lott, yes?)

When Reagan took office, he and his conservative cohorts simply switched around cause and effect. Welfare wasn't an effect of poverty. No, no, no. Welfare was now the *cause* of poverty. Reagan's message was simple. The economy in 1981 was a mess *not* because the government had spent trillions on a war in Asia it couldn't afford and lost anyway. Nope, the economy was a wreck because of poor people: Social welfare programs like food stamps, medicaid, and Aid to Families with Dependent Children (AFDC) were the root cause of stagflation. Welfare in particular, according to these guys, encouraged women to have children out of wedlock by as many different men as possible and to avoid decent jobs at all costs. According to this logic, it was crucial to reduce and eventually eliminate AFDC.

Remember, AFDC was the social program with the highest percentage of women as clients or recipients, and it suffered the largest decline in spending under Reagan.[43] In 1973, nearly 85 percent of children living in poor families collected AFDC; by 1986, that number had declined to 60 percent. Benefits fell considerably: The purchasing power of AFDC benefits dropped by a third between 1970 and 1986, because they didn't keep up with inflation or they were cut. Between 1981 and 1986, the Reagan administration slashed the budgets for education, nutrition, and health programs by $36.5 billion.[44] By tightening eligibility requirements, the administration forced as many as five hundred thousand working-poor families off of welfare, and four hundred thousand people lost food stamps.[45] According to one estimate, one-third of the increase in poverty since 1979 would not have occurred had these government cutbacks not taken place: The government went from helping one in seven black women out of poverty in 1979, to helping only one in fourteen by 1987.[46] Let's put it another way: In the first three years of Reagan's presidency, the number of children living in poverty increased by 16 percent, rising to one in five kids, the highest rate in American history since the government started keeping records.[47] Yet when infant mortality rates increased, when poor women could no longer get prenatal care or birth control information, when poverty rates worsened, it was the poor woman's fault.

As the 1980s and '90s progressed, there were a few pat roles, in addition to "the queen," that welfare mothers were assigned to play in the news media. Drawing from the "praise Jesus" storytelling frameworks of the new evangelicals then in power, the news media gave us the "born-again" welfare mother. This was the workfare success story, complete with the epiphany that came from being dunked in the sacred river of employment. Such stories showcased the mother who, as a former recipient, now saw the light (say amen, somebody) and denounced welfare as promoting indolence and robbing a woman of all self-worth. Ever since his California days, Reagan had been a big champion of workfare—making recipients work for their checks—and increasing numbers of states adopted such programs in the 1980s. So we started seeing upbeat stories about welfare mothers who were resurrected through a workfare program with a name like "GAIN" or "PRIDE" or "America Works."

Some workfare stories focused on men, but increasingly they put the spotlight on mothers. They featured a mix of women: Slightly less than half were white, slightly more than half were African American, and a few were Latina. But the narrative structure and emotional states were the same for them all. They hated welfare, they had had no self-esteem (a word used repeatedly to give workfare the requisite pop-psychology patina) and no pride, and then they got into a workfare program, which was economically and psychically redemptive. Workfare was "better than sitting home—you work for your check," noted one woman, while another said that staying home was not living, it was just existing.[48] (This at the exact same time that *Good Housekeeping* was widely promoting its "New Traditionalist," the middle-class white woman who chose to stay at home because that was the right thing to do, dedicated herself to her kids, and never had an idle moment.) "I made up my mind to get off the pot and do something for myself," emphasized a black mother who got off welfare after six years.[49] In a story about getting mothers "off the welfare crutch," as millionaire Connie Chung put it, one white woman confessed, "I felt trapped and helpless, like I had no control over my life anymore, I had no self-esteem left." But now "I feel great, I feel very strong, very confident."[50] So welfare mothers themselves reinforced the stereotype that welfare mothers were lazy, "sat around," did nothing, even though, in real life, they were raising kids, often in the most dangerous, depressing, challenging circumstances.

The networks especially favored soundbites in which the mother claimed that working made her kids look up to her in way that had simply not been possible before. (We never heard from a child who said, "I miss my mommy. I don't want her to have to work." That sentiment was reserved for middle-class white kids only.) A Latina woman in another story testified, "Now I feel part of society again, I am a complete human being." [51] (So welfare mothers themselves reaffirmed that when you are on welfare you are an outcast, certainly not a citizen.) "If I can work, so can they, so can they," insisted a recently employed African American mother. Added a white woman in 1993, "Now I'm on the other end I can say 'Get a job, I know you can. You can't give me an excuse for why you're not working.' " [52] Again and again, rugged individualism conquered poverty, joblessness, racism, and sexism. If these mothers could do it, any welfare mother could, if she just pulled herself up by her bootstraps.

Now it goes without saying that for millions of welfare mothers, getting a decent job was and is vastly preferable to dealing with the system, which treated most welfare mothers like lepers, criminals, or both, and didn't pay them enough to live on. (They were also treated like lepers when they bought groceries with food stamps and identified themselves and their kids as medicaid recipients at the local hospital.) But the networks usually profiled workfare and training programs that provided decent childcare, medical benefits and transportation to and from work, and slotted women into jobs that paid a bit more than washing out toilets at the Comfort Inn. (We did not see workfare stories about mothers forced to get on a bus at 6 A.M., before their kids were even up, ride an hour or so to the workfare job, and get home at 8 P.M., just in time to put the kids to bed.) And again, these few women were meant to stand for all welfare mothers. The stories' repeated discourse of self-actualization—*these* women took initiative, if they can do it, anybody can—masked the fact that in some areas, there were no jobs, period; in other areas there were only minimum-wage jobs that paid less than welfare and didn't provide health care for your kids; in some areas, there was either no day care or horrible day care or hideously expensive day care. In real life, it wasn't only up to a mother's determination or motivation. Poor women's choices were especially hemmed in by geography.

And what if they felt, as did millions of middle-class mothers, that they were the best people to take care of their kids when they were little?

In our review of three decades of network news stories about welfare mothers, only one, which aired on NBC in October of 1969, featured a welfare mother saying that she didn't want "just anybody" coming into her home and watching her child and finding that "things were different from what they're supposed to be" when she got home at night.[53] Such a concern was a luxury poor women were not supposed to be able to afford. And, of course, having undergone a workfare makeover, it was crucial that the redeemed workfare mom testify, as someone who should know better than anyone, that welfare made you lazy and was a system recipients themselves now blamed for their previously sorry lot.

By the late 1980s and early 1990s, a much less sympathetic stock character increasingly overshadowed both the "queen" and the born-again workfare mom in the news: the unwed teenager who, whoops, had a baby and then, whoops, had another and made the decent taxpayers of America pay through the schnozz forever for her seconds of unprotected, thoughtless pleasure with some irresponsible, layabout black boy, himself increasingly stereotyped on reality shows like *COPS* and *911* as a drug-dealing criminal. At first, in the mid-1980s, most stories about welfare mothers and unwed teen mothers were in separate categories. The "epidemic" of teen pregnancies was illustrated by visits to high school programs designed to keep girls in school, and we saw a fair mix of black and white teens. But when the stories talked about some of these girls going on welfare, invariably the face that we saw was black.[54] And gradually these stories merged into one giant pathology of a metastasizing welfare system pushed to its limits by irresponsible, oversexed black girls.

Even though only 1.2 percent of welfare mothers were under eighteen when they received benefits, and teens accounted for about 5 percent of welfare caseloads, the unwed teen, preferably one whose mother and grandmother had also been unwed teen mothers on welfare for life, was to conservative politicians and the networks what Princess Diana was to *People* magazine: a constant attention grabber.[55] We first met her in 1985, when NBC introduced us to Gloria from Cabrini Green in Chicago, who was born when her mother was sixteen and first became pregnant herself at fourteen. She, her two kids, and her mother were all on welfare, and it was here that we may have first heard the phrase "children raising children." These children were "trapped in a cycle of crime, isolation, and welfare." The term "culture of dependency" (which suggested that poor black mothers were inherently shiftless and unproductive and, as with sickle-cell anemia, they transmitted this diseased, deviant lifestyle to their vulnerable offspring) became a part of the new common sense about welfare.

Now, most people agree that it is not a good idea for fourteen-year-olds to have babies. But really, what were Americans thinking? Take one large teenage population, inundate them with barely clad models in Calvin Klein ads, characters on soap operas who live to hump, sitcoms at 8:00 P.M. (the old "family viewing hour") with jokes about odd-shaped penises, masturbation, and hookers, bumping and grinding movie videos with giant boobs and stuffed crotches, prime-time soaps like *Melrose Place* where everyone really was in bed 24/7 with whoever was handy (they, like, wrote memos and sealed mergers in bed), news "documentaries" like NBC's "Scared Sexless" (1987), romanticized depictions about getting swept away by passion, and the never-ending acts of copulation in the movies, and you are kind of conveying a relentless message that sex is the nation's most popular recreational activity and the one that confirms that you are attractive, worthwhile, and cool. Simply put, beginning in the 1980s, the media seriously overemphasized the importance of sex in everyday life. Now, add to this a really incomplete, underfunded, often-censored sex-education system, which, when it does exist, often promotes abstinence as the only alternative to unprotected sex (an approach that research has repeatedly shown does not work), spotty information about and access to birth control and decreased access to abortion, and millions of teenage girls without adequate health care. (In Utah in 1985 it was illegal to teach about contraception.)[56] Finally, also add an increasing barrage of media images geared exclusively to females that suggested that having a baby is a sure way to find unconditional love and is the most important thing that you, as a female, can do in your life, and what might the outcome be? You got it: by the mid-1980s, the highest rate of teen pregnancies of any industrialized nation.

So we are not about to minimize a very serious problem for millions of adolescent girls in the country. But a reality check is required here as well. Teen pregnancies—which had become quite normal in postwar America as women married and had children younger—began to decline in the 1970s as more middle- and upper-middle-class women postponed marriage and childbirth. So the teenage birth rate had actually *declined* from its baby boom high in 1960: by 1985, it was the lowest it had been since 1940.[57] So there was no new epidemic of teenage pregnancies. What *was* different was the increasingly high proportion of teenagers who were not married when they gave birth. Also vastly underreported was how many of these young girls had been impregnated by older men in their twenties and thirties, sometimes through abusive or predatory family relationships. This rise in unwed teenage pregnancy was used by Republicans to attack all single mothers (remember *The Daily News* headline: DAN QUAYLE TO MURPHY BROWN: YOU TRAMP!) and to paint an even more negative picture of welfare mothers that justified a highly punitive form of welfare "reform." Ironically, it was when the unwed teen birth rate began *declining* in the United States, starting in 1991, that the media drumbeat about this "epidemic" increased.[58] And the news media rarely reported about what might be called the African American Murphy Brown phenomenon: the fact that the number of black single mothers *not* on welfare grew in the 1970s and early 1980s just as rapidly as those who were.[59]

The unwed teen welfare mom had her media-scripted role, too. She got pregnant by "not thinking," she regretted it now, she hated the father, it was very hard to be a good mother, welfare had made it all possible, and she had no idea nor could care less that the taxpayers were footing her bill, and it was indeed costing "us" a fortune. At first, she was simply clueless and irresponsible. By the early 1990s, conservatives changed the story. She could have gotten pregnant by "not thinking," but more likely she saw the fabulous financial benefits of welfare and deliberately got pregnant so that she, too, could become one of those jackpot-winning welfare moms. In other words, the news frame that made these young women so unsympathetic was one that suggested they were deliberately *choosing* to go on welfare rather than do anything else. At the same time that middle-class mothers were seen as planning their pregnancies with the precision of a moon landing so as to mesh with career trajectories, sibling spacing, and financial capabilities, teen welfare mothers came off as refusing to make such calculations—except for the one that guaranteed them welfare if they had a baby. As one white male sociologist told CBS News, the message that teenage mothers got was that "someone" would pick up the pieces, "not me, not the boy who got me pregnant, not my family, the state will pick up the pieces."[60] Or, as Betty Rollin of NBC put it, "have a baby, get a reward."[61] Rollin neglected to add that the "reward" was usually a life of poverty.

No television program was more central to the vilification of black teenage mothers, and indeed of the black family itself, than Bill Moyers's highly influential and controversial documentary, "The Vanishing Family: Crisis in Black America," which aired on CBS during prime time in January of 1986. (Moyers, a liberal in so many areas, was outraged by teen "illegitimacy," and even did an on-air commentary in 1995 arguing for a cutoff of all benefits to unwed teenaged mothers.) [62] The show resurrected the highly controversial and offensive arguments put forth by Daniel Patrick Moynihan—another "liberal"—in his 1965 report *The Negro Family: The Case for National Action*. The Moynihan Report, as it came to be known, also characterized the black family as a disaster, with the all-dominating black matriarch who had "too many children too early" and emasculated the men in her life, as the cause for this "tangle of pathology." [63] Welfare, of course, was also destroying the black family. Like Moynihan, Moyers focused on how the "pathology" of the black community—rather than discrimination, crappy schools, racist banking practices, lack of jobs, and unavailable birth control—kept black folks down. But unlike Moynihan, Moyers could *show* Americans what he meant.

Moyers's cameras brought "us" into the depths of Newark, New Jersey, in the same way that a safari leader might have taken us into the heart of the dark continent. Moyers asked a group of young black women with babies in their laps, "Raise your hand if you're married." None did. "Raise your hand if you'd like to be married to your baby's father." None did, and one woman nearly dragged her arm to the floor to emphasize how distasteful this prospect was. The entire tone of the show was accusatory, the girls cast as freaks. "For much of black America, the traditional family has vanished," intoned Moyers, meaning, presumably, the nuclear family that plantation owners had been so devoted to preserving for their slaves and that welfare policy had also sought to foster. [64] The show simultaneously implied that the "white family" was some bastion of stability and harmony (you know, like the Osbournes), while also projecting a host of fears about the collapse of the white family onto blacks.

This show marked a real turning point in blaming the girls themselves, and, more pointedly, a cultural bankruptcy within the black community, for the perpetuation of poverty. This place was presented as a world unto itself, so alien, so sordid, that it needed shutting down. Nothing less than "America's future" was at stake. Once the news media discovered the "national crisis" of teenage pregnancy, linked it to welfare, and racialized it as a peculiarly black problem, the image of welfare mothers, and economic aid to them, were doomed.

This was the news frame Charles Murray, darling of the right and author of *Losing Ground* and, later, the infamous *Bell Curve* (which argued, basically, that blacks are inherently dumber than whites), had been pushing for years. Right-wing think tanks like the Heritage Foundation, the Olin Foundation, and the Cato Institute—to name just a few—learned how to get their talking heads on the news with the same frequency that Whoopi Goldberg appeared on *Hollywood Squares,* and they presented visions of cultural pollution brought on especially by welfare mothers. In 1985, in an NBC "special segment" on black America, Murray insisted that whites "can't ignore the special problems posed by blacks in our country" and asserted, without any evidence, that welfare itself had "caused the dramatic increase in unwed mothers." [65] Nine years later, with the 1994 Republican "revolution" blowing wind in his sails, Murray argued more emphatically for ending all welfare altogether. "I want to make the behavior of having a child when you aren't prepared to care for it extremely punishing again." [66] In a 1994 rant on CBS, he again posed the threat of contamination: their behavior was going to infect "us." "We will have white urban neighborhoods that look and feel pretty much like the black urban neighborhoods do now. And that is a disaster for everyone." [67]

By the late 1980s, again taking their lead from the conservatives' agenda, the news emphasized how much these girls' babies were costing "us." Welfare got reframed as if AFDC was in dad's wallet and these girls snuck in and stole the money that never belonged to them. "The cost to the rest of us," intoned Diane Sawyer in 1989, who would shortly be making $7 million a year, "is enormous," and Carole Simpson added in the same report that "the economic burden of teen pregnancy is staggering," an estimated $19 billion in welfare payments. [68] No breakdown of this figure was given. (In 1990, it cost $289 billion to support the defense department, just for the sake of comparison.) [69] In 1994, Betty Rollin on CBS said "the national tab" (you know, like the kind you'd run in a bar) for unwed teen pregnancies was $30 billion a year, although viewers had no idea where the figure came from or what it included. [70] To New Jersey Governor Florio, welfare mothers were "the anchor around our neck" that "the nation can't afford." [71] And these teen girls—inheritors of the "queen" mantle—were now depicted as pushy, conniving, and brazen adolescents who felt they had every right to get knocked up at the public's expense.

Sadly enough, women reporters weren't any easier on these girls than the men—in fact, often they were tougher—and it was female reporters who got these beats. Indeed, Linda Douglass, Rebecca Chase, and especially Betty Rollin seemed particularly damning in their reporting about these girls. Just to cite one way in which words were put into these girls' mouths, a Latina girl told Linda Douglass on CBS that it was hard for many girls to avoid getting pregnant. Douglass translated this into the teen having "no trouble asking taxpayers to bail her out . . . she feels that having children is her right. She expects to support herself someday, but expects the government to be there if she can't." [72] Now this poor kid didn't say anything like this on camera; the attitude of entitlement was imputed to her by the reporter. Rebecca Chase asked a single welfare mother in 1992, "Do you feel like you owe the taxpayers anything for them helping you support your children?" The woman smiled and looked a bit incredulous. "I never really thought about that, that never came to my mind." Such inconsideration and ingratitude was about to change, warned Chase, as welfare reform would "force recipients to think about their obligations." [73] For professional women, especially those whose success had been made possible by feminism, these girls represented a throwback, a failure or refusal to take advantage of what the movement had sought to make possible. Whether the struggles of white women reporters to land jobs in their field equal to those of men while also raising kids produced a judgmental stance against these girls is unknown, but by middle-class, feminist standards, unwed teen mothers were a disappointment politically and individually: they set themselves, and all women, back. It would hardly be surprising if these women reporters, whether consciously or not, allowed such judgments to inform their coverage.

There were exceptions to the overwhelming emphasis on African American women, as the networks were already sensitive to charges of racism. So the other welfare poster mother we saw was the indolent, overweight white woman who often lived in a trailer. For example, in a 1995 edition of CBS's 48 Hours, titled "The Rage Over Welfare," we met two doughy white women who lived on welfare in New Hampshire. The very first shots we saw—just to let us know the kind of lazy, selfish moms we were in for here—were close-ups of hands shuffling a deck of playing cards and, next, a mom lighting a cigarette. The white male journalist badgered one of the women, who said she couldn't work because she had epilepsy and arthritis. "Well, people with epilepsy work. People with arthritis work, they *do,*" he scolded. As she answered, "I don't know what kind of a job I could find to do," the camera again cut to her hands shuffling the cards, suggesting, perhaps, a bright future in the casino industry if she'd only apply herself.

Finally, by the early 1990s, the media began to reinforce the equation between welfare and child abuse. Tom Brokaw reminded viewers in his series "Families in Crisis" that unwed teen pregnancy was happening to all groups "but especially to black, inner-city teenagers." The story then cut to a young African American woman named Sonya, a "third-generation single mom," who admitted "I'm not the best mom." As the story opened we saw her yelling at her kids, hitting one, and then telling him to "shut up." [74] We also met "Deborah B.," a black pregnant welfare mother of seven, who had lost custody of all her previous children because of neglect and abuse, and was now being ordered by the court to relinquish the new baby as soon as it was born so she wouldn't have the chance to abuse it. [75] Other more upbeat stories about parenting classes for single welfare mothers nonetheless cast such mothers as "inherently unfit and even affirmatively harmful to their children." [76] Such stories were not countered by images of welfare mothers tucking their kids in at night, giving them advice, or telling the reporter all that she had to do to feed, clothe, and protect her kids.

But the most sensational confirmation that black, inner-city welfare mothers were utterly degenerate aired on February 2, 1994. Chicago police, looking for drugs, entered an apartment where they found nineteen black children "living like animals." The cops reported that the kids were hungry, cold, and "living in filth," and that there were roaches everywhere, which was clear from the revolting photographs of the trash-strewn floors, a filthy mattress with no bedding on it, and kids "surrounded by garbage and dog excrement." One cop reported that there was hardly any food in the house, and that the food that remained was being fought over between a dog and the children. [77] ABC reported that cuts, bruises, and cigarette burns on the children's bodies also testified to abuse. [78] The mothers—all black welfare recipients—were arrested and the kids put into foster care. The networks reused the footage in other stories about child abuse and the need for welfare reform, as ABC's Rebecca Chase did when she cited the case as a shocking symbol of all that is wrong with the system: "Their mothers received more than $5000 a month in welfare," yet, as we saw, seemed not to spend a cent of it on their kids.[79] Of course these mothers were appalling; but again, they came to stand for most welfare mothers, not for the exceptions.

With Bill Clinton's rise to power and his mantra during the 1992 campaign—that we needed to "end welfare as we know it"—coverage of welfare became even more frequent, and more negative, and public opinion followed accordingly. Diane Sawyer, who by then *was* making at least $7 million a year, referred to teenage welfare mothers on a 1995 broadcast as "public enemy number one." Jonathan Alter of *Newsweek* said they were a "threat to the fabric of this country," and a subsequent issue likened unwed teenage mothers to drunk drivers.[80] Beginning in 1991, opposition to welfare spending shot up from approximately 18 percent to nearly 50 percent by 1994, as measured by a question about whether the government was spending too little, about the right amount, or too much on welfare.[81] By 1994, polls showed that of those people who believed most recipients were black, 61 percent believed that people were on welfare because of "lack of effort" and 65 percent believed it was because "they don't want to work." [82]

By now, the belief that welfare mothers were congenitally predisposed to make sure that they and all their children remain on welfare forever and ever was a given. And by now it had become a news routine to present the sensational exception as the rule, however inflammatory or inaccurate. Rebecca Chase on ABC emphasized, for example, that in 1991 (during a recession) there were more people on welfare than ever before, virtually all of them women and children. "Nearly 25 percent of them have been there for more than five years," she intoned, without emphasizing that a much larger figure, 75 percent, hadn't. In 1992, Chase illustrated the cycle of dependency by taking us to the home of an African American woman named Marsha who had been on welfare for twenty years. "The nature of the problem can be seen in the Hankerson apartment, where Marsha's fourteen-year-old daughter is eight months pregnant."[83] Chase actually used the exact same footage twice—once in April 1992 and again in October 1992—of a black teenager saying matter-of-factly, "My mother had me when she was sixteen and I had him when I was sixteen," thus further pepetuating the exaggeration of how many welfare recipients were unwed teens whose mothers had also been on welfare.[84]

While there was no evidence, despite years of research on welfare mothers, that women got pregnant to go on welfare or had more kids to increase their benefits, reporters showcased the infuriating exception. Betty Rollin found a woman who was willing to say, on camera, "I'm one of those people that had another baby just for the extra sixty-four dollars."[85] Even when Rebecca Chase reported on a statement by seventy-nine social scientists in 1995 that disputed the connection between welfare and illegitimacy, she warned "numbers can be deceiving," and then brought us a welfare mother whom she asked, "Do you think some women have babies just to get on welfare or get more money?" "Yeah, I know a couple that do."[86] So much for those clueless social scientists. Hearsay trumped research any day.

The other place that welfare mothers appeared was in the newsmagazines, and they fared no better here. The newsmagazines, in cover stories about the "black underclass," reproduced the same media frameworks, about "the cycle of single motherhood and dependency" in which a "matriarch" was "receiving a welfare check for a household of children and grandchildren," illustrated by a photo of four unsmiling African American women and five children all living under the same roof.[87] George Will, in a 1990 *Newsweek* essay titled "Mothers Who Don't Know How" (as if that little worm ever wiped up projectile vomiting), deplored "the family pathologies that drive the intergenerational transmission of poverty" and claimed to know about "a childcare—actually noncare—product popular in some ghettos . . . a pillow made to hold a bottle next to an infant so the infant can take nourishment without an adult in attendance."[88]

In her unwelcome starring role as the celebrity mother's evil twin, the news media's version of the welfare mother reinforced one of the most unwarranted stereotypes of all: Black mothers are bad mothers. As Dorothy Roberts has shown in her powerful indictment of the child welfare system, *Shattered Bonds,* the assumption that most black mothers are unfit has prompted the state to remove thousands of black children from their mothers and put them in foster care. As Roberts notes, "We seem to have regressed in our thinking about poor families."[89] We used to think it was our responsibility to help them. Now, they should help themselves or be destroyed.

One of the most important trends that we found during this period was that the attacks on the maternal qualifications of welfare mothers increased, over the years, in direct relationship to the increased emphasis on the new momism. There is little doubt that for working mothers, especially white working mothers, these highly negative portrayals of welfare mothers enhanced our own self-esteem at a time when we, too, were very much under attack. By the late 1980s and early 1990s there were raging debates about what constituted a good mother. A woman could be a good mother and still work outside the home; no, a good mother stayed at home with her kids. A good mother did phonics with her three-year-old; no, a good mother didn't push her kids. A savvy mother allowed her teenager to dye his hair lime green; no, the savvy mother put her foot down. And so on and so forth, ad infinitum. In other words, the stereotype of the lazy, irresponsible, neglectful, and promiscuous welfare mother became so important in the 1980s and beyond because however insecure we felt in our identities as "mothers," we suddenly (if briefly) felt very confident and virtuous when juxtaposed to this other, bad mother.[90] Our exclusion of her from the "perfect mom" club ensured our own membership, even though we knew we weren't perfect. Compared to the scowling, dark-skinned mother of five who made her kids sleep in their own feces while she got high on crack, we were transformed, purified, the Madonna herself. We may have screamed at the kids last night, picked them up a half hour late from day care, or fed them Frosted Flakes for dinner, but at least we didn't do *that*. The construction of the identity "mom," then, was and is often based on vehemently excluding certain types of people from that identity, and then establishing a hierarchy in which one group is on top and the other is way down at the bottom.[91]

Once welfare reform passed in the summer of 1996, under the hectoring title "Personal Responsibility and Work Opportunity Reconciliation Act," control over welfare went to the individual states in the form of block grants, and recipients now faced strict work requirements and time limits on receiving benefits. The law required states to move one quarter of welfare recipients into jobs or work programs within one year, and half into jobs by 2002. Adults who did not find work within two years would be cut off, and no one would receive cash assistance for more than five years. States were allowed to deny benefits to women who had additional children while on welfare, and to unmarried women under eighteen.[92] Once welfare reform passed, welfare mothers disappeared from the national stage. Congress had to reauthorize the welfare act in the fall of 2002, but remembrances of 9/11, the build-up to the war on Iraq, and the congressional elections headed the national agenda. As of August 2003, Congress remained deadlocked over welfare reform. President Bush and the Republicans in the House backed a proposal called, with typical Bush cynicism, "PRIDE" (Personal Responsibility and Individual Development for Everyone), which would require that welfare mothers increase their working hours from thirty to forty a week, did not contain additional funds for childcare, but would pour millions into programs that allegedly promote marriage. Senate Democrats and child-welfare activists from around the country have objected to such punitive measures in the face of soaring unemployment and nose-diving state budgets.

So what do we know so far about these women and their kids? Welfare reform was declared a huge success, with a 59 percent drop in the rolls between March 1994 and July 2001.[93] The robust economy helped enormously, as many mothers were able to find jobs that actually paid them more than welfare had. They worked primarily in service or whole-sale/retail jobs. Their median income in 1999 was $13,788, which was roughly the poverty level for a family of three in 1997.[94] Only 23 percent of them had health insurance through work.[95] Many states allowed mothers to combine welfare and work, increasing the amount they could earn and still collect some benefits. But many of these mothers still could not make ends meet on their salaries, and used food stamps, some welfare, and money from family and friends to get by.[96] Many remained poor.[97] Mothers reported going without medical or dental care for themselves, and one-third of former welfare mothers had to cut the size of the meals they served or skipped them altogether because there wasn't enough food. Half of these mothers said that sometimes food didn't last until the end of the month and they didn't have money for more.[98] Once the recession began in the spring of 2001, to be exacerbated by the aftermath of 9/11, forty out of fifty states saw their caseloads increase—some, like Nevada's, up 69 percent.[99] The unemployment rate for single mothers rose 60 percent from December 2000 to December 2001.[100]

Childcare remains an enormous problem for poor women. The Center for Law and Social Policy reports that only about 15 percent of those children eligible for federally funded childcare assistance actually get it.[101] More than a quarter of former recipients were working mostly night hours in 1999, and we all know how easy it is to find decent care then.[102]

Repeatedly, former welfare mothers have to choose between their jobs and the safety of their kids. The kinds of jobs they have don't have the same flexibility and autonomy as, say, college professor, real estate agent, or computer programmer. Some mothers battle the stereotype that they don't want to be working, so if their kid is mildly sick, they'll give her a Tylenol to mask the kid's fever, take her to day care, go to work to show that you do want the job, and then wait for the call from the childcare provider. Some are not allowed to take phone calls on the job, so they never even find out if their kid is sick.[103]

Here's a story we didn't see on the nightly news in 2002. A former welfare mother, now working, left her twins, as usual, at a home-based day care. The center took the kids to the circus. At the end of the day, they forgot one of her kids there and never realized they had left him behind; she found her child through the police. Needless to say, she had to find another provider. (Imagine the media hoopla if this had happened to someone with the financial profile of, say, Patsy Ramsey.) All too many mothers have to rely on kids age ten, eleven, or twelve taking care of smaller siblings: that is their before- and after-school childcare.[104] When these women's childcare was unreliable, they missed work, and then they lost their jobs. One issue never mentioned in the news coverage of the need for welfare mothers to go to work no matter what, was what might happen to their adolescent children once Mom was away ten to twelve hours a day. Researchers have reported that the combination of increased childcare duties and the lack of supervision has proved stressful and risky for many of these kids.[105] In the winter of 2000, New York City registered the highest number of homeless people ever, and most were women and children. As the end of the five-year limit for welfare starts approaching for millions of women and their kids, we will see, in the years ahead, what the consequences of "welfare reform" might be, especially given the budget crises in the states.

As part of our collective history as mothers, we need to reconsider how repeatedly damning media portrayals of these mothers—most of whom loved their kids, had very few people or places to turn to for sympathy and support, and were terrified of going off welfare completely because they would lose health care for their children—hardened so many of our hearts toward them (and they were indeed cast as "them"). Most powerful of all in these media myths about welfare mothers was the discourse about choice: that welfare mothers had some vast array of options but *chose* to go on the dole. So now that we look back on it all, do we really believe, as mothers, that only some kids deserve to go to the doctor, go to bed with food in their stomachs, own books, and get a new toy now and then? Do we believe that only certain mothers should have to worry about crappy childcare, empty refrigerators, the phone being cut off, or losing her job because her kid is sick? Do we really believe that these mothers "choose" to be poor, and have their kids be poor too? Do we?

SEVEN

The "Mommy Wars"

On October 22, 1990, Tom Brokaw opened a special segment on "Mom at Work," with the by-now moth-eaten bromide about women trying to "have it all," meaning a job and a family, which were "two full-time jobs." The reporter, Betty Rollin, introduced us to a mom who was a lawyer at Goldman Sachs. "Unlike most working mothers, she does not feel pulled between work and home," as if every mother felt that pull, was supposed to feel that pull. But this mother had eluded the pull because she worked only three days and was "among the growing number of working mothers unwilling to sacrifice motherhood for the fast track." (No figures from, say, the Bureau of Labor Statistics were offered to support the "growing number" assertion.) "My children are young, they'll never be this age again, and I really don't want to miss out on that," she told Rollin. "The beauty of my way is that I have everything," she added with a glowing smile. Rollin reported that, for women, part-time work is "a new version of having it all. . . . The superwoman version, which is by no means dead, often led to exhaustion, guilt, and as-yet unknown effects on the children." (These, then, were our choices: either work part-time or be an exhausted superwoman who has probably scarred her kids for life.) The story then cut to a mother who worked for Steelcase in Michigan, which now offered employees job sharing and flex time. She used to work full-time, but there was "no time" for her son. "I had no life," she observed, and then added the kicker for working mothers. "Everything was so rushed, that I don't really think he knew who his mommy was."

Welcome to the era of "the mommy track," that period in the late 1980s and early 1990s when story after story announced that for working mothers, career success—even working outside the home, for that matter—was not all it was cracked up to be, and mothers were allegedly retreating en masse to the domestic bliss of home. Everywhere one looked, from *Ladies' Home Journal* to *The Wall Street Journal,* there were articles about professional women—lawyers, managers, newspaper editors—who had successful careers but happily left the workplace because domesticity was much more fulfilling and because somewhere along the way they had come to believe that doing so would be better for their children. *Fortune* featured a cover story on WHY WOMEN ARE BAILING OUT (which actually they weren't), and marketing consultant Faith Popcorn coined the term "cocooning" to describe women's allegedly newfound love of "nesting."[1] Since the workplace was not going to accommodate the needs of parents, mothers (not fathers) would have to give up some of their income and the possibility for advancement. It was now time, simply put, to reposition women back in the home.[2]

Such stories coincided with what Nina Darnton of *Newsweek* dubbed in 1990 "the mommy wars." In one corner was the working mother, in the other, the stay-at-home mom. The working mother supposedly saw her opponent as a boring, limited woman who had just said "uncle" to patriarchy, spent too much time fondling Tupperware, and because she didn't work was a poor role model for her kids, especially her daughters. The stay-at-home mom supposedly saw her opponent as a selfish careerist who neglected her kids, was too stressed out when she *was* with them, and deserved whatever guilt she felt.[3] Every decade has its media-staged cat-fights, and this was the one for the 1990s: mom versus mom.

Both the "mommy track" and "mommy wars" divided mothers up into two mutually exclusive and combative camps, when studies showed that millions of mothers moved back and forth between these categories at different times, appreciated from a first-person basis the pluses and minuses of staying at home versus working, and thus would have to be just as much at war with themselves as with other mothers when the battle cry went forth. This either/or schema suggested that women—presumably because their brains were too small—could only cope with one, unchanging orientation, worker or homemaker.[4] Thus it masked the ambivalence mothers had about work *and* child rearing, and suggested that if mothers remained in rigid, unchanging roles, then businesses hardly had to become more flexible.

As part of these wars, we also saw the rise of the new sun-drenched domesticity—i.e., the Martha Stewartization of America—in which impossible images of uncluttered, immaculate, breeze-filled, lavender-scented, voile-curtained homes invited women to pour themselves into decorating and crafts, and to see the home as the one, true, most rewarding domain to master. *Good Housekeeping* launched its "New Traditionalist" campaign in the late 1980s, in which pictures of serene, upscale mothers flanked by their docile, obedient kids suggested that new, postfeminist mothers had discovered that June Cleaver, in spite of her predilection for shirtwaist dresses, had really been on to something. Cutting through these media images was the boll weevil of the "mother in jep," as the TV industry put it: made-for-TV movies, almost of all them starring Patty Duke, Melissa Gilbert, or Valerie Bertinelli, in which mothers (especially but not solely working mothers) were in constant danger of losing their kids and thus had to refocus on the domestic sphere and their kids like a laser beam or lose it all.

Beginning in the late 1980s, and steamrolling through much of popular culture in the 1990s, was a new glorification of domesticity and over-the-top levels of hypernatalism. The movies *Parenthood, Baby Boom, Look Who's Talking* (all seventeen of them), *Three Men and a Baby,* babies being born on *Murphy Brown, L.A. Law, Mad About You,* the never-ending parade of celebrity moms: babies, babies, babies were everywhere. Maternal yearning—i.e., "baby lust"—saw a resurgence in magazines like *Glamour* and *Mademoiselle.*[5] In academic and popular writing, there was the emergence of what came to be called "difference feminism," as exemplified by Carol Gilligan's highly influential, often misunderstood *In a Different Voice,* and the appalling *Men Are From Mars, Women Are From Venus.* (Did you ever see the author? He was from Neptar.) According to difference feminism, women really were more nurturing, more cooperative, more intuitive, less competitive than men. Some saw this difference stemming from socialization; others, of course, from planet of origin. And there were feminists who disagreed with these conclusions. But difference feminism trickled into magazines and public discourse, too, in the early 1990s, fueling the hypernatalism.[6]

But it was at this exact same time, in the late 1980s and early 1990s, that television brought us the greatest number of defiant mothers who tackled the backlash against women, and the new momism, with the force and fury of William "The Refrigerator" Perry. *Roseanne,* in particular, mooned romantic notions of motherhood week-in and week-out, as did *Married with Children, Grace Under Fire,* and *The Simpsons.* Shows that made fun of the "perfect mom" ideal, and news accounts and entertainment programming that suggested that mom couldn't do it all, so might as well go back to the kitchen, both served to eradicate the "supermom" as an icon. The "supermom"—a media construction—was not what feminists had hoped for as a model. Feminists didn't think mom should suddenly do everything—work outside the home and clean the house and care for the children and make gourmet meals. Feminists thought maybe dad and the government should participate too. But we got the media's version of the feminist, "have it all" mom anyway. Then when it turned out that real women could not and would not actually be supermoms, the supermom was discredited as something we had allegedly aspired to but couldn't achieve, and thus we were supposed to go back to the kitchen. The supermom was imprisoned in the House of Maternal Corrections, and the battle between the mommy-track moms and the rebellious-sitcom moms raged. But once Murphy Brown, caricature of the hardened career woman, sang "You Make Me Feel Like a Natural Woman" to her newborn infant, we knew what direction the battle was taking.[7]

Now, before proceeding, let's just get a little reality check on how many working mothers *were* calling it quits. According to the Bureau of Labor Statistics, the proportion of women working, which had risen steadily for three decades, did stall slightly between 1989 and 1991, and then again in 1993. Aha, you say, see! Well, here are the details. Those figures were for *all* women. But guess which ones were not entering the labor force at their usual rapid rates? First, teenage girls. The economy stunk and there weren't as many jobs for them. Second, women between the ages of twenty and twenty-four, many of whom were staying in school longer before starting work. The vast majority of these young women did not have husbands or children. As the Bureau reported, "marital status or motherhood appears to have little to do with this decline." Or, to put it another way, "Women are not leaving the workforce to return to the lifestyles that prevailed more than thirty years ago." In fact, just the reverse was true. The so-called "traditional" family, in which the husband was the sole breadwinner, was *less* prevalent in 1992 than in 1987.[8] Nor was there a decline in dual-income families. What did increase—get this—

was the number of two-parent families in which the *father* was not working outside the home!

In 1989, Felice Schwartz published "Managerial Women and the New Facts of Life," which appeared in the January/February issue of the *Harvard Business Review*. With a title like that, you wouldn't expect the piece to take on the qualities of a Molotov cocktail. Schwartz, who had in 1962 founded Catalyst, an organization designed to promote women's entry into the workforce, very much saw herself as a feminist. She had consulted with corporations for years, and by the late 1980s felt that most companies did a very poor job of accommodating their female employees who were also mothers, often of small children, and needed more flexibility at and support from work than was currently available. So far, so good. But the article opened with the assertion that "The cost of employing women in management is greater than the cost of employing men," because women went on maternity leave and men didn't. (Schwartz never provided a numerical comparison of the actual cost of maternity leaves, versus, say, the cost of absenteeism due to alcohol or drug abuse, which affected a higher percentage of men than women, or the cost of supporting men who had had heart attacks, strokes, or other stress-related ailments that kept them out of work.) However, it was her proposal for how companies should deal differently with "career-primary" women versus "career-and-family" women that made Schwartz a pariah among many women. Companies should allow the latter type of woman to drop out of the fast track while their children are young so they could spend more time with their children. They could return to the fast track later.

The New York Times dubbed this "the mommy track," a term Schwartz herself never used, and the media frenzy was on. Feminists charged that the mommy track would encourage discrimination against women and ghettoize mothers into dead-end jobs. They asked why there wasn't a comparable "daddy track." Why did all women have to fit into one or the other category? What about women who were managing to do demanding jobs and raise their kids? Schwartz got a worse rap than she deserved because of media distortion of her key point—corporations were indeed rigid and clueless when it came to the needs of mothers. Her mistake, which she corrected in her subsequent book *Breaking With Tradition: Women and Work, the New Facts of Life,* was focusing on mothers instead of on parents, and on mothers instead of government failings and corporate workaholism. But before such mea culpas, in 1989, Schwartz did go on the network news claiming that women were willing to trade higher pay and promotion for flexible hours.[9] (Well, sure, some were. For others, them were fightin' words.)

As a result, her article and the way the media hammered home the term "mommy track," even when reporters did so critically, was a real setback for working mothers. The implication lingered that having a career and having small children were utterly incompatible. And the "mommy track" perpetuated the stereotype that child rearing was strictly a woman's responsibility. Worst of all—and again, Schwartz did not say this herself—was the suggestion that deep in their hearts, mothers with careers were finding it all too stressful and, if given a choice, would quit in a heartbeat. In fact, in his CBS story on the "mommy track," Richard Schlesinger claimed that companies often made it so difficult for managers who also become mothers that they'd rather quit.[10] (The fact that plenty of fathers found their jobs and bosses unbearable and wanted to quit too was not noted.) The "mommy track" became a news peg for the press, and examples of women leaving top jobs, however exceptional such stories were, circulated through *The New York Times*, *Fortune*, and the nightly news.

To cite just one of many of these mom-chucks-it-all-stories, NBC on August 28, 1993, reported that "many women are now experimenting with ways to spend more time at home with the children" such as sharing jobs or working at home. "Now an increasing number of women are deciding to take time out from their careers," intoned anchor Brian Williams, citing no back-up statistics, no figures on just exactly what "many" meant. The story, titled "Mom's Home," opened with a white female Ph.D. and teacher now staying home to raise her baby. "Like a lot of women" she had "bought into" the notion that you could do everything simultaneously. But now, noted reporter Wendy Rieger, "some women believe there's more to life than having a career." Rieger then cited a Yankelovich poll asking women if they would stay home if they could afford it, and reportedly 56 percent said they would, up from 38 percent who said that in 1989. Rieger noted that the stigma of staying at home was fading. "For years women were told they had to do it all, be supermom," she reported; "now the word is sequencing—you still do it all, but you do one thing at a time." In other words you work, then because you're a woman *you* stay home with the kids until they're in school, and then, poof, it's back to the office where a plum job allegedly awaits you.

Paving the way for the mommy track was the critically acclaimed, innovative, often addictive, and highly annoying show *thirtysomething*, which debuted in the fall of 1987 and targeted that recently identified market niche, the yuppie. After seeing pedophile priests, crack mothers, and unwed teen welfare mothers on the nightly news, we could, the same night, retreat into the secure, white haven of *thirtysomething* where children were treasured because the new momism had triumphed. In this show, a woman's place was in the home, but not because she was forced to be there, oh no: She had "freely" chosen to return because of women's moral obligations to children.[11] Set in Philadelphia, it followed the lives and loves of two couples, Hope and Michael (Mel Harris and Ken Olin) and Nancy and Elliot (Patricia Wettig and Timothy Busfield) and their single but ever-dating, ever-involved friends Melissa (Melanie Mayron), Gary (Peter Horton), and Ellyn (Polly Draper). *thirtysomething* was one of the few TV dramas that placed motherhood, fatherhood, and the dilemmas of raising kids at the center of the series. With its soft lighting and adorable blond children, the show simultaneously romanticized child rearing while also acknowledging how time consuming and stressful it was. Even the audio track was punctuated by the sounds of baby babbling and gibberish so you were reminded of the presence of children.

The show celebrated and reinforced the norms of intensive mothering at every turn. From the opening of the title sequence with its innocent and upbeat recorder-and-guitar theme song—in which Michael was lying on the floor, his wife, Hope, was lying on top of him, kissing him passionately, and then their baby came crawling up next to them and they smiled with delight—a happy, fulfilled marriage (that even still included sex!) was defined as one that must include kids and stay-at-home moms. The mothers were always attentive to their kids' needs, praising their art work, constantly getting them juice and ice cream. These moms got down on their hands and knees to play with their kids, they ran around the house with them, crawled under tables after them, sang "Teddy Bear's Picnic" to them during diaper changes. They were fun moms. In addition, Hope and Michael's friends seemed to come over regularly to play with Janey, change her diapers, put her to bed, and so forth. But just as the mothers exemplified intensified mothering, so did the fathers embody intensified fathering, and the show's story lines and female characters rebuked them when they failed to live up to this standard. Fathers regularly bathed the babies, watched them, read to them. As Melissa said to Michael, "You've done more for Janey in her first year than your father did for you your entire life."

The nobility of these mothers was what you wanted to emulate. It also made you want to throw paving stones at the TV. Let's take just one example. By 1988, Elliot had left Nancy. Their son, Ethan, who was about five or six, was having nightmares that monsters lived in his closet. Nancy reached out to him, offering to take him out for ice cream, for example, but because he was really pissed about his parents' separation, he kept rejecting her and her offers. At home he defied her authority by refusing to obey her orders to shut off the computer and go to bed. At one point we saw Nancy walk into his room, chastise him about the mess, start to say "you're getting just like . . ." and then stop herself from saying "like your father," because as a fair-minded and enlightened mother, she knew she was not supposed to dis Dad to the kids, even though she wanted to murder him. Moments like this were frequent throughout the series, fleeting vignettes straight out of the advice columns in *Parents* about how to perform the role of motherhood, as if you were a saint.

This particular episode was, indeed, like one big dramatized advice column from Dr. Lee Salk. Ethan wanted Nancy to tell him a story, but only the one Dad told him, "The Prince." She said she knew some stories of her own, but he told her to "forget it." So she left, and then he started imagining the monster in the closet. Nancy got Elliot to tell her the story, so she could tell it to Ethan. The next night, while he was playing on the computer and continuing to be insolent to her, she overlooked this behavior (no "time outs" ever in *thirtysomething*), and told him she now knew the story, but didn't think she knew all of it, and if he could help her out, "I would really appreciate that. Do you think that you could do that, maybe, help me out a little bit here?" As a savvy mother, then, instead of beating him with a plank for being a little jerk, she sought to empower him by putting herself in the supplicant's position and him in the position of the one with knowledge and power. And she used the qualifying language of women—"Do you think," "maybe," and "a little bit," to further minimize the impression that she was trying to get him to do something he didn't want to do.

He refused to respond. So she persisted by telling what she knew of the story, while he continued to bang away on the computer keyboard making explosion sounds with his mouth. (Imagine Roseanne or Clair Huxtable putting up with this!) She then said she knew that something was missing in the kingdom and the prince had to look for it, but she didn't know what was missing. He still refused to talk to her. She guessed that what was missing was a rose, the most beautiful rose in the land, and he responded in the snottiest tone possible, "It was not." Okay, so not a rose, then she went for something really ridiculous—"magic broccoli," because as a savvy mom who had read every book on child psychology ever published, she knew this would really get a rise out of him, which it did. "Oh, please," he snarled in derision. "So, come on Ethan, help me out, what was it?" "You're so dumb," he replied, "it was the sun."

See, it was worth it to be ignored, demeaned, and insulted by a six-year-old to get the information out of him that she wanted and to move him along in a conversation with her. "Oh, the sun," she smiled with joy. Later, at bedtime, she asked him if he wanted to do more of the story, and he snapped, "No." But then he added, in a tone of voice Tony Soprano might use to order a hit on someone, "Maybe tomorrow." She smiled with delight because she knew her strategy—her mom-as-therapist, psychologically shrewd, I'm-willing-to-eat-shit-to-help-my-son-through-this-crisis parenting approach—was working. The next night, Ethan actually called for her when he was afraid of the monster in the closet and she reassured him there was no one in there. Then she started telling him the story, and he started helping her with the details. So she was stepping into the dad's role and clearly doing it as well or better than he. Ethan fell peacefully asleep. Her sensitive, caring, perceptive strategy had worked perfectly. The next day he was joking around with her and we saw them chasing each other around the house. Then they started drawing a picture together. She was able to drop everything to fully engage with her child. She then suggested that they make a book together out of the drawings. "Would you like that?" He nodded. "Me too," she says.

The next night (sorry, it really went on like this), when Ethan had seen his Dad with another woman and had freaked out, Nancy went to see if he wanted to talk about things. He didn't. So again, in her best child-psychologist mode, she realized that he could probably best deal with his fears and anger by forging ahead on the story. He saw the monster in his mind's eye and started screaming. She hugged him and told him to look straight at the monster. Then, in the story, as the monster approached, the prince (Ethan) looked at the monster and said he was not afraid of him. The monster was crestfallen and walked away, but then asked for help with an injury, and the two became friends. Thus the story ended, and we knew that Nancy had helped Ethan conquer his fears. As she was tucking him in, he now asked her to tell him another story—a big turnaround from just the other day when he told her how dumb she was.

Now, here's the best part—the real test of maternal nobility. It turns out that Elliot, who still clearly had unfettered access to the house, had sneaked up the stairs and peeked inside the room, but lurked just outside it, where Nancy couldn't know that he was there. Ethan asked to hear the story about the day he was born. Here the mother had to tell a story that involved the dad, whom she wanted to run over with a tractor, and who was now spying on her. How would she behave? What might she say about him to her kid, not knowing he was there? This was the ultimate trial of her fairness, of her ability to rise above her own furies and sadness for the sake of the kids, putting their emotions before her own. She said that she really wanted a boy, and that when he came out of her tummy she was so happy.

"You changed it," chided Ethan. Yes, she admitted with regret, and the camera cut to Elliot listening outside, also with regret. She then got back in bed with him and retold it the way she had when she and Elliot were still together. "We wanted a boy," she began, emphasizing the we, "and every night your daddy would lean down and say to my tummy, 'I love the baby.' " Then she said how happy "we were" when Ethan was born, and then Daddy leaned down and said "I love the baby," and she said that Ethan smiled because he had heard it so many times before, in utero. She had preserved the loving image of the dad for the child. She had not said that Dad was a jackass. The soft lighting, the slow, melodic, Segovia-on-Quaaludes acoustic guitar melody in the background, all drove home how successfully she had reestablished the house—rent by separation—as a haven nonetheless.

She left the room to discover Elliot sitting there. He knew she had been selfless in recalling their past unity, and she knew that he knew. Downstairs, she reassured him that he was a good father, which was crucial to him. Having been put under surveillance by her husband, she was now put under surveillance by her son. Ethan had snuck out of his bed to overhear his mom's generous reassurance to his dad, and their friendly parting. The final shot of the episode was of Ethan, lying in his bed smiling. For that was the most important character here, the person whose happiness counted most—not Nancy, not Elliot, but Ethan.

Hope was, to many, the most irritating character on the show; she nearly had a nervous breakdown after Janey stopped nursing, she was so bereft by the loss. She had quit her job to be a stay-at-home mom (Nancy was a stay-at-home mom too) and was what some shrinks in the 1950s might have called "overidentified" with the baby. In one 1988 episode, Hope and Michael were going to go away for a long weekend without the baby, and left her with Nancy. This was clearly very, very hard for Hope, who, as she walked to the car, looked like her right arm had been ripped off. She then moped at their gorgeous seaside hotel, pining for Janey, instead of soaking in the hotel hot tub or heading to the bar like a normal person.

By the next season, Hope was working part-time as a researcher/writer, but she was also thinking about having another child. In what came to be a classic narrative pattern for the show, someone would lay out the perils of domesticity and motherhood for women, only to have those trumped by what presumably were the irresistible undertows of child rearing. In this episode, Michael tried to have sex with Hope before she could grab her diaphragm, but Hope told Michael that it was a hard time for her to get pregnant again. "Do you know how good it feels to be back at work, to feel like I'm contributing?" They fought on about whether she should get pregnant again. "You know, you hang around with two-year-olds long enough, you start to feel like a two-year-old . . . You lose your confidence and your competence," Hope charged. But you know she's going to give in. So, what made her change her mind?

To think that so many of us bought this story line credulously, with tears in our eyes, is pretty embarrassing. Hope had found the diary of a woman who had lived in the house during World War II and had become pregnant when her husband came home on leave. He was then listed as missing in action, and she lost the baby. He finally returned home, and the diary stopped. So here's what did it. Hope hallucinated going back in time and meeting the woman before she moved out of the house. In this daydream (or whatever), Hope "learns" that the woman was pregnant again. Hope took this to be a sign that she should cast aside doubts based on rationality and agreed to get pregnant again too. About two episodes later she was.

It was a given that women who didn't have children lusted after them with all their hearts. In a 1988 episode about "baby lust," Melissa, Michael's single cousin, took Nancy clothes shopping, and stared enviously at the pregnant sales clerk, a mother kissing her baby and toddler, and another mother chasing after her toddler in the store. Anyone who has tried to go shopping for herself with a toddler in tow knows that it's easier to herd snakes on a bed of petroleum jelly. There is never *any* reason to envy a mother shopping with a small child. But here, through Melissa's eyes, it looked to be the most transcendent activity possible.

Over and over, the show staged a point-counterpoint between the new momism and some version of a feminist worldview. Melissa knew she wanted kids, but Ellyn asked why kids were necessary to a good relationship. She pointed out that Michael was a good father, but "Hope is home with Janey and the dirty laundry, he's out working with the grown-ups, it might as well be 1956 again. . . . Hope's the one with the baby puke in her hair," and some women in the audience might have been saying "right on." But Melissa countered with the Truth: "Have you ever seen the way that Janey looks at Hope? Hope walks in a room and Janey's whole body comes alive, Hope's too. It's like there's an electrical current running between them . . . they're like a little universe all to themselves. Can you imagine being that close to someone?" Ellyn insisted, correctly, "It's not always like that." For Ellyn, giving herself over to something like that was scary. Melissa retorted, "What scares me is missing out on loving that much. On being loved that much." Q.E.D.

While fathers weren't quite as kid-centric as the moms, they nonetheless personified the new ideals of fatherhood seen way more often in TV shows and movies than in real life. Here's a classic example that we were actually supposed to believe. Elliot, still mourning his separation from Nancy and his kids, was in the office with Michael, and asked what time it was. Michael responded, "One-fifteen." With a faraway look in his eye, Elliot answered, "One-fifteen; Ethan's just getting out of gym class—dodgeball." Elliot was such a psychically involved father that he had memorized his son's school schedule and the specific activities for each day. Now if all fathers in America were stopped dead in their tracks and asked, "It's 1:15: What's your kid doing in school right now?" what percentage would you bet could answer correctly? More to the point, what percentage of mothers could do that? Talk about upping the ante on the extent to which we were all supposed to internalize our kids' entire lives.

Fortunately for all of us, there were antidotes to this: *Married With Children* (1987 premiere) and *Roseanne* (1988 premiere), the former possibly paving the way for the latter, *The Simpsons* (1989 premiere) and *Grace*

Under Fire (1993 premiere). All reveled in a much more transgressive version of motherhood. In the TV mommy wars, these shows sized up the new momism and said, "Give me a break." Taking deliberate aim at *Father Knows Best* et al. (and the often staid networks that had produced them), *Married With Children* brought us an appalling TV family that violated every sitcom norm, not to mention those of the Christian Coalition. Airing on the fledgling network FOX, which got its start by targeting young, urban (and also African American) audiences, the show reflected the cynical sensibilities of those who felt the older networks' idealized nuclear families had been little more than bourgeois propaganda. *Married With Children* was an instant hit for FOX, despite efforts by a small group of offended viewers to boycott the show and its sponsors.

The father, Al Bundy, was an unsuccessful and physically unappetizing—some might say revolting—shoe salesman held in contempt by his wife and kids. His wife, Peg, was probably the best antimother ever to appear on TV: Her décolletage, skin-tight pedal pushers, and sky-high teased red hair suggested "hooker," she openly lusted after other men, she couldn't cook (and usually refused to), never shopped for food for the family, neither worked outside the home nor ever did housework, smoked cigarettes, and lived for trash TV like *Wheel of Fortune,* which she watched while eating bonbons. She lived on the sofa. When Al came home and asked, "Anything for dinner?" Peg sneered "Get a wife," or, in response to "Any food?" answered, "Yeah, there's a six-pack in the fridge." When she did cook, her cigarette ashes—or the butt itself—fell freely into the food. Peg openly ridiculed her husband's lack of sex appeal. The children, Kelly and Bud, fought constantly, and unlike the good daughters of TV yesteryear, Kelly was a stereotypical dumb blonde, an avid sexpot who walked around in black leather bustiers and micro-mini skirts and was thicker than a stump. (She was, for example, unable to comprehend the directions for making Jell-O.) When Peg wanted to get rid of the kids, she snapped, "Go away—dinner will be in two weeks." Family dialogue consisted of serial insults, and sex (or lack thereof) was a central topic of conversation, including among the kids. Peg and Al forgot their own kids' birthdays. There was nothing even closely resembling the milk of human kindness in this family: Everyone was out for him- or herself.

And then, of course, there were *The Simpsons* (1989), possibly the greatest antidote to *Father Knows Best* (not to mention Pat Robertson) ever aired. The word "subversive" has been used repeatedly to describe the show, and with good reason. *The Simpsons* was a weekly send-up of the delusions put forward by the family-values crowd: that small-town life is wholesome, that work is rewarding, that the nuclear family is the embodiment of Christian values, that the "typical" family is an oasis of love and support, that children are little angels who are a joy to raise, and, of course, that Father—in this case the utterly hapless Homer—indeed knows best and thus should be deferred to at all times. Marge Simpson, the mother with the blue beehive the size of the Chrysler Building, didn't so much attack intensive mothering as she ignored it. She and the kids ate TV dinners while lying in the living room watching violent cartoons; in one episode she paid scant attention as the baby Maggie wandered into the woods and was abducted by a grizzly bear. Marge was a caring, usually stay-at-home mother whose son, Bart, was nonetheless a smart-mouthed, belching juvenile delinquent. One early episode, "There's No Disgrace Like Home," simply said "oh please" to the mythically perfect family. The Simpsons had to go to the annual picnic held by Homer's contemptible skinflint boss, Mr. Burns, who scrutinized his employees to see if they exemplified the "family unity" he demanded of his workers. Marge quickly ran into another mother of a baby who suggested they dump the kids in the nursery and go get some punch. When Marge asked, "Should we leave the kids unsupervised?" the other mother said, "Oh, yeah," and turned on the TV set. They then proceeded to a rather large bowl of highly spiked punch, which Marge drank increasing amounts of as she listened to some insufferable mother brag about her perfect kids. In short order, Marge was plastered.

As they left the picnic, Homer became dejected over the contrast between his family and the supposedly ideal ones all around him. As Bart and his sister Lisa fought over who would get into the car first, and as Marge nearly barfed out the car window, Homer saw the children at the next car say "After you," "Oh, no, after you," as they got into the backseat. The family drove off happily singing "Bingo"; a shot inside the car showed them all sporting angels' wings and halos, and then a huge shaft of sunlight—the hand of God—shone on their car. When Homer moaned, "Sometimes I think we're the worst family in town," Marge suggested, "Maybe we should move to a larger community." "The sad truth," offered the ever-precocious Lisa, "is that all families are like us." When they sneak around town to spy on other families and see them all eating together at a dinner table (with napkins, no less) or "having a conversation—they actually enjoy talking to each other," Bart concludes, "these people are obviously freaks."

The Simpsons provided (and still does) scathing social satire about the lies many of us want to believe—or feel are shoved down our throats—about the family. Married With Children was meant to be total farce, a giant, rude raspberry to the notion of "family values." No moral messages at all were embedded in the show, and it was not meant to be an argument for including different kinds of families and mothers on America's media screens. Roseanne was different. Becoming famous for her deadpan "domestic goddess" stand-up routine in which she proclaimed "if the kids are alive by 5:00, I've done my job," Roseanne topped the TV ratings charts in 1988 when her sitcom Roseanne premiered. It was the biggest new hit of the late 1980s, and was either number one or among the top four shows in the Nielsen ratings from 1988 to 1994.[12] After the sanctimonious saccharine of thirtysomething, how delicious to have a TV mom who ate too much, was stuck in the kind of crappy jobs most women got relegated to, and said to her kid, when asked why she was so mean, "'Cause I hate kids . . . and I'm not your real mom." The difference between Roseanne and Married With Children was that Roseanne explicitly sought to give representation to working-class families and, thus, made claims for being "authentic," which Married With Children never did. Roseanne also meant to give legitimacy to a more ambivalent, frank, even jaundiced portrayal of motherhood and, thus, to offer women a different kind of permissible role model. Married With Children in many ways reaffirmed the virtues of a more selfless motherhood by showing the unspeakable consequences of refusing the self-abnegation of the new momism. The show's humor depended on viewers recognizing two equally ridiculous alternatives: Mom can devote her every waking moment to the cultivation of her children's psyche, or she can totally ignore them and, instead, just lie on the couch eating candy.

Roseanne offered the latest TV version of the unruly woman, a type brought to perfection by Lucille Ball and reworked on shows like Maude. But unlike Lucy, who mainly wanted to break out of the home into the vibrant challenges of the larger male world, Roseanne attacked sexism by name and the suffocating, hypocritical norms surrounding the new momism straight on. "Good" mothers, in the media, were endlessly supportive of their kids, never yelled, endured their kids' misbehavior with adoring bemusement, never put their kids down, didn't ever put themselves before their kids, were slim and trim, and mostly provided support from the background, from the wings, so their kids could take center stage. Roseanne, by contrast, took up as much space as she wanted without apology, she cackled, yelled, and delighted in the insults she hurled at her kids, and, unlike the mother in most other family sitcoms, she appeared often in the workplace as an actual working mother.[13] At home she was Everywoman exposed, but without an iota of shame or embarrassment: rollers in her hair, bitchy from PMS, content to serve her kids bologna sandwiches for dinner, unmoved by her kids' whining and griping, indifferent to the rules of etiquette. As Roseanne told one interviewer, she especially wanted to challenge TV shows in which what we saw was "a male point of view coming out of women's mouths."[14] To another she said, "I was so damned sick of all the bullshit portrayals of women and mothers in sitcoms. They were either too passive or always absent in the lives of the family. The truth is, the mother is the center of the family."[15]

Some episodes deliberately pitted the messy, rollicking, loud, smart-mouthed, Cheese-Doodled Conner household against the supposed ideal, which was shown to be overly restrained, judgmental, and just plain fake. For example, new neighbors moved in next door from Chicago, and their son befriended D.J. When the mom—blond, slim, and perfectly coiffed—came to look for him, she walked in on Dan emitting a belch that would have shaken a Sequoia. Roseanne invited her in, but she refused. Then she sneezed—little, squeaky, thwarted sneezes, like something out of a squeeze toy, and told Roseanne she was allergic to dust as she surveyed the living room. When she left, Roseanne quipped that she was so uptight, "you couldn't drag a needle out of her butt with a tractor."

Her son Todd and D.J. returned home from a bike ride; they had gone to a construction site, which Roseanne had explicitly told D.J. not to do. When Todd went home with a cut arm, the uptight mom, Cathy, came over to reprimand Roseanne for not keeping an eye on the kids. The exchange was a classic battle over the expectations of the new momism. "You allow your son to just leave whenever he wants?" she yelled. "Yeah, I encourage it," she shot back. Cathy said she always asked her son where he was going, and if the place sounded dangerous she said no. Roseanne responded, "Well, you're finally coming over here, but it's to tell me that you're a better mom than I am." Cathy said she always knew where her son was. "Well, I have three kids and a job and I can't be everywhere, so I've gotta trust my kids and they're still alive so I've obviously done something right." "So now you're a better mother because you have more children?" asked Cathy in disbelief. "Yes," answered Roseanne instantly, "Yes, I have three, you only have one, three to one, I win, get it?" (Here the audience erupted into laughter and applause.) "You probably still sneak into Todd's room to check if he's breathing," Roseanne charged. "Yes," gasped Cathy. "Amateur," Roseanne shot back. They agreed that the boys couldn't see each other. As Cathy left, Roseanne yelled, "You think you're too damn good to live next door to me. Well, you're not. You're just some stressed-out, overprotective snob who paid way too much for her house." (Here the audience applauded and hooted approvingly again.)

But D.J., of course, missed Todd, so Dan asked Roseanne to go apologize to Cathy "for the good of the kids." "Oh, cut the telethon crap, Dan," Roseanne sniped, again a swipe at the phony, smarmy way people exploit the vulnerability of kids for their own ends. But Roseanne did have to apologize to Cathy, who refused to concede anything and made Roseanne admit that she was wrong, which Roseanne indeed did do, for the sake of her son. The episode explicitly staged a battle between the new ideal of intensive, overprotective mothering versus the necessarily more laissez-faire style of working mothers, especially lower-income working mothers, and argued that the latter approach was superior because it helped your kids become more self-reliant. And it was the working-class mom who had the heart here, who, despite her wisecracks, cared enough about her kid to eat crow so he could be reunited with his friend. In *Roseanne*, the new momism was portrayed as overly obsessive, snooty, and piously judgmental of the mothers who, especially because of class position, could not or would not conform.

Of course the audience loved Roseanne's attack on the sanctimonious bourgeois mom and all that she embodied—it was cathartic. In real life, everyone knew that because mothers, especially working mothers, were under such relentless surveillance, it was Cathy who would indeed be deemed the "good" mom, and Roseanne the one who would be seen as too blasé for her kids' own good. Although *Roseanne* was meant to be more realistic than other sitcoms, it was actually a utopian show, providing a little oasis where mothers could rebel against the suffocating ideal of the "perfect mom," an ideal that dogged them day in and day out.

Roseanne provided an opening for *Grace Under Fire* (1993), starring the equally mouthy comedian Brett Butler. *Grace* pushed the envelope on TV motherhood even further: She was the single mother of three whose ex—"my knuckle-dragging, cousin-loving, beer-sucking redneck husband"—had physically abused her. She worked in an oil refinery with a slew of unreconstructed male chauvinists whose missing-link attitudes toward women provided Brett—ironically named Grace Kelly in the show—with the opportunity for withering feminist ripostes. Her house was distinctly down-market and often a mess, and her life chaotic, but the show took on the stereotype that single mothers were inadequate mothers and instead dramatized how women and their kids might be a hell of a lot better off without a plastered, abusive man in the house.

Female characters who are too fat, too loud, too outspoken, too sexual, too self-centered—especially if they are mothers—have usually been the source of revulsion in popular culture, and have often been punished by the end of the story. But precisely because they are so defiant, they also help undermine the existing order of things. They give real-life women permission to speak the truth, to talk back. The mothers of *Married With Children* and *Roseanne,* despite their differences, conveyed the pleasures of thumbing your nose at the new momism, if only vicariously and for half an hour. Here was an alternative—however remote—to the obsessive, guilt- and competition-driven maternal regimen mothers felt compelled to follow. These TV mothers were outliers who refused to parrot the line that being a mother was an endlessly renewing, transcendent, ever-joyful experience that trumped everything else all the time.

Yet however much people enjoyed *Roseanne* the show, Roseanne the person, the one who sang "The Star-Spangled Banner" off-key and then grabbed her crotch à la Madonna, or claimed to be an incest victim, or moved rapidly in and out of several marriages, made many uneasy. The tabloids, and even the mainstream press, routinely vilified the "real" Roseanne for her excesses. Strong women on TV—and Brett Butler faced similar negative coverage of her personal problems—are especially likely to be eaten alive in the press. The "real" Roseanne was not someone most mothers wanted to emulate, however much they cheered her sassy comebacks on her show. In fact, the tabloids and the news media so horrified by the "real" Roseanne conveyed this message: You can inhabit the sassy, defiant persona of Roseanne while you watch the show, but you had better take it off and put it away once the credits roll.

In other words, mothers who identified with the character Roseanne's acerbic—and feminist—point of view about motherhood had to domesticate that fury in real life, because stacked against *Roseanne* was the avalanche of other media fare reaffirming the nobility of the *thirtysomething* take on being a "mom." Not surprisingly, subsequent TV shows, like the enormously successful *Home Improvement,* offered a tamed, hybrid mom, one who was toned and pretty and was rarely seen working outside the home (even if she did) but who got to hurl sarcastic zingers at her husband and kids.

Premiering in 1991, *Home Improvement* instantly became one of the top-rated shows of the early and mid-1990s. Tim Taylor (Tim Allen) was the host of a home fix-it cable show called *Tool Time,* and thus believed himself to be superior to his wife, Jill (Patricia Richardson), in most things domestic (except, of course, for cooking, laundry, and toilet scrubbing) because he wore a big, swinging tool belt around his pelvis, knew how things worked and how to fix them, and she didn't. Every week, she disabused him of this notion. Some of her lines were straight out of Roseanne, as when Tim wondered about his son, "Where did I go wrong with him?" and Jill shot back, "Don't worry about it—he's not yours." But the show was a postfeminist compromise, an indicator of how the war between the mommy-track mom and the rebellious mom would be resolved in the media by the mid- to late 1990s. Dad, however ridiculous at times, was the center of the show. Relationships with the kids were peripheral to most of the situations, and Mom's power was channeled through, and restricted to, one-liners designed to keep Dad from thinking he knew best. Nor, except for insisting that the kids do their homework, did the show offer many normative messages for how to be a mom, or critiques of how others thought we should be as mothers. It was in dramatic shows, and especially made-for-TV movies, where morality tales about what it took to be a good mother got acted out.

By the early and mid-1990s, fueled by news stories about custody battles between biological and adoptive parents, about surrogacy, about women stalked by husbands and boyfriends, and of course by the cascade of stories about children being abused, kidnapped, and the like, a new movie genre emerged on TV: women-in-jep films (short for jeopardy), also known as fem-jep. Designed for women who did not want to watch semi-armored beefalos butting into each other on ABC's *Monday Night Football,* these movies migrated effortlessly from NBC and CBS to Lifetime in the late 1990s. So you'd know right off that women or their kids were in for trouble, these made-for-TV movies had titles like *Fatal Vows, One*

Woman's Courage, With Harmful Intent, Because Mommy Works, When He Didn't Come Home, Someone Is Watching, and *The Other Mother: A Moment of Truth.* Although there may have been some that starred women of color, we didn't find any. These were about the dangers awaiting white, middle-class mothers.

The plots of the jep movies—invariably "based on actual events" to give them gravitas—went something like this. A single mother was courted by a handsome, charming man who seemed also to dote on her kid, so she married him. He then turned out to be a murdering mobster who controlled her life and scalded her kid's hands in boiling water as a threat against her ever ratting him out. Or a single mother and her child moved into a new house, only to be stalked and terrorized by a crazy person. Or a mother of older kids (this was/is Patty Duke's specialty) discovered that one was missing and when the police proved to be utterly indifferent to the crime and inept at solving it, she had to do it herself. Or the single mother of kids must confront a newly rematerialized biological mother who deserted the kids years ago but now wanted them back. Or the single mother of kids decided to search out the child she gave up for adoption years before. You get the idea.

It's easy to make fun of these made-for-TV movies, as *Saturday Night Live* regularly has, because they were, and are, so formulaic and often shlocky. They also often staged the "mommy wars" by having different kinds of mothers compete over the same children, with the audience put in the position of rooting for one or the other. But these movies did acknowledge that mothers lived in a society routinely insensitive to their needs and that it often took heroic efforts for them to protect their kids. Patriarchy in these films was personified by men who were either indifferent to the needs of women and children or out-and-out dangerous. You could always tell who these bad men were because they smoked cigarettes. But there were good men too, the nurturing, thoughtful ones who had been changed for the better by feminism, and they undercut the notion that patriarchy was a systemic problem for mothers.

Nonetheless, it was the male-dominated institutions that supposedly protected kids—the police, especially, but also hospitals and the entire medical profession—that repeatedly came off as worthless in these movies, and required mothers to take matters into their own hands. Drawing from news stories that repeatedly portrayed state licensing agencies, the child welfare system, and the courts as inept when it came to protecting kids, the plots of these films featured cops and other male authority figures who refused to believe a mother when she reported a child in danger. In the classically titled *Fatal Vows: The Alexandra O'Hara Story* (1994), a mother had her son taken away by social services because she failed to protect him against his abusive stepfather (the mobster who burned the boy's hands with scalding water). She had tried to get help from the cops but they wouldn't believe her. In the end, after conducting her own investigation, suffering various forms of abuse (including poisoning), and agreeing to wear a wire, she did more than the cops to put him behind bars so that she could get her son back. In *Race Against Time: The Search for Sarah* (1996), Patty Duke's daughter, in her early twenties, went missing. (Your kids are never safe; you can never stop worrying.) The cops refused to believe that Sarah had been hurt or kidnapped, and suspected she had just gone off with friends for a while and would turn up. But Mom always got "these feelings," like ESP, when anything went wrong with her kids, and she had that feeling now. So she and her family posted missing-person signs everywhere, questioned people and followed up clues, and continued to badger the cops, who told the mom she was being too aggressive. In the end, the family found Sarah just in time, forcing the cops to apologize for not believing them: "You did it," admitted one cop, "you stuck together and you did it." While women and their kids were vulnerable and victimized during, say, seven-eighths of the film, in the end it was women's perseverance, complete dedication to their kids, defiance of men in authority, and fearlessness that saved their children. The movies dramatized the same story mothers saw on the nightly news: They had to do it alone.

Of course, mothers were pitted against each other. Unlike most sitcoms (and much more in line with *thirtysomething*), these movies showed us what distinguished a good mother from a bad one. Good mothers rough-housed with their kids, they tickled them, marched in indoor parades with them, took them to the zoo, handmade their kids' Halloween costumes, and joked around with them, asking if they wanted a "monster brain sandwich" in their lunchbox.[16] Good mothers were always in a good mood and ready to play. Good mothers never bad-mouthed their ex-husbands in front of the kids, no matter how despicable these cads were. Bad mothers wore fancy business suits (red ones were a dead giveaway of evil), carried briefcases, and put too much pressure on their kids to excel at school. Bad mothers kept a messy house. Bad mothers resorted to store-bought Halloween costumes. Bad mothers did not listen to their kids, yelled at them, and were not adequately empathetic. Bad mothers were status-conscious and only concerned about appearances; bad mothers were too materialistic. Bad mothers got home too late and didn't have dinner on the table in time. If the director wanted you to know right away that a woman was a bad mother, he (and yes, directors of women-in-jep films were almost entirely men) had her—you guessed it—smoking cigarettes. When biological mothers vied with adoptive mothers who had actually raised the kids, the movies came down on the side of the adoptive mothers, because in these movies emotional investment trumped genetics.

One of the better women-in jep films was a real tearjerker (and blood pressure raiser), *Because Mommy Works,* which aired in November of 1994 just after the nation learned that Susan Smith had killed her kids. Motherhood, good and bad, was on people's minds. The movie was especially distressing because it was based on actual custody battles in which working mothers had lost custody of their kids to husbands who had remarried stay-at-home moms. Abby (Anne Archer) was a divorced mother and nurse raising her six-year-old son, Willie. We saw her smiling face in the morning as she stuffed celery sticks with peanut butter for his lunch, hugged and kissed her son, strapped him into his seat belt and took him to school: no doubt about it, stellar mom. But Ted, the dad (yes, he smoked), decided to move back to town because "he misses being a daddy," as the saintly Abby told Willie. (Ted had been gone for three years, and Abby did not wonder out loud in front of Willie why the lout had not "missed being a daddy" then.) It turned out, of course, that Ted had gotten remarried to Claire, a stay-at-home mom. You know how this came out. Pretty soon Claire was hand-making Willie's Halloween costume and preparing his lunch for school. At first Ted wanted joint custody but in the end got full custody because he was able to demonstrate in court that Abby's job as a nurse interfered with her motherly duties. "How could a nurse who takes care of sick people be too busy to take care of her own son when he's sick?" was just one of the increasingly surly questions her ex-husband asked when she needed him to cover for her while she went to work.

The movie came down squarely in favor of the working mom, in part by showing that the supposedly perfect stay-at-home mom's kids were mean-spirited, spoiled brats. In an updated version of the wicked stepmother, the movie showed the stay-at-home mom allying herself with the father (i.e., with patriarchal prejudices against working mothers) and against Abby: Claire supported the heartless removal of Willie from his own mother's house and care. Willie hated it at his dad's and missed his mom. Yet he was able to parrot the line working mothers dread hearing, "Daddy says you care more about your job than you do me. Daddy says if you really loved me, you'd stay home with me." So Dad was willing to bad-mouth mom in front of Willie, which the noble Abby refused to do right to the end, even when she was packing Willie off to move in with his dad and stepmom for good. The movie ended with the announcement that "many" divorced, working mothers were losing custody because they work. While the "many" was misleading—mothers still got custody most of the time—the movie sought to portray the human costs of the Neanderthal notion that working mothers were bad mothers. But it also threw more fuel on the "mommy wars" by dramatizing that working mothers were under real attack from stay-at-home moms, who wouldn't stop at guilt tripping them, but would actually take their kids away from them.

Just over a year later, in March 1995, Marcia Clark, one of the prosecutors in the O. J. Simpson case, saw her personal life dragged before millions when she had to request a scheduling change because of childcare pressures. Please note that no male in high-profile cases has been subjected to such an invasion of privacy or to scrutiny about parental performance. Was Marcia Clark a good mother? Her estranged husband, who was threatening to sue for custody, said no, because she was now working too much.[17] While the news coverage was mostly sympathetic to Clark, it also pitted work against motherhood as a choice individual mothers had to make. Working long hours was not acceptable for mothers, ever, end of story.

At the same time that the news media were hyping the mommy track and suggesting that once women had spent some time in an office they realized how gratifying it was to make Jell-O "Fun Shapes," a new magazine appeared on the newsstands in 1991: *Martha Stewart Living*. Bashing Martha, which had already begun through tell-all biographies like *Martha Inc.* (in which we learned that Martha allegedly once called her husband "fucking stupid" in front of company because he stacked the firewood improperly), *Saturday Night Live* skits, and parodies of *Living*, reached new levels with the ImClone insider-trading charges in 2002. We, ourselves, freely admit to finding Ms. Stewart and her raise-your-own-purebred-chickens, hand-print-your-own-toilet-paper version of domesticity to be its own best parody. But she didn't build an empire on grumps like us—millions of women found her promise of domestic control and serenity quite compelling. Why? What was Stewart offering mothers at this moment?

From the beginning, Stewart brought uptown sensibilities to the downtown crowd, suggesting that if we just had voile antimacassars and shams made out of cotton from the south of Portugal, we would automatically be mistaken for the moneyed classes. The lifestyle you could create by studying *Living* was a cross between the dressed-down New England of Louisa May Alcott and the dressed-up New York of Henry James. Grafted onto this, improbably, was the can-do spirit of the pioneer women who made bread out of birch-bark flour and, presumably, backyard gazebos out of sod.

On one page of *Living* an eclectic array of jars filled with fresh-picked-huckleberry preserves cools on a "distressed" kitchen windowsill, while a ceramic bowl of celadon-hued eggs and the lingering feather from the underside of a broody hen suggest a recent trip to the chicken coop. A mound of plump, dewy English peas atop a plank kitchen table await shelling. Soft breezes blow through the curtains like a little puff from Mother Nature herself. The next page features the results of various techniques of wall marbleizing, a look heretofore accessible only to those who, in 1906, escaped the heat of their townhouses on Washington Square for the seaside gardens of their "summer cottages" in Newport. But with Martha there is a big difference. To be a true domestic goddess, you can't buy all these things, you have to make them yourself, no matter how busy or rich you are. (Of course you do have to buy some antiqued pie plates or poached egg trimmers from Martha herself.) So even wealthy women cannot escape the do-it-yourself edict of Martha's version of the new momism. *You* are the one who has to marbleize the bedroom walls and weed the Japanese lactiflora.

Stewart first made a splash with her 1982 book *Entertaining*. In 1991, *Living* appeared and reached a circulation of more than two million. The TV version of *Living* went on the air in 1993, first as a weekly show and then, in 1997, as a daily show with a weekend edition as well. Prior to *Martha Stewart Kids* there was *Martha Stewart Wedding, Martha Stewart Baby*. Then Martha Stewart at Kmart. Martha, Martha, Martha.

Feminists, in their appraisal of the plight of the housewife, criticized the fact that her work was never-ending, crucial to family maintenance, yet terribly undervalued, both financially and ideologically, because people thought anyone could wash a floor or do the laundry. Magazine articles in the 1970s about juggling work and family, even in those women's magazines most dedicated to domestic order, suggested that the first thing to slide should be housework. By the late 1970s and early 1980s, many mothers, especially those who worked outside the home, were indeed telling these magazines that they delegated more housework to the kids, to their husbands (who couldn't see dirt, so this was a problem), and felt it was necessary—and fine—to abandon the Swiss-operating-room standard of cleanliness. Some even used their newfound wages to hire someone else—who would actually earn money to mop the floor—to help clean the house.

Stewart intervened here in ways that were simultaneously feminist and antifeminist. On the one hand, she insisted that domestic work was not just necessary drudgery any drone could slog through. She elevated the value of domestic work: It was an art form, a set of craft skills. It took time, knowledge, care, talent, and, especially, management skills. The woman who managed her home was not a drudge. She combined the abilities of a chef, a maître d', an interior decorator, an art teacher, a seamstress, a handyman, a sommelier, a set designer and, at times, a farmer. Stewart, in other words, reclaimed domestic work as a set of tasks combining a "womanly" touch with masculine, careerist abilities. This work was hard, time consuming, creative, and required discipline. She also retrieved "arts and crafts" from the garishly colored, kitschy, crocheted-toilet-paper-cover offerings of, say, Family Circle in 1972. The things you made with Martha were classy, sophisticated items out of the Rhode Island School of Design, not from a recent cub-scout meeting. A central part of Stewart's unspoken message was that just because women have traditionally been the ones to tend to the home, that was no reason whatsoever to devalue that labor. On the contrary, Martha sought to rescue domestic work from sexist dismissals of it, and to elevate it to a profession.

On the other hand, of course, in the process of doing this, Stewart also contributed to a backlash against working women (even though she was one of the most successful ones in the country) because she reasserted domesticity as central to women's lives and identities. This was a proactive domesticity, one that appealed to those women who were discovering that the workplace was not accommodating itself to the realities of family life. Just when we had seen the last of those obnoxious "ring around the collar" ads from Wisk (in which *his* dirty rings were somehow *her* fault), just when we had figured out how to avoid ironing altogether, just when we decided we could live without curtains (not to mention "window treat-ments"), in came Martha. Though Martha offered the home as more of a haven and less of a trap than the suburban nightmare of the 1950s, she opened a new arena of domestic competition. Sure, some women might decide to follow Martha to the chicken coop, but most couldn't, whether they wanted to or not. Nonetheless, it simply was no longer good enough to have a house and kids that would not be condemned by the board of health. Now flowers needed to accent every corner, chairs needed to be ac-cessorized with chenille throws, and you and your children needed to make Faberge eggs for that Easter-egg hunt, sew your own Christmas tree garlands out of pomegranate seeds and gold dust, and shape napkins into Pilgrim hats for Thanksgiving dinner.

Yet the vision of the home conveyed in *Living,* and then in all the imi-tative catalogues from Pottery Barn, Crate and Barrel, and even L. L. Bean (which should have stuck with mukluks), suggested that there was some-thing Zen about folding sheets, arranging the flowers just so, making your own envelopes with your children.[18] Your home—peaceful, protected refuge, a temple—was a place where domestic drudgery morphed into a Buddhist ritual of self-actualization. This was your place, under your command, no one else could override you or undermine you. Unlike the workplace—disorderly, usually ugly, artificially lit, often without win-dows, filled with stress and with all manner of jerks, the pace of your day out of your control—here was your domain, a place of beauty, order, and autonomy. (Never mind that your own efforts to follow the "easy-to-make" instructions resulted in cakes resembling cow pies and throw pil-lows that looked like Chewbacca had made them.)

By the 1990s, the tone and sheer volume of childcare advice columns had changed too. Clearly, kid shrinks could no longer get away with the mom-is-a-dotard-and-always-to-blame stance they took in the early 1970s. In fact, *McCall's* in the early 1990s finally dumped Lee Salk and replaced him with Ron Taffel, Ph.D., a Manhattan-based therapist and author of *Parenting by Heart,* who wrote a monthly column, "The Confident Par-ent." Compared to Salk's mantra that everything required professional help, Taffel repeatedly emphasized his faith in mothers' intuition. He at-tacked media messages that guilt-tripped working mothers. He reassured them that it's okay to discipline your kids and warned, possibly with Salk in mind, "I'm afraid we are turning into a generation of therapists to our children" with "an overdeveloped sense of fairness" that made parents reluctant to punish their kids when they needed it.[19] Talk about a breath of fresh air.

But Taffel was an exception. An avalanche of advice that put you, Mom, and even the tiniest, most insignificant aspect of child rearing under surveillance was everywhere, even on TV magazine shows like *20/20* or *Dateline NBC*. There was a totally right way and a totally wrong way to handle everything: sleeping problems, chapped lips, food allergies, head lice, nosebleeds, soccer sprains, cradle cap, trench mouth, bad manners, sledding, TV viewing, clutter, and playing with rattles. By 1990, *McCall's*, which in 1970 had had no monthly columns dealing with motherhood, now featured (in addition to its monthly kid shrink column) "Ask Dr. Mom" by Dr. Marianne Neifert (mother of five and a pediatrician at St. Luke's Hospital in Denver) and "The Mother's Page," in which readers submitted essays about motherhood. The January 1990 issue alone featured, "40? You're Not Too Old to Have a Baby," "Postpartum Depression: Beyond the 'Baby Blues,'" "Plan Ahead for a Healthy Baby," and "Is Your Workplace Endangering Your Baby?" *Redbook* in 1970 offered "The Expectant Mother" every other month; by January 1992, it had a whole section titled "You & Your Child," with anywhere from four to six articles on everything from kids' health, child-rearing trends, teen rebellion, and dawdling, which may have undermined the message on the January 1993 cover with Demi Moore, headlined WHY EVERY MOM SHOULD FEEL THIS SEXY.

But there wasn't just an increase in the established women's magazines in articles or advice columns about child rearing. Multiplying like rabbits, entirely new child-rearing magazines—some geared to specific ages like birth to three—vied for Mom's attention with headlines suggesting you just might be doing everything wrong. *Parents* had been around since 1926, but the German company that bought it in 1978 gave it a major face-lift, nearly doubling its size, making it much more glossy and more "authoritative."[20] *Parenting* in the 1990s inaugurated monthly safety pullout sections: "Poison Alert: Pullout Safety Guide," "Protect Your Kids From Drowning," "Age-by-Age Guide to Childproofing," "Hidden Danger: How Safe Is *Your* Home?" "8 Simple Steps That Could Save Your Child's Life," and so forth. By the turn of the twenty-first century, mothers could choose among *Working Mother, Family Life, Baby Talk, American Baby, Fit Pregnancy, Mothering, Child, Early Childhood*

Today, Parent and Child, Parenting Your Stepfamily, Twins, Christian Parenting Today, Family Adventure, Family Fun, Adoptive Families, and *Pregnancy,* and, worst of all, *Martha Stewart Kids* and *Martha Stewart Baby.* (And this doesn't include the panoply of on-line magazines, from www.mainstreetmom.com to www.athomemothers.com.)

And what did these multiple bullhorns proclaim? Childhood is filled with peril, but motherhood is fun, fun, fun. You didn't even have to open the magazines, some of which were wall-to-wall advice columns in some form or other: the Spanish Inquisition–type questions and the exhortations to produce endless pleasure for your kids were right on the cover. "Is Your Child Eating Enough?" "Can Your Family Pass Our Stress Test?" "Is Your Baby Normal?" "Your Child's Personality: Can You Change It? Should You Try?" and "Is Your Child Addicted to TV?" and, of course, "Are You a Good Parent?" demanded the headlines, warning that you'd better be obsessing about and micro-managing this kid-raising business to eliminate any, *any* threats to or bad influences on your kid. But you also had to be as carefree and peppy as a camp counselor, and armed with as many activities, too. Because the same magazines offered "Fun & Games: The Ultimate Summer Guide," "Boo! 96 Easy Ideas for Halloween Fun" [96??], "Fun Crafts, Cards and Treats to Make Together," "Y2K With Kids: 38 Cool Ideas to Plan Now" (Let's play "back up Mommy's hard drive"?), and "Get Ready to Rumble! Why Kids Need Rowdy Family Fun." Maybe we were deprived children, but with the exception of teaching us to knit or sew on a button, our mothers' idea of arts and crafts was getting out a pad, scissors, glue, and some crayons, and crossing their fingers that we would leave them alone for an hour. It never would have occurred to them that making funhouses for us in the basement or a replica of Cirque du Soleil in the backyard was a sine qua non of being a good mother. And it didn't occur to us kids, either. Not to be left holding moldering copies of Dr. Spock, the publishing industry discovered mothers too, and opened the spigot full blast. In the early 1970s, there were maybe four or five new books published a year on motherhood (some years as few as two). The number of titles gradually increased in the early 1980s, but 1988 was the turning point, with the phrase "enough to choke a horse" coming to mind as one counted up more than forty books then and more than sixty in 1995.

The beatification of the home and motherhood also reached new levels in advertising, although white knights galloping through kitchens and giant, bald genies appearing in the bathroom had certainly dramatized what women's most important duties were. But beginning in the 1980s, and adhering with the goopiness of the Exxon Valdez oil spill, was the rise of ads showing people bonding powerfully and emotionally through, or because of, products.[21] Usually, these ads tried really hard to make you cry, and they relied on tugging at the sentimentality surrounding the mother-child bond (although there were dads in here too). If there was original music, the jingle was sung by a guy with a deep, gravelly voice who could make his voice catch on just the right emotionally charged word. Think Folgers ads, when the mom woke up in the butterscotch tones of morning to discover (get this) that her baby had been sleeping peacefully on his dad's chest much of the night. Think GE ads, in which Mom and the kids danced around folding the laundry as sunbeams illuminated their faces because "GE brings good things to life." These bonding ads often focused on key, emotionally powerful moments in one's personal life—a baby's first steps, a daughter's first prom, a son's graduation, a fiftieth wedding anniversary—and then implied that it was the product that made such moments and such emotions possible.

This strategy relied especially, for mothers, on images of mothers cuddling with their kids and, most frequently, holding their infants in the air above them as the arc of pure bonding oscillated between them. This image was de rigueur for Gerber's or Johnson & Johnson, but even an ad for the new SteamVac Widepath vacuum cleaner from Hoover sold its product with this romanticized image of infancy.[22] In the 1960s and 1970s, ads directed at mom most often focused on the product, like the box of Tide, or the cleaner clothes Tide allegedly produced, or on the mother using the product. But by the 1980s, the relationships that the products allegedly made possible were front and center. And those close, loving relationships were made possible, of course, by the product, but also by mothers who empathized with and anticipated their kids' every need. The ads implied that in the 1990s, mothers should never let one nanosecond pass without her kids feeling loved. Hallmark urged mothers to buy a stash of "To Kids With Love" cards, "the first cards designed specifically for grown-ups to give to kids." Mothers were supposed to "keep extras on hand so you're ready for any occasion" because "whether they applaud a job well done, offer a word of encouragement, apologize for a misunderstanding, or simply say you're thinking of them, 'To Kids With Love' cards touch children in a way they'll never forget."[23] Then there was the cell phone ad where the cutest little girls in the world wanted to go to the beach, but Mom couldn't because she had to meet with a client. "When can I become a client?" asked one of her daughters plaintively. That was it. Mom packed them off to the beach and brought her cell phone, which permitted her to be a perfect nurturing mom *and* a responsible, professional career woman. This ad was a perfect poster for what moms were now supposed to be—ever ready, spontaneous respondents to their children's every desire.

Ads also repeatedly showed mothers as teachers and emphasized how important it was for them to make sure their kids didn't fall behind. Even laundry products could play on this. "Who are the brightest kids in America?" asked an ad for Vivid. In the small print we learned that "brightest" referred to the cleanliness of their clothes, not their IQs. Anheuser-Busch placed an ad in *Good Housekeeping* admonishing mothers to talk to their kids about drinking and driving as soon as the kid started learning how to ride a bike.[24] Even changing diapers got converted into a learning experience. Huggies in 1995 introduced "the training pants that really help you teach." Now there was a label on the back of their disposable training pants that said "back" so the kid knew which side went where; this "helps you teach dressing skills" (and reminds you that if your two-and-a-half-year-old can't read yet, you had better get to work). An ad for Gyne-Lotrimin, a yeast infection treatment, showed a smiling mother with her child at a potting wheel, teaching her how to do ceramics.[25]

Few events in the early 1990s captured the importance and stupidity of the debates revolving around working mothers, and the rise of single mothers, than Dan Quayle's instantly infamous attack on the TV sitcom character played by Candace Bergen, Murphy Brown. On the campaign trail in California in May 1992, Quayle, already regarded by many as dumber than a gerbil, singled out Murphy Brown as a terrible role model because she had chosen to be a single mother and was thus "mocking the importance of fathers." The bulk of the speech, which came just as "welfare reform" was picking up steam, was actually an attack on poor, inner-city (read black) unmarried mothers who were responsible for the "lawless anarchy" and "lack of structure in our inner cities." Marriage was "the best antipoverty program of all," Quayle lectured, ignoring that perhaps decent salaries for women and subsidized day care might be even better antipoverty programs. But it was his criticism of a sitcom character as if she were real that got Quayle on the front pages of *The New York*

Times, USA Today, and *The Daily News.* Diane English, creator of the show, immediately shot back, "If the Vice President thinks it's disgraceful for an unmarried woman to bear a child, and if he believes that a woman cannot adequately raise a child without a father, then he'd better make sure abortion remains safe and legal." [26] Quayle ended up looking like a fool, and was forced, for PR purposes, to watch the premiere of *Murphy Brown* with a group of single mothers in September.

But the Quayle brouhaha at the time missed the point. Why did Murphy Brown have to have a baby in the first place, husband or no? Was she really incomplete as a woman without a child? The baby-saturated media landscape seemed to think so. And after the first few episodes of her as a mother, her son, Avery, drifted into the background, making no difference in her life the way a real baby would. In one episode when he did appear, Murphy had just decided to call off a planned marriage to a coworker. After the coworker left, Avery came downstairs, and Murphy swept him up in her arms, singing "You're All I Need to Get By." As media scholar Bonnie Dow noted tartly, here the show descended "into a profound romanticization of motherhood," by suggesting that a child can provide a woman with all of her emotional needs.[27] Who needs a man when you can have a baby instead?

The new momism also found its way into hit dramatic shows like *N.Y.P.D. Blue* and *ER,* mostly in the form of abusive or neglectful mothers whose failure to get with the program had heart-wrenching costs. In the early years of *ER,* for example, maternal villains included: a mother who had adopted a baby from an eastern European country but abandoned it at the hospital once she learned it had AIDS; a mother who had burned her daughter's hands on the stove after discovering her masturbating; a mother who suffered from Munchausen syndrome by proxy and thus kept forcing her kid to take medicine and go to the hospital in an effort to make (and keep) the kid sick; and so on. Here the ER was beset by an epidemic of maternal sickness. *N.Y.P.D. Blue* had a stable of neglectful, abusive mothers, many of them African American, who also served as a warning that motherhood was really on the skids.

Many in the media biz argued that all this "women-centered" media fare, from *Roseanne* to *Living* to women-in-jep films, spoke to and reaffirmed women's newfound strength. What it really did was indicate the importance of women, especially mothers, as a market. And while it might seem that women solving missing-person mysteries or building their own henhouses was empowering, there is a better word for what most of this media fare in the 1990s was: reactionary. The discourse of individual-ism—if mothers wanted anything better for their kids, moms had to achieve it on their own, by themselves—suggested that feminism and sis-terhood were irrelevant and the government did not have to give women's needs high priority—or any priority at all. And the sepia-toned images of Mom relocating her priorities back in the nursery and the kitchen because she chose to—well, this was the feminine mystique dressed up in padded shoulders and a PalmPilot. Mothers were supposed to lower their expec-tations about career success and increase their expectations of their job performance in the home.

Of course, most working mothers continued to work. Many women thought the "mommy track" was a load. And they hooted with delight at Roseanne because they desperately needed, if only for twenty-two min-utes, to rebel against the new momism. Torn as many of us were between our need to work, our deep love for our kids, and the escalating standards of the new momism, many felt an increasing identity crisis in the 1990s about whether we were good mothers and whether it was even possible to be one, whether we worked outside the home or not. All of these other media forms and outlets presented such a powerfully interlocking set of norms about motherhood, and suggested they were shared by everyone "out there" (except for Peg Bundy and Roseanne), that you would be a deviant—and a condemnable one—if you didn't conform. The fantasies about the sainthood and contentment you achieved if you donned the new momism, coupled with the dire warnings about what happened if you didn't, meant that whatever contradictions real women felt over this tug-of-war, the new momism was going to pull you in.

By the late 1990s, then, the struggles of the 1980s and early 1990s were over, and postfeminism had won. Whatever tensions there were in the family as a result of both parents working, or mom being single, the lack of childcare, paid parental leave, and so forth had to be resolved by women themselves. "Privatization" here meant "Mom will handle it." [28] It was sheer common sense that motherhood was central to women's lives whether they worked outside the home or not, and that a woman was, as in the 1950s, not a "real" woman until she had a child. Very simply, woman equaled mother. [29] The supposed universal desire among all women for children had become, once again, so taken-for-granted that you couldn't even imagine women wanting anything else. [30] It was women, not men, who were once again innately better suited to have primary responsibility for raising the kids. What was central to the women-in-jep films was that the women, despite whatever threats they faced, preserved and buttressed their identities as good mothers. That's what was really at stake.[31]

This romanticizing of homemaking and motherhood, in *thirtysomething*, in Folgers ads, in *Living*, encouraged women to become so invested in upholding particular, unattainable standards of motherhood, that they stopped—or didn't even begin—to question a set of practices, backed up by the government and much of corporate America, that, as we used to say in the olden days, oppressed mothers. Yet because we saw a new TV breed of cuddly, fun dads who bathed their kids and read to them, we were supposed to believe that the old, bad, stinky patriarchy that had kept Betty Friedan's generation down was a thing of the past. The "mommy track" gave credence to the notion that mothers could not do it all.

The "mommy wars" suggested that mothers could never unite across divides, like whether they worked or not, let alone across the divides of class and race, to fight for a more kid- and parent-friendly society. We were *supposed* to resent each other. Mothers who failed to get with the twelve-step momism program were supposed to be seen as outgroups encased in stereotypes that were rarely true. The fact is that millions of mothers who stayed at home with their kids were sympathetic to and sometimes envious of mothers who worked, while millions of those who worked outside the home were sympathetic to and envious of those who stayed at home. But in the 1990s, with its mom-versus-mom catfight storyline, that kind of supportive mutuality was cast as, like, *soooo* 1960s.

But as the 1990s turned into the beginning of the twenty-first century, there developed a strain of intensive mothering that became unremittingly obsessive and oppressive. But before we see just how nuts things have gotten, let's address the $64,000 question: Why, over thirty years after the women's movement, do we still not have a remotely decent day care system?

EIGHT

Dumb Men, Stupid Choices— or Why We Have No Childcare

Lock the kids in the basement, grab a glass of wine, put your feet up, and imagine this. It's time for work. You take your toddler to her childcare center, as usual. But you also drop off some clothes that need mending, because there's a mending center there. Because there's also a medically staffed immunization center, your toddler will get her shots today, saving you a trip to the pediatrician's. At the end of the day, when you pick her up, you can also pick up a ready-made dinner from the center's take-away counter that features casseroles, roasted chicken, and the like. Bags of groceries are also waiting for you, prepared by the center's shopping service according to the shopping list you left in the morning. The next day, when your toddler is sick and you have to—*have to*—be at work, you don't panic, because the center has an infirmary where she'll be well taken care of.

Hard as it is to believe, such centers existed right here in the United States in 1945. They were established to assist the six million women, many of them mothers, who entered the workforce during World War II. There weren't many of them, it's true, but they were a crucial start. When the war ended, the government, with the speed of a heat-seeking missile, shut them all down and withdrew its financial support for childcare. By the 1970s, Denmark, France, Italy, and Sweden had a national system of nursery schools or day care centers. But not us. No siree. That'd be comm'nist.

When you sit back and think about it, isn't it really beyond belief that for over forty years the idea of providing preschool care for American kids was always accompanied by images of Joseph Stalin or Chairman Mao? The argument was simple: Day care centers, as agents of the State with a capital S, only provided highly regimented, one-size-fits-all care that stifled the individuality of the child and instead turned him or her into an undifferentiated robot (who then, of course, would be putty in the hands of communists trying to take over the world). When you go to any decent day care center today, and see one child sticking her hair into some Plaster of Paris to see what a braid fossil looks like, while another one is lying on the floor painting the underside of a table because he thinks he's Michaelangelo, and another group of kids is snuggled in "story corner" listening to a teacher read *Ask Mr. Bear,* the notion that day care kids are being "Sovietized" is truly from the planet Neptar. Here, in what is supposedly one of the leading industrialized countries on the planet, addled folklore—not research, not the experiences of other countries—based solely on Cold War hysteria, guided American policies for decades.

Once the Cold War was over and the "Sovietizing" rhetoric was suddenly beside the point, we got to hear that day care centers were overrun by Satanists and would turn all kids into bullies or underachieving cretins who hated their mothers and were incapable of love. In an updating of the Sovietizing line, Bob Dole said day care "discriminated against the home-maker" and meant the "long arm of the federal government" would be telling parents how to "treat their children."[1] If you opted for a nanny, she would shake or bludgeon your kids to death. All this because you, Mom, were a selfish careerist who cared more about her job than her own kids.

Of all the domestic-policy decisions made from 1970 to the present, those regarding childcare have done the most to guilt-trip mothers into embracing the new momism. If parents hear over and over that day care is (somehow) un-American and dangerous, *and* the government withholds all but the most pitiful funding for day care so that parents are left to make ad hoc, often unsatisfactory, costly arrangements for the care of their children, then shouldn't Mom just chuck it all and stay at home? If Mom "chooses" to work in spite of these obstacles, at least she will feel perpetually guilty and stressed.

Here are the questions before us, and they go straight to the heart of how the media frame our innermost feelings as parents, as well as our notions of what's commonsensical and possible. Why is it that mothers, most of whom have wanted, with all their hearts, a truly decent, caring, educational childcare system in the United States, feel incredibly guilty about childcare? And why is it that the politicians who have for decades thwarted decent day care don't feel bad at all? Why have mothers been in the media bull's-eye, and not them? What kind of media tales turn us against *ourselves* and not against the guys who have never gone to work with spit-up on their lapels, and certainly have never been fired for missing too many days at work caring for a sick child?

And let's put forward one caveat right away. The question is not—as it has often been posed by the media—what's better, kids staying at home or kids going to day care. As such, the question makes no sense: Better in what respect? According to whom? If the available day care makes the old Chicago stockyards look good by comparison? If the kids won't have food on the table unless the mother works? If the kids are at home in front of the television set all day or go to day care where there are sand tables, dress-up clothes, and a child-staff ratio of 4 to 1? The question also ignores the economic reality of life on Main Street USA: For most mothers, work is an absolute necessity and so, hello, Earth to Congress, some reliable form of childcare is also an absolute necessity. Our purpose here is to acknowledge that reality, and then to talk back to that Greek chorus of politicians, policy makers, child development experts, CRAP members, and media outlets who have feathered their own, comfy nests by championing the view that day care was equivalent to child neglect.

At the same time, the news and women's magazines did often hammer home the desperate need for decent day care and politicians' failure to act. It is in these contradictory messages about the perils and merits of day care that we see the struggles between feminism and the new momism quite dramatically fought out. As various conservative politicians attacked feminism, and sought to put uppity women in their place, their serial assaults on and defeat of childcare legislation provided the platform through which they would insist that the only appropriate caregiver to children was Mom herself. Millions of mothers and fathers rejected this antediluvian position. Nonetheless, once it became clear, as it did after 1990, that the federal government was not going to do anything significant to support and regulate a national day care system, the new momism picked up even more steam as mothers became, yet again, the ones expected to address childcare on their own.

Forget Martha Stewart's make-your-own diapers from organic cotton that you have grown in your backyard. It is time for the mothers of America to design their own childcare dartboard and to remind ourselves and those who make the decisions about our family lives, that the personal (raising decent, healthy kids) is still political (sustaining a decent, healthy country). The pantheon of men whose faces should grace said dartboards include but are not restricted to: Pat Buchanan, George Gilder, Gerald Ford, Charles Murray, Ronald Reagan, David Stockman, Strom Thurmond, George Bush (the dad), Bill Clinton, and George Bush (the son). Richard Nixon goes in the bull's-eye as he is more responsible than any other single politician for thwarting a national childcare system. Phyllis Schlafly gets to be an honorary man here, since she fought like a feral animal against childcare (and since she's probably really Pat Buchanan in drag anyway). Next to that, set up a small shrine with the portraits of Walter Mondale (D-MN); Senator John Brademas (D-IN); Senator Jacob Javits (R-NY); Representative Gus Hawkins (D-CA); Senator Birch Bayh (D-IN) and his wife, Marvella, who campaigned tirelessly for a national day care program; Teddy Kennedy (D-MA); and, with a halo around her, Marian Wright Edelman, head of the Children's Defense Fund. Mondale, probably best remembered for his disastrous presidential campaign against Reagan in 1984, when he thought a really cool soundbite was "Where's the Beef," should also be remembered for his determined campaign to establish federally funded, high-quality childcare.

You probably don't have the spare time—not to mention the inclination—to review what those half-wits in the District have had to say, over the years, about mothers and children and how best to serve them. So we thought, as a public service, that we would provide you with a little Whitman's sampler of fabulous policy bonbons from the folks who have ensured that we have the worst infant mortality rates, childcare programs, and maternity-leave policies of the industrialized world. Most of our nation's politicians haven't done squat—well, maybe that's all they've done—for the 25 percent of American children who live in poverty. And they haven't done much more, either, for middle-class kids who also need and deserve decent preschool care.

As women watched the news, read magazines, watched TV, or went to the movies, what stories have they seen about childcare since the 1980s? Mostly really scary ones about what happens to kids when they are cared for by someone other than their mothers. Stories blamed mothers for taking our kids to day care in the first place, and for failing to investigate, monitor, and improve them with the rigor of a UN inspection team. Even when studies came out purporting to show that good day care actually improved kids' language and cognitive skills, reporters looked for the findings, however small, however buried, that suggested day care turned some kids into Hannibal Lecter, Marilyn Manson, or Mike Tyson. After 1984 and 1985, when the news was flooded with stories of abuse at day care centers, the panic did abate, but not without leaving a residue of paranoia within mothers' psyches. The media turned that paranoia inward in the 1990s, when we saw footage from a black-and-white surveillance camera (the "nanny cam") of a baby-sitter beating the child in her care with a wooden spoon, and saw more lurid stories about murdering nannies.

In addition to these attention grabbers, the media were also filled with more measured—and more contradictory—images of childcare. Women's magazines, especially *Working Mother,* understood mothers' needs and advocated for better childcare policies. Editors of these magazines formed a coalition to pressure Congress into action. Television news, often led by women reporters who may have known a thing or two about finding decent day care, featured highly sympathetic and reasoned accounts of the perpetual lack of quality childcare in the United States. These, however, were punctuated by poorly researched and hyperbolically reported stories about "studies" purporting to show how day care makes kids do poorly in school, hate their mothers, and punch other kids in the face. Only rarely have Americans seen comparisons between our pathetic childcare "system" and what other countries provide for their parents and kids. Nor has media attention been directed at the scandalously low wages we pay the people, mostly women, who care for the kids of the country. In only one story over a thirty-year period did one network, CBS, report that childcare workers earned less than parking lot attendants and pet care groomers.[2]

In the end, childcare, as it has been squeezed out of the media pastry bag, has taken four major, often overlapping forms in the news. First, of course, were the highly sensationalized melodramas about sexual abuse. Next were the advocacy stories beginning in the late 1980s about the desperate need for more and better day care. Third were the "effects" stories: the potential effects, detrimental or salubrious, on the kids. Fourth were the cost stories: day care, however much it was needed, was simply too damn expensive. These stories encouraged two responses. One was fatalism: This was an impossible problem, too controversial, too costly, too messy, for any kind of governmental solution, so parents, and especially mothers, were on their own. The other response, evoked in stories with titles like "Daycare Nightmare," in which Tom Brokaw looked at you from his newsroom throne and asked "How safe is your child if that child is in day care?," was guilt. If you sent your kid to day care you were warehousing her, depositing her someplace with the same care and attention you would devote to dropping off your dry cleaning. Even stories emphasizing the desperate need for more and better day care often contained this little burrowing worm of accusation.

At the beginning of this chapter we painted a pretty picture of day care during World War II, so first, let's review the unsurprising bad news. Most women struggled with childcare, as too little was done for them by the government or corporate America. In 1941, Congress passed the Lanham Act, which provided funds for social services and public works to those towns and cities especially affected by the rise of war-related work.[3] In 1942, with the then-desperate need for women war workers, the scope of the Lanham Act was expanded to funnel money into childcare.[4] More than forty-four hundred communities did establish some form of childcare, which included more than three thousand centers serving six hundred thousand kids, but this didn't even begin to meet the need.[5] Often the hours were too short to cover a full working day, or the centers were in out-of-the-way places inaccessible by foot or public transportation. Many centers were overcrowded and understaffed. *Collier's* reported in early 1943 that ten thousand kids in Seattle still needed day care, and that San Diego, "packed to its roofs with war workers, wants one day-care center within a radius of every three blocks . . . and expects to open more nurseries at the rate of one a week." So, three quarters of the kids who needed day care got it in private homes through relatives, friends, or neighbors.[6]

But the Kaiser Company in Portland, Oregon, where 60 percent of the workers were women, got it right. Doris Kearns Goodwin reports that Eleanor Roosevelt herself was responsible for talking the Kaiser family into setting up a model system.[7] At the Portland and Swan Island shipyards in 1943, Kaiser established a six-day-a-week, fifty-two-weeks-a-year center staffed by trained teachers and nurses. It took kids from eighteen months to six years, and eventually became a twenty-four-hour site to accommodate women on the graveyard shift. It had a kitchen, a cafeteria, and an infirmary. Sick children went to an isolation room staffed by nurses and visited by a pediatrician every day. There was an additional program for kids ages six to twelve during school vacations and the summer. And at the end of the day mothers could pick up their kids and a fully cooked dinner to bring home. During its first year the center served two thousand kids.[8] Kaiser boasted—rightly—that the centers "were among the first places where people of average means have been able to afford good nursery education for their children."[9]

While the Kaiser centers were models, they were not alone. The director of the childcare centers in Baltimore County noted that working mothers "were breaking down under the strain of working at an eight- to ten-hour job—a job which by itself has always entitled a member of the stronger sex to the best armchair by the fire and his pipe and slippers at the end of a hard day!" But working mothers came home to mending, laundry, cleaning, and cooking, getting to bed at midnight only to have to get up at five the next morning. (Sound familiar?) So, after a series of meetings with stressed-out working mothers, the Baltimore childcare centers provided the following services. The mother left her shopping list, money, and ration points at the center in the morning, and at the end of the day her groceries were ready for her. The centers would pack lunches for kids, take kids to the barber, dentist, or doctor, handle the mother's laundry and dry cleaning, shop for kids' clothes, provide a "clubhouse" for schoolchildren who had no place to go after 3:00, and, of course, provide a hot evening meal to take home, "our most popular service."[10]

Once the war ended, and the government withdrew all funding to support day care centers, the Cold War rhetoric about childcare centers being tiny factories that would produce carbon-copy versions of little Ivans and Svetlanas became the American "common sense" about day care. That common sense held sway for nearly twenty years. Beginning in the 1960s, a coalition of Americans began to push for federal funding for day care centers. Head Start, the preschool program founded in 1965 and designed for disadvantaged kids, had already proved such a success that some child advocates began to think preschool would be great for middle-class kids, too. After all, day care centers introduced kids to a variety of other children; they learned about a range of behaviors; learned how to share and to play in groups; learned their colors, numbers, and the alphabet.

It is now the twenty-first century. The U.S. government, which happily spends millions on military bands, on subsidizing cigarette advertising to children in Thailand, on bombers that don't work, and an estimated $125 billion on corporate welfare, regards the funding of day care as too expensive and unnecessary.[11] The words most frequently used by policy analysts and academics to describe the American childcare system are "patchwork," "haphazard," and "piecemeal." [12] As a result, parents throughout America still scramble to find decent day care. About two-thirds of preschoolers are in home-based care at relatives, neighbors, or friends, while only between 20 and 25 percent are in centers. (Guess who uses centers most? Educated middle-class and upper-middle-class professionals.) There is a desperate shortage of childcare in rural areas as well as in cities like New York.[13] The Children's Defense Fund reported in 2002 that 80 percent of childcare was substandard, and 87 percent of care for infants and toddlers inadequate.

But wait, you say, isn't it true that most Americans don't believe the government should be involved in childcare? Wrong. Huge majorities support federal funding for childcare, especially for lower-income families (86 percent), and most Americans—get this—would pay higher taxes in exchange for quality early childhood care. Go look at the Children's Defense Fund Web page, Harris Polls, and *Parent's* magazine if you don't believe us. Nine out of ten adults polled said finding quality childcare was difficult for most families and one in four parents didn't think their childcare was good enough.[14] But never mind what parents think, especially if those parents happen to be mothers, or worse yet, feminists.

In 1970, the White House Conference on Children, which convened every ten years, was especially rowdy, rebellious, and productive, filled as it was with four thousand delegates, which included black activists, feminists, childcare activists, Native Americans, Chicanos, and pacifists, all eager to force "the new" Richard Nixon to confront the sorry state of government services for children and their parents. There were three times as many delegates as there were at the 1968 Democratic convention. They met over five days in three different hotels, and when they were done, presented Nixon with twenty-four recommendations to act on. One was the establishment of "universal day care, health and early learning services in which parents and the neighborhood would play a major role." The Conference asked the government to fund the training of fifty thousand additional childcare workers over the next ten years.[15]

The rising number of employed mothers, feminists or not, prompted the news media and some politicians to realize there was a day care crisis that needed fixing. In the summer and fall of 1971, Congress considered several childcare bills, some of which drew heavily from the recommendations of the White House Conference and others from three years of Congressional investigation, which included 1,715 pages of testimony by 166 experts.

There was also a real shift in thinking about what childcare was and who needed it. In the 1960s, and particularly with the prominence—and success—of Head Start, childcare was thought of as something disadvantaged kids needed, a way to make up for a deficient home life. But by 1970, childcare advocates and politicians like Walter Mondale were emphasizing the importance of early enrichment programs for all kids. In other words, the justification was shifting away from childcare as rehab for the poor to childcare as a developmental advantage for all children.[16]

This sensibility made it into the news media, which admittedly gave only moderate coverage to the need for day care. In May 1971, Roger Mudd of CBS News reported that "day care centers for preschoolers have become almost a necessity for millions of working mothers who are counting on the Nixon administration for help." In the story that followed, Daniel Schorr cited the shortage of good centers and emphasized that the center he visited stressed "not just baby-sitting, but education, not just custody but child development in the critical years that can make or break a child's future." The new push for centers was "not just for convenience of parents, but for the development of the child." Yet the Washington, D.C., center featured in the story was entirely black, reinforcing through images the still-prevailing notion that day care was primarily for poor, inner-city children. Walter Mondale, in language that seems so quaint and alien today, especially coming from a politician, noted how many kids were hungry, lived in substandard housing, and had their early developmental needs ignored. How we can "mangle" children today, "and still claim to be a just society, I don't know," Mondale wondered. He then said that providing quality childcare to all women and children who wanted and needed it was "the most important single new area of public policy needed today." Schorr ended the piece by noting, "the day of day care may be approaching in America."[17] Don't we wish.

That December, Congress passed the Comprehensive Child Development Act with broad bipartisan support, marshaled by its cosponsors, Walter Mondale and Jacob Javits, Republican Senator from New York (remember moderate Republicans?). It made childcare available to all children as an extension of the Economic Opportunity Act. The federal government would have provided funding to local groups—from local governments to community groups to Indian tribes—to establish childcare centers; poor kids would go for free, and middle-class families would pay fees on a sliding scale, according to their salaries. Wherever possible, the centers would have been administered by parents and neighborhood groups—the federal government paid the tab, but control was local. The bill would have provided prenatal care for women unable to afford it, and also would have funded after-school centers for older children. The initial authorization was for $2 billion. The Comprehensive Child Development Act was Congress's "first major effort . . . since the Second World War to respond to the nation's childcare needs." [18]

Nixon vetoed it. [19] Please glue face to dartboard. To bull's-eye. (The Senate fell seven votes short of overriding the veto. Mondale denounced the veto as "a cruel blow to children and working parents.") [20] Clearly imagining day care as some place staffed by hippies who passed out joints to toddlers wearing tiny Chairman Mao jackets, Nixon declared he was unwilling to commit "the vast moral authority of the national government to the side of communal approaches to child rearing over . . . the family-centered approach." He denounced the bill as fiscally irresponsible, a threat to the family, and unnecessary, since he saw no real need for childcare. [21] Journalists were taken aback. Dan Rather reported Nixon's assertion that there was no demonstrated need for childcare with an air of barely restrained disbelief. [22] *The New York Times* denounced the veto, and Jack Rosenthal, also writing for the paper, was startled by the "vehemence" of the veto's language. [23]

As well he might have been—because guess who wrote most of the veto statement? Pat Buchanan, the Republicans' "family values" pit bull. According to historian Mary Frances Berry, Buchanan and Charles Colson (of Watergate fame) feared that some right-wingers might challenge Nixon in the 1972 Republican primaries. So they urged him to veto the legislation to "buy ourselves maneuvering room with the right wing," as Colson put it. [24] In other words, placating the likes of Strom Thurmond, who charged that the bill would put "our preschool children under the strong influence, if not control, of the HEW bureaucrats," was more important than providing quality day care for millions of the country's kids. Conservative commentator James Kilpatrick made the point more explicit: "this is a bill to provide, Soviet-style, for making children virtual wards of the state." [25] The Nixon veto meant that no childcare bill would be enacted for years, and left the childcare advocacy groups demoralized and uncertain about what, if anything, they could do next. When the Day

Care and Child Development Council of America asked Pat Nixon—its honorary chairwoman—to account for her husband's veto of the bill, she gave one of those tight little smiles she was so good at and resigned.[26] For good measure, Nixon imposed a federal ceiling in 1972 on spending for day care, just when the cost of food and fuel were going through the roof.[27]

In 1975, clearly a glutton for punishment, Senator Walter Mondale (again) and Representative John Brademas (also again) proposed the Child and Family Services Act of 1975. It would have provided $1.9 billion in federal funds for day care services, prenatal care, training for parents, medical care for handicapped kids, and other educational and health services.[28] The bill was supported by the PTA, the AFL-CIO, the U.S. Catholic Conference, the United Methodist Church, and the National Education Association.[29] Little did Mondale and Brademas know that this bill would instigate one of the biggest controversies of the Ninety-fourth Congress.

From somewhere deep within the foul, twisted catacombs of American culture, an anonymous, mimeographed flyer emerged claiming that the bill would force parents to turn over their children to government-run centers, would mandate "communal forms of upbringing," and—get this—encourage children to sue their parents if they required them to attend Sunday school. In fact, the flyer warned, the bill gave kids "the freedom to insist that they be taught nothing, or any ideas, about God." (The 1971 Act, the one Nixon vetoed, would supposedly have "removed children from their parent's instruction shortly after birth.") The flyer also said that the bill would give children the legal right to organize a labor union against their parents and to sue them if the kids had ever been punished. The bill supposedly contained a "Charter of Child's Rights" that would allow kids to disobey their parents. "If the mother or father asked the child to take the garbage out and the child doesn't want to, the parents have no right to insist on it," the flyer warned. "Take the trouble to write [to your Congressman] or suffer the consequences of your silence," the flyer cautioned.[30] Some versions of the flyer had subheadings that asked, simply, "Can the Government Take Away Your Children?"[31] Amazingly, lots of people believed the flyer. Newsweek reported that Mondale had to hire two extra staff members to answer the two to six thousand letters he got every day protesting the legislation.[32] He wasn't alone. Other members of Congress were also deluged by mail from constituents completely freaked out by the right-wing smear campaign. Senator Charles Percy of Illinois reportedly got twelve thousand letters about the bill between the end of 1975 and the beginning of 1976.[33] At the time, Mondale referred to the campaign as "one of the most distorted and dishonest attacks I have witnessed in my fifteen years of public service."[34]

Where did this dementia come from? The awakening giant of the Christian Right. Another picture for the dartboard, this time of a place: the virulently racist and reactionary Bob Jones University. One of its august publications featured hysteria inducing "facts" about the bill, as did the *Christian Crusade Weekly,* which came out of Tulsa, Oklahoma, and had ties to the John Birch Society.[35] Reporters learned that the flyer had been distributed at churches, schools, factories, and revival meetings.[36] This loony-tunes flyer succeeded in killing childcare legislation.

While most in Congress denounced the flyer, many still objected to supporting day care on grounds not all that dissimilar from the Birchers. Representative James Broyhill of North Carolina was opposed to putting the federal government "into the baby-sitting business."[37] "Is there really a large-scale public interest in massive federal funding for day care?" asked Representative Bob Wilson of California rhetorically, assuming the answer was no. For one thing, it would produce "red tape of nightmarish proportions." The government, he concluded, should not "be in the day care business."[38] Why is federal funding always "massive" when it goes to women and children, but not when it goes to tanks and subsidies for agribusiness? Mondale and Brademas had to abandon their push for the bill.

Another face for the dartboard: Gerald Ford. Constantly depicted by the news media (and Chevy Chase on *Saturday Night Live*) as a bumbling, head-banging, golf-ball-hurling, yet utterly endearing dope, Gerald Ford, as a consequence, gets off the hook for his record on women's issues. So let's remember that he was a states' rights Republican, and like the guy who put him into office, Richard Nixon, vetoed a childcare bill in April 1976, the Child Day Care Standards Act.

This puny little act provided additional funding only to existing day care centers that served primarily low-income or welfare mothers in order that these centers meet new federal guidelines for staffing, health, safety, and nutritional codes that Congress had passed and Ford had signed into law on January 4, 1975. In other words, having imposed these codes on day care centers, Congress and the President could actually help close them down by refusing to provide the money necessary to meet the new standards. The amount was a mite-sized $125 million. The House overrode Ford's veto 301 to 101, and the Senate followed suit, 60 to 34. Voting to support the veto? Jesse Helms, Bob Dole, James Buckley, Bob Packwood, Strom Thurmond, Sam Nunn, and Barry Goldwater, all of whom had succeeded at working outside the home on minimum wage while changing diapers and packing lunches.[39] James Buckley, brother of William F., noted, "significant damage can be done to infants who are in effect warehoused in institutions supervised by an inadequate staff." The image of babies lined up in a Wal-Mart aside, the act was meant to increase and improve staffing. He then had read into the record an article titled "At Home" by Daniel Oliver that had appeared in his brother's rag, *The National Review.* Here Oliver unburdened himself of the opinion that "modern day care seems designed mainly to liberate women from their family responsibilities."[40]

Because of feminism, welfare-rights activism, children's advocacy groups, and the fact that Democratic politicians used to have that body part known as a spine, the early 1970s witnessed increasing public acceptance of a new idea: that childcare centers were not only necessary for millions of families, they were also a great addition to early childhood education. But because this idea included the notion that the federal government had a responsibility to invest in such programs, conservatives worked assiduously to pull this new idea out by its roots. Instead, they sought to plant a new common sense about childcare that child development expert Uri Bronfenbrenner referred to as the "Anglo-Saxon mode" (close cousin to the missionary position?). In this "mode," childcare is viewed as a private responsibility; it is best handled privately and individually. Because it's handled individually, it somehow promotes the rugged individualism that distinguishes America from those pansy, socialist dupes on the other side of the Atlantic. Leaving childcare provision to "the market," according to this view, magically increases families' choices (even though *all* the evidence contradicts this). What's more, childcare is really a "special interest" issue, because it is only about women who "choose" to work. It is clearly "antifamily."[41]

Just in case enough damage had not been done, Ronald Reagan's policies put a stake through the heart of federal support for childcare. For starters, Reagan really didn't think women should work at all. When asked to comment on unemployment during 1981–82, when the country went through the worst recession since the Great Depression, Reagan blamed women. "Part of the unemployment is not as much recession as it is the great increase in people going into the job market and, ladies, I'm not picking on anyone, but because of the increase in women who are working today. . . ." [42] If Reagan thought that the further decimation of childcare would drive women back into the home, he was wrong. Between 1980 and 1986, federal funding for childcare programs declined by 18 percent, which was especially disastrous since the number of working women with preschool children increased by 29 percent during the same time period. [43] Of Reagan's proposed budget cuts and tax reductions, totaling $44 billion, one third directly hurt poor women and their children. Government-sponsored training programs for childcare workers were eliminated, funding for the Child Care Food Program was cut (remember, this was when ketchup was designated as a vegetable for kids?), and support to welfare mothers and their kids was cut as well. [44] Reagan's answer to all programs that might help mothers—especially working mothers—was "privatize it." The very moment when poor and middle-class women needed more support from the government than ever before was the same moment when whatever support existed was slashed. Under Reagan, the childcare shortage got much, much worse. And because of his economic policies—cut taxes, especially for the rich and corporations, but increase military spending dramatically—the nation faced a huge budget deficit by the late 1980s. Given that the country was more in hock than it had ever been, proposing a major new federal childcare initiative faced more obstacles than ever. Ultimately Reagan's impact on the sorry state of American childcare lasted well beyond his actual reign.

In 1984 a coalition of childcare experts and women's rights groups formed the Child Care Action Campaign (which included the editors of major women's magazines) to push, once again, for a national system of day care. [45] Marian Wright Edelman, head of the Children's Defense Fund, also put together the Alliance for Better Child Care, which included 122 groups, from religious organizations to business groups. The news media took note. On January 9, 1984, ABC did a story on the lack of decent day care in the U.S. "Who is taking care of the nation's children?" asked Peter Jennings. He noted that 56 percent of the nation's mothers were working, and thus day care had become a pressing issue. "When you look outside the family for help, it is hard to find." In this sympathetic story by Rebecca Chase, ABC noted that too many centers had huge wait lists, weren't open when mothers needed them, or were unaffordable. With demand for day care far outstripping supply, ABC reminded viewers that the Reagan administration had cut direct federal aid to day care, but the illustration they used for this was the White House, not the one they should have—a big picture of Reagan with a bolt in his head.

CBS also covered the issue in April 1984. As the story opened we saw a mother and her seven-month-old baby "about to say good-bye for the day. It's a ritual more and more infants and their mothers are having to get used to," Phil Jones reported, as if this was a necessary evil. We saw her stroking her baby's cheek as they said good-bye. Like ABC, CBS emphasized that the demand for childcare was increasing dramatically while availability was not, and reported that the number of working mothers with babies under one had risen 30 percent in just five years, with 45 percent of mothers of babies under one working outside the home.[46] (Many women who started families then will recall putting their names on the wait list of a day care center just when they started *trying* to get pregnant, in the hopes that by the time the baby came they would have moved far enough up the ladder to actually get their kid in.)

While "some are proposing more government subsidies for childcare," Jones reported, "others are proposing that the problem be solved by a return to the ways of yesteryear." In a typical journalistic nod to "the other side," we then saw Linda Burton of "Mothers at Home," an organization whose membership we did not learn, but whose size had to have been minuscule compared to the number of working mothers. Burton declaimed, "We strongly suggest that another approach to the problem be investigated. That of bringing home the many mothers who do work who would rather be at home, who would rather not have their children in day care in the first place." (And what, put them on welfare?) But Burton did not get the last word. That went to a widowed mother of an infant who had not yet found decent care for her baby and had been given one month by her employer to find day care or lose her job. "What can I do? I can't stay home," she insisted indignantly. "What am I going to live on? I'm the sole support of this family." The story ended by noting that too many women would be seeking day care that they could barely afford. While this was another sympathetic story on the subject, viewers were left with two individual women pitted against each other over a problem that seemed insoluble. There was nothing in the story about what other governments around the world did to make it possible for parents to work, no pressuring questions of politicians on how they might address this problem, and no mention of the Reagan cuts.

Of course, in March 1984 the McMartin story broke, with the accompanying witch hunt surrounding childcare centers and child molestation, so the push for federal childcare legislation became doubly crippled, by Reagan's attitudes and public panic. One of the district attorneys in the McMartin case, for example, told NBC News that there's a "substructure of people who are child molesters and through that substructure of life, that underworld of life, people can be brought in, recruited for the school." Evoking images of secret covens and cults, he added, "people who do not come from that subculture or underworld would not be hired at that school." [47] Molestation—real or imagined—was one of the biggest stories of the year, and vastly outnumbered and overshadowed stories about the still-desperate need for childcare by millions of families.

In fact, that need was now necessarily framed within the context of the ever-present potential for sexual abuse. In a special segment on day care that NBC aired September 5, 1984, Tom Brokaw introduced the story by reminding viewers—just in case they had forgotten—that "it is an explosive subject these days," because a number of day care centers "have been involved in outrageous child molestation cases." (Whether he meant to or not, Brokaw thus conveyed that they were already guilty.) Nonetheless, Cassandra Clayton reported that good day care remained expensive and hard to find. "This is a generation of children, six million of them, who have to look after themselves." Viewers then saw a small clutch of African American kids glued to the TV in their home, all alone. The boy said "we just sit in the house, all alone, nuttin' to do," and his sister added that it got scary sometimes because you had to look after yourself. But this poignant portrait did not mean the government had to help, according to Margaret Heckler, Reagan's Secretary of Health and Human Services. If we were to impose a single, universal system of childcare on the states "we would lose the advantage of innovation that we have," she opined, leading some, at least, to wonder whether the kids stuck home alone or the allegations about sex abuse were the kinds of "innovations" she had in mind. Why, "the private sector" was a "dynamic force" for new childcare facilities. But NBC's Clayton nailed her. "The facts suggest otherwise," she countered, observing that only eighty corporations had set up childcare centers while six million other corporations—that's right, six million—had no programs at all. Nor did Clayton fail to mention the

$65 million in funding cuts for day care for poor working women. She ended her piece by showing a single, white mother who paid half of her salary to day care, so she quit and went on welfare. She wanted to work, she liked to work, but she couldn't afford it. Many women reporters were especially good at conveying how ridiculous the American situation was.

So here were news viewers, buffeted around by shocking accounts of sexual abuse at day care centers around the country, assurances by the Reagan administration that the all-knowing, all-seeing, beneficent "market" would take care of everything, stories that suggested childcare was still primarily an issue for low-income women, and stories that insisted this was a huge middle-class problem, too. A real pessimism hovered over all the stories—that the problem was huge, and that nothing could be done. Because the news media focused on the plight of individual mothers, and on political elites like Heckler, without also showing the work of childcare activists or what other countries did (hey, we're the center of the universe, who cares?), viewers got little sense of what to do or that change might be possible. Despite the undoubtedly good intentions of these stories to cover this enormous social change, the news media's endemic reliance on "individualism" to frame stories meant that the basic lessons mothers should take away were these: one's going to help you, collective action is un-American and futile, so figure it out yourself.

However, the day care scandals, once they began to settle down, also drove home the need for improved centers with higher standards. But such stories also raised questions about whether the government could really be entrusted with the welfare of children. One recurring theme of the overheated media coverage—once they got past children being forced to drink blood and pose naked—was the failure of federal and state agencies to license and inspect centers. For example, in the 1984 Minneapolis case involving charges that a children's theater director molested kids, ABC reported that the director had been under investigation for two years, but the state would not permit theater officials to inform the parents.[48] A Bronx district attorney investigating a mother's charges that her five-year-old was sexually abused in a day care center maintained that hiring procedures were "lax." The center claimed that it screened employees, but "the screening failed."[49] In Tuscon in September 1984, a man who had been convicted twice of child molestation was released from jail after only three years, and someone matching his description was seen in the neighborhood where a little girl had gone missing.[50] No one—not the jails, not the licensing agencies (when there were any), not the courts, not the DAs—could protect your kids. It was up to you, and even you could be fooled or thwarted by the state. Did people really want any arm of the government, under these circumstances, funding and regulating day care?

Though the rising tide of new momism was undoubtedly augmented by the pervasive assault on day care, the need for it just wouldn't go away. Some politicians, even in the 1980s, sought to meet the need. By the late 1980s childcare was the fourth largest household expense after housing itself, food, and taxes.[51] Pollsters in the fall of 1987, just a few months before the Iowa caucuses and the New Hampshire primary, identified "children's issues," and especially the need for day care, as a possible huge sleeper issue.[52] Because the news media increase their coverage of an issue when Congress takes it up, stories about childcare exploded again in 1988, when more than a hundred bills dealing with childcare in one form or another were introduced into Congress, and Christopher Dodd (D-CT) and Dale Kildee (D-MI) plus at least twenty additional cosponsors introduced the ABC Bill, the Act for Better Child Care Services, in November 1987. This bill would have authorized $2.5 billion in federal funds for the states to support much higher quality childcare and would have expanded tax credits for childcare for working parents. Money would have gone to centers in the form of low-interest loans and grants to help them improve their facilities. The bill also provided money to train childcare workers and would have established national standards for centers, like child-staff ratios and qualifications for providers. Even Orrin Hatch, Utah's crown prince of conservatism, cosponsored a bill—more stingy, mind you—that would have given childcare vouchers to working mothers and $250 million in grants and loans to centers, plus even he would have centers regulated and licensed by the states.

Now remember, gang, 1988 was an election year, Dukakis versus Bush, and people were paying attention to something called the "gender gap," which meant that the Republicans were a lot less popular with women than the Democrats. Despite all the "family values" hooey, many women thought that they and their kids were getting screwed because of the right wing of the Republican party, a perception that was correct. So it was important that both candidates look like they supported childcare, especially when a Gallup poll in May 1988 showed that a plurality of likely voters would back a candidate who supported more day care services, and a *New York Times* poll that July showed 52 percent of respondents supporting increased federal spending for day care.[53]

So Bush dutifully declared his support for childcare while smearing Dukakis with the now infamous Willie Horton ad campaign, while Dukakis himself said little about childcare and instead devoted himself to looking like Dennis the Menace in a tank. (Let it be known that Dukakis, a liberal, was worthless on the childcare issue.) Once Bush got elected, here was what he actually supported: giving tax credits to parents for childcare, with poor families getting direct payments if they earned too little to actually pay taxes. Even a five-year-old can see that tax credits do absolutely nothing, nada, to increase the supply and quality of childcare.[54] But with tax credits you can look and sound like you care about childcare (although primarily for the middle and upper-middle classes) without doing squat about it. And then pretend you are a mother without a high school education, or a mother with a college degree, or any mother without her own personal accountant, and you have to figure this out: "Families with incomes below $13,000 would have to choose between an expanded dependent-care credit or a new credit capped at $1000 for each child under the age of 4 and based on 14 percent of earnings."[55] Say what?

Of course, the right did not want *any* childcare bill, and would resort to the most craven and cynical lengths to undermine it. How about running this up the family values flagpole: The bill constituted "blatant discrimination against the mother who takes care of her own children." Phyllis Schlafly ridiculed the ABC Bill as "the federal baby-sitting bill."[56] In 1985, her Eagle Forum began sponsoring a "Full-time Homemaker Award" in each of the fifty states; only women who used "her husband's name," stayed home full-time, and earned less than $500 that year were eligible.[57] Bush repeatedly threatened to veto any bill like ABC, and it indeed croaked in Congress.[58] Now, in fairness, one must note that the Senate did pass ABC, while the House dickered around about another version of a bill. But then they had to be reconciled, and to make a really long story short, the Omnibus Budget Reconciliation Act of 1990 (that sounds like childcare, right?) was passed in October, and Bush signed it.

Some hailed this as "historic childcare legislation."[59] You decide. The Child Care and Development Block Grant that was part of the Omnibus Act earmarked a puny $732 million in federal funds for block grants to states for fiscal year 1991 to improve the availability of childcare to low-income families. There was also money for states to upgrade their licensing requirements. Most of the money was earmarked directly to low-income families themselves to support their getting day care from a licensed provider (which, again, does not increase the amount of day care available to them). Tax credits for childcare were also expanded to give larger credits to working families.[60] There was also a small amount of funding for before- and after-school "latchkey" programs. But after you subtracted the money for these programs and for administrative costs, only about $494 million was actually available to support childcare. Or, to put it another way, only about 220,000 additional kids would be served by this legislation.[61] So, some low-income families as well as middle-class families got a financial break on childcare, and some money went to upgrading facilities. But this bill—the first childcare bill actually, finally enacted since the Lanham Act—did almost nothing to expand the amount of quality day care or to improve the pay its workers got. In the end, the legislation provided "only the most minimal help for parents trying to balance jobs and children."[62]

In June 1990, President Bush vetoed the Family and Medical Leave Bill that would have required firms with more than fifty workers to provide employees with unpaid leaves of absence without losing their jobs for the birth or adoption of a child, or to care for a seriously ill child. Patricia Schroeder and Christopher Dodd pushed for the legislation. By the time it was passed, it contained so many provisos that it would have affected only five percent of employers and 44 percent of employees. Why did Bush oppose it? Well, besides the fact that businesses claimed the bill would ruin them (remember—we are talking *unpaid* leaves), Republicans objected to the fact that the bill was gender neutral, thus implying that fathers took care of children, too, that fathers might need such leave time. Republicans suggested that they would support the bill *only* if it referred to mothers and maternal leave.[63] It is at moments like these that we can see how deeply ideological the new momism was and is.

Unlike the push to "end welfare as we know it," with childcare, the news media did not fully follow the party line set out by politicians, especially conservative ones. Unlike welfare, in which major class and racial divisions separated most of the journalists from the issue at hand, childcare was a problem that cut across class lines, affecting even reporters who made salaries equivalent to the annual budget of Des Moines. But there was one fundamental way that the network news in general did parrot the Republican framework encasing day care: that the U.S. simply couldn't afford it. So we got these on-the-one-hand-on-the-other-hand stories that emphasized the "desperate" need for childcare and yet the impossibility of actually getting it.

Nineteen eighty-eight was "the year of the kid," reported Morley Safer on CBS, and predicted that "legislation will likely pass and will offer working parents some kind of affordable day care." But then Dan Rather asked him, in his most serious investigative mode, how much it would cost. It was in stories about childcare and welfare when reporters really enunciated the "b" in billions, to punctuate from the bowels of the national piggy bank what an unaffordable luxury this was. Safer responded that it depended on which bill passed, but the Democratic bill would cost two and half BILLION, nearly blowing Rather's hair out of place with the air jet from the "b." "Expensive any way you cut it," noted Rather. "Any way," affirmed Safer.[64] This closing, which undercut Safer's story about Americans' desire for day care, was typical—all too many stories mentioned the cost without, say, showing what other things the country had been able to afford, like bailing out the shysters and criminals in the savings and loan industry, for example.

But by 1989, there were other problems with day care, and these warnings also fueled the new momism and its insistence that mom inhabit her child's inner life. In addition to stories about children who became blind, paralyzed, and brain damaged at their day care provider's hands, or those who out-and-out died, we learned from male researchers that even average day care caused "psychological harm." Jay Belsky, a psychologist then at Penn State, who has been at the forefront of the "day care is bad" line (most recently the author of the "day care produces bullies" soundbite), went on the news saying that he used to believe that day care benefited small children but changed his mind after doing some research. (Beware the convert!) As we watched footage of children crying their hearts out as mom dropped them off, Belsky asserted that children who went to day care as infants didn't do as well as those who stayed home with their mothers. Kids in day care have "an increased risk for feeling insecure in their relationships with their parents," but it was really the "insecure attachments to their mothers" that made them "have trouble in later life." Invoking the specter of "irreparable damage," Belsky asserted that such kids grew up to be "noncompliant, disobedient, and aggressive." Child "expert" Burton White flatly asserted that babies should be raised by their families (meaning mothers). Another male researcher's advice to mothers? "The later they can postpone returning to work, the better." [65]

The reporter, Robert Bazell, acknowledged there was "another side" to the story but featured no researchers with different findings about day care (such as the findings that some kids who had gone to day care since infancy did better than those who had stayed at home with mom, which CBS reported in 1991).[66] In fact, there were already scholars quite critical of Belsky's research and of his unproven assertions that day care caused kids to snub mom and pistol whip the dog, but they did not get air time.[67] In fact, less than 10 percent of articles on day care cited research that indicated that the effects of day care either were not detectable or were positive.[68] At the end of the story a pediatrician reported that some guilt-ridden parents woke their kids up at midnight (!) to play because they didn't have enough quality time with them. Now really, how many could this possibly be? Stories like this, circulating with those about how impossible it was for the government to establish a high-quality system, turned the spotlight on mom, on her selfish "choices," on her failings, and away from those in Washington who had done nothing to help us.

Belsky got on the air again in 1994, continuing to sound the alarms.[69] "How do you know your day care is good?" asked ABC News, following up with, "What is the impact on children of spending long hours, often in large groups, with someone other than a parent?" The story immediately cut to a mother who admitted, "Yes, I think there's going to be a price to pay," and continued ominously, "I don't know what it is." So the story opened with a tone of concern and guilt. Belsky, identified as "a pioneer in the field," reported that kids in fact do well in "high-quality" day care, but that most day care in the U.S. was "of limited to poor quality." Kids in such places probably didn't get the attention they needed and "the consequences can be serious." Infants left in "average" day care (whatever that meant) for twenty to thirty hours a week were likely to be "less attached" to their parents and, by age three, likely to be more aggressive and disobedient. (No statistical evidence was offered, nor were studies by other researchers which contradicted these findings reported.)

Why might stories like this—which did admit that at least some day care centers (presumably those run by Penelope Leach herself) were *good* for kids—make you feel guilty anyway? Well, let's consider what we saw on the screen and how images on TV news might have more staying power than what is said. The text that got pulled from the story and projected onto the screen said "more aggressive" and "more disobedient." No text was projected onto the screen that said "enhance intellectual and social development," which was a finding reported about the results of "high-quality" day care. If one was walking back and forth from the den to the kitchen, watching the news between breaking up double half-nelsons between warring siblings, and saw on the screen "more aggressive" and "more disobedient," what do you think the major message taken from the story might be?

The story closed with Belsky worrying that "more and more children at younger and younger ages" spend "more and more hours a day" in day care and "the quality of that day care is remarkably limited." Of course, Belsky had a point: There was, indeed, not enough "high-quality day care." But at no point did Rebecca Chase buttonhole any politicians who had consistently voted against government support for child care. This was now, effectively, a private concern. Instead, the story urged working parents, in their vast reservoirs of spare time, to go monitor their kids' day care to assess how well it was doing. And despite the fact that some care was "average" or "low quality," viewers never learned what those terms meant. The specter of the "average" or "low-quality" day care loomed as an undefined menace. Could you ever be sure that your day care center was one of the "high-quality" ones? How could you be?

In another story a few years later, Chase asserted that only 14 percent of day care was high quality "in part because parents do not know what to look for." We know which parent that would be. (Nothing in this story about mothers having to settle for what was nearby, and nothing about the government's stonewalling.)[70] In fact, according to the news, parents—i.e., mothers—were self-deluded when it came to childcare. "While most parents believe they are getting good quality day care, all too often they are wrong," warned John Blackstone of CBS. An "alarming report" on the state of day care in the U.S., covered by all three networks in February 1995, reported that 70 percent of day care centers provided "mediocre care" that "may compromise a child's ability to learn." In large text on the screen we read "40% Infant Centers—Dangerous" and "1 in 7 Promotes Healthy Development." Yet, as one expert reaffirmed, yet again (and this in 1995 when the economy was strong), the government could not step in to help because "it's going broke all over the place."[71] Of course a study just over one year later, "the most comprehensive study yet," found that leaving a child in day care did not interfere with a child's attachment to its mother.[72] But no big text on the screen ever emphasized the good news.

Even when studies found, as Tom Brokaw reported in 1997, that "children actually thrive in day care centers where the environment is stimulating," the news flashed the spotlight on those "other problems." This too was "the most comprehensive study ever conducted," and it warned that "some" mothers of kids in day care were less sensitive to their children's needs and "some" of those kids were, in turn, less affectionate with those mothers. How many? What percentage? Who knows? Were there other factors at work here besides day care? Who knows? Whatever.

NBC then emphasized that infants begin learning as young as six weeks, so they "must be introduced to music and math and foreign languages at this age because by nine or ten" the "windows" that were open to learning at these early ages would be closed.[73] Get to work on *that*, mom. (Never mind the previous generations of kids who had not learned to read or add until first grade and had still managed to learn calculus and read Shakespeare in high school.) ABC, which featured the report on day care as its lead story, also emphasized the "insensitive mothers" angle (what about Dad? Where was he in this study?) and noted that "the mother's temperament" was crucial to how kids did in day care. This story concluded that high-quality day care "can be good" for kids—when the study affirmed that, in fact, it *was* good for them.[74]

When the news did turn its attention to what other countries did, we learned that even "the best childcare system in the world . . . run and paid for by the Swedish government" didn't really work, because it too did not have enough openings for kids who needed them. Even though Sweden spent three times what the U.S. government did, according to ABC's Rebecca Chase, they still had long wait lists and so parents were "failed by the government." "So what can America's mostly private system learn from Sweden's day care?" Chase asked. "That even with unlimited spending, government alone has not met the demand." (In addition to raising the specter of a bottomless money pit, "unlimited spending" evoked cribs with Armani bed linens and, well, decoupaged high chairs.) Sweden needed more "private alternatives." (In whose opinion?) Of course no system, not even Sweden's, was perfect, but such stories encouraged us to let the politicians and the government off the hook, throw up our hands and say "Jeez, I'll just have to muddle through this by myself, best as I can." Chase also reported, erroneously, that Swedes paid 80 percent in taxes to support such a system.[75]

Finally, in the spring of 2001, we got the following headlines: DAY CARE LINKED TO AGGRESSION, YOUR CHILD CARE COULD BE TURNING YOUR CHILD VIOLENT, or, more to the point, FROM BABIES TO BULLIES.[76] Once again, a quite small and unproved negative finding from a preliminary study—whose main thrust was that there were many beneficial effects of day care—grabbed the headlines. (In fact, one of the main findings was that the more hours kids spent in day care and the better it is, the higher the kids scored on language and cognitive tests.) And once again, Jay Belsky, now at Birbeck College in London, worked the press, much to the dismay of his many coinvestigators. Belsky and a team of researchers were part of a long-term study of day care funded by the National Institute of Child Health and Human Development. In April 2001 they were scheduled to present their preliminary findings at a conference for reactions and comments and, in a move most now regard as a really bad mistake, had a press conference about the unpublished findings in which Belsky was only one of two spokespeople for the whole project. By all reports, he dominated the press conference and gave the study its spin.[77] He also gave the impression that he was the lead investigator in the study, which he wasn't.

Forget the good news. One of the preliminary findings, which was based on observing kids cared for in day care, or by their grandmas, or by their dads, versus observing kids cared for by their mothers, was that 17 percent of kids cared for by anyone other than mom for more than thirty hours a week showed more "disobedient" or "aggressive tendencies" (which, by the way, included "can't stand waiting" and "wants attention"), while 6 percent of those cared for by their mothers showed these tendencies. In other words, the difference between the two was 11 percent of kids. Meanwhile, child researchers emphasized that 83 percent of kids in day care for more than thirty hours a week *didn't* show these tendencies, and that 17 percent was a pretty average representation of kids, day care or not, who might shove another kid in line or knock over a castle she had made out of blocks. (These findings were released again in the summer of 2003 with the misleading lead, "The longer young children spend in day care, the more likely they are to be overly aggressive." Buried farther down was this: "For the vast majority of children, the behavior was within normal limits.")[78] Because of Belsky's emphasis on kids who fought, bit, or kicked, complained one child researcher, "What the press picked up on was the most aggressive of behaviors . . . when these were only among many, many items on the list of behaviors."[79] Belsky's recommendation? More mothers should stay at home longer with their kids or work part-time.

Several of Belsky's colleagues experienced highly elevated blood-pressure levels over what turned out to be his own disobedient and aggressive behavior, and they sought to get on TV and in the press to contradict his spin. (According to one account, many were no longer on speaking terms with him after the fiasco and some charged that his behavior was unprofessional.)[80] But it was the "day care produces bullies" soundbite that carried the day, and right-wing pundits were as happy as pigs in cow flops. The findings "do not bode well for the brave new world originally engineered in the name of feminism. . . . there is a steep, possibly prohibitive cost in the so-called 'liberated life' of countless American women who . . . have seen fit to warehouse a whopping 75 percent of the nation's youngsters . . . to further or maintain full-time professional careers," huffed the conservative *Washington Times*.[81] Phyllis Schlafly (a working mother throughout her life, by the way) praised the study, and conservative pundit Robert Novak gloated on CNN that the study was "a blow for the feminists, who defend dumping their children in a day care center."[82]

Another update of this study is due out in 2004. Expect bad news and scary headlines, no matter what the study actually says. And if you see Belsky on TV, hit the remote—the guy is bad for your health. And by the way, in case you were wondering how fathers figure in the equation, you will undoubtedly be shocked to hear that there has been a singular absence of front-page headlines guilt-tripping the fathers of America about how much time they spend at work. So you will be interested to know that a 1999 study by Ellen Galinsky of the Families and Work Institute found that kids actually felt fine about the amount of time they spent with their mothers, whether they worked or not. It was Dad they were missing; it was Dad they wanted more time with.[83]

So, here were your choices. Join hands with those neglectful, child-hating feminists and consign your child to a day care center that resembled, most closely, one of those dark, satanic English orphanages staffed by sharp-nosed hags and warlocks that Charles Dickens might have described. Or stay home. It's your choice.

Now, if you had decided, because your budget allowed it, to go the high-class, Princess Diana route and get a nanny or full-time baby-sitter rather than "warehouse" your kid, you were in for trouble too. Stories about killer baby-sitters and murdering nannies were hot stuff, presented as a service to parents, but helping, of course, to increase ratings and sell newspapers and magazines. (And maybe making those of us who couldn't afford nannies feel like we weren't missing much?) In 1992 we met Heidi Jensen, arrested for beating a baby to death with a hair clipper, and a Swedish nanny (how classy could you get?) indicted for allegedly setting a three-year-old girl on fire. In the most chilling footage from a crude black-and-white surveillance camera—which CBS aired in 1992 and again in 1993, and NBC used in 1994—we saw a baby-sitter beating a two-year-old and throwing her to the floor. CBS acknowledged that "these are exceptions" but then added that "with more women in the workplace, increasingly there are fears about who's minding the baby-sitter." (Whose fears? Evidence for the increase?) To drive home the sense of danger mothers should feel (and to add the imprimatur of reality?), CBS then showed a clip from a shameless (and really cheesy) Hollywood melodrama, *The Hand That Rocks the Cradle* (1992), and emphasized that "the movie hits all the maternal hot buttons, not only fears of violence but the guilt and jealousy that working mothers inevitably feel." (No matter that the mom in the movie didn't work, but got a nanny so she could build her own greenhouse the size of Madison Square Garden in her backyard.) Although CBS conceded that "not every nanny story is a horror story," NBC, in 1994, ran a story about background checks on nannies that reported that 7 percent of the applicants were rejected because of criminal records or child abuse, and that even convicted murderers and drug dealers had applied to become the next Mary Poppins.[84] The biggest story broke in 1997, when British nanny Louise Woodward was accused of killing eight-month-old Matthew Eappen by shaking him to death. Although Woodward was convicted of murder, she maintained her innocence; a judge reduced the charge to manslaughter and let her return to Britain. If you can't trust a British nanny, who can you trust?

* * *

Throughout all the negative, pessimistic, or fatalistic coverage of childcare in the news media, there were surprisingly very few representations of childcare in TV shows or movies, given how central childcare had become to most parents' lives. There were really cool housekeepers like Alice in *The Brady Bunch;* or the fantasy hunks Tony (Tony Danza) in *Who's the Boss* and Charles (Scott Baio) of *Charles in Charge* who worked in that frequently-seen line of work, the male governess; or the English house-keeper *Mr. Belvedere;* or the live-in painter Eldin on *Murphy Brown,* who took care of her son, Avery. (*Charles in Charge* and *Who's the Boss* both premiered in 1984, high point of the McMartin scandal, when producers probably didn't want to feature day care centers as part of their sitcom landscape.) In *Look Who's Talking,* Kirstie Alley hired John Travolta to be her baby's nanny. And the short-lived sitcom *Day by Day* (NBC, 1988–89), about a stockbroker and his attorney wife who quit their jobs to set up their own day care center so they could spend more time with their own kids, seems mainly to have helped launch the careers of Julia Louis-Dreyfus and Courtney Thorne-Smith. Whether day care had been too tarnished in the news media, or was still somehow thought of as too controversial, it was simply avoided in TV Land. Even the kids in *Rugrats* didn't go to day care. Where are the after-school programs for, say, *Malcolm in the Middle*? Who takes care of Elinor and Lindsey's new babies on *The Practice*? Only Peter Benton on *ER* seemed to have a regular relationship with a day care center. And he, after all, was a forlorn, single dad.

Several movies, however, either made fun of the quest to find a decent childcare provider or, as in *The Hand That Rocks the Cradle,* gave us a nanny who made Norman Bates seem well adjusted. Claire, a stay-at-home mom who seemed to have stepped right out of one of those *Good Housekeeping* "New Traditionalist" ads, and Michael Bartel (Annabella Sciorra and Matt McCoy) had an adorable, never-whining, ever-agreeable daughter, Emma, around five, and a three-month-old baby, Joe. As noted above, Michael suggested that Claire get a nanny because now that she had a new infant, she naturally wanted to build her own greenhouse in her spare time. Miraculously, the next day, a gorgeous blonde, Peyton (Rebecca De Mornay), stepped out from behind Emma's school bus saying she wanted to be the Bartels' nanny. So Claire (Hello? Earth to Claire?) invited her in and hired her that night. No messy stuff like check-ing references. For the next hour-and-a-half of the movie Peyton sought to steal the affections of Claire's husband and kids while driving Claire nuts.

This movie capitalized on "the danger of the imposter" theme that was such a favorite both in Hollywood and in the news media. When it comes to childcare, a woman can fake it: She pretends to be a nurturing caregiver when in fact she is a murdering psychopath. The other old chestnut here was that childless women wanted to "steal" the lives of those who had kids because a woman is nothing—even if she looks like Rebecca De Mornay—if she doesn't have kids. And finally, of course, once Peyton was rampaging through the house with a shovel and a fireplace poker à la Jack Nicholson in *The Shining,* it was up to the mom, Claire, to save her kids all by herself by yelling the immortal line, "This is *my* family, Peyton," and then hurling Peyton out the attic window.

Childcare was the impossible dream in *Baby Boom* (1987). The potential nannies Diane Keaton interviewed were either bimbos, lunatics, or former Gestapo members. In *Mrs. Doubtfire* (1993), once the most perfect nanny in the world is revealed to be Dad, the unforgiving careerist bitch mom, Miranda (Sally Field), has to find a new housekeeper. The one we meet looks like the wicked witch of the north and hisses "I don't do laundry, I don't do windows, I don't do carpets," and ends her long list with "I don't do dinners, and I don't do reading." In *Beethoven* (1992), the mom decided to go back to work and left the kids with the baby-sitter from hell, an old bag who made the kids listen to her sing "Voulez-Vous Coucher Avec Moi" while the youngest wandered off and nearly drowned in her pool until Beethoven—the dog—came to her rescue. Dog teaches Mom a lesson. Mom realizes that work isn't for her.

By 1995, 75 percent of kids under five were regularly watched by someone other than their parents.[85] Today, childcare centers with postmodernist play structures, teachers with degrees in environmental education, a Little Tikes "activity center" for each infant, baby goats in the "farm area," and piped-in Mozart violin concertos are geared toward and used by primarily white, middle-class, often professional families. Lower-income parents can't afford them, and rely on home-based care, especially by relatives.[86] African American and Latino mothers must rely on their extended families. In general, working-class parents use more informal arrangements, like relatives or neighbors.[87]

The Reagan administration was no friend to women and kids, especially poor ones, but the Bush II team makes him look like Mr. Rogers.

Even conservative politicians have had to concede that Head Start is a proven winner for preschoolers, but not Team Bush. They proposed giving four-year-old participants in the program "tests" to see if they've learned anything and, if not, implied that Head Start could be "defunded," as they say in D.C. As it is, in 2003, only three out of five preschoolers who were eligible for Head Start could get in the program.[88] They also proposed dismantling the whole program at the federal level and letting the states run it as they saw fit. The budget Bush proposed in the winter of 2003 would slash taxes for the rich while dismantling childcare and after-school programs that serve five hundred thousand kids. As Bob Herbert of *The New York Times* put it, "In the arena of bad ideas that one is a champion."[89] According to Marian Wright Edelman, head of the Children's Defense Fund, the cost of Bush's proposed tax cut on stock dividends (also for rich people) "is enough to provide comprehensive health care for all 9.2 million uninsured American children and Head Start for all unserved eligible preschoolers."[90] Bush even proposed cuts for his own cynically titled "No Child Left Behind" program, which should be renamed "Piss On the Little Bastards."

Despite the fact that many more fathers now do drop off and pick up at day care, the prime responsibility for this remains the mother's. Every day millions of women must organize their time and their space—where they go to, when, and for how long—in an often highly strategic fashion. They try to arrange to have shorter commutes to work, make more trips between work and day care, and time these so that trips to the grocery store, drug store, and dry cleaner can also occur.[91]

So, when all is said and done, as we review this sorry history, a clear villain emerges—the far right wing in the United States. Now, sophisticated academic and governmental analysts who have devoted their careers to studying all the multiple reasons why we do not have a national childcare policy in this country would call this simplistic. They would point to very real debates over whether day care should be set up in the public schools, whether childcare should be administered by the federal government or the states or even smaller units like towns and community groups or by private companies. They would note that there have been debates about who should set childcare standards, the feds or the states. They would remind you that there have been important debates about whether religious-sponsored centers should receive federal funding, given the church-state separation issues we have here. They would note that America's tradition of individualism and its emphasis that the family be a private unit independent of the state (when, of course, it isn't) have worked against most Americans seeing childcare as a pressing collective need. They would make these points in spite of the persistent and wide gap between public opinion polls and what our "leaders" choose to do. Finally, they would note that in a country like France, which does provide neighborhood-based day care, the children turn out to be, well, French.

Despite all these complexifying (as Bush II might say) factors, there is no denying that it was Nixon who vetoed childcare, then Ford; Ronald Reagan who cut its funding. It was George Bush I who vowed to veto childcare legislation, ensuring that it wouldn't pass. And besides, their faces fit much better on a dartboard than some piece of paper that says "individualism." So call us simplistic. (We're used to it.)

But let's not let the media, especially the news media, off the hook here. Yes, they were ahead of many politicians on this issue, beating the drum about the pressing need for better-quality day care. But whether they were hamstrung by the codes of objectivity which require "two sides" (and only two sides) to be represented in a story, or whether they had simply bought into conservative arguments about day care—that it was unaffordable, that it wasn't really the government's business anyway—their stories encouraged us to be politically resigned on this issue, to agree that however serious the situation, nothing could be done.

It is a direct result of feminism and mothers' need to work that millions of children and their parents today have access to high-quality day care centers with a trained staff—yes, a few of them even male—and a creative, developmentally nurturing curriculum. But as a result of the Republicans' insistence on the new momism, there remain millions of parents who want such day care and have no access to it, and "by and large the poorest children who could benefit most from professionally run, stimulating child care have the least access to it."[92] Many young mothers who need a salary—and, frankly, time away from the kids—feel they have no choice but to quit their jobs, either for the sake of the kids, or because they simply can't afford the childcare near them.

Remember that glass of wine you were supposed to have at the beginning of the chapter when you were envisioning a childcare center that also made dinner and did your shopping? As our last pitch for day care, we treat you to the true story of WearGuard Corporation, the nation's largest direct marketer of work clothes, in Norwell, Massachusetts. Here's what is included in the benefits package for its thirteen hundred employees, along with the vacation, health insurance, and pension plans: on-site day care, a snow-day program, an accredited kindergarten, a school vacation program, a summer camp program, carry-out dinner, and a dry-cleaning drop off. And get this. In December, the childcare director has slumber parties for the kids on weekend nights so that the parents can do their holiday shopping in peace. According to their human resources director, " 'We believe we get better work from employees who aren't worrying about problems at home.' " [93] Hey, isn't that a quote from the Communist Manifesto?

To emphasize how truly backward our society is as a result of dumb men making really stupid choices, let's finish with a little quiz. Let's do it like *Jeopardy*. In 1990, this government required companies to give a new mother a year's leave at 90 percent pay. Answer: What was Sweden? This country provided nurseries for most children over eighteen months. Again: What was Sweden? Nearly half of the children under three in this country were in publicly financed nurseries, and nearly 95 percent of children three to six were (and are). Answer: What is Denmark? In this country, 95 percent of children aged three to five are in preschool. Answer: What is France? This country provides care for one quarter of children under three in wholly or partially subsidized nurseries. Again: What is France? [94] In 1984, this country gave workers twelve weeks of maternity leave with pay. Answer: What is Brazil? (Yes, Brazil!) This country mandated eight weeks of maternity leave *with pay*. Answer: What is Kenya? (You heard us, Kenya!) [95] This country provided none of these things; instead, to help mothers and small children, its magazines featured profiles of rich celebrity moms who could show women how to do it all. Answer: What was the United States?

The moral of the story: Don't listen to anyone who says that the parents and children of the United States, whatever their income, race, or ethnicity, don't want, need, or deserve such centers. And the next time someone suggests that day care is just too darn expensive, ask how much Kenneth Lay paid for his various ski lodges in Aspen, his château in France and the jet to transport him there, or tote up how much one year of war in Iraq costs at $3.9 billion (with a *b*) per month. Activate the deflection shields. When it comes to childcare, do not take the new momism for an answer.

NINE

Moms "Я" Us

Now would be an appropriate time to do what most of us loathe doing—go walk into your kids' room(s) and take a good look. Go ahead. Most of them look the same—as if a grenade had exploded in the middle of Toys "Я" Us, Target, and/or Abercrombie & Fitch. Look at all that crap. Now, instead of cursing under your breath at your child, yet again, for having zero concept of what the term "clean up" means, or cursing at yourself for utterly failing to make your home look like those breeze-kissed rooms in the Pottery Barn catalog, think about how all that crap got there.

We bought it because advertisers urged us not to miss one tiny developmental step in matching the right toy with the right stage; we bought it because our kids have been so effectively and relentlessly marketed to that they've learned how to nag the living breath out of us until we cave (the toy industry actually has developed a category of cheap items they call "shut-up toys");[1] we bought it because we needed them to be distracted while we made dinner, did the laundry, got ready for work, and answered phone calls from telemarketers. And we bought it because we have been all too ready to equate buying plastic, fake fur, and sandblasted denim with demonstrating just how much we love our kids, a trend and a weakness that has accounted for the stupefying explosion of the profits of the toy and kid clothing industry since the 1970s. We also bought it because a host of business-friendly deregulatory moves during the Reagan administration made it much, much easier to apply a host of stealth targeting to our kids, and therefore to us.

The new momism gained momentum in the 1980s because of media panics about endangered kids, the lack of institutional supports for families, and because of right-wing attacks against working mothers. But let's not also forget that a key tenet of the new momism—that it was crucial to invest in as many goods and services for your child as possible—was very, very profitable. The spread of cable TV, which brought distant UHF stations and kid-specific channels like Nickelodeon, Disney, The Cartoon Network, Fox Family, and MTV into the home, made targeting mothers and kids much easier, and more incessant. The ever-ballooning standards of good motherhood were inflated even further by the simultaneous exhortations to buy more, buy better, buy sooner.

A review of the tactics and profits of the toy industry since 1970 shows the decisive role they played, too, in promoting the new momism. Of course we enjoyed getting our kids stuff, seeing their faces light up at the new doll or the new Delia's shirt. But the toy and other kid- and teen-related industries have hijacked those pleasures into year-round, daily pitches that have made this element of the new momism especially insufferable. If you feel, as a mother, that every year the barrage gets worse, guess what—you're right.

See that child of yours across the room? That is not a child. That is, in the parlance of toy advertisers, "a guided missile of marketing."[2] As Peggy Charren, President of Action for Children's Television, put it in 1985, "The whole world of childhood has become one huge sales pitch. It's nauseating." Children have been marketed to throughout the twentieth century, although targeting children escalated dramatically with the rise of radio and after-school programming that hawked decoder rings generously made available by the program's sponsors. Mothers in the 1960s and '70s who had to take their kids with them to the supermarket noticed that more toys were being hawked at A&P (remember the A&P?) and Food King. The toy sections were aimed directly at the kids, not at their mothers because, as A&P executive Larry Kaufman put it, "Kids can't pass toy sections without picking something up. What mother could refuse to buy her child a toy?" So books, model kits, water guns, Play-Doh, doctor kits, yo-yos, dolls, and the like were dropped from the higher shelves to lower shelves where kids could see them immediately and then break into the requisite whining.[3] Some shelves were redesigned on an incline so more toys could be displayed at a better angle, and toys were also put in the cereal aisles where marketers knew kids were helping Mom pick out the breakfast fare. End-aisles facing the front of the store were also a favorite for toy marketers. Something called a "Planogram" helped suppliers decide which toys to display when and, of course, the shelf space in supermarkets for toys tripled just before Christmas.[4]

So bombarding the kids was hardly new in the 1970s and beyond. But niche marketing was only in its infancy, a consumer safety movement was just beginning to hit the kids' product market, and, of course, more mothers were spending more time away from the kids. As increasing numbers of mothers went back to work, the toy business figured out quite well how to profit from their guilt, as well as from their reduced amount of time to shop. In 1980, the toy business was a $5 billion industry; by 1992 it had more than doubled, to $13.5 billion.[5] And get this figure: In 1982, our country accounted for a full one-half of the entire planet's toy sales.[6]

Several powerful trends collided in the 1970s and '80s that got manifested in pitching toys to Mom and the kids. Experts in the toy industry simultaneously capitalized on and intensified the emergence of the new momism. Educated parents and those influenced by the women's movement wanted their children to be raised playing with nonsexist and nonviolent toys. They also wanted to shield their children from excessive materialism and consumerism. At the same time, however, they didn't want their kids "falling behind" in any way, and they were sitting ducks for toy companies that knew it and hawked a host of toys and games claiming to be educational. On the other end of the toy philosophy spectrum, the Reagan team's bellicose militarism, backed up by military interventions both ludicrous (Grenada) and lethal (aid to the Contras in Nicaragua), and coupled with its hairy-chested antifeminist backlash, cleared the way for toys far more sexist and violent than those from Howdy Doody days.

Just as the battles over redefining motherhood were a struggle between prefeminist norms and feminist challenges to the MRS, so too did the changes in the toy industry reflect major struggles between feminist and antifeminist visions of how to raise children. In other words, at the very same time—the 1980s—when millions of women were struggling to redefine a mother's place, and what it meant to be a good mother, especially if you needed or wanted to work, the toy industry simultaneously surrounded her kids with nonsexist, educational toys and with toys that were more retrograde than ever. Whatever she was doing, her kids were getting very mixed messages about the proper roles for boys and girls, the proper roles for mothers and fathers.

In addition, marketers offered mothers from different socioeconomic classes different kinds of products, exploiting the knowledge and education of middle-class and professional women, while figuring that working-class and poor mothers wouldn't care about which toys were developmentally appropriate, nonviolent, and nonsexist and, if they did, couldn't afford them anyway. In the process they reinforced another "us" versus "them" division, this one based on class. Just as the tobacco companies in the 1970s pitched low-tar cigarettes in *The New York Times* magazine while wallpapering poor, inner-city neighborhoods with Camel billboards, so too did toy makers target the home planetarium to upscale mothers and toy bayonets to those with lower incomes. Mothers like us—college-educated with decent salaries—were especial suckers here because the makers of all those "good" toys flattered us as women who were smart and "knew better" and so would of course buy the nontoxic doctor kit over Barbie's Beauty Salon. Now, given our class position, we *do* think the doctor kit is the better choice; others might disagree. But it is especially important for women like us to see what was fobbed off on other mothers and their kids, how that stuff got into our own homes whether we liked it or not, and how toys, clothes, and all the rest mark an increasingly rigid hierarchy among kids over who is special and who is not.

As the 1980s and '90s progressed, distinctions based on conspicuous consumption and brand names became even more fine grained. Kids themselves started to appreciate ever earlier, with the help of all the intensified advertising geared just to them, that they were supposed to look privileged even if they weren't. They had to learn how to make others envy, even resent them, and Ralph Lauren, Calvin Klein, and Nike were there to do just that. Their parents, meanwhile, obsessed with what Barbara Ehrenreich brilliantly diagnosed as the "Fear of Falling," helped them understand the pecking order based on the fine gradations between a Toyota Camry, a Ford Expedition, and a Lexus. The ones lower down on the ladder got razzed for not having the brand name signifiers of those higher up. But once those in the middle started sporting the Polo logo, then the kids higher up the income scale had to display even more expensive and uncommon logos and products. So what was a "good" mother under these circumstances? One who got her children all those educational toys when they were little so they'd have a head start and then, when they were teenagers, bought them clothes and other crap that proclaimed, through their logos, that they were better than the other kids?

Once the Reagan administration came into power, with its mix of machismo and let-the-market-decide ideology, there was a new environment perfectly suited for intensified marketing to children, and thus the intensified beleaguerment of mom. Reagan's FCC, under Chairman Mark Fowler, was dedicated to as little regulation of broadcasters and advertisers as possible, especially around children's programming. Reagan's Federal Trade Commission (FTC), which monitors advertising, also rescinded restrictions on advertising to children, extending the number of minutes per hour that could be filled with ads to kids, and making it much easier to sell to them more often using more visual tricks. The religious right, so concerned about the sanctity of motherhood and the morality of women working outside the home, was apparently much less squeamish about using children as stealth marketing devices in the home. The Christian Broadcasting Network in 1977 advised advertisers to sell to parents by selling to their kids. "Whether it's toothpaste or toy trucks, burgers or bionic dolls," the ad on the network advised, "Charlie's mom is buying. But you've got to sell to Charlie first."[7] Thus, the deregulation of children's television under Reagan gave mother yet another new job: one-woman media critic and regulator, stauncher of the flow of commercialism and stealth advertising into the home and her kids' psyches.

Mothers have found themselves caught between these powerful cross-currents. We don't want our kids to feel deprived, we want them to have as many games and toys as possible that promote as many skills as possible, and yet we believe that in doing so our kids have started to acquire stuff with the same greed and mindlessness that Imelda Marcos collected shoes. In various polls, parents have said, basically, that try as they might to pile up the anticonsumerist sandbags, the endless entreaties to their kids still come pouring over the dikes. Eighty percent of respondents to a Time/CNN poll in 2002 said they believed children are more spoiled today than ten years ago, and 68 percent admitted that their own kids were very or somewhat spoiled. Seventy-one percent said their kids were exposed to too much advertising. And two-thirds of the respondents bemoaned the trend we all find dispiriting: that our children too often "define their self-worth in terms of possessions."[8]

Yet a good mother is not supposed to allow her kid to feel like a dork because he or she doesn't have what the other kids have. Nor should the good mother let any opportunity go by that might give her kid a leg up when it comes to reading, math, spatial relations, geography, problem solving, vocabulary building, negotiating, strategizing, cooperating, compromising, competing, computer programming, sports, learning music, acting, sculpting, or building small electric motors. Because advertisers have divided kids up, demographically, into micromarkets—the one- to two-year-old market, the two to fives, up to tweens and so forth—there are age-appropriate, necessary purchases for pretty much every three-to-six-month period.[9] In addition, marketers have cultivated the "collecting" mindset in kids—no kid can have just one Barbie or just one Beanie Baby or just one American Eagle T-shirt. The consumerist aspects of motherhood—certainly a challenge in the 1950s—have become much more daunting because mothers and their kids are more bombarded than ever before by sales campaigns, and mothers struggle to find that fine line, given one's budget, of buying the right kinds and amount of stuff without socializing our kids to think of themselves, first and foremost, as shoppers.

It is in the realm of toys and other goods and services for kids that the stark contradictions inherent in the new momism seem especially impossible to reconcile. Our homes are supposed to be havens from the everything-has-a-price, everyone-is-defined-by-commodities values of the marketplace. Mothers are meant to be self-sacrificing, embodying the value of altruism and putting others before ourselves. Our kids are priceless, their value to us completely outside market calculations. And yet, our devotion as mothers, our commitment to our kids not falling through the cracks, our kids' own sense of self-worth and our love for them, all have been and are measured by how many and what kinds of goods and services we buy for them. If we get them too little they are deprived, and if we get them too much they are spoiled. Either way, we fail.

The increased onslaught of toy marketing began with the megastores, in which guys like Charles Lazarus, the founder and CEO of Toys "Я" Us, applied the techniques of the supermarket chain to toy stores and pitched his stores as the bargain-hunter's dream. As Lazarus put it, "When I realized that toys *broke* . . . I knew it was a good business."[10] In 1968, Toys "Я" Us (founded in 1949) had four stores; in 1978, there were seventy-two stores, with twelve more planned for 1979.[11] These stores were huge, averaging thirty-six thousand square feet, seven to ten times the size of other specialty stores built then. In 1978 alone, earnings for the company were up by 77 percent, with sales at $350 million.[12] That same year, the retail toy industry brought in about $6 billion, and the figures for 1979 showed a 15 percent increase, despite a still crappy economy.[13] In 1979, the toy industry spent $244 million hawking its wares, a 17 percent increase over the previous year.[14] By 1982, Toys "Я" Us had one hundred twenty stores, offering eighteen thousand different items for sale, with profits still booming.[15] Although most toy stores did 50 to 60 percent of their business just before Christmas, electronic toys and games, which began to catch on in the late 1970s and early 1980s, opened up a year-round market, especially for teenagers and young adults.[16] Toys "Я" Us sought to capitalize on and cement this trend. The store began stocking necessities like Pampers and baby food and selling them at cut-rate prices with the knowledge that once the poor sucker parents were in the store for diapers, additional impulse buying was inevitable, especially if there was a whining, fit-throwing toddler along for the ride.

The strategy at Toys "Я" Us was to lay out the stores in an identical pattern, so that a New Jersey woman visiting her daughter in Ohio could walk into the Midwest store and know exactly where to go to find the Hot Wheels or the baby dolls. One way this was made obvious was through color-coding. Just as feminist mothers were seeking to overthrow sex-role stereotypes through records and books like *Free to Be You and Me,* Toys "Я" Us featured aisles of Barbies and My Little Ponies painted bright, shocking pink, juxtaposed to neighboring aisles, black, gray, or camouflage-colored, lined with trucks, tanks, and G.I. Joe.

By the early 1980s, a new parental concern shaped the toy business: worries about the declining standards of the country's public schools. White flight to private schools accelerated in the 1970s in response to court-ordered desegregation. And the tax-revolt movements—Proposition 13 in California, Prop 2 1/2 in Massachusetts—cut the money available to public schools. Meanwhile, stories about "Why Johnny Can't Read," press coverage of declining SAT scores, and evidence that five-year-old Japanese kids could do advanced calculus while American high schoolers thought Greenwich Mean Time was a new rock band all worried parents that their kids would be left behind in the competitive dust. Many mothers were a ripe market for educational toys.

Also, there were mothers who didn't necessarily want their kids playing with toys they thought would encourage them to think of themselves as soldiers of fortune or brainless sexpots, like Little Johnny Flame Thrower or Las Vegas Barbie. Hasbro Toys, for example, got 65 percent of its total revenues from G.I. Joe in 1965; by the early 1970s, sales had plummeted because of antiwar sentiment. But then Hasbro and others looked at the demographics of the mid-1980s—baby boom women reaching their prime child-bearing years, women who had postponed having children but now were ready. As one analyst put it, "With smaller families and more working mothers, there will be a tendency to spend more money on fewer kids." [17] Toy producers began to suspect that if they promised enrichment, they could also charge more money.

While it was certainly true that many mothers were looking for toys that were stimulating and compensated for the fact that America still had no national day care or nursery school system, the toy industry always suggested that the new marketing trends were entirely driven by mothers. "There's a great push to build the better baby," noted Helen Boehm, child psychologist and toy consultant. Or, as another toy executive put it, "mothers want . . . superbabies." (Because they themselves are supermoms?) So new phrases began appearing in toy ads that hadn't been there in ads for Silly Putty in 1960: "word recognition," "hand-eye coordination," "verbal skills," and "creative play." As one toy executive put it, "Mothers like to be assured that their child will get something out of the toy." So the toy industry took these concerns and, of course, magnified and packaged them in ways that we liked (unisex carpentry sets) and in ways that made us nuts (phonics for infants, trigonometry flashcards for two-year-olds). Some such toys, like that plastic ball you'd get from Johnson & Johnson that had three smaller balls that fit inside, came with a twenty-page instruction manual so you would use it in developmentally appropriate ways. What was wrong with just rolling it across the floor?

Brand names like Fisher-Price became very important. "A parent may think a familiar name means a quality product and will buy it to keep the kid happy because they feel guilty about not spending time with him or her," noted the editor of *Toy & Hobby World*. There was a new emphasis on toys for preschoolers, which became one of the fastest-growing segments in the toy industry in the early 1980s. [18] One study showed that spending on toys was increasing not because people were having more kids, but because they had more income, especially with Mom working. Also, as parents divorced, toy companies understood that parents sometimes competed with each other over who would get the kids the coolest—

and the most—toys.[19] Fisher-Price was no fool; in 1985 they increased their advertising budget 40 percent, heavily targeting first-time mothers.[20] They also developed a new line of arts-and-crafts toys specifically for preschoolers.[21] In the 1970s, Fisher-Price might introduce only twenty new toys a year for all age groups; by 1985, the company was introducing thirty new toys specifically for the preschool market.[22] Hasbro's doll for boys, My Buddy, featured shoes with real laces that needed to be tied and Velcro attachments on the shirts that help the boy learn how to dress and undress the doll. When we were kids, we practiced this on ourselves, or on our cats. By the mid-1980s some stores had seen a 50 percent growth in the sale of preschool toys over previous years.[23]

In 1981 Johnson & Johnson, projecting a 26 percent increase in births by 1985, staked out the infant toy market.[24] And the niches got smaller and smaller. By 1985 some stores were separating infant toys along six-month increments, and preschool toys by one-year increments. Now mothers could walk into stores with newly installed "learning centers," which showcased the educational preschool fare. In short, mothers who were, in general, older and more affluent, were spending more money on toys per child than ever before. In 1981, consumers would spend 6.8 billion on playthings, a 60 percent increase over 1977.[25]

A key part of the new marketing strategies during the 1980s was to encourage Mom to see things from the baby's or child's point of view, to put herself in her baby's position, so she could properly anticipate his or her current and future developmental needs. For example, in 1985 Fisher-Price marketed a crib mobile "from the baby's point of view." This meant that the animals on the mobile faced down into the crib, staring directly at the baby. This was designed, in part, to develop the baby's eye tracking more quickly.[26] As *Advertising Age* quipped sarcastically, the toy companies were "going beyond their role as marketers of playthings, assuming a position as child development expert."[27]

By the late 1980s, mom and the kids didn't even have to go out—every week, your mailbox would be stuffed with kid catalogs that sold everything from rattles and blocks to diapers made out of stonewashed Alpaca fur. Several of these catalogs, like HeartSong, were dedicated to educational, nonviolent, and nonsexist toys. Others, like the one from F.A.O. Schwartz, specialized in $500 dolls. Millions of mothers welcomed these catalogs, in part because they avoided the torture of shopping with small children, and because many of them offered things Toys "Я" Us wouldn't touch because they were too safe or too educational. But now there was a new phenomenon in the home: Very small children could sit on the sofa with items targeted specifically to them and say, "I want this," "I want this," and "I want this."

At the same time, of course, crass commercialism, with absolutely no pretense to enrich anything except the manufacturers' bank accounts, became even bolder. Advertisers and/or the entertainment industries carefully tutored children in the art of nagging (their conferences actually included sessions titled "The Fine Art of Nagging"),[28] of wearing down maternal resistance, of interposing the voices of outside authorities between the kids and the mother, usually to the kids'—and the outside authority's—advantage. One child marketing expert calculated that kids aged five to twelve, between their requests while out shopping, at home, or on vacation, pestered their parents for stuff about three thousand times a year.[29]

Ironically, mothers were themselves looking increasingly to these outside authorities for advice on child rearing, on being good wives and mothers. So mothers were in a bind—new, multiple voices of authority were coming directly into the home, especially through women's magazines and cable TV. Some of these voices mothers respected, and looked to for guidance, but other voices were suspect and not to be trusted. So there were more demanding gatekeeping functions imposed on mothers. Advertisers, especially when addressing mothers in parenting magazines, did and do encourage mothers to see themselves as informed savvy consumers who, if they're smart, will indeed buy the best things for their kids. But at the same time, the advertisers were also approaching the kids this way, and you can't have two authorities in the house, now can you? These marketing pitches—one set to Mom, the other to the kids—were inherently and highly contradictory, reaffirming the mother's authority on the one hand but undermining it on the other.

One notorious and wildly successful campaign aimed at Mom and the kids was for that 1983 break-down-the-toy-store-doors sensation, the Cabbage Patch Kids. One thing neither of us recalls from our childhood is any of our parents participating in a toy riot. But in 1983, Cabbage Patch dolls turned normally well-behaved adults into crazed swarms of toy-seeking locusts. The news media cast the mass Christmastime parental panic to locate one of the dolls as some inexplicable and sudden hysteria, but Coleco's $2 million promotional campaign to pitch the dolls was anything but haphazard. First—and important, given how toys in the 1980s came to be pitched—each doll was unique, "one of a kind," so one kid's was different from another's, and you could own more than one. Why, you could own dozens and none would be identical. Kids also "adopted" the dolls, so they didn't just get the doll, they got the doll's birth certificate, name, baby footprints, and a parenting guide. There were male dolls too, some in little football helmets or baseball caps, to try to lure in boy buyers. A full array of accessories also sang their siren song: Cabbage Patch strollers, slumber bags, clothes, and baby carriers.[30]

The press launch of the doll included events like staged adoption ceremonies at Boston Children's Museum. Coleco's press kit included advice from child psychologists on the importance of pretend play and the value to children of "the bonding process." Such pitches resonated perfectly with the editors at women's magazines, and *Working Woman, Woman's Day, McCall's, Parents,* and *Essence* all featured the Kids as a great Christmas gift idea. Leaving little to chance, however, Coleco sent a letter and a doll to Jane Pauley, hugely popular cohost of *Today,* whose pregnancy Americans were following week by week. A five-minute spot on the show featuring the dolls shortly followed. Sixty percent of the television advertising for the dolls was targeted to mothers during daytime and early evening programming. As Christmas approached and demand increased, television news began showcasing stories about craven parents on the verge of insurrection in Toys "Я" Us if they couldn't get the doll. Demand soared even higher. The campaign was brilliant, and brought Coleco, according to one marketing analyst, $100 million in free advertising.[31] The dolls that seemed so anticommercial, because they were "homely" and had a handmade look, took the country by storm precisely because the marketing scheme behind them rivaled the planning for the twentieth anniversary of the Super Bowl.

As some companies sought to increase sales, and the amount of loot in junior's bedroom, by guilt-tripping mothers or suggesting that all playtime should really be about home schooling, other companies set their sights straight on the kids and their guilty pleasures. In what was called licensing, toy makers took an already established character with built-in media exposure, like Mickey Mouse or Winnie the Pooh or E.T., and created toys based on that character. The licensing of characters for toys boomed, from a $6.6 billion industry in 1978 to $20.6 billion in 1982.[32] But a new ploy emerged in the early 1980s that did not amuse children's activists like Peggy Charren, president of the now defunct and much-missed Action for Children's Television. This stratagem was called syndication, in which a TV show for kids was based on a toy, like Mattel's He-Man and Masters of the Universe, or Kenner's Strawberry Shortcake. In 1970 the FCC had warned broadcasters against airing shows based on toys because they were, in fact, program-length commercials. Similarly, the FTC had in 1971 forbade toy companies from using camera techniques such as slow-motion, freeze-frames, or stroboscopic lights to make their toys look way cooler than they really were. (Some consumer activists thought it might be deceptive to show Johnny Lightning cars capable of drag-strip speeds in the ads, only to get the cars home and watch them move with the velocity of a slug.)

But this was the early 1980s, and mothers were in Reagan country now. Reagan's FCC, in 1983, simply eliminated guidelines for children's programming, regarding them as wasteful and burdensome regulations. Reagan's FTC lifted the 1971 camera restrictions in 1984, letting the toy companies determine for themselves what might be deceptive or misleading.[33] And at least eight shows based on toys and other merchandise premiered on Saturday mornings in 1983. See, the FCC's line, parroted straight from broadcasters and toy companies' position papers, was that deregulation wouldn't really change kids' programming all *that* much because competition in the marketplace would keep everyone in line.[34] We guess they were right: Between 1983 and 1985, the number of toy-based shows jumped from fourteen to forty.[35] By 1985, sales figures showed that cartoons based on toys, and the toys they were based on, sold much, much better than toys without TV tie-ins.[36] ACT noted that if ABC's prime-time show *Hotel* were called, instead, *The Marriott,* people would be up in arms about crossing the line between advertising and programming. But because these were shows for kids, who cared?

Toy manufacturers were perceptive enough not to advertise Ms. Shortcake the toy on the same show in which Ms. Shortcake was also the headliner. Nonetheless, Peggy Charren and others argued that such shows were simply half-hour or hour commercials instead of actual programs, and filed a complaint with the FCC. The National Association for Better Broadcasting labeled the He-Man series "the heaviest load of outright commercial exploitation that has ever been heaped on America's children."[37] Although Charren was trying to prevent the country's children from becoming "guided missiles of marketing," she also thought that maybe the networks could come up with something a little more edifying for kids than musclemen punching each other out at Castle Grayskull.

A Mattel executive suggested that critics like Charren had "rocks in their heads," and stated, "You have to construct good entertainment" (e.g., quality programming like *He-Man and Masters of the Universe*) "and if that's based on a toy . . . that's what should be used." He further added that the show was exemplary fare for kids because "we don't want anyone getting killed," and each episode ended with He-Man coming on and giving "a little moral lesson."[38] Added an executive from Kenner, "Advertising directly to children helps make them 'more responsible consumers.' The decision-making process . . . is part of the growth process."[39] So for those of you who suffered through sons nagging for a fifth Skeletor figure, Sy-Klone, Prince Adam, and Moss Man, rest assured that your boys were just exhibiting a newfound maturity and ascending to new, enlightened developmental heights.

Mothers didn't stand a chance in the 1980s. A year after Charren filed her complaint, Hasbro was offering TV shows in 1984 based on their toys My Little Pony, Charmkins, and the newly revived G.I. Joe (war was safe again). Most toy-based shows were sexist, often blatantly so, so mothers who cared about equality between the sexes were awarded two new jobs by the toy-based cartoons: fighting off the pleas to buy, and fighting off the gender stereotypes in which they trafficked. Some toys like Transformers and Go-Bots were featured in TV specials that then evolved into regular series, and the toy makers had no problem getting such shows—hour-long commercials—aired. By 1987 there were seventy—count 'em, seventy—toy-based TV shows.[40] The shows were key in training children to accept no substitutes or knockoffs. As one market researcher put it, these shows were "instrumental in recruiting, eliciting, and encouraging young consumers to accept only the original product. . . . Such strong product identity makes generic alternatives unacceptable."[41] Although all of these shows were, of course, predicated on offering kids the finest in quality entertainment, let it not be overlooked that Hasbro, within the first year of launching its Masterpiece Theater for kids, *Transformers,* raked in over $100 million in sales of the hunks of plastic that converted from robots to armored vehicles, making this the most successful toy introduction ever.[42] Transformers were a different kind of toy from Hasbro's old faithful of the 1950s, Mr. Potato Head.

Toy industry executives consistently maintained that the success of these action figures was completely consumer driven. Little boys wanted to fantasize about being bigger and stronger, and Mattel, Coleco, and Hasbro were just giving them what they wanted. This claim is more than just a disingenuous account of these toys' supposedly inevitable success. It also makes the return to sexist gender roles for kids seem perfectly natural too, driven utterly by little boys' inherent, unmediated desires that feminists were somehow seeking to thwart and deny. So let's consider the careful premeditation behind *He-Men* and *Transformers,* and why they (and Mattel) were so smart (and venal).

Feminists, supported by shows like *Sesame Street,* asked why boys couldn't play with dolls and girls with trucks. But the main thrust, if you will, of the Reagan administration was to remasculinize the presidency (after the flaccid failures of Ford and Carter) and American foreign policy. Hollywood reinforced this chest-beating machismo through "hardbody," Michelin-muscled films like *Die Hard* and *Rambo.*[43] In this new cultural regime, there were no wusses allowed. There really was still fear that if boys played with dolls, they would all grow up to be gay (instead of growing up to be, say, *fathers.*) So even though these five-inch pieces of plastic "he men" were referred to inside the industry as boy dolls, you never, ever said that out loud: In public they were "action figures." Next, by showcasing the "action figures" in a cartoon series, Mattel embedded the toys in premade narratives that boys could copy, draw from, or modify. The kids didn't just have the dolls and the accessories—they had story lines, too. And once you know the story line—He-Man fighting Skeletor and so forth—you really had to have all the figures, like Stinkor and Mer-Man, so you could play the story just right.

But then, how could you really play the game properly unless you also had the weapons and vehicles you'd seen in the cartoon, like the evil warrior vehicle with jaws called the Land Shark? And then where would you go? You had to have Skeletor's evil stronghold Snake Mountain, and He-Man's pied-à-terre, Castle Grayskull. (This was known as having a "synergy of items" in your toy line.) The He-Man collection began with eight action figures and four accessories. Within three years it featured thirty-six figures and twenty-one accessories. In 1985 Mattel released a feature-length film based on the toys, *The Secret of the Sword.* As the trade journal *Madison Avenue* put it, the toys benefited from "marketing magic and unparalleled exposure." By 1985, Mattel was selling forty million He-Man action figures worldwide, plus one thousand licensed items that totaled one billion—you heard us, one billion—in annual retail sales.[44]

While it is certainly true that there were millions of boys who loved the toys, it was also true that the marketing blitz, and especially the cartoon in which the heroes could do anything and go anywhere in the universe, made the toys especially seductive. It is not true, however, that millions of parents also loved the He-Men. Of course there were those who saw no problem with their sons playing a game based on creaming someone else with your bare hands and a "basher ball." However, if you didn't want your son to model himself after the He-Men, but all the other little boys had He-Men, and maybe your son got one for his birthday from one of those kids, or he nagged and begged and cried and then ratcheted up to incessant whining and pulling, you might just say to yourself "oh screw it" and return from Toys "Я" Us with Buzz-Off and his mates. This was, of course, what Mattel was counting on.

So begins the story of turning our kids into serial buyers. Now you didn't just need one Barbie or one He-Man, you needed them all. The idea of kid as serial consumer would come in very handy in the 1990s to the makers of Beanie Babies and Pokémon cards. As for the heroic Peggy Charren, the FCC in 1985 dismissed her complaint that shows like He-Man were program-length commercials, and refused even to hold hearings on the issue, agreeing with Mattel that "there is no evidence that exposure to programming based on products harms the child audience." [45]

By the mid-1980s, then, not only were TV shows based on toys, but toy companies, cereal companies, fast-food joints, candy companies, and whoever else had an interest in selling stuff to kids collaborated much more systematically to cross-promote their different products. Advertising budgets to sell to kids continued to increase. As one trade journal put it, "The battle for the children's cereal market becomes a fight among children's favorite TV and toy characters." [46] Ralston Purina put $15 million behind G.I. Joe cereal; Coleco licensed Rambo for a new line of action figures (Yo—don't go calling Rambo no doll).[47] Such cross-promotion increased the visibility of both companies and their products, often in places or during everyday activities where mothers and kids had not seen or thought of the product before.

Mothers were also up against increasingly sophisticated market research that sought to identify kids' tastes and desires and turn them into profits. In the olden days—the early 1970s—toy makers would design a product, advertise the hell out of it between October and December 24, and hope for the best. No more—by the mid-1980s such an approach was regarded as utterly innocent. The toy industry had become much more like the fashion industry, with fads and styles now changing every few years. In fact, by the late 1980s, the toy industry changed 50 percent of its product line every one to two years.[48] As toy companies merged, they were able to combine their resources to develop high-level research, development, and marketing plans, sometimes called "concept fulfillment studies." As one toy executive put it in 1985, "When I was at Mattel in the 1970s, they had a very limited research budget. Now they probably spend close to $1 million on marketing research." Hasbro spent $8.8 million on research and development in 1983, a 40 percent increase over the previous year.

This meant tons of "upfront" work before the toy ever got a berth at Toys "Я" Us. First there might be focus groups, with kids as young as five, to find out what they wanted to play with and what they thought would be cool. Based on that, some prototypes might be developed. Then, using two-way mirrors, researchers would watch how—and whether—the kids played with the toy.[49] The play sessions were usually videotaped. These "observation sessions" were, as one snuggly type in the business put it, "invaluable in staging effective play simulation for commercial adaptation," meaning the way the kids played with the toy determined how the company advertised the toy on TV. Possible names for the toy would be test-marketed to kids, and how it was packaged would be test-marketed too. One Brenda O. Dailey, the manager for product testing at Milton Bradley, bragged about her company's "product viability studies," which gauged "the overall playability" of the toy or game. Sounding more like General Schwarzkopf than one might like, she then noted that this research offered information on "establishing the primary targets" (that would be your kids) for the product. Her company would test-market the commercials before they were aired to measure for "recall, believability and message communication."[50]

Cereal companies in the mid-1980s also tried to hit two age groups with one ad campaign: thus could Mom be double-nagged. They figured that with more mothers working, older siblings were now helping with food purchases, including Super Sugar Crisp and Cap'n Crunch. To get the older kids to buy their brand of cereal, the companies ditched the practice of sticking a chintzy plastic toy in the box, and instead invited the older kids, through TV commercials, to enter contests that featured video games and computers as prizes. For kids aged two to five, in whom companies like General Mills or Kellogg were trying to establish lifelong brand loyalties, "jingles and cartoons . . . have been effective in helping the child form an early brand identification."[51] And there was more skulch and sugar-coated styrofoam than ever trying to pass for food. "Cookie Crisp was an amazingly successful product in its first year and a half," reported one industry analyst. "Basically, you were offering kids cookies for breakfast: Who could ask for anything more?"[52] By 1987, Heinz ketchup was spending an extra $2.5 million to advertise to preteens; Kool-Aid doubled its ad budget for kids.[53]

Executives for toy companies, but also for candy companies, cereal companies, and other faux-food firms, now had to plan their advertising and marketing campaigns with the precision of a presidential campaign because so many mothers were working outside the home. Some products could be marketed directly to the kids, other products could only be marketed to Mom, while others were pitched "to an all-family audience." This meant buying time on Saturday morning, late afternoons, and early evenings, during soap operas and daytime game shows, and finding the best shows to deliver the best mix of potential buyers.[54] In an especially exploitative act of cross-promotion directed at moms and their kids, the makers of Care Bears and the magazine *Woman's Day* teamed up in September of 1985 to launch the "Care-A-Lot Kids" campaign. *Woman's Day* readers were asked to write in about kids who had committed " 'special acts of kindness, caring, valor, or love.' " The five winners would get $5000 and, you guessed it, a special limited edition of the Care Bear doll from Kenner, and would be mentioned on the Care Bears TV show.[55] Talk about the effort to commodify, and profit from, the sweetness of little kids! You were nice to someone recently? Hey, sell it!

Companies also devoted more ad dollars to hitting Mom directly upside the head in magazines like *Working Mother, American Baby,* and *Working Woman.* While Mattel was singing the siren song to your three-year-old son via the TV show *He-Man,* the company now used women's magazines and prime-time programming to pitch you more educational, cuddly toys, especially those for infants who couldn't quite yet grasp ad copy. It used to be that companies like Mattel blanketed the airwaves and print media just before the holiday season. By 1985, advertising during the first nine months of the year had increased from 10 percent to 40 percent of the company's ad budget. Hasbro countered by sponsoring "Mothers' Minutes" on ABC daytime TV, in which Joan Lunden, then host of *Good Morning America,* gave parenting advice for thirty seconds or so, followed by a Hasbro ad.[56] As we now know, this was all just the beginning of what was to evolve into the current, massive cross-promotion and cross-marketing campaigns aimed at our kids, where Star Wars characters or mini Beanie Babies appear in Happy Meals, or where Rugrats dolls are prominently displayed in Blockbuster when a new Rugrats movie is out because Viacom owns Nickelodeon and Blockbuster.

As the success of the *He-Man* and *Transformers* TV shows and toys suggests, sex-role stereotyping made a resounding comeback during the Reagan years. *Advertising Age* reported in 1982 that military toys were more numerous at that year's Toy Fair than in any other year since the Vietnam war years. Toy executives attributed the change to "the Reagan era's renewed emphasis on defense spending and to the rise in antiterrorist activities globally." An executive at Mega Corporation felt that World War II–inspired toys were now dated, but "given the news coverage on antiterrorism," the company introduced a line dubbed "Eagle Force," and in 1982 Hasbro reintroduced G.I. Joe, who had clearly been to the steroid outlet since his initial appearance in the 1960s. (Sales tripled in three years, from $45 million in 1982 to $125 million in 1984, the year his TV show debuted.) A company called Nylint brought out "Army Search & Rescue" sets that included military uniforms and guns. Model plane companies showcased build-'em-yourself AWACS, combat planes, and missile launchers. Then there were Action Jack military figures, Super Battle action sets, Sgt. Rock action figures, and a radio-controlled Power Command tank. Even *M*A*S*H,* which boomers may recall was an antiwar satire as a film, and equally critical of and irreverent about combat as a TV series, was licensed as a toy brand name in 1982, affixed to action figures, vehicles, canteens, and flashlights.[57]

In 1985, Coleco (maker of Cabbage Patch dolls) gave America's sons the Rambo doll and, as a Coleco spokesperson put it, promised to give Rambo "weaponry and vehicles, all that create a proper play environment."[58] Kenner toys brought out a Chuck Norris doll in 1986 with the following claim: "The Chuck Norris figure represents the self-discipline of karate, which is good for kids to emulate." By 1986, kids could see approximately two hundred fifty episodes of war cartoons a year, and learn a simple lesson: War is fun. One study found that children who played with action figures like He-Man and the Transformers were twice as likely to get in fights and indulge in other antisocial behavior. But one child psychiatrist countered that the toys were especially "good figures for children" because they "helped children to figure out sex roles—what's masculine and what's feminine." And anyway, she insisted, why worry about the violent play these dolls inspire because a child's "moral development . . . doesn't happen until adolescence." [59] Added Mel Ciociola, who headed his own ad agency that specialized in advertising to kids, "toy commercials must come to terms with the reality of male chauvinism among children." [60] In the mid- to late 1990s, in the wake of a series of school shootings by boys, Columbine being the most notorious, the media made much of the fact that many of the shooters had recently been obsessed with violent video games or movies, as if Mortal Kombat was a single hypodermic needle filling a boy with murderous rage. Few, however, wondered about the cumulative effects of an onslaught of violent toys and games that these boys could have imbibed day in and day out from their toddler days in the 1980s, and that would have repeated the same aggressive scripts about how to deal with people and resolve conflict. [61]

In February 1986, the controversy around war toys prompted CBS to cover the phenomenon, reporting, "The sound of battle now engulfs many living rooms. Toys that glorify war and other fighting are on the march, each with a TV show to keep the kids combat ready." There was an "arms race" in kids toys, with about half of the best-selling toys having a weapons theme. Some parents had become so concerned that they launched demonstrations at the 1986 Toy Show in New York. But we didn't hear from them on CBS. Instead, one promoter described a toy helicopter as "completely outfitted with its own arsenal of bombs and weapons." Toy representatives dutifully noted that kids know the difference between fantasy and reality, and needed such toys to get their aggression out. Only one mother appeared, who said she was tired of other parents "sticking their noses in raising my children" and added that it was "baloney" that she was raising an aggressive child. While CBS did bring attention to the soaring militarism of kids' toys, those opposed were trivialized as throwback "toy doves." [62] Two years later, in 1988, the industry saw the launch of the most successful action-figure line in U.S. history, the Teenage Mutant Ninja Turtles. [63]

* * *

If mom had to fight off the militarization of her son's room and psyche, she also had to combat the sexual objectification of her daughter. Play cosmetics targeted to girls between four and nine became a controversial yet heavily promoted item. Explained Mattel spokesman Jack Fox, "Little girls have forever been getting into their mothers' cosmetics and making a mess of the products, as well as their faces. Play cosmetics are a safe, nontoxic, easily-washed-off substitute." To help them design and market the products, Mattel, Hasbro, and others hired cosmetic experts from the adult makeup biz. They apparently helped consult on the prices, too. When women were being urged to spend $30 on 1/32 of an ounce of some wrinkle cream that was made in the French Alps from extract of edelweiss and pig urine, they could also shell out twenty-five bucks in 1981 for Hasbro's Fresh'n'Fancy makeup kit. Execs admitted that the cosmetics displays in toy stores were "as slick as any in the cosmetics department." But this was *really* about respecting girls' intelligence. As one toy exec put it, "We see no reason to talk down to little girls." This was about nurturing the child's development. "The more realistic the toy is, the better. . . . If it's sophisticated, it's a better tool to help the child learn how to cross the bridge into adulthood." [64] So *that's* why she needs to learn the fine points of applying eyeliner before her fifth birthday.

Mattel also realized that since Barbie "is no feminist" (really?) and seemed, well, a bit "one-dimensional" (except for her boobs) by the early 1980s, she would need to be updated just a tad. Mattel's marketing research staff tripled from 1980 to 1985, and these employees would bring girls into a play area equipped with a two-way mirror and watch what they did with Barbie. The girls also participated in focus groups. In addition, two research teams canvassed mothers around the country to see if a "more liberated" Barbie would fly. The answer was a resounding yes. So, by the mid-1980s, there were many different kinds of Barbies and many more accessories—a calculator, business cards, computer, cordless phone—to suggest that despite the fact that the interaction between the size of her feet and the size of her boobs would make her unable to stand erect in a real office, now Barbie was a new woman. We also got Great Shape Barbie in her leotard and leg warmers (thanks a lot, Jane Fonda), Barbie TV News Reporter, and Astronaut Barbie. Thus, girls needed many more Barbies and many more Barbie accessories, and mothers concerned about Barbie's Playmate-of-the-Month proportions could feel better because at least now she had the NASA seal of approval over her left DD.

Toy manufacturers claimed, with some accuracy, that boys and girls liked to play with different toys. And they were determined not to give "sex-role stereotyping" (as we used to call it) a rest. Because, as one put it, "boys and girls are as different as night and day," gender-specific marketing was "a fact of life" for toy marketers. This was an especially important "fact" because it demanded the manufacture, and then the purchase, of completely different toys for boys and girls. The toy makers and their advertisers, by repeatedly hawking bucket loaders to boys and mini shopping carts to girls, made the "William Wants a Doll" campaign of the *Free to Be You and Me* years seem like a pipe dream. William might have indeed wanted a doll at two, but as soon as he started taking in the Saturday morning TV fare, he would realize that his very masculinity was at stake. Toy makers seemed to believe that the preference for pink (or lilac as a fallback) was wired into the rods and cones of girls' eyeballs. Thus a new line of Duplos introduced in 1993 for girls was pink; the Strombecker Corporation offered a pink-and-blue girls' version of its double-holster cap gun and a pink cowgirl outfit; and Strombecker also brought out a "bubble sword" for girls, emphasizing that "we made sure to include lots of pink . . . to make the sword attractive to girls." [65]

Indeed, when the wildly popular TV show *Mighty Morphin Power Rangers* premiered in August 1993, it was clear that the toy/entertainment execs had figured how to appease the gender police and the EEOC. Five friends from a juice bar in the town of Angel Grove, California, were given Power Morphers by Zordon of the planet Eltar, who was hell-bent on ridding the universe of evil (the first incarnation of which was Rita Repulsa). Able to transform their bodies into magical suits empowered by the spirits of dinosaurs, the five teens were convinced of the danger, and agreed to become the Mighty Morphin Power Rangers. Of the five original Rangers, two were white guys, one was a black guy (who, not surprisingly, got to wear the black suit), one was a black girl, and one was a white girl. If you guessed that the Pink Ranger was a white girl, well, you were right on. If you guessed that she was Southern California pretty, you were right on again. The main attraction of the Power Rangers was their ability to execute karate moves that would put any ordinary black belt to shame. But guess which Ranger had the best (i.e., most lethal) moves of all? Yup, that would be Jason, one of the white guys. Guess who was the brainiest Ranger? Yup, that would be Billy, the other white guy. The show, which featured evil doers such as Cyclopsis, Oysterizer, and Polluticorn, spawned not only costumes but also fighting gear, board games, video games, action figures, stuffed toys, bedding, cartoons, wallpaper, and feature films, themselves morphing as new Rangers and new evildoers replaced the old. The racial and gender diversity of the show hardly compensated for the endless kung-fu levels of violence. Once again, parents were faced with major episodes of kickboxing in the living room.

But, of course, things could be worse. Unlike *Power Rangers* and *Ninja Turtles*, which could be absorbed while delivering roundhouse kicks to the houseplants, Nintendo and PlayStation required kids to sit on their butts. Maybe that's why it seemed natural to kick up the violence another notch. Electronic games like Pac-Man, pioneered in the early 1980s by Atari, enjoyed a sudden but brief success in 1982 and '83, and then fell in popularity. By the 1990s, there was an entire new generation of computer and video games for boys, all too many of them inviting boys to kill and maim new generations of evildoers on the screen. Sales of software for Nintendo tripled between 1987 and 1989. Sega entered the scene, and by 1992—when the video game market was a $4.9 billion industry—had stolen 40 percent of the market from Nintendo. That same year, Sega's $300 CD player for video games flew off the shelves at Christmastime.[66]

It wasn't only commercial television that began capitalizing on the toy–TV tie-in. PBS, which many parents of toddlers and preschoolers favored over commercial TV because it was nonviolent, nonsexist (although nearly all the Muppets on *Sesame Street*, from Elmo to Big Bird to the Count, were male), and taught your kids numbers and the alphabet, began marketing its main kiddie characters as well. Parents who nearly gagged on their coffee listening to Barney sing every morning could now have the pleasure of having a stuffed Barney right in their homes. Thomas the Tank Engine from *Shining Time Station* quickly followed. Again we see the divisions, particularly along class and educational lines, in marketing toys to kids. As Forbes put it in 1993, "PBS is a hot marketing tool, in many ways far better than commercial television. Rationally or not, parents who wouldn't let Donatello the Teenage Mutant Ninja Turtle anywhere near their impressionable offspring feel comfortable with toys born out of public TV." The shows and the toys—especially in the wake of He-Men and Veterinarian Barbie—conveyed "an aura of noncommercial respectability." So even kid zones previously outside the marketplace got colonized by sales pitches. Because many parents, especially of boys, were looking to alternatives to the testosterone- and nitroglycerin-infused offerings of Hasbro et al., Thomas toys in 1993 had sales that rivaled the heavily hyped Ninja Turtles and G.I. Joe.[67]

In the late 1980s, the birth rate increased to its highest level since 1964, meaning more little customers.[68] With PBS-inspired toys straddling the divide, there was by the 1990s and early 2000s a huge gulf between two kinds of toys: those sold through blaring, strobe-lit commercials on TV and those too decent, too educational to be hawked on the idiot box. The first kind of toy, Mom bought and then threw it and junior into the den while she did something else. (We know what kind of a mother *she* was.) With the second kind of toy, whose sales soared in the 1990s, the purchase was part of an extended research and development process. First, Mom had to read articles in *Parents* or *Better Homes & Gardens* (even *U.S. News & World Report* got into the act) with titles like "How to Choose the Best Playthings for Your Child, Age by Age." These articles relied on the advice of multiple Ph.D.s and MDs who were child-development experts at places with names like the Einstein–Marie Curie Center for Baby Genuises or the Stanford-CalTech Childhood Cerebellum Expansion Project. They were quoted as saying things like, "Today's children . . . need to play with the toys that shaped successful people like yesterday's Thomas Edison or today's Colin Powell or Connie Chung."[69] Subtitles in such articles read "Stick to Age-Appropriate Learning," "Think Fast," "Test for Success," "Strive for Balance," and "Think of Toys as Tools."[70] Fun? Fun was for the hapless, neglected kids of lazy, down-market moms.

"Toys are not just things. They're vehicles for learning," such articles advised. And you, Mom, had to start stimulating the proper firing of your baby's brain synapses in infancy, or she would end up a semiliterate counter girl in Dunkin' Donuts for life. Toys became a marker of cultural capital. They designated which kids, thirty years hence, would drive a Lexus, eat radicchio, advise heads of state, be profiled in *The New Yorker,* and read Proust in the original while lounging in their villa in Arles. They also imparted a halo around those mothers who had been savvy enough and dedicated enough to make that happen. For your infant, "it's best to offer a variety of materials—wood, cloth, plastic—as well as those with interesting textures like raised dots or nubby fabric." You weren't thinking of giving your baby a plain old rattle, were you? Jeez, don't you know that noisemakers must "connect a sound to an action whenever possible.

... When your baby shakes a rattle harder, for instance, the clacking should grow louder too." In addition, "the best infant toys match different textures to visual cues: a fabric ball might have a panel of smooth red satin and a rough corduroy panel in blue." But too much stimulation was bad too, and you must "limit the number of toys that blink, or light up." [71] One toy, the Funny Honey Bee rattle, included a set of directions called "Instructions from Baby" that told parents "how to get the most out of playtime." [72] It goes without saying that Mom must "anticipate the ways your child might abuse a plaything before you purchase it" and thus you really had to "try it yourself." "Do all of the sorting shapes fit easily through the holes?" was just one of many things to ask yourself as you took the toy for a test drive while a toddler whined at your feet. And, of course, "make sure that your child's playthings give her the chance to exercise her imagination as well as her muscles." [73] (While you were struggling to make the toy work, your toddler was much more interested in the box it came in.)

Once your advanced research was done, you could only go to a toy store like Zany Brainy or The Learning Center or Imaginarium that specialized in developmentally appropriate toys. Just taking your toddler inside Toys "Я" Us could lower his IQ and corrupt his fledgling sensibilities. Or you could order through one of those catalogs whose titles ("One Step Ahead" or "The Right Start") suggested that purchases from its pages ensured your kid a slot in the entering class of Harvard eighteen years hence. But your work had only just begun. After the toy arrived, "you may need to modify [it] when you first bring it home." (This invariably involved multiple screwdrivers, a hammer, Krazy Glue, and a string of expletives.) You had to play with the toy with your child and absolutely keep to a minimum toys "designed to replace you" as a playmate. (Hey, isn't that what toys are for? So you can get five minutes to unload the dryer?) Encourage the child to "get messy" with blocks, bead sets, and arts supplies that "provide wonderful opportunities for building motor and thinking skills." After all, Mom, "you can always turn clean-up time into a game." [74] (Could anyone, no matter how besotted by the new momism, really believe this?)

Once your kids hit the preschool years, you had to "focus on toys that teach broader concepts." Puzzles show kids "how to make comparisons" and "memory and matching games help with logic and concentration. Board games reinforce turn-taking and cooperation." (Oh yeah? How about cheating, crying, and name calling?) By the time your child was six, it was "time to get your child hooked on a hobby" and you absolutely had to get "craft, science, and nature kits that you can work on together." [75] Did your kids have the toy that promoted "their ability to build in 62 directions in space"? Could your kids "construct models of cells, crystals, DNA, domes and bridges"? [76] No??

Advice like this fed off of the worsening, embarrassing news about declining SAT scores and the deterioration of the country's public school system. Bush the First felt compelled to proclaim himself the "education president" in the wake of highly publicized, annual rankings of academic achievement around the world in which American high school students knew less science and math than first graders in China and Burkina Faso. There was much breast-beating about how in the world U.S. kids, when they grew up, would be able to compete with others when they didn't know the century—*century*—in which the America Revolution happened, where on the globe Greece or Australia was, or that the periodic table was *not* a feature at the Old Country Buffet. [77] Your kids were in a highly individualized do-or-die race to the top, and if they couldn't do square roots or diagram sentences by age four (let alone distinguish Schubert from Beethoven) it was a reflection on you: on your genes, of course, but also on whether you had been an attentive, intellectually nurturing mother or a lazy, neglectful, ignorant slut of a mom.

So, the market for educational toys grew steadily in the 1990s, with Mother enlisted as early childhood educator whose job it now was (on top of everything else) to ensure that not one fleeting second passed that was not an enriching learning experience. What the entire governments of Denmark or France offered to all kids—namely, preschool—American mothers had to do on their own. They had to buy Science Guy Junior Scientist Lab Kit, Science for a Week Aerodynamics Kit, Brain Quest's "Be a Know It All," MathSafari, and the Smithsonian Institution's Crystal Growing Set. The words "genius," "brainy," and "smart," never, ever used to sell Blockhead, Colorforms, or even Clue, increasingly appeared on toy boxes directed at Mom. Psychobabble got a new life with these toys, as when toys you could pull apart now introduced "another important concept, part/whole relationships." [78] Blocks introduced "math and physics through spatial relationships." [79] Remember when we were kids and, when stuck in the backseat during a long car ride, were told to shut up and play the license-plate or alphabet game? Now mother had to design an entire kit filled with stimulating activities for the whole ride, lest that potentially brain-boosting time be wasted. Or she could buy the KidsTravel "back-seat-survival-kit" that taught geography and, probably, quantum mechanics.

Then there was the whole Mozart problem. Researchers exploring the relationship between listening to certain kinds of music and cognitive development found their work hyped as "the Mozart effect," which meant, basically, that listening to classical music (and especially Mozart) gave your baby a real leg up.[80] So it wasn't enough to pipe the Flute Concerto in D Major into your uterus throughout your entire pregnancy. Once out and able to manipulate blocks, your toddler just had to have the Mozart Music Cube ($70). When the child got the blocks arranged in the correct order, the Cube played "Eine Kleine Nachtmusik" as a reward.[81] Think this is stupid? Well, have a look at Shazad Mohamed, age fifteen, profiled in USA Today in 2002. Shazad's mother piped classical music into her belly, and now her son was a CEO of an Internet company who oversaw "the 19 employees of GlobalTek Solutions." "I can remember back to just about when I was born," he told USA Today. "I also noticed things, like paintings and music, that seemed familiar. It turned out my parents exposed me to them when I was in the womb."[82] (How did he get to see the paintings, exactly?) So, were you really going to balk at the $70 price tag on the Mozart Cube? Wouldn't you be sabotaging your child's future life opportunities?

Clearly, it was not enough just to talk to your baby. You also had to take her to foreign language classes, even though she didn't even understand English yet. Monica Langley, writing for The Wall Street Journal, hilariously recounted in 1999 her visit to the Language Workshop for Children in Manhattan (tuition: $500 for fourteen weekly classes), where mothers were told to bring their six-month-old children, even if they did sit in class "like a potted plant." "Early exposure to a second language actually grows more connection in the baby's brain," mothers were told, and you had to start immediately, in infancy, or the window of learning would slam shut—in fact, by ten months it was all over, according to one expert. The BBC multimedia language course for infants ($169) warned, "Your child's window of opportunity is right now."[83]

By 2002, USA Today found that 42 percent of parents polled felt "pressure to raise smarter kids" and announced "The Race to Raise a Brainier Baby: Parents Clamor for Educational Toys."[84] One of the bestsellers was LeapPad, a $50 talking book from LeapFrog Enterprises; Mattel, now owner of Fisher-Price, offered Kasey the Kinderbot, a $70 robot designed to "help preschoolers prepare for school"; and LeapFrog offered the Imagination Desk, "an electronic coloring book that teaches preschoolers reading and math," as well as My First LeapPad for three-year-olds.[85] One company was, indeed, named Baby Einstein, and specialized in videos and flash cards for infants (yes!) that provided (according to the company) a "stimulating introduction to classical music" or in the case of Baby Newton, "baby's first introduction to geometry!" Guaranteed to grab the attention of the "youngest infant," the videos are full of "interesting effects that will keep your baby engaged while the music creates a delightful mood." You can buy the ten-DVD set for only $179.00. In 2000, Target and *Parents* magazine launched their Play & Learn Discovery & Development toy line designed to "challenge newborns [!] and infants up to 2-year-olds."[86] In fact, educational toys were the fastest-growing sector of the industry by 2002, their sales increasing by 10 to 15 percent annually in the late 1990s and early 2000s.[87] The toy business had swelled to a $25-billion-a-year industry.[88]

Like many educated mothers, we confess to having been suckers for a lot of this stuff—although not the French lessons at three months. But our desires to do a bit better by our kids than what laser swords or Potty Dotty had to offer were exploited with a vengeance. Millions of us found ourselves harassed at every turn about what we *weren't* doing properly with our babies at seven months, what we *were* neglecting at thirty-two months, and how the kids who played Brain Quest were going to get into Stanford while ours would be lucky to get into clown school. The educational toy folks weren't just selling to us. They also capitalized on the fierce competition the new momism begat, pitting mother against mother with her kids' math, science, and linguistic achievements the badges of which mom had done best. In this competition, money and Mom's time were no object.

Because of the way mother and the kids were sold to, the playroom became a sight of striking contradictions. Developmentally encouraging and nonsexist toys like Playmobile schoolhouses lay right next to an Air Hogs Helicopter and the Bratz Stylin' Salon 'N' Spa (which included a pedicure station and a smoothie bar). Many a mother wanted the toys she saw in *Working Mother* that promoted reading, or problem solving, or creative play. The kids wanted the dreck they saw on TV, hawked with rap music and soaring camera moves. Because of the war between progressive versus market values, toys began to get mapped onto the kid population more and more along class lines. In the 1950s, unless you were really rich, most kids had the same stuff: Roy Rogers cap guns, Tiny Tears, hula hoops. But in the 1980s, '90s, and beyond, as the rich got richer and the poor got poorer, and the gap between the classes became wider, so too was it the case that affluent children with progressive parents wore unisex clothes and played with developmentally appropriate toys ordered from HearthSong, while more financially strapped working-class parents could go to Kmart and choose from T-shirts that said FUTURE MISS AMERICA and shelves stacked with toy AK-47s. The "good" mother chose the former, enlightened products, not the latter, crass commercial products. So through toys, good motherhood was equated with savvy consumption, money, and taste.

If you as a mother felt that you were getting bombarded much more on a year-round basis—not just before Christmas—you were right. Increasingly toys were tied in not just to TV shows but also to blockbuster movies—especially hoped-for summer blockbusters like *Jurassic Park,* or *Last Action Hero* with Arnold Schwarzenegger. The toys came out simultaneously with the movie so the kids could nag virtually every month for something new. By 1993 Mattel reported record first-quarter sales (traditionally the postholiday doldrums for the industry) with a 13 percent increase over the previous year.[89] In the 1980s and beyond, given this full-bore marketing offensive, it is not surprising that parents and children came to internalize more than ever before the equation between buying and loving.

In 1999, it was estimated that the annual disposable income of children ages twelve and under was $27.5 billion, but that in fact they influenced anywhere from $200 to $500 billion in adult spending. Spending on advertising targeted to children grew at 15 to 20 percent a year in the mid- and late 1990s. By the summer of 2001, the amount of money spent annually on advertising to kids—a whopping $3 billion—was more than *twenty* times the amount spent in 1991.[90] One of the fastest growth areas in retail clothing was specialty retailers for kids—upscale, designer-label shoes, T-shirts, jeans, and the like for "fashion-minded children with considerable discretionary income." On *InStyle Celebrity Moms,* which aired on NBC in April 2001, Cindy Crawford introduced viewers to the new designer lines for infants and toddlers, so we could see "what Hollywood's next generation is wearing." Companies now routinely run focus groups for children ages eight to twelve, and even younger, to tap into fads and desires and figure out how better to sell to them. In the fall of 1999, approximately sixty members of the American Psychological Association petitioned its officers to amend the organization's code of ethics to censure the use of psychologists and psychological techniques to help corporations market and advertise to children.

But as any mother of a teenager knows, kids between twelve and eighteen are the real prize catch. They reportedly spent, in 2002, about $140 billion; they go the mall, on average, fifty-four times a year (the average for all shoppers is thirty-nine times a year). Demographers predict that by 2010 there will be 33.9 million teens—a record number.[91] American Eagle, Tommy Hilfiger, Abercrombie & Fitch, Hollisters, Target, Pacific Sun, Hot Topic, Delia's, Claire's, all bombard them with images of bare-bellied girls and bare-chested boys about to have an orgy on the beach, to which only those who have bought the right products are invited. *Teen People, Cosmo Girl,* as well as old standbys like *Seventeen,* plus *Maxim,* to say nothing of MTV, sell them an image of coolness through consumption that they resist at their peril. Added to everything else required of the new momism, each mother is also a lone David figuring out how to moderate the influence of the media Goliath on her own unsuspecting children.

By entreating Mom to inhabit and anticipate all of the current and future developmental needs of her child, the toy industry insisted she be a home schooler, a child-development expert, a phonics teacher, an arts-and-crafts specialist, and the constant gatekeeper of the other, less-edifying garbage it was selling directly to her kids. We were supposed to see the world through their eyes and indulge them, yet be on the lookout for bad toys and police their desires. We felt this contradiction every time we went to the toy store. Your kid wanted the talking Thong Barbie that said "I'm too dumb to count" or the Rambo Collateral Damage game. You said no, deeming them inappropriate on multiple fronts. Then the kid started crying and whining about his or her friend having one and it's so cool and please, Mommy, please, please, Mommy, I want it so much. Wasn't it just easier to give in? If you were a working mother, resisting such entreaties made your kids very unhappy and thus tarnished the time you *did* have with them. Give in, and you're a bad mother for contaminating them with such garbage. Don't give in and you're a bad mother for denying their simple pleasures and making them cry. Again, another no-win situation for mothers.

Most of all, the toy and other kid-related industries insisted on further commodifying not only the mother-child relationship, but also the child's relationship to everyone else to whom he or she had to sell him or herself as well. Some kids may have felt that they were still "free to be you and me." But most felt that they themselves were products whose value was determined by what they played with, drank, and wore. Mothers became challenged, on a daily basis, to add to their duties that of consumer cop, as they drew, and redrew, a line in the sand that conveyed, somehow, that yes, they loved their kids and were willing to indulge them, and no, they were not going to let their kids become spoiled tyrants and promoters of shameless sexism. This, too, was yet another full-time—and loathsome— job for Mother.

TEN

Dr. Laura's Neighborhood:
Baby Wearing, Nanny Cams,
and the Triumph of
the New Momism

When we were raising babies and toddlers in the 1970s and '80s, back with the panics about missing children, razor blades in Halloween candy, and pedophiles running day care centers, we thought the climate of fear around mothering had reached its peak. No way. By the early twenty-first century, the terrors had metastasized and become even more deadly. Murdering nannies. Vaccinations that kill. Flesh-eating bacteria. Lethal dirt in your baby's nostrils. More missing children, abducted children, children snatched from their beds or their front yard. Internet predators. Freak dancing. Air travel and SIDS. Circumcision and SIDS. Pets and SIDS. SIDS and hiccups. SIDS, SIDS, SIDS.

Gaining enormous momentum from the incessant newsflashes about such dangers, the new momism has emerged nearly triumphant in the early twenty-first century as an ideology few women can escape. And now, from Dr. Laura to the Internet to the dozens of niche magazines geared to "kinds" of mothers, the new momism offers innumerable points of entry. It draws strength from our fears and anxieties, and in the process, has become an increasingly reactionary ideology, resembling the feminine mystique more with each passing year. Having said that, the new momism is not about subservience to men. It is about *subservience to children*. And there's nowhere to run, nowhere to hide. On the surface, the call to motherhood seems more liberated, if you will, than the stifling housewifery of the 1950s. And in a way it is. But beware what lurks beneath. Whether you are a married religious fundamentalist, a partnered lesbian, a divorced secular humanist with a Ph.D., or a single twenty-year-old trying to make it in the big city, if you are a female human, the new momism has circled the wagons around you. This is not to say that young mothers today are any less savvy than their predecessors in seeing through media hype. They are simply surrounded, in a way their mothers were not, by efforts to commercialize virtually every step of pregnancy and childrearing.

First-time mothers today, if they read publications like *Baby Years* or *Pregnancy* or go to the one-hundred-times-infinity Web sites about parenting, are besieged by blood-chilling warnings and ads for all the products that will allow them to be more vigilant, to protect their baby better. Products unknown to mothers just fifteen years ago—clock radios that are really surveillance cameras to monitor your baby-sitter; the "Germ Doctor," a sanitizing zapping box which, if you put your baby's pacifiers and toys inside, will "kill 99.9% of germs" on them "in just 30 minutes"— now routinely accost the readers of parenting magazines. The grim reaper lurks everywhere, just one maternal misstep away. So it is hardly surprising to overhear, as one of us did, a young mother saying to her friend at a playground, "You can't be too overprotective."

By the mid-1990s and early 2000s, the various warnings that had emerged to police mothers in the 1980s had become a battery of interrogation lamps aimed directly at us, demanding to know whether we were doing everything possible to defend our kids from harm. This happened well before September 11, 2001, yet since the attacks, the Brothers Grim of corporate America and the news media still emphasize the threats from within. The paranoia about your children's health and safety, the fear that you aren't tending to their developmental needs, the nervousness that you aren't doing enough arts and crafts or baking enough cakes in the shape of Hogwarts, the worry that they don't have the right toys or a nursery that is color-coordinated with their personalities, and the concern that you simply aren't spending enough time with your kids and demonstrating in countless ways each and every day that you really, really love them—all of these have now inflated to near-bursting, Michelin Man proportions.

At the same time, images of the hip, relaxed, spontaneous and, yes, sexy mother who is confident, serene, and above such nagging doubts, who has it all under control, whose teenagers are her best friends (like the mom and daughter in WB's little piece of hokum, *Gilmore Girls*), also fly at us from ads, women's magazines, and the ongoing celebrity profiles. We are supposed to be as vigilant as Michael Corleone's bodyguards, but appear as relaxed as Jimmy Buffett in Margaritaville.

One way to survive these contradictions is to buy as many child protecting/enhancing products as possible. Reasonable precautions have morphed into unrelenting, wallet-emptying paranoia. Overindulgence has become equated with safety, as well as with educational success and emotional fulfillment. The sheer number of new products for mother and child just since the 1980s would, if piled up, no doubt dwarf Mt. McKinley. Many of the sales pitches hurled at parents could, with only the most minor tweaking, serve as skits on *Saturday Night Live*. Conspicuous consumption has conquered childhood, motherhood, and the nursery, making just the normal acquisition of a plain old crib and stroller seem, well, negligent, or at the very least, withholding. Any mother who suggests to her teenager that every trip outside the home does not require spending money is lower than Scrooge.

Most parents' most desperate fear is that their child will die—that hasn't changed. When we had babies, there was of course that moment when our relief at an unusually long nap was transformed into a panic that our babies had succumbed to SIDS, and in we ran to their rooms, sometimes putting the proverbial mirror under the tiny nostrils to check for breath. Later, there were additional moments of terror induced by a toddler disappearing in the aisles at Kmart or falling off the slide at the playground or waking up at 3:14 A.M. with croup. Various companies have discovered, not surprisingly, that there are profits in such fears. And mothers, as a market, are being increasingly segmented into more specialized, target markets, and thus can be serially bombarded with admonitions about the amounts and kinds of surveillance they are now meant to provide. In the 1980s, the marketing expert Rena Bartos had divided adult women into four demographic groups: the stay-at-home housewife, the plan-to-work housewife, the "just a job" working woman, and the career-oriented working woman.[1] But that was only a start. Just as that category "kids" was increasingly broken down by niche marketers, so too did the category "mother" get partitioned into profitable subsets by the number of kids she had, her employment, lifestyle, food preferences, fabric preferences, race, age, geography, zip code, class and, yes, specific parenting "styles."

Some of this niche marketing is simply the natural progression of target marketing nationwide; it is easier and more efficient for those selling, say, Clearasil to advertise on MTV and in *Seventeen* than on CNN or CBS, where such ads might be wasted on the Metamucil set. But companies and their advertisers have also responded to, and capitalized on, a powerfully anticommercial trend—people's use of the Internet to do an end-run around consumer culture, to gain information and locate and build communities. People who suddenly found themselves the proud parents of triplets could go on-line and find out how two adults survive three infants with colic. Or parents sick of the hypercommercialism surrounding childhood could find like-minded parents and share strategies about convincing their teenagers that there are, in fact, other cultural institutions in the United States beside the mall and other ways to spend time than watching *Cribs* or *Spring Weekend Topless Barforama* on MTV.

But in their efforts to form communities on-line with other parents with particular concerns and interests—adoption, surrogacy, allergies, a visceral hatred of anything plastic—these parents also identified themselves as niches with product needs: nursing pillows for twins, 100 percent cotton SPF 40+ cover-ups for sun-sensitive kids, and the like. And businesses found them on-line. This dance of becoming a target, dodging the big corporate darts, and yet welcoming some commercial darts because they provide what Toys "Я" Us doesn't, has led to an explosion of more products and more anxieties than Clair Huxtable could have ever imagined.

Companies that address parents' worst fears are simultaneously providing tools to allay anxieties, and are, through their ads, articles, and Web sites about their products, dramatically inflating the paranoia already very much in the air. The risks and problems a minority—sometimes a very tiny minority—of babies and children might face become instantly universalized to be potential risks for every single baby and kid there is. For example, there is now a product called the Angelcare Movement & Sounds Monitor by BebeSounds that sells for a hundred bucks. You place a sensor pad under your baby's mattress, and if your baby does not move for twenty seconds, an alarm sounds in your room (or wherever you are in the house, as the "parents' unit" is portable). The Baby-Be-Safe Crib Sheet—the "only one of seven crib sheets to pass the Good Housekeeping Institute's test"—stays secure to crib mattresses and fits over an elevation sleep wedge for baby that "reduces the fear of choking on spit-up or vomit" (note—reduces not the choking itself, but the *fear* of it) and "helps relieve pain and discomfort associated with a multitude of childhood diseases." Generations of children have grown up without these, yet now the fear is, If I don't have these products, am I unnecessarily putting my baby at risk?

Both of these products address the terror of Sudden Infant Death Syndrome (SIDS), the top killer of babies ages one month to one year in the industrialized world.[2] Having said that, however, the incidence of SIDS in the United States declined approximately 20 to 30 percent between 1992 and 1994 alone. SIDS declined by nearly 40 percent between the 1970s and early 1990s. In 1992, the American Academy of Pediatrics recommended that healthy infants be placed on their backs for sleep, and this, plus warnings about smoking near babies, seems to have reduced the rate of the syndrome. In countries where only 5 to 10 percent of babies sleep on their stomachs, the reduction in the SIDS rate has approached 70 to 80 percent. By 2002, the death rate from SIDS had declined to 75 per 100,000 live births.[3] Studies also report that the one intervention that has been proven *not* to work has been the physical monitoring of the baby in the crib.[4] So here are young parents, in a world in which SIDS has declined dramatically and in which prevention, not monitors, works best, accosted by products that increase their fears.

You can also worry, and electronically monitor your baby, before he or she even emerges from the womb. It used to be that a woman at risk of miscarriage or premature birth might be given an at-home fetal Doppler kit to check her baby's heartbeat. Now anyone can have peace of mind and rent one for anywhere from $30 to $49 a month.[5] You get the works: that gloppy, ice-cold ultrasound lotion, of course; a CD or tape to help you learn how to distinguish between "maternal sounds and fetal sounds"; an instruction manual; and a tip sheet. As one of these products, Baby Beat, exclaims, "Listen to your baby's heartbeat at home! High quality Doppler just like the doctors use."[6] In other words, having the Doppler is as much for entertainment purposes as it is for safety. Bebe-Sounds, the same company that makes the crib monitor, offers a "prenatal heart listener" that allows you to "record your unborn baby's sounds" including "heartbeat, kicks and hiccups" so that you can add the tape to the prebirth "memory box" that you will surely be making if you really care about your kid.[7] The Stork Radio Fetal Ultrasound Doppler System helps "to create a special bond between expecting parents and their child."[8]

How about DomesticSpy.com, which offers clock-radio- or VCR-shaped surveillance cameras that allow you to "inconspicuously monitor babysitters, nannies, maids or housesitters"? The firm offers hidden cameras as well. The ad warns, "Incidents of child abuse committed by parents and other caretakers make up about one-fifth of violent crimes against juveniles," and adds, "the majority (73%) of these parent and other caretaker crimes are physical assaults, and 23 percent are cases of sexual abuse."[9] So in addition to spying on your sitter, you can also spy on your partner or spouse.

Then, of course, there are the organic products for baby. We are very sorry, Mom, but plain old cotton simply will not do anymore. And that pink Johnson & Johnson baby lotion? Please! Doesn't your baby deserve pure, natural, synthetic-free, talc-free, non–animal tested, nut-oil free (?), nonpetroleum, non–mineral oil, artificial fragrance–free products? Of course, some kids do have delicate skin or allergic reactions to stuff. But now *all* babies should have a skin-care regimen to rival Cleopatra's or Cher's. There's Baby Spa, "based on the principle that every child needs and deserves the natural touch." Baby Spa offers massage oil and aromatherapy for baby, as well as "bath care" and "luxury textiles."[10] Arizona Babies also offers "the natural way to love your baby" (through all-natural skin-care products) and has a product we could have used, a lotion called Tranquil Time, which allegedly will "help baby sleep."[11] Erbaviva offers a sachet for baby filled with oatmeal, powdered lavender, and rose petals. (What this does, exactly, is unclear, but you have to have one.) Burt's Bees offers primarily honey-derived formulas. With these products mothers are meant to "prepare baby's room by misting the air and bed linens lightly." Then mom should "lovingly pamper" baby "with an aromatherapy massage."[12] Ecobaby Organics offers "chemical-free wools" and "everything natural you need to raise a healthy baby."[13] If you're not using these natural products, then you yourself are a know-nothing patsy of the Dupont corporation, a throwback of a mother whose child will grow up to be chemically contaminated and covered with scabies. And don't even think about using baby powder on your babies. Does "black-lung disease" mean anything to you?

At the same time, you have to be worried about the threat of germs. Perhaps the most terrifying product is VIROFREE, "The disinfectant every parent has been waiting for." It's a pocketsize disinfectant spray that "kills not only germs, but viruses, on surfaces." This stuff allegedly annihilates everything—"staph, strep, E. coli, salmonella, HIV-1, Influenza A, A2, B, and C and the common cold." Attentive parents will spray it on "shared toys, public toilets, shopping cart handles and restaurant high chairs." [14] God knows what's in VIROFREE, but it seems odd to massage your baby with oil from organic olives that can only come from the southern shores of Santorini and then blast her toys and the shopping cart with something that the CDC should probably classify as a weapon of mass destruction.

It's also never too soon to begin educating your infant, and you certainly don't want him or her to fall behind those other overachieving babies who will be able to spell *eustachian tube* or distinguish among Chopin's piano concertos at age two, thus leaving your child in the dust. If you join the Gentle Revolution, you can "Teach Your Baby to Read!" The ad shows a nine-month-old reading flash cards. For real. If you get the Bee Smart Baby video series, you can get—for an infant—the Baby Math, Vocabulary Builder, and Action Words videos to "Boost your Baby's Brain Development!" The videos feature classical music and are "designed by educators to build receptive language." Alleged parent testimonials in the ad brag that because of the videos, their toddlers are way, way ahead of those other, dimwitted rugrats who "could only verbalize a few words" or "could not clap five times." [15] Or here's a chilling proposal: "Convert Your Computer into a Child's Activity Center!" (Yippeee! Kid drool on the keyboard!) Baby Type changes your computer into a series of interactive games for infants starting at six months that allow him or her to identify animals, shapes, and so on. [16] Hmm—we just talked to our babies and parked them in front of *Sesame Street,* and they learned to talk and count just fine.

Possibly the creepiest trend of all is the fetishizing of baby. Now you don't preserve the baby's shoes, you preserve body parts of baby himself. You too can transform his or her fist, foot, or fingerprint into a charming amulet right out of Papua New Guinea. This, mind you, is nothing like the little clay hand imprints that your kid brings home from preschool. If you go to Fingerprintcharm.com, you can order a wax fingerprinting kit and take your baby's print. Then their "skilled craftsmen" will turn it into silver or gold and superimpose it onto a charm in the shape of a boy's or girl's head, so you can walk around wearing your kid's print on a necklace. If you go to Imagesoftime.com, you can—get this—order a kind of plaster of Paris kit in which you stick baby's hand for three minutes (go to the website if you don't believe us!) and produce a tiny and terrifying mold of a cut-off hand. ("Treasure your baby's hand forever—3 easy to follow steps in less than 3 minutes.")[17] Of course we all adore our babies' tiny fingers and toes, and want to sear the images into our memories. But really—these look like grotesque miniversions of the jungle trophies Dian Fossey was trying to eliminate. Or you can "Make a Proud Belly Cast!" That's right, girls, you can buy a plaster kit for *yourself,* smear the cement on your pregnant gut, and make a belly cast of the protuberance that prevents you from seeing your feet for five months. This belly cast is "a beautiful keepsake."[18] Talk about generational differences. Making a memorial out of your swollen girth would have seemed weirdly obsessive in the 1980s. Today, such a product just seems like a natural extension of marketers' efforts to capitalize on every single aspect of childbirth. So some young mothers find the belly cast fun, even kitschy. But women of the Erma Bombeck generation might ask "Where would you put it, over the fireplace next to the moose head, or do you turn it upside down and fill it with Doritos?"

Back in the olden days (like ten, fifteen years ago), just before the baby came, you got a crib, a changing table, a diaper pail, a baby monitor, and a year's supply of paper towels, and if you were a really romantic sucker, a rocking chair. That was about it for the baby's room, aka the nursery. Crib designs, furniture companies, and nursery accessories we never heard of in 1990 (we were probably too busy summoning the dog to clean off the highchair) bombard mothers with an array of upscale designer choices once reserved for viscounts and shahs. PoshTots.com sells an orange dresser in the shape of a carrot and a Fantasy Bed Coach that is a bed inside a replica of the globe-shaped carriage that took Cinderella to the ball.

Now here's why you're supposed to spend the GDP of Liechtenstein on the nursery. You're not trying to keep up with the Joneses, no, no, no. You are "decorating the spaces where your child lives, laughs and dreams"; you are doing this to stimulate his or her imagination.[19] But you are also "reflecting" the child's imagination. Of course, you can't know what is especially compelling to your child's imagination until he or she is born, has been around for a while, and can talk, but never mind. In "Creating a Dream Nursery" in *Pregnancy* (which reads like a sales pitch for one company, cradlebee.com), we learn that in addition to the crib (which must be chosen very carefully because it "dictates the look of the room"), we need to get a mobile that is "coordinated with bedding sets," "hand-painted stools," toy chests "painted with various themes," "decorative clocks" (because "clocks can be a fun way to reflect a theme or inspire the imagination"), "wall accessories to reflect the child's personality" (remember, kid not born yet, personality unknown), "heirloom-quality hand-painted canvas wall hangings," or a "traditional permanent mural" which "can be personalized with Baby's name or initials." In addition to the crib, you'll want a Moses basket "woven from natural fibers, such as cornhusks" (ouch!) or "organically grown cotton." Hold on, toots, you're not done yet. You also need decorative "drawer pulls, tissue-box covers, wall plaques and designer wastebaskets" to "evoke a sense of harmony." Because "lighting is a key mood-setting feature," you also need to do some lighting design that provides "soft focal illumination." [20]

At the vanguard of the new momism is the movement that insists that your job isn't done until you've home schooled your kids. Talk about upping the ante! Now mother is supposed to be omniscient and fluent in quadratic equations, the XYZ affair, and when Banquo's ghost appears in *Macbeth*. There has been a dramatic increase in the number of families who home school their kids, from an estimated 360,000 in 1994 to about 850,000 in 2001. [21] Only 1.7 percent of the country's fifty million school-children were home schooled in 1999, but that's a two-and-half-time increase in just five years. Most home-schooled kids live, obviously, in one-income families, since someone, usually Mom, has to stay home and be the teacher. [22] Parents choose this educational route for all kinds of reasons, such as horrible public schools, a desire to tailor-make their child's learning, or an insistence that their kids never encounter the words *evolution, birth control,* or *Oscar Wilde*. In a government survey, the number-two reason parents gave for home schooling, after the desire to provide a better education for their kids, was their religious beliefs. (Perhaps because we are such losers, our children greet our efforts at homework help with, "Leave me alone, you're ruining it, you're doing it *all wrong,* now I'm going to look stupid," so we have no idea how any parent spends the whole day attempting to impart knowledge to her kids.)

In the olden days, if you thought that the public schools were doing a lousy job, you joined the PTA and gave the local school board hell. Or, if you had money, you might send your kid to private school. But under the banner of the new momism, those are cop-out alternatives. Of course, for some parents today, home schooling is the best and sometimes the only option they have, and they do it without an ounce of self-righteousness. But in the hands of some zealots, home schooling has become the most perfect indicator of maternal virtue. If you really care about your child, if you truly see the world from his enlightened perspective, you necessarily understand that consigning him to the Mudville public school system—no matter how good it is judged to be—is tantamount to squelching his individuality and dimming his intellectual lights. You, and only you, Mom, can provide your child with a learning environment uniquely designed with him in mind. And that is because you have succeeded in adopting his worldview, which momism insists is the only one that matters. Forget about demanding the rehabilitation of public education. Forget about the fact that you can't remember the Pythagorean theorem, let alone have a clue as to how you might teach it to somebody else. Forget about the enrichment that kids derive from seeing themselves as part of a group, as eventual citizens. And certainly forget about experiencing the relief of knowing that whatever else Monday might throw in your face, at least the kids are back in school for the week.

Now, how are we to account for this explosive rise in protectionism and, indeed, narcissism around our kids? What we've seen since the early 1990s is a hyperindividualized emphasis on how truly, exquisitely unique and precious our child is, the Hope diamond, more special than the others. Yes, attitudes toward the preciousness of children have come a long way since the days when six-year-olds worked in factories rolling cigars or shucking peas. (One of our grandmothers used to yell routinely to her son back in the early 1920s, "I'll paint the walls with your blood," and "I'll tear your arm out and beat you with the bloody stump," two disciplinary ploys not recommended today by *Parents* magazine.) We agree that it's not a very good sign if you don't think your kid is deserving of the best that life has to offer.

But this more recent version of culturally constructed and commercially promoted maternal love has a nasty underside: the compulsion to have your kid step over the others, be the envy of others, rise above the mass of the others—to be, and to be seen as, well, a star. Kids come into the world feeling that they are the center of the universe. For years, shrinks told us that a parent's job is simultaneously to give the child love and confidence and also to disabuse him or her, over the course of the toddler and preschool years, of the notion that he or she is the Sun King. Since our kids do have to get on with others, and are, in fact, not Prince William or Prince Harry, and when they grow up will have to deal with the Division of Motor Vehicles, voicemail menus, and the nursing shortage just like everyone else, this advice seems sound. But because mothers today are urged to inhabit and identify with the child's inner subject positions and cater to them, they are pushed to reinforce the notion that he's the center of the universe, his thoughts and feelings the only ones worth considering, the ones that cut in line before everyone else's.

There are important cultural and political reasons for this shift, too. "Our" government has, over the past thirty years, simply refused to ensure that the nation's children are treated with decency. The rejection of any communal, collective ethos around the care and education of children leaves mothers one alternative: individual effort and vigilance on behalf of your own kids. It's every mom for herself. It only takes a village if you, Mom, aren't doing enough by yourself. We are in a competitive fight to the finish, pitted against all the risks and dangers "out there," pitted against each other, scrapping over ever-scarcer resources, from conception to commencement—and beyond.

The advertising industry, of course, uses competitive individualism to sell products—do you want to be the first one on the block to have the new improved model or, conversely, be the only one on the block with the mortifying old one? Except in the domain of reproductive rights, Americans are barraged with the idea that having a plethora of "choices" is fundamental to their "freedom." So the ideology of "the market," rather than the government, taking care of social needs and concerns has powerfully fueled these changes in attitudes toward children and child rearing. And this in spite of the absolute failure of the market to provide even better-off Americans with a "child friendly" infrastructure for ordinary life. The Ronald McDonald Playground may lure you in on Saturday afternoon after exercising your freedom of choice over the dazzling array of breakfast cereals at Safeway, but it'll do nothing for you on Monday morning when you have to go to work and your teenager informs you that her little brother is "blowing chunks" all over the bathroom floor. Then, you're on your own.

What you should do, according to Dr. Laura, Mussolini of domesticated motherhood and chief spokeswoman for right-wing momism, is quit your job and stay home. On the remarkable chance that you have escaped her talons, Dr. Laura Schlessinger is a radio talk-show hostess whose syndicated program, begun in 1994, rapidly drew a listener base of nearly twenty million, which by 1998 rivaled that of Rush Limbaugh. Despite the fact that Dr. Laura might respond to a tearful plea for advice with "How stupid can you be and still be able to chew your food," tens of thousands call in each day for guidance.[23] Every day she doles out invectives against "shacking up," working mothers, abortion, nonmarital sex, high school dating, gay parenting, Murphy Browners, women who consider divorce because they are sick of being enslaved to their husbands, and "mixed marriages" (which seems to include any marriage not between a man and a woman of roughly the same age, race, religion, ethnicity, class, and dietary predilections). But above all, Dr. Laura proclaims herself to be on the side of the "kidlets."

Dr. Laura has come under fire, most famously, for her vehement on-air homophobic remarks in which she has insisted, for example, that homosexuality and incest are exactly the same thing. She has come under less fire for her hypocritical—might one even say transgendered?—promotion of patriarchy circa 1954, in which women assume the position of doormat, especially when it comes to their kids. Dr. Laura herself is a cutthroat viper (an "ogre," according to a former colleague)[24] and shrewd businesswoman who has made millions of dollars from her radio show, books, T-shirts, coffee mugs, fan club, speaking engagements, and endorsements. But never mind all that. She is, through and through, first and foremost, above all else, a mom. She opens every segment with her signature remark, "I am my kid's mom." Only the densest caller fails to realize that whatever slim hope she has of getting a sympathetic response from the Great and Powerful Doctor depends on announcing, before she asks Dr. Laura her "question," that she, too, is her kid's mom. Dr. Laura (whose graduate degree in exercise physiology apparently qualifies her as an expert in everything else) wants her listeners to believe (just as Phyllis Schlafly wanted when she was away from home touring the country 24/7 for years, campaigning against the Equal Rights Amendment) that she is the paradigmatic mother, always there when her little Deryk needs her. Despite the fact that Deryk will be able to vote in the next presidential election, Dr. Laura's anecdotal references to him imply that she is taking your call during a quick break in a game of peekaboo.

Dr. Laura is a born-again religious zealot (she reclaimed her Jewish roots), a born-again political conservative, and a born-again antifeminist, and the combination is formidable. She claims to have once been a feminist, but now "they nauseate and sicken" her because "they've destroyed the family."[25] She knows how easy it is to be lulled by feminism into thinking, for example, that it might be okay to leave your one-year-old with a baby-sitter for a couple of hours so you could visit a friend in the hospital. Babysitter!!! Are you kidding??? What did you think when you signed on to motherhood??? That you could just dump your kid somewhere and go gallivanting around??? These tirades end when the caller, who inevitably began with a testimonial to Dr. Laura's transformative powers, allows as how she thought that it was probably a foolish idea, but she just wanted to check because she was feeling a little bit sorry for her sick friend.

The very best moms, the ones whose lives are totally defined by self-sacrifice, win an "I am my kid's mom" T-shirt or a free membership in the I Am My Kid's Mom Club (which we are all encouraged to join by visiting Drlaura.com or by calling 800-DRLAURA). You qualify for a freebie only when you call in to say that because of Dr. Laura, you not only renounced all thoughts of being anything other than a mom, but now make all your clothes out of old bedsheets to save money because being a real mom requires total self-denial. Besides, since you are home schooling your kids, learning to sew can be incorporated into the home-economics curriculum. Wearing a size-two Armani suit, her hair perfectly coiffed, her body toned by a two-hour before-dawn workout, the empress of the airwaves only congratulates those callers who have resisted the siren song of self-indulgence and instead heeded their biological destiny.

Sometimes Dr. Laura gives reasonable advice, as long as you don't think too hard about the terms of the question. It's not your job to tell your husband's sister that your family won't be attending her wedding since she and her fiancée have been "shacking up" (i.e., living together) for two years. It's his sister, so it's his job. Fair enough. Sometimes she dishes it out to men who are stupid enough to call up and ask her opinion about spending money on a vacation with their new girlfriend instead of paying child support. But her rise to power is based, at least in part, on her recognition that she could capitalize big-time on the successes of the 1980s CRAP crusade to vilify feminism. She zeros in on women's ambivalence about work and motherhood, an ambivalence that is exacerbated by the government's blockade against support for family services. She resolves the ambivalence by reaffirming the sexual division of labor: women are moms, men are CEOs (or soldiers, or police officers, or rabbis); women arrange playdates, men watch football; women weep, men stonewall; women change diapers, men change tires. Estrogen makes it possible for women to care for children by identifying completely with them. Testosterone does not.

Dr. Laura's dictatorial, Big-Mother-is-watching-you stance treats mothers—er, we mean *moms*—as though they themselves are children. By addressing her listeners as developmentally arrested nincompoops, she establishes her "professional" superiority and her moral authority. As fabulous as children are, they don't know very much. Their moral universe tends to remain kind of black and white for quite some time. There are good guys and bad guys; if you're not with us, you're against us. Moral ambiguity, or any ambiguity for that matter, fits uncomfortably in a child's worldview. Mothers, however, are surrounded by ambiguity and often beset by ambivalence about child rearing, work, their marriages or relationships or, for that matter, the merits of microwave dinners. Therein lies the genius of Dr. Laura. By constructing a simplified, childlike world for her listeners, she can dismiss ambivalence as either stupid or irrelevant to the governing dictum "I am my kid's mom." She appeals to some women's longing for a clear sense of purpose, for an escape from the doubt—and stress—that indeed result from the tensions between feminism on the one hand and the backlash against it on the other. She offers pure moral oxygen delivered in short, angry spurts.

Despite her success, there are also millions of women who loathe her. They hate her insistence that mothers not work when this is either impossible or undesirable for millions. They find it insufferable that, as a female, she assumes the role of patriarch who dishes out paternalistic diatribes designed to keep women down. But mostly they despise her glib self-righteousness (especially when they learn that she herself ditched an earlier marriage, reportedly lived with her second husband before marrying him, and refused to patch things up with her estranged mother, who died alone in her apartment but was not found until two weeks later). Many see Dr. Laura as representing a fringe, right-wing version of the new momism that has a clear, conservative political agenda. And that is indeed the case. Dr. Laura's new momism is too explicitly restrictive, too tied to her own version of religious fundamentalism to become a majority position. Having said that, however, her holier-than-thou "I am my kid's mom" mantra is a vital tributary feeding the basic, mainstream value of the new momism: that always putting your child first and obsessively anticipating his or her every need is essential to raising remotely healthy, happy children.

And don't think the other minions of CRAP are resting on their laurels. The latest salvo in the beloved sport of mother-bashing comes from Mary Eberstadt, whose *Policy Review* article "Home-Alone America" will soon accost you as a full-length book. You do have to hand it to Eberstadt—she has elevated the "cheap shot" to breathtaking new levels that even Howard Stern might envy. The very first line of her article reminds readers about the spate of horrific school shootings culminating with those at Columbine, and then quickly moves in for the kill. Guess whose fault all those were? You got it: absentee, working mothers. In Eberstadt's "home-alone" world, working mothers are, by definition, never present, inattentive, delinquent mothers and are responsible for—in addition to school shooting sprees, of course—supposedly skyrocketing rates of teen suicides, child and adolescent mental problems, "conduct disorders," child sexual abuse sexual promiscuity among teens, poor performance in school, and all depression, anxiety, and drug use among kids.[26] Neglected, in her tirade about working mothers ruining the children of America are, again, those pesky things called facts. Government figures showed in 2003 that unwed teen pregnancies are actually *down,* smoking among teens continues to decline, the death rate for adolescents in 2000 hit an all-time low, drug use among teens is down, the number of teens taking honors-level courses has increased "significantly" since the 1980s, and the percentage of young people in their twenties who earn a bachelor's degree or higher is also at an all-time high.[27] Hmm, with this kind of data—and if one was in the business of making what social scientists call spurious correlations—one could argue that mothers working outside the home has been the single best trend to hit the U.S. in thirty years.

Why, in Eberstadt's universe, do mothers work? Well, a few "mothers in extremis" work out of "genuine necessity," but most "prefer to arrange their lives that way" because, well, they just really don't want to spend time with their kids. Eberstadt has apparently never attended a school play at 2:00 P.M. whose audience is filled with working mothers who have rearranged their entire schedules to be there; never seen a working mother help her kids with their homework; never seen a working mother discipline her kids, hug them, lavish them with love, or have heart-to-hearts with them about everything from sex to drinking to why their best friend might indeed be a jerk.

To find a community slightly different from Dr. Laura's neighborhood, or one somewhat less craven about designer nurseries than *Pregnancy*, many mothers have turned to the Internet. While it isn't possible to provide any precise figures about the number of mom Web sites there are, suffice it to say that a Google search for *mom* results in ten million hits, while *dad* gets six million, many of which are for sites like "Digital Age Design." *Father* gets almost as many as *mother*, but there's not much of relevance to parenting once you eliminate Church Fathers, Founding Fathers, and Web sites that give you ideas about what to give your dad for Father's Day. There is the usual vast array of sites, from huge commercial ones like Babycenter.com, which convey the extent to which the Web has been turned into an electronic strip mall, to tiny sites created by individual women to display family photos, recipes, and tips about toddlers.

Taken as a whole, the motherhood Web reflects the cultural tensions that fuel the new momism. On the one hand, mom Web sites do provide women with sources of information, advice, solace, and encouragement from other women who are facing similar challenges. Especially for mothers facing illnesses in their children, such as autism, or even those less devastating, like ADD, the Web indeed offers a crucial node of connection and information rarely available elsewhere. Some of these motherhood Web sites are even dedicated to talking back to the new momism. On-line, mothers get to talk to each other, not just listen to some supposed expert, and the outpouring of support you see women giving each other, about everything from diaper rash to homework assignments (including links to relevant Web sites), truly embodies what we used to call sisterhood. Mothers look to each other for affirmations of what is "normal" in kids and for sympathy about insensitive, uninvolved fathers, and they get it, with a lot of heart.

On the other hand, many chat rooms and "community forums" encourage an obsessive fixation on the details of child rearing and domestic life that ultimately results in Even More Work for Mama. What may begin as collective spirit is ultimately diverted into a never-ending set of exchanges on the merits of air versus machine-drying organic diapers. There are mom Web sites that serve as forums for women to challenge the received wisdom of experts and the utopian claims of marketers and advertisers, but many more mom Web sites are plastered with ads for bionic baby bouncers and links to fitness sites that themselves hawk postpartum toning videos. Worse still, and in total opposition to the notion of sisterhood, except with those who are exactly like you, are the sites that are driven by an us-them, "mommy wars" mentality.

The Internet has allowed people to find like-minded others in cyberspace to make up for the fact that compatriots might not be living just around the corner. The Internet has also encouraged people either to assume new identities or cement the ones they have as they interact with distant others on-line. One such on-line persona goes by the Internet argot the SAHM: the stay-at-home mom. And on-line, she often comes out fighting. She is the heart and soul of the new momism. Unlike many flesh-and-blood stay-at-home mothers we know, the on-line, faceless, self-proclaimed SAHM is often unbearably goody-two-shoes, overtly impressed by her own virtue in the face of those mothers who have gone to the other side. She is the mom who has kept the faith in the face of the mythical feminist onslaught against the family. A soupçon of the media's version of feminism does get folded into the on-line SAHM's worldview: Choice is important. You can choose the right way to be a mother, or you can choose the wrong way. The wrong way, invariably, is to work outside the home. Homebodies.org, founded by Cheryl Gochnauer, author of *So You Want to Be a Stay-at-Home Mom*, bills itself as "helping parents find their way home," though we doubt her advice is directed at Dad.

Many of the mom Web sites reinforce the sense of collectivity, of higher purpose, characteristic of the new momism. But like so much else on the Internet, mom Web sites have become increasingly partitioned into identity niches: African American SAHMs (AASAHMs), Christian SAHMs, home-schooling SAHMs, valley SAHMs, organic SAHMs, metro SAHMS, and so forth. Lots of mom Web sites function, then, as virtual clubhouses, except instead of hanging a sign on the door that says GIRLS ONLY—NO BOYS ALLOWED à la fourth grade, they sport a more refined set of inclusions and exclusions. Only those who share the same product preferences, religious affiliation, demographic niche, or parenting styles (or prejudices) will be comfortable logging on. Within these narrow, like-minded congregations, self-righteousness and myopia flourish.

Momsview.com, for example, has economy shopping as its raison d'être. It offers zillions of web coupons, and links to sale sites and "free things." Being a mom, after all, requires a lot of shopping, and this Web site enables mom to shop even more. But it also has a "community" section that includes discussion groups and message boards. You can choose "Prayer Requests," "Moms Get Fit," or "Moms Get Organized," which turns out *not* to be a call to march on Washington for paid maternity leave, universal health care, or mandatory flex time, but is rather a call to organize your purse. Step number one? "First, pick a nice size purse." Responses include, "Thanks, Barbara. You gave me some inspiration for organizing my purse today!" There is further advice on organizing your home-schooling materials: "Color code each of your kids and yourself. In your binder, you can put reminders to yourself to peel and stick three pounds of carrots for dinner while you are teaching algebra." (Shoot us now.)

Except in discussions like "Youngest Angels," where women exchange heartbreaking stories about miscarriages, stillbirths, and the death of their young children, discussions often impossible elsewhere, many SAHMs write to each other with a "you go girl!" determination. A "happy SAHM of four" writes in to say that she wants to have a fifth child but she wonders what to do about the people who will undoubtedly accuse her of overindulgence. "Go for it!" "It's your choice!" or "I have five kids and I have never lost one of them!"—a remark that suggests a different angle on the problem of overpopulation. Here, any expression of commitment to intensive, obsessive mothering is rewarded with an outpouring of "You know you are doing the right thing!" and advice to ignore the naysayers. Waning resolve in the face of being at home all day with small children is answered by new entries to the list of "Boredom Busters" because "Moms Do Get Bored Sometimes." And lest you think that all Momsview.com moms think alike, there is the "Kitchen Table Debate" where moms can butt heads on issues such as whether or not it's okay for the Muppets to talk about HIV (everybody said "no") or whether anybody supported the mother whose drunk, bare-breasted daughter was featured on a *Dateline* episode about parents who let their teenagers go to Cancun unsupervised for spring vacation (no one did).

One rarely sees direct attacks on working mothers on these sites. Rather, one can see that the incessant self-justification comes, indeed, from how little American society supports or values motherhood—and these mothers know that. Hence the names of forums like MOTHBoard—for Managers of Their Own Homes—which tries, through rhetorical flourish if nothing else, to elevate the status of caring for children. More tellingly, some of the chats involve unselfconscious critiques of patriarchy—although, God forbid, that curse word would never be used—as women ask each other how they can be, simultaneously, submissive to their husbands (good wife) yet stand by and watch that husband refuse to give their child the attention he wants and deserves (bad mother). So while working mothers might indeed find many of the SAHM Web sites aggressively pious, to coin an oxymoron, we can also see that many of them are documents of the sheer rage women feel at doing such an important job that is so consistently taken for granted and devalued. In the process, of course, we see on the Web, possibly more clearly than anywhere else in the media, the extent to which some mothers themselves revel in and inflate the new momism.

At the very top of the SAHM heap are the moms of "supermultiples," namely, women who are "blessed" with five, six, seven, or (the record) eight babies. How much more overblown can the new momism get? Nowhere is the gap between candy-coated imagery and a Herculean parenting challenge more stark than in the reverential genuflecting to the multiples in the crèche. Because of fertility drugs (i.e., the miracle of modern medicine), the number of multiples increased in the 1990s, yet the most prominent supermultiple mothers, and the superSAHM Web sites that beatify them, prefer to erase the role played by science and simply cast these children as divinely wrought miracles (forget the "modern medicine" part). There are those in the medical profession who regularly refer to these as "litter babies," but you would never see such a sobriquet on the cover of Good Housekeeping or on MOMSBoard.com. There are Web sites devoted exclusively to superSAHMs, and lots of Web sites have discussion forums for the extreme challenges that face these mothers: financial chaos, logistical nightmares, and seriously premature infants with developmental problems that will affect them their entire lives. But in the sunlight-shafting-through-clouds world of the new momism, these crises are eclipsed by the enormous halo emanating from the supermultiple mom. We are hardly saying that these mothers do not deserve support and respect given what they are up against. But their stories push the struggles of such women out of purgatory and into heaven, where idealization reigns supreme. And unlike welfare mothers, who with two kids were cast as irresponsible baby machines, these mothers came across—and sometimes presented themselves—as innocent vessels of God's will.

The most super of the superSAHMs is Bobbi McCaughey, the canonized mom of the famous septuplets, who have, since their emergence in 1997, graced every cover of the holiday issue of *Ladies' Home Journal*. (Other supermultiples aka "Little Miracles" like the Collins sextuplets occasionally take the place of the latest celebrity mom, but with less regularity).[28] The "seven from heaven," as their parents refer to them in their book of the same name, resulted not from divine intervention but were, in fact, the products of high-tech fertility drugs and a medical team of about forty. When women become pregnant with so many embryos, doctors routinely advise "selective reduction" because of the enormous risks to mother and fetus of carrying more than two or three babies to term. Bobbi McCaughey refused to do this. Instead, to maintain this very high-risk pregnancy, she spent the last three months of her confinement lying upside down in a hospital bed, fed intravenously, and wired to a bank of monitors rivaling the controls of the USS *Constitution*. The babies were delivered by c-section, and then each one of them was wired to his or her own extrauterine life-support system. Given that their average weight was one pound, most of the babies spent their first year in the hospital, at the cost of well over a million dollars. (Unlike the children of welfare mothers, we never heard about the cost "to us" of the care of these needy babies, even though insurance companies routinely pass on to the consumer—us—the fiscal consequences of such high-risk pregnancies.) The McCaugheys were deluged with corporate and community largesse, all of which helped to ease the transition from one child (three years old at the time) to eight. There was only one acceptable, prescribed reaction from most of the media, and certainly in the SAHM Web sites: admiration and awe.

Now, talk about a maternal drama that exemplifies a single-minded commitment to Motherhood with a capital M! Insisting on carrying, delivering, and raising seven children at once is the ultimate in giving yourself up for children. Because of this embrace of extreme momism, Bobbi McCaughey was controversial, some finding her irresponsible (and nuts) and others seeing her as a saint and a beacon. "If Bobbi, a SAHM of eight, can do it, I can't complain, can I?" According to this strain of new momism, Bobbi McCaughey really does it all. Take the November 2002 discussion of the McCaugheys on the Web forum MOMSBoard. Mom2kt: "I was just reading an on-line article about them. In the article, the mom states that they don't do Santa, and she has chosen to home school all seven children! . . . I have always been very impressed with this family and this just takes my respect for them one step further." Adds Sunrise: "I too love to read about this family! They are truly a testimony for Christ and it is a blessing to see how the Lord uses them to bring glory to Himself!" Whatever one thinks of this imputing to the Great Almighty what was made possible by human-made drugs, such comments express many SAHMs' need for deities who affirm that staying home and raising kids is indeed heroic.

Because of the Christian right's determination to return all women to the barefoot-and-pregnant era of world history, they have embraced the McCaugheys, themselves fundamentalist Christians and conservative Republicans, as the embodiment of family values. The McCaugheys were proud to be featured on the Web site of the Family Research Council, "Defending Family, Faith and Freedom," then headed by archconservative Gary Bauer, who resigned to become a Republican presidential candidate in 2000. Indeed, Bauer made a special campaign stop in Iowa to meet with the McCaugheys.

There are other ways to achieve, or to attempt, the new momism than to be a fundamentalist Christian SAHM of septuplets. Perhaps no one has contributed more to its ascendancy among an often quite different group of women—college-educated high achievers—than William Sears, MD. Along with his wife, Martha Sears, RN, he has made an industry out of what they refer to as "attachment parenting." When it comes to properly nurturing your child, these two make the likes of T. Berry Brazelton or Penelope Leach look like Conan the Barbarian and Nurse Ratched. The Sears philosophy is as simple as it is impossible: Reattach your baby to your body the moment she is born and keep her there pretty much until she goes to college. If you do not do this, your child will fail to bond properly to you and you to her, and the rest is a road straight to the juvenile detention center for her and the Betty Ford Clinic for you. Dr. Bill and Martha, as they prefer to be called by their "little patients," are the parents of eight children, two of whom, Dr. Bob and Dr. Jim, have also become pediatricians. The Searses are authors of *The Baby Book,* the "parenting bible of the '90s," according to their Web site, Askdrsears.com. Dr. Bill contributes as well to Parenting.com, is a consultant to *Parenting* and *BabyTalk* magazines, and has authored or coauthored a stack of other books for parents and for kids. Martha calls herself (what else?) a "professional mother," and in answer to those who question her decision to have eight kids, says, "The world needs my children." [29]

A mom achieves the goal of attachment parenting first by "Creat[ing] a

Peaceful Womb Experience" because "[i]n the past twenty years there have been new and exciting discoveries about the fetus's sensory and emotional awareness. Mother and her unborn baby share emotions. When mother is upset, baby may be upset. If your pregnancy is cluttered with emotional stress (especially the last three months), you have a higher risk of having a child who is anxious." [30] (This reminds one of the "old wives' tale" that if you got scared during your pregnancy your baby would be born with a scar). Then there is "baby wearing." You wear your baby in a special sling until she wears you out, at which point you put her in the "family bed" and get in with her to "co-sleep." If there's not enough room, your husband or partner can go to the couch. You can purchase the "original" Dr. Sears sling on-line at the Dr. Sears Store, or you can order a custom sling from one of the many Web sites, like Mamaroobabysling.com.

Now we admit—we did not wear our babies and, except for the odd bout of night terrors or simply passing out from exhaustion with a baby at our side, we did not co-sleep with them. Not only did we worry about smothering them, and not only did they manage to occupy the space of a sumo wrestler with restless leg syndrome, co-sleeping was "out" then, not on the list of "must do's." *We* were told that if they didn't learn how to sleep without us, they would become spoiled tyrants. So our point here is not to bash mothers who find these options comforting or convenient. It is to see attachment parenting as a fad, like the Zone Diet (as so many of these child-rearing trends are), and to say *excuuuse me* to a whole host of practices that, in addition to demanding that you see the world only through your children's eyes, insist that you remain physically tethered to them pretty much all the time.

While Dr. Bill leaves one with the impression that he and Martha kind of invented attachment parenting, he wants to reassure us that it is also primal (African women who haven't yet been corrupted by the demands of civilization wear their babies), natural (kangaroos and primates do it), and at the same time a reflection of the very latest medical and psychological research. While the "bonding literature" had been largely discredited (yes, if you deprive infants of responsive and consistent caregiving, they aren't going to do too well, but it doesn't follow from that that they need the very same person—the would-be mom—providing the care at every moment), it has seen a renaissance in the new momism. Now, not only are you enjoined to keep your baby out of anyone else's arms, but you have to keep her glued to your torso at all times.

Visiting with Dr. Bill on his Web site, moms are fed a harsh purgative disguised in the soft glow of shameless maternal romanticism. "The time in your arms, at your breast and in your bed is a relatively short while in the life of a child, yet the memories of love and availability last forever." In other words, rid yourself of your selfish thoughts and desires! Enlightened motherhood demands it! Hoping to get your baby on a schedule? Only a selfish antimom would subject her child to "sleep training." A mother might brag that "He sleeps through the night," but this mother, by failing to heed her child's cry, has cruelly cut off communication with him. The consequences? "The result of this lack of communication is known, ultimately, as 'failure to thrive.' 'Thriving' means not only getting bigger, but growing to your full potential emotionally, physically, and intellectually." [31] Are you on the verge of buying a size 2T straightjacket for your two-year-old? That's because you are failing to "Get behind the eyes of your toddler." For example, "as you enter the kitchen, you see your two-year-old at the sink splashing water all over the floor. You could sink into a 'poor me' mind-set: 'Oh, no! Now I have to clean up the mess. Why does she do this to me?'" But here, according to Sears, is "a healthier choice." Instead of first considering your own inconvenience, immediately click into your child's viewpoint. You need to say, " 'This is fun. Look at all the different things you can do with dishes and water.' Getting out of yourself and into your child saves mental strain. You don't have to clean up the mess in your mind along with the water on the floor." [32]

By the time a woman has endured the entreaties, threats, and predictions embedded in Dr. Bill's discussions of breastfeeding (the longer, the more, the better! If your kid still wants to nurse before his violin recital, well, *get behind his eyes*), how are you going to feel when you move to the section on pumping breast milk, a section clearly designed for those misguided moms who "choose" to go back to work and so "must" be away from their babies for hours at a time? Worse yet, what if a woman can't nurse? They get "A Word About Bottlefeeding," in which there is, indeed, only one short paragraph and it does boil down to one word: *loser*. While Dr. Bill and Martha do acknowledge that working mothers are real and do refrain from saying anything explicitly condemnatory about them, the massive edifice of attachment parenting that they construct is one that no working mother can fully scale and conquer. Unlike Dr. Laura, Dr. Bill is not on an antifeminist, antiabortion, family-values crusade to increase the ranks of SAHMs. But at its core, attachment parenting pushes many of the same buttons and has the same effect. Women who would never think of wearing a T-shirt that says *Proud SAHM* nonetheless find themselves making homemade baby lotion out of elderberry extract and wearing one kid while getting behind the eyes of another. Especially if you are accustomed to high achievement and to cutthroat competition, attachment parenting opens the door to standards of excellence that would put any law partner wannabe to shame. If you are going to be a mom, well, you'll show *them* how it's done, no holds barred. In the baby-wearing neighborhood, where Mom must prove her mettle, Dad is best relegated to the role of "helper" (as he is called in attachmentese) and gets kicked out of the bed, if necessary, once Junior moves in.

Meanwhile, there are now an estimated two million fathers who stay at home with young children while the mother is the breadwinner. But look at the on-line moniker they get: SAHDs (maybe they should be SAHPs—stay-at-home pops). If you visit one of the few SAHD Web sites, you will see that this persona lacks the chutzpah of the SAHM. In fact, one of the Web sites is called Slowlane.com, which simultaneously takes a swipe at Dad's lifestyle choices, his sex drive, and his mental capacities. Here you will discover almost immediately that "SAHDs' risk of death from heart disease is 82% higher than that of men who work outside the home." Hmmm—what lesson should we take from this?

Given that the new momism had bulldozed through the news, talk radio, *People,* and the Internet much like the tanks in Tiananmen Square, one would think that by 2001, no mothers would dare stand in its path. But that summer, on June 20, a story broke that suggested, however briefly, that the new momism, as a cultural value and as a dictum for mothers, had gone too far. Tom Brokaw informed viewers, "There is a horrible situation in Houston tonight, a tragedy." [33] Across the network news, we were alerted to a "stunning," "chilling," "shocking," "horrifying" story, and only someone who had slept through 1994 could fail to think of Susan Smith. Andrea Yates, thirty-seven-year-old mother of five children, ages six months to seven years, had systematically drowned each and every one of them in the bathtub of her suburban Houston home. Yates was, by all reports, an exemplary mother, wife, and daughter. According to *Newsweek*'s Dirk Johnson, who was interviewed by *Today*'s Ann Curry, Yates ". . . had been a caretaker not only for her five young children as a home-schooling mother, but had also taken care, her mother told me, of her ailing father who had Alzheimer's. She would go to her parents' house every day for seven or eight years. She would help change her father's clothes, bathe him, help feed him. She was a woman—a young woman, her mother said, who always tried to do everything for other people." [34]

As it turned out, Andrea Yates had a history of postpartum psychosis and suffered from chronic major depression. She had been hospitalized on several occasions, once for a suicide attempt. But Andrea continued to have children because, as her husband Rusty put it, "That's where she got her fulfillment." [35] Andrea had been valedictorian of her high school class, a swimming star, and a nurse at a cancer clinic. But after the birth of their first child, Rusty "wanted her staying at home," according to their neighbor Sylvia Cole. [36] For a time, home was a converted school bus, sold to Rusty by Michael Woroniecki, the fundamentalist preacher whose flock Rusty had joined while a student at Auburn University. Woroniecki had raised his family in a bus as he preached his way through the South. Although they eventually abandoned the bus for a suburban ranch house, the Yates family continued to follow Woroniecki's strict teachings, especially about family life. They were determined to "have as many kids as nature would allow." [37] All worship and schooling were done at home. What many people do in the public realm—schooling, worship—Yates was asked to fold into the private realm of home and motherhood, and take all of this on—all of it—herself.

According to Andrea Yates's own account, she killed her children because she was constantly being told by Satan, who was inside her, that she was a failure. Her children "weren't developing correctly." She had been considering murder for two years, "[s]ince I realized I have not been a good mother to them." After she was jailed, she continued to hear the voices telling her that she was a lousy mother, that she had "failed her children." Only her execution would save her "from the evil inside her." [38] The birthday cakes and chicken potpies from scratch, the homemade costumes, the hours of schooling, nursing, cuddling, cleaning, none of it seemed to matter in the face of the unquestionable indictment of her mothering. Two weeks before she killed her children, she had been taken off her antipsychotic medication.

While there was the obligatory chorus of voices demanding that she fry, especially on right-wing radio talk shows, most of the media and public responses were quite unlike those to the Susan Smith case. Her clear history of serious mental illness and the particular form that it took made it difficult to see her as a wanton predator. In fact, the killings, and the reasons she gave for them, rallied women all over the country to see the case as an indictment of the new momism and its demands for endless self-sacrifice. Anna Quindlen in *Newsweek* movingly condemned the "insidious cult of motherhood" that gave a woman no space, when she was overwhelmed or exhausted or depressed, "quietly going bonkers in the house with five kids under the age of seven . . . to admit what she's really feeling." [39]

Readers flooded *Newsweek* with letters, and while they of course condemned the murders, they thanked the magazine for its "compassionate coverage of the Yates case." And despite the media's emphasis on Yates's shaky mental health, many women refused to dismiss Yates's desperation as only stemming from some medical disorder. Asked one, "Have we romanticized motherhood so much that we can't acknowledge the harsh reality of what women actually experience?" A stay-at-home mother of three children under the age of four charged, "For anyone who has condemned Andrea Yates as a bad mother or one who did not love her children, you must walk a mile in her shoes in order to know what her world was like." Other mothers identified with "the personal hell" they felt Yates had been going through and warned, "Somewhere, right in your own neighborhood, is a mother of young children struggling to make it through each day." But the most damning letter about the media's version of the new momism came from Meredith Berlin, someone in the know. "I can only say it's about time someone finally had the courage to tell the truth about what I call women's dirty little secret. As the former editor-in-chief of *Seventeen,* and the mother of three children who were once simultaneously under the age of 3, I have always felt that women, women's magazines, indeed the entire media, must do a better job of telling the full story of what mothering is about—warts and all. Unless we start admitting to ourselves and each other that it's not always a walk in the park, our guilt, anger, fear and depression will continue to go underground. And as we have learned, that is not a healthy place for them to be." [41]

Newsweek was hardly alone—from ABC's *Nightline* to *Redbook* to *People*—the case provoked serious discussions of postpartum depression and even, at times, of the burdens of motherhood itself. (Although Yates suffered from postpartum psychosis, a much more rare form of mental illness usually accompanied by delusions, the bulk of the coverage focused on postpartum depression, which can affect up to 20 percent of new mothers, but rarely results in their killing their children.) Katie Couric, a mother herself not unacquainted with loss, read the address of the Andrea Yates defense fund on the air. The case struck a nerve. Despite huge cover headlines like the one on *People* that screamed VILLAIN OR VICTIM? millions of women refused to reduce this to an individual question about whether this sole woman was a lunatic or an evildoer, and instead saw it as evidence that the institution of motherhood once again had to be addressed.

As part of *Newsweek*'s original cover story coverage, the magazine also published a confessional piece by Marie Osmond, who in 1983 appeared on the cover of *Good Housekeeping* with the euphoric headline, HAPPINESS IS HAVING A BABY. Now, however, Osmond recounted her near-immobilizing siege of postpartum depression, "the darkest place I've ever been." Even with money, fame, and support from friends and family, Osmond at first found it extremely difficult to seek out help, because motherhood was supposed to be euphoric. "We need to dispel the motherhood myth," she wrote, and acknowledged how difficult caring for a small child—let alone several—really is.[42] Coming from a celebrity who had herself previously contributed to the myth of ever-joyful maternity, Osmond's story briefly pulled back the curtain, suggesting a darker side even to celebrity momism.

While the Yates case revealed that many women felt overwhelmed by the duties of and expectations surrounding motherhood, it did not reignite demands for universal health care, or for a national, high-quality day-care system, or for reorganization of the workplace to make it more accommodating to the raising of children. There was one charge that lay buried under the outpouring of empathy for Yates' plight: Why do our political and economic institutions get away with doing so little for mothers and children? How have we, as a society, allowed mothers and children to be forced into such isolation? Why have we embraced what others would have be our fate as if it were our own invention? Mothers are left to their own devices until something goes horribly wrong, and then they are brought out as an object lesson. We listen up, take note, and then go back and try harder. Why?

How far have we come, really, if we can go back to Adrienne Rich's *Of Woman Born* (1976) and read that "good" mothers, when they see another mother driven to the brink, "resolve to become better, more patient and long-suffering, to cling more tightly to what passes for sanity . . . to assume that I, the individual woman, am the 'problem.' " [43] In her analysis of a thirty-eight-year-old mother of eight who, in June 1974, murdered her two youngest children, Rich asked what anyone, including psychiatrists, could have done for her, given that she was trapped within an institution of motherhood utterly defined by patriarchy. "What woman, in the solitary confinement of a life at home enclosed with young children, or in the struggle to mother them while providing for them single-handedly, or in the conflict of weighing her own personhood against the dogma that says she is a mother first, last, and always—what woman has not dreamed of 'going over the edge'?" [44] If we could look inside mothers "we would see the embodiment of rage, of tragedy, of the overcharged energy of love, of inventive desperation, we would see the machinery of institutional violence wrenching at the experience of motherhood." [45]

In the 1970s, feminists confronted institutions—federal, state, and local governments, the press, the workplace—and demanded a host of structural changes that would improve the everyday lives of millions of women and children. But today political fatalism seems the only sensible option because the political big boys have extinguished—or as Harry Potter would say, disapparated—public activism for better social programs as a course of action. By the early twenty-first century, the country's political culture (and the omnipresent right-wing pundits) have successfully established the taken-for-granted notion that it is now ridiculous to look to the government to solve any major societal problems (except for color-coding terrorism warnings as if they are home-schooling folders). Mothers are supposed to be resigned to the fact that the government has plenty of money for weapons and corporations, but none for our kids. Although the Yates case fleetingly revealed that millions of mothers were chafing— or worse—under the new momism, in the end, being at the end of your rope remained an individual aberration.

Over the past thirty years—at least—women have taken in mixed messages from the media that have urged us to be, simultaneously, independent, achievement-oriented, successful, the equal to any man and yet appealing to men, selfless, accommodating, nurturing, the connective tissue that holds all families together and, of course, slim and beautiful. We really were supposed to become some hybrid between Mother Teresa, Donna Shalala, Martha Stewart, and Cindy Crawford. Talk about straddling contradictions! But the thing is, millions of us did it and are still doing it—except we are hardly saints, cabinet officials, CEOs, or supermodels. In fact, even though stress and self-doubt are facts of life for most of us precisely because of these multiple, conflicting demands, we also do harbor some pride over the fact that we were told "do it all" and a lot of us did—a whole lot of it. We are used to the contradictions, comfortable in them, despite the pressure. Now, however, as the new momism gains reactionary momentum from political and economic instability, we're being told to abandon these contradictions, that we can't really straddle them, and that we should opt for something simpler. This is exactly the opposite direction women took in the late 1960s. Then, fueled by collective determination, women claimed their autonomy. Now, in the solitary confinement of the new momism, we are supposed to give it the heave-ho.

Raised to be "anything you want to be," cutting their teeth on Holly Near vinyl, finessing the soccer ball into the goal, and outshining the boys at the science fair, today's young mothers grew up holding their own in a world defined by competition and self-empowerment. But against a drooling infant, there is no contest. Ironically, the African proverb "it takes a village to raise a child" circulated through the media during the 1990s in large part because Hillary Clinton adopted it as the title for her best-seller *It Takes a Village*. But the proverb's collective spirit was eclipsed by the increasing wattage of the new momism.

Forget the damn village. The new momism insists that the formation of a child into a successful, happy person is exclusively the handiwork of one person: "Mom." Mom—however lofty her own hopes for herself, and whatever her financial circumstances, whatever embattled neighborhood she lives in, however scarring her own upbringing, however lousy her educational options—must simply make the right choices. If she doesn't, too bad for her kids, and for her. In a society where autonomy and success go hand in hand, isn't it just a little bit suspicious that successful motherhood requires relinquishing one's autonomy to a sometimes dangerous, always preposterous view of women and children? The many-headed hydra that is the new momism alternately lures and terrorizes us into second-class citizenship, making us wonder whether we are back in 1954.

Yet, there are cracks and fissures in the new momism through which you can glimpse the ghost of Erma Bombeck, hear echoes of Roseanne, and hear new voices that capture a different experience of motherhood. You stumble on them, you hear of them from a friend, who heard of them from her sister. You find them on a Web site that has come up gasping for air from the virtual swamp of the new momism. They emerge unexpectedly from the idiot box (as our fathers used to call the TV), in a book, a movie, and, on those odd days when it snows in Hades, from a mainstream news report. *Working Mother*, having ended its "best mom" competition, replaced it with the "Raising a Ruckus Awards" for mothers with "moxie" who are "making some noise and making a difference." Mothers—real and fictional—are ripping off the blinders of the new momism that direct our attention within, and urge us to obsess endlessly over our own supposed inadequacies while ignoring the truly desperate situation of millions of mothers and children in the United States (and elsewhere). Some mothers are reclaiming an identity that the new momism seeks to take from us: that of citizen. They are looking askance at the "mom is a dunce" cap from the 1950s that the new momism exhumes and saying, firmly, that they refuse to go near it.

The mothers on *Malcolm in the Middle, Life with Bonnie,* and *Everyone Loves Raymond,* for example, are hardly subservient June Cleaver types, and their sarcastic asides often raise that question: "How did I get here?" And once Rachel—a single, unwed mother—on *Friends* had Emma, several episodes acknowledged the toll a baby can take on sleep, dating, hanging out in coffee shops, and sex. (However, since the ongoing challenges children provide are often the kiss of death to a sitcom, we started seeing a bit less of Emma once these jokes were exhausted.) There is currently an orange juice commercial that opens with a phony, black-and-white image of a calm, harmonious breakfasttime circa 1957, only to erupt into the in-living-color reality of the chaos of real families' breakfasttime: It makes fun of the gap between image and reality. At Parentcenter.com you can read regular installments of "Bringing Up Ben & Birdy" or "Raising Eleni," literary journals written by women who convey the day-to-dayness of motherhood with insight and humor, and without the overlay of sentimentalism, sainthood, and indictment typical of the new momism. Catherine Newman, mother of three-year-old Ben and new baby Abigail (aka "Birdy"), writes about being stuck indoors for weeks during the dead of a very cold winter. "But in some ways, Ben's such a trooper—totally game and willing to make the most of the winter. 'Come on, Mama,' he shouts from under a blanket. 'Be a bear with me in my bear-hive. Come and hibernacle with me.' I see the confusion between 'cave' and 'hive,' but I have no idea how 'hibernate' ended up morphing into 'tabernacle.' Go figure. But we play lots of hibernating games, which—since they mostly involve lying around on the couch and snacking—I really can't complain about."

Here's an approach to motherhood that assumes there is something of yourself left over even after giving in to the care and feeding of a small, inscrutable, mesmerizing, needy creature. In this case, a mother's bemused inability to account for her kid's inventive word splicing establishes a self-preserving distance between them. In that space, there is room for her (and for him) to maintain a foothold, to see that her desires and his, though they are mutually satisfied by lying around and snacking, are simply not the same.

This is the maternal strategy that has made Anne Lamott's life raft to mothers, *Operating Instructions: A Journal of My Son's First Year,* a perennial best-seller. Lamott, a single mother who refuses to set aside her distinctive and compassionate honesty, details the experience of a new mother that leaves the institution of motherhood in a shambles but her own sensibility intact. "Sam is two weeks old today. His umbilical cord fell off. I'm probably supposed to feel that it is something lovely and natural, but I must say that I'm going to be able to live without it somehow. It's like something a long-haired cat would get stuck in her tail." (Pretty soon, *Pregnancy* will be selling kits that allow you to varnish and frame the scabby little thing.) She admitted, "I've decided that the reason Sam is so gorgeous is that God knew that I wouldn't be able to fall in love with this shitting and colicky little bundle if he looked like one of those E.T. / Don Rickles babies." And then the astringent honesty: "I'm crazy tired. I feel as stressed out by exhaustion as someone who spent time in Vietnam. Maybe mothers who have husbands or boyfriends do not get so savagely exhausted, but I doubt it. They probably end up with these eccentric babies plus Big Foot skulking around the house pissed off because the mom is too tired to balance the checkbook or give him a nice blow job." [46] Not quite the sentiments one would find in *Baby Years*.

In the fall of 2002, Barnard hosted a conference on the status of mothers that commanded media attention and brought women from all ends of the political spectrum together who registered a fed-up, end-of-my-rope exasperation with the devaluation of motherhood in the "real" world not inhabited by Hollywood's "sexy" new moms. The conference revealed that various women have formed organizations like the Motherhood Project, the Motherhood Movement, and MOTHERS (Mothers Ought to Have Equal Rights). Many women are going to activist Web sites, whether it is Welfare Warriors, The Children's Defense Fund, or Ann Crittenden's, which has excellent links to a variety of crucial sites and list serves. And many are doing none of this, but are starting to say snide things to the latest *InStyle* feature on Hollywood moms more frequently and loudly than they used to.

Welfare Warriors, an organization of mothers fighting against the dismantling of the welfare system, who never get on the nightly news, do have a kick-butt Web site. During the holiday season, they encourage us to join together for some strategically placed caroling. "Our Kids Need Guarantees," from their Wisconsin chapter, is sung to the tune of "Little Drummer Boy." [47] Sample stanzas begin:

Mothers work—we are not bum-bum-bum-bums
And yet they treat us like we're scum-bum-bum-bums

and conclude with:

We buy our formula, not rum-rum-rum-rum
Yet TV Six shouts out we're scum-bum-bum-bums
The legislators join ha-rump-pa-pum-pum
Our families won't run, pa-rum-pa-pum-pum,
rum-pum-pum-pum, rum-pum-pum-pum
So we're here today, Pa-rum-pum-pum-pum
    Together we've come!!

Such sentiments do not help sell Oil of Olay or Ford Expeditions, nor do they promote in media audiences the complacency required to let the Big Boys handle things for us. It is the corporate media's job to seal off these cracks in the new momism's façade. At the same time, since resentment of the new momism is deep and wide (as the Yates case temporarily revealed), the media—to keep selling to us—have to provide some images that acknowledge mothers' resistance while containing it through jokes, wise-ass comments, and plot lines where mom gets to triumph for a few fleeting minutes. Media forms and outlets below the corporate media's radar screens *do* debunk the new momism, but in their pure forms cannot get on FOX or CBS. What's left, then, is the Battle of the Media Moms, with the compliant mother who has joyfully capitulated to the new momism in one corner, and the rebellious mothers armed with nothing more than zingers and snappy backtalk in the other. [48]

The news media's addiction to stories about child endangerment, our commercial culture's emphasis on indulging yourself and your kids while surpassing the Joneses, the niche-market magazine-and-cable assault on mothers, Dr. Laura's hypocritical harangues, our government's refusal to see us as citizens with quite pressing needs and demands: All this adds up to a rather huge block of interests, and a manufactured common sense, to take on. But we can do it. And the first step is to name the new momism every time and everywhere you see it, to ridicule it (preferably out loud, in front of others), and to tell yourself and other mothers you are doing just fine. Each of us needs to take a critical look at her own concessions to the new momism, and to imagine where women might be if we refused to keep our mothering on the straight-and-narrow of the mommy track. Talking back—in the supermarket, in front of the TV, with friends at the playground or at the soccer sidelines, to those in Congress—may not seem like much. But it is a crucial start: naming and denouncing the enemy. As Adrienne Rich put it nearly thirty years ago, "This is where we have to begin."

Exorcising the New Momism

It's Thursday night, 8:00 P.M., five years or so from now, and you have just tuned into the latest "reality" TV show women have turned into a smash hit—*Survivor: Motherhood Island*. Ten men in their thirties and forties are taken to Motherhood Island (which is *not* tropical) and each is deposited into a house with a two-day-old infant, a four-year-old, and a thirteen-year-old. The winner—who will get a million bucks if he and the kids survive till the end of the series—must provide food, clothing, and shelter for the family, but must also be voted the most devoted, loving, self-sacrificing father by the viewing audience (here *Motherhood Island* takes a leaf out of *American Idol*'s book). To get those votes, the "dad" must always smile at the kids, never lose his temper, listen closely and be ever understanding, and always put himself last.

Before being taken to their new homes on the island, the contestants are put in isolation chambers where their only reading material are books on the absolute necessity of attachment parenting and bonding for men, and magazines that feature an endless parade of male sports figures, actors, and businessmen, photographed swirling their babies in the air and proclaiming that "fatherhood is sexy." Many of these cover-boy dads "confess" that being a father is much more rewarding than being in the NBA finals or winning an Academy Award, and say they are going to give it all up and become househusbands. Inside these magazines, how-to articles warn the contestant that if he doesn't build a tree house out of bird's-eye maple for his kids, wear his baby until she's five, drop everything to be at the school play, and volunteer to be the class parent, he will be a failure—not just as a father, but as a man. The isolation chamber is also equipped with a radio, from which Dr. Larry upbraids all the male callers for being bad fathers because they have not quit work to stay home with their kids and do not walk around proclaiming "I am my kid's dad."

Once this brief training is done, the fun begins. First, each "dad" must decide whether to take his two-month unpaid paternity leave to take care of his infant, or go back to work so there will be food on the table. (Each man is fitted with prosthetic breasts and is required to breastfeed the baby every two hours.) He has two childcare options on Motherhood Island: The Little Mensa Center, with one trained staff member for every two children, that costs $2000 a week and takes infants, or Brunhilda's Kid Grotto, staffed only by the toothless, alcoholic Brunhilda herself, but at a cost of $100 a week. After Dad faces this challenge, he confronts the next one. In two days, he has a meeting at his Motherhood Island job that he absolutely, positively cannot miss; he will be demoted or fired if he does. At the exact same time, his thirteen-year-old has a band performance he has been practicing for three months and if Dad does not attend, he will be deemed a careerist lout and voted off the island by the viewing public. (Cameras will zoom in for a close-up the child's face, searching the audience for a dad who had failed to show, the tears now welling up in his eyes.) Dad #1, who has been given the job of lawyer, gets a very high-profile and lucrative case to try. The only way he can stay in the running for the million, however, is to turn down the case so he won't be spending too much time away from the kids. Dad #2, caught by the cameras reading an interoffice memo during the half-time of his child's soccer game, is voted off the island immediately.

Each dad gets one "lifeline" telephone call to his Motherhood Island Congressman, but this is just a gimmick so the audience gets to see Dad squirm some more. When one dad uses his lifeline to call to ask for a day-care center cheaper than Little Mensa yet less criminally negligent than Brunhilda's, the Congressman laughs out loud and says Motherhood Island can't afford to provide any day-care center like that because Motherhood Island needs a lot of missiles, its millionaires need a $90,000-apiece tax cut, and the Motherhood Island corporations need tax breaks so they can market cigarettes and Fatty Burgers in Thailand. When another dad uses his lifeline to say he really needs to have his eight weeks of paternity leave be paid or his kids will be living on blade-of-grass puree, his Congressman doubles over in giggles, asking whether Dad fully understands that this would bankrupt Motherhood Island. One dad cheats and uses his lifeline to call a woman off island to beg her to come and help him out. Not only does she give him her most withering "been there, done that" look, all the women in the audience vote him off for being a weakling and a throwback.

The challenges mount. On the same day that his boss tells him—at 4:55 P.M.—that he needs a foot locker full of information prepared and organized for a meeting at 8:00 the next morning (and Brunhilda's doesn't open until 8:30), Dad #4 discovers that his four-year-old has just gotten a double ear infection *and* head lice, and the thirteen-year-old has to bring "snack" the next morning for a classroom of twenty-five kids. His prosthetic breasts have been leaking on and off all afternoon and the clean shirt he put on this morning—his last one—is a wreck. When he gets home, his mailbox has been stuffed with *Michael Stewart Living, Dad* magazine (whose cover shrieks THE TEN WORST MISTAKES DADS MAKE and STRESS-BUSTERS FOR THE HARRIED DAD) and male *People,* where Bill Gates proclaims, "It's more fun being a dad than a billionaire!"

Every few nights the dads have to convene around a campfire, where the Motherhood Island host, Rambo de Sade, makes them repeat: "Only fathers can raise kids properly, women don't know how," "My children always come first, my children always come first," "Fathers must read their children's minds," and "I'll never be a good-enough dad." Each father must enumerate all the ways he has failed to be a truly loving, empathetic, fun-to-be-with dad. Then de Sade tells them that the guy who is really going to win the million bucks is the one who home schools the kids.

Just when the *Survivor* dads think it can't get any worse, several of them have their Motherhood Island jobs taken away and are relocated to roach-infested apartments that are also, conveniently, fifty miles away from any childcare center. These dads are all painted green because, on Motherhood Island, everyone knows that green fathers are bad fathers. These dads now have to ask for Motherhood Island welfare. But they learn that they have to work forty hours a week to get the welfare money, which is one-fifth the amount they used to earn. They know they're really going to lose now because they have to get on a bus at 6:00 A.M. to go to the workfare job and can't get home until 8:00 P.M., so they can't have any "quality time" with the kids that will get them the votes they need from viewers.

One by one, the dads quit and flee from the Island, yelling "take this show and shove it." No one wins the million. In fact, this is the fourth version of *Survivor: Motherhood Island* that has been aired. Each time, the fathers make it through the first several weeks of challenges and then start leaving en masse so that no man makes it to the end. Suspense and interest mounts as viewers wonder whether this time, some man can indeed "do it all."

Survivor: Motherhood Island has become such a hit because it makes fun of the bad old days of the late twentieth and early twenty-first centuries. But ever since the presidency of Frances Roosevelt, Eleanor and FDR's great-granddaughter, the importance and centrality of mothering is part and parcel of public policy. Roosevelt got elected after the disastrous John Ashcroft / Charlton Heston administration, in which they shut down all the day care centers, abortion clinics, and OB-GYN practices in the country, passed out handguns to every kindergartner, made Dr. Laura Secretary of Health and Human Services, and enacted a law mandating that mothers who worked outside the home would lose custody of their kids. But it was the leaked "momism papers" that really did them in. Once *The New York Times* printed a purloined copy of *How We Sold Momism and Put Women in Their Place,* coauthored primarily by Ashcroft and Dr. Laura with help from Pat Robertson, all hell broke loose. (Dr. Laura's infamous boast—"The propaganda campaign has worked! They are all cowed, they constantly obsess about whether they are decent mothers, and they'll never ask the government or business for any help again. They have bought the new momism hook, line, and sinker—the suckers!"—was seen as especially inflammatory.)

"Exorcise Momism" groups sprang up all around the country, and women brought in magazines, childcare manuals, clips from radio and TV shows and movies as well as news reports and denounced the new momism everywhere they saw it. E-mail groups and Web sites fanned the insurrection. Mothers realized they were, indeed, good-enough mothers just as they were. In response to the scandal surrounding the momism papers, the Exorcise Momism coalition mounted a huge, nationwide strike that started on Mother's Day. They refused to go to brunch, costing the restaurant industry billions. But then they issued their demands. Until the government enacted paid, three-month paternity and maternity leaves, established a national, regulated, high-quality day care system and a national preschool program for all children, universal health care including prenatal care for all, decent housing for all poor women and their kids as well as a living wage for them, a thirty-five-hour work week, and revitalized the public schools of America, they were going on strike. And they did.

Things got ugly fast. Diapers piled up everywhere, kids were stranded because there was no one to drive them to day care, school, or girl scouts, and heartburn and flatulence gripped the land since everyone was eating at McDonald's. Businesses from banking and real estate to restaurants, beauty salons, and department stores came to a halt because the mothers who worked there were on strike. Motels and hotels closed because there were too few chambermaids. Schools and government agencies shut down. The smell of rotting laundry, unbathed children, uncleaned hamster cages, and food putrefying in the refrigerators of America hung over the land like a pong.

At first President Ashcroft said this was traitorous and that all the mothers should be deported to Guantanamo. The government could not meet any of these demands, he snarled, because of the tax cut for Jack Welch and the four-hundred-trillion-dollar Buck Rogers missile shield the country had to build. But after the Million Dad March, when they came to Washington and rode Ashcroft out on a rail, and with the entire economy at a standstill and the Dow down to 1700, Congress figured they had better do something. This was an election year, after all, and Ashcroft's approval rating was 4 percent, while Frances Roosevelt's, the Democratic challenger who supported the strike, was 95 percent. The rest, as they say, is history.

The new momism quickly became an object of study in the academy, with feminist scholars tracing its rise and fall. Debates raged over what finally did in the new momism and whether it would return in some new form. But several conclusions garnered widespread agreement. Yes, the government in the early twenty-first century had gone too far in cutting funding for day care, after-school programs, housing subsidies for poor mothers and their kids, and child health services for about thirty million low-income children while proposing, at the exact same time, an average tax cut of $89,000 for each millionaire in the country.[1] Their efforts to "defund" Head Start, a program even the dopiest Golden Retriever knows works, angered mothers. After seeing *Bowling for Columbine*, many people appreciated the inhumanity of forcing welfare mothers to work even longer hours for their workfare checks. Increasing numbers of people were indeed concerned—and embarrassed—that 37 percent of American children (twenty-seven million) lived in low-income families and sixteen percent (over eleven million) lived in poverty, four million of them under the age of four.[2] Many parents were sick and tired of the huge gap between people's need and desire for decent day care and the government's refusal to provide it.

But the feminist historians agreed that what was truly necessary to the new momism's demise was a change in consciousness among women themselves. Resistance began to take many forms, from talking back to the TV to mothers joining groups and e-mailing their Congresspeople. The scales began to fall from mothers' eyes, and they began to name the new momism for what it was. They started doing this in checkout lines, on the phone, and at work. Around the country, they gathered to burn their copies of *The Baby Book* and to construct funeral pyres consisting of toy sanitizers, Barbie Talking Ovens, G.I. Joe breakfast cereal, and celebrity-mom issues of *People*. They began imagining a different future. They stopped believing that feminist struggles were a thing of the past. They became convinced that motherhood remained the unfinished business of the women's movement.

In Steven Spielberg's epic about the overthrow of the new momism, *Moms of New York,* Reese Witherspoon, Halle Berry, and Nicole Kidman play the heads of the Exorcise Momism coalition. In the final scene, John Ashcroft is climbing up the side of the Empire State Building, trying to escape the pitchforks being hurled by the furious mothers below. A small plane, piloted by Oprah, dive-bombs him, and he begins to fall. Kidman says, "The plane got him." But Berry responds, "Oh no. It was mothers killed the beast."

NOTES

INTRODUCTION: THE NEW MOMISM

1. *People*, September 21, 1998.

2. *Good Housekeeping*, January 1995.

3. *People*, July 8, 1996.

4. Kristin van Ogtrop, "Attila the Honey I'm Home," *The Bitch in the House* (New York: William Morrow, 2002), p. 169.

5. "Motherhood Today—A Tougher Job, Less Ably Done," The Pew Research Center for the People & the Press, March 1997.

6. Philip Wylie, *Generation of Vipers* (New York: Holt, Rinehart and Winston, 1942). See also Ruth Feldstein's excellent discussion of momism in *Motherhood in Black and White: Race and Sex in American Liberalism, 1930–1965* (Ithaca: Cornell University Press, 2000), especially chapter 2.

7. Hays's book is must reading for all mothers, and we are indebted to her analysis of intensive mothering, from which this discussion draws. Sharon Hays, *The Cultural Contradictions of Motherhood* (New Haven: Yale University Press, 1996), p. 4.

8. For an account of the decline in leisure time see Juliet B. Schorr, *The Overworked American* (New York: Basic Books, 1992).

9. Patricia Heaton, *Motherhood & Hollywood* (New York: Villard Books, 2002), pp. 48–49.

10. See Katha Pollitt's terrific piece "Killer Moms, Working Nannies" in *The Nation*, November 24, 1997, p. 9.

11. Hays, pp. 4–9.

12. Based on an On-line Computer Library Center, Inc., search under the word *motherhood*, from 1970–2000.

13. Susan Faludi, in her instant classic *Backlash*, made this point, too, but the book focused on the various and multiple forms of backlash, and we will be focusing only on the use of motherhood here.

14. Robert Lekachman, *Visions and Nightmares: America After Reagan* (New York: Collier Books, 1988), pp. 118–121.

15. For a superb analysis of the role of mother-blaming in American politics, see Ruth Feldstein, *Motherhood in Black and White*, especially pp. 7–9.

16. V. Spike Peterson, "Gendered Nationalism: Reproducing 'Us' versus 'Them,' " in Lois Ann Lorentzen and Jennifer Turpin, eds., *The Women and War Reader* (New York: New York University Press, 1998).

17. This contradiction is central to Hays's argument.

18. Hays, p. 9.

19. Ibid.

20. Ibid., p. 9, p. 18.

21. Most notable are Ann Crittenden, *The Price of Motherhood* (New York: Metropolitan Books, 2001); Diane Eyer, *Motherguilt* (New York: Times Books, 1996); Susan Chira, *A Mother's Place: Choosing Work and Family Without Guilt or Shame* (New York: Perennial, 1999); Susan Maushart, *The Mask of Motherhood* (New York: The New Press, 1999).

22. As reported in "Wondering If Children Are Necessary," *Time,* March 5, 1979, p. 42.

23. Ken Auletta, *Three Blind Mice: How the Networks Lost Their Way* (New York: Vintage, 1992), pp. 457–60.

24. Jonathan Alter, "Who's Taking the Kids?" *Newsweek,* July 29, 2002 on-line edition; see also in the same issue Andrew Murr, "When Kids Go Missing," p. 38.

25. Alter.

26. *Redbook,* April 1988; *Redbook,* June 1988.

27. This information based on a content analysis of the January, March, May, July, September, and November 1970 issues of *Ladies' Home Journal* and *McCall's,* and the January, March, and May issues of *Redbook.*

28. Cited in Hays, p. 58.

29. *Redbook,* September 1990.

30. Ibid.

31. Ibid.

32. Ibid.

33. We are grateful to Kris Harrison for pointing out this research. Melissa Milkie, "Social Comparisons, Reflected, Appraisals, and Mass Media: The Impact of Pervasive Beauty Images on Black and White Girls' Self Concepts," *Social Psychology Quarterly,* June 1999, pp. 190–210.

34. John Thompson, *Media and Modernity* (Stanford, CA: Stanford University Press, 1995), ch. 7.

35. Hays, p. 8.

36. Interview, Letty Cottin Pogrebin, February 2001.

37. See Susan J. Douglas, *Where the Girls Are* (New York: Times Books, 1994), ch. 1.

38. For an excellent discussion of postfeminism and the media see Andrea Press, *Women Watching Television: Gender, Class and Generation in the American Television Experience* (Philadelphia: University of Pennsylvania Press, 1991), pp. 38–49.

39. Peggy Orenstein, *Flux: Women on Sex, Work, Love, Kids and Life in a Half-Changed World* (New York: Doubleday, 2000), pp. 105–6.

CHAPTER 1: REVOLT AGAINST THE MRS

1. Lauri Umansky, *Motherhood Reconceived: Feminism and the Legacies of the Sixties* (New York: New York University Press, 1996), p. 38.

2. "Wages for Housework," Rosalyn Baxandall and Linda Gordon, *Dear Sisters: Dispatches from the Women's Liberation Movement* (New York: Basic Books, 2001), p. 258.

3. "Women's Lives Will Change in Every Way," in "What Kind of Future for America," *U.S. News and World Report,* July 7, 1975, p. 47.

4. Danielle Crittenden, *What Our Mothers Didn't Tell Us: Why Happiness Eludes the Modern Woman* (New York: Touchstone, 2000), p. 15.

5. Crittenden, p. 20.

5. Crittenden, p. 13; p. 16.

6. Cited in Robin Morgan, ed., *Sisterhood is Powerful* (New York: Vintage, 1970), p. 536.

7. Susan J. Douglas, *Where the Girls Are* (New York: Times Books, 1994), p. 55.

8. Arlene Skolnick, *Embattled Paradise: The American Family in the Age of Uncertainty* (New York: Basic Books, 1991), pp. 108–9.

9. On this final question see Alix Kates Shulman, "A Marriage Agreement," in Baxandall and Gordon, p. 219.

10. Susan J. Douglas, *Where the Girls Are,* Ch. 8.

11. ABC News, August 25, 1970.

12. Marcia Cohen, *The Sisterhood: The Inside Story of the Women's Movement and the Leaders Who Made It Happen* (New York: Fawcett Columbine, 1988), p. 351.

13. Reprinted in Morgan, p. 550.

14. Carol Hanish and Elizabeth Sutherland, "Notes from the First Year," http://scriptorium.lib.duke.edu/wlm/notes.

15. See the insert "The New Feminism," *Ladies' Home Journal,* August 1970, pp. 63–71.

16. Jane O'Reilly coined the term "*click!* experience" in her article "The Housewife's Moment of Truth," *Ms.,* May 1972, 54–55, 57–59.

17. *Ms.* letters collection, Kathleen Phillips Satz, El Cerrito. CA, November 1982 issue. Quoted in Ruth Rosen, *The World Split Open* (New York: Viking, 2000), p. 212.

18. Letty Cottin Pogrebin, "Motherhood!", *Ms.,* May 1973, pp. 47–51, 96–97.

19. Alix Kates Shulman, "A Marriage Agreement," in Baxandall and Gordon, pp. 218–20.

20. Alix Kates Shulman, "A Marriage Disagreement, or Marriage by Other Means," in Rachel Blau Du Plessis and Ann Snitow, eds., *The Feminist Memoir Project* (New York: Three Rivers Press, 1998), pp. 294–95.

21. "Is the American Family in Danger?" *U.S. News & World Report,* April 16, 1973, p. 74.

22. "Ties That Bind," *Time,* September 1, 1975, p. 62.

23. "New Marriage Styles," *Time,* March 20, 1972, p. 56.

24. John P. Hayes, "Marriage Contracts: Why Couples Want Them and How to Write Your Own," *Glamour,* January 1978, pp. 20–22.

25. Pam Moore, "Marriage Contracts—New Twists on an Old Idea," *Psychology Today,* August 1975, p. 29.

26. "Men of the House," *Time,* February 18, 1974, p. 76.

27. Eric Larsen, "When Dad Becomes a 'House-Husband,'" *Parents,* July 1978, pp. 48 ff.

28. Letty Cottin Pogrebin, "Househusbands," *Ladies' Home Journal,* November 1977, pp. 30ff.

29. Jo Ann Hoit, "Speaking of Spock," Baxandall and Gordon, pp. 226–27.

30. ABC News, January 25, 1972.

31. Marylin Bender, "How Much Is a Housewife Worth?" *McCall's,* May 1974.

32. Clare Booth Luce, "Equality Begins at Home," *The Saturday Evening Post,* October 1977, pp. 16–17.

33. Maureen Orth, "The American Child-Care Disgrace," *Ms.,* May 1973, p. 88.

34. Ibid., p. 90.

35. Louise Gross and Phyllis Taube Greenleaf, "Why Day Care?" in Baxandall and Gordon, pp. 234–36.

36. Ti-Grace Atkinson, "The Institution of Sexual Intercourse," in Firestone and Koedt, eds., *Notes from the Second Year* (New York: New York Radical Women, 1969), p. 43.

37. Shulamith Firestone interviewed by Conchita Pierce for a CBS News special report on the feminist movement, March 1970.

38. Shulamith Firestone, *The Dialectic of Sex: The Case for Feminist Revolution* (New York: Bantam, 1971), p. 206.

39. Ellen Willis, "To Be or Not To Be a Mother," *Ms.*, October 1974, p. 34.

40. Jeffner Allen, "Motherhood: the Annihilation of Women," in Joyce Trebilcot, ed., *Mothering: Essays in Feminist Theory* (Totowa, N.J.: Rowman and Allanheld, 1983).

41. All letters from "Dear Jane Alpert," *Ms.*, February 1974, pp. 58–60 and 100–106. One woman warned, "Motherhood is the biological capacity to bear children; no more, no less. To believe it is our identity, our strength, our political tool to free us from male oppression is to believe that we must once again obscure ourselves in the guise of a time-honored, pro-patriarchal role." Another put her objections more succinctly: "Women will not be free until the family is completely eradicated." Another added that because women are responsible for raising children they are unable to participate in society more broadly. Thus, "children are used as political weapons to oppress women." But another argued, "Really, it is as Mother (Woman) that we must speak at this time and with all the firmness and assurance of the mother; for today's world 'order' is the product of the immature male child." She continued, "I don't know, at this time, of one male-female relationship in which the woman is not emotionally and spiritually more mature than the man. . . . It really is time for women to take the lead in establishing a world order based on love instead of oppression." Alpert surrendered to authorities in 1974.

42. Jane Alpert, "Mother Right: A New Feminist Theory," *Ms.*, August 1973, pp 92–93.

43. Adrienne Rich, *Of Woman Born* (New York: Bantam Books, 1977), pp. 280–81, p. xv.

44. Ibid., p. 1.

45. Ibid., p. 292.

46. "Free to Be You and Me," music by Stephen Lawrence, lyrics by Bruce Hart, in *Free to Be You and Me*, Marlo Thomas and Friends (Philadelphia: Running Press, 1997).

CHAPTER 2: MOUTHING OFF TO DR. SPOCK

1. Stephan Segal, "The Working Parent Dilemma," *Personnel Journal*, March 1984, p. 50.

2. Howard Hayghe, "Working Mothers Reach Record Number in 1984," *Monthly Labor Review*, December 1984, p. 31.

3. *Monthly Labor Review*, December 1984, p. 33.

4. Marianne Walters and Nonny Majchrzyk, "When Women Raise Families Alone," *Good Housekeeping*, March 1982, p. 92.

5. Howard Hayge, "Rise in Mothers' Labor Force Activity Includes Those with Infants," *Monthly Labor Review*, February 1986, p. 43.

6. Carol Tavris and Toby Jayaratne, "What 120,000 Young Women Can Tell You About Sex, Motherhood, Menstruation, Housework—and Men," *Redbook*, January 1973, pp. 68–69; "American Women Today," *Ladies' Home Journal*, February 1984.

7. Helen A. De Rosis, "Guilt-Free Motherhood: A Psychiatrist's Guide," *Ladies' Home Journal*, May 1974, p. 64.

8. Diane Eyer, *Motherguilt: How Our Culture Blames Mothers for What's Wrong with Society* (New York: Times Books, 1996), p. 59.

9. Benjamin Spock, "What Mothers Should Know About Breast Feeding and Weaning," *Redbook,* September 1977, p. 28.

10. Benjamin Spock, "Working Mothers: Some Possible Solutions for Child Care," *Redbook,* September 1970, p. 34–43.

11. Diane Eyer, in particular, has debunked bonding/attachment theory. See *Motherguilt,* pp. 100–104, and Eyer, *Mother-Infant Bonding: A Scientific Fiction* (New Haven: Yale University Press, 1992), passim.

12. Benjamin Spock, "How Mothers Learn to Love Their Newborn Babies," *Redbook,* May 1976, p. 22–29.

13. Benjamin Spock, "What Mothers Should Know About Breast Feeding and Weaning," *Redbook,* September 1977, p. 24.

14. Benjamin Spock, "How Does a Mother Know When to Let Go?" *Redbook,* May 1978, p. 106.

15. Diane Eyer, *Motherguilt,* p. 220.

16. Bruno Bettelheim, "Dialogue with Mothers," *Ladies' Home Journal,* March 1972, p. 30; April 1972, p. 32.

17. Bruno Bettelheim, "Dialogue with Mothers," *Ladies' Home Journal,* April 1972, p. 33.

18. Ibid., p. 32.

19. Lee Salk, "You and Your Family," *McCall's,* June 1978, p. 109.

20. Lee Salk, "You and Your Family," *McCall's,* October 1978, p. 107.

21. Lee Salk, "You and Your Family," *McCall's,* April 1978, p. 51.

22. Lee Salk, "You and Your Family," *McCall's,* December 1978, p. 70.

23. Lee Salk, "You and Your Family," *McCall's,* August 1972, p. 52.

24. Lee Salk, "You and Your Family," *McCall's,* February 1974, p. 19.

25. Lee Salk, "You and Your Family," *McCall's,* March 1974, p. 34.

26. Lee Salk, "You and Your Family," *McCall's,* March 1976, p. 52.

27. Lee Salk, "You and Your Family," *McCall's,* May 1974, p. 62.

28. Lee Salk, "You and Your Family," *McCall's,* August 1974, p. 36.

29. Lee Salk, "You and Your Family," *McCall's,* February 1978, p. 72.

30. Roberta Brandes Gratz and Lindsy Van Gelder, "Double Jeopardy: The Working Motherhood Trap," *Redbook,* July 1974, p. 38.

31. Geraldine Carro, "Mothering," *Ladies' Home Journal,* February 1975, p. 40.

32. Nancy Dailey, "Going Back to Work Made Me a Better Mother," *McCall's,* March 1979, p. 80.

33. Felice N. Schwartz et al., "How to Go to Work When Your Husband Is Against It, Your Children Aren't Old Enough, and There's Nothing You Can Do Anyhow," *McCall's,* March 1972, p. 27.

34. Letty Cottin Pogrebin, "The Working Woman," *Ladies' Home Journal,* June 1971, pp. 46, 108ff.

35. Letty Cottin Pogrebin, "The Working Mother," *Ladies' Home Journal,* August 1974.

36. Letty Cottin Pogrebin, "How Do Children Really Feel When Their Mothers Work?" *Ladies' Home Journal,* June 1979, p. 31.

37. Kathryn Keller, *Mothers and Work in Popular American Magazines* (Westport, CT: Greenwood Press, 1994), pp. 61–62.

38. Mary Ann O'Roark, "How Children Feel About Their Working Mothers," *McCall's,* September 1978, p. 91.

39. Ibid.

40. Interview, Letty Cottin Pogrebin, February 2001.

41. Gratz and Van Gelder, pp. 40–42.

342 NOTES

42. Bess Myerson, " 'Someday I'd Like to Walk Slowly': A Conversation: Bess Myerson Talks to Working Mothers," *Redbook,* September 1975, pp. 72–80.

43. Dailey, "Going Back to Work Made Me a Better Mother," *McCall's,* March 1979, p. 80.

44. Keller, p. 60.

45. Jane Adams, "New Ways of Taking Turns," *McCall's,* September 1978, p. 92.

46. Laura Engel, "Four Single Mothers: Together on Our Own," *McCall's,* December 1978, p. 26, p. 174.

47. Keller, pp. 60–61.

48. Virginia Barber and Merrill Maguire Skaggs, "A Bill of Rights for the Mother Person," *Redbook,* August 1976, pp. 91, 194.

49. Lynn Caine, "Single Mothers," *Ladies' Home Journal,* October 1977, pp. 104, 106.

50. Georgia Lee Cox, "Confession of a Wicked Stepmother," *Ladies' Home Journal,* March 1971, pp. 104, 198.

51. Judith Viorst, "How to Behave When Your Kids Don't: The Confessions of a Mean Mommy," *Redbook,* September 1977, p. 48.

52. Andrea Press, *Women Watching Television: Gender, Class and Generation in the American Television Experience* (Philadelphia: University of Pennsylvania Press, 1991), p. 37.

53. See Susan J. Douglas, *Where the Girls Are* (New York: Times Books, 1994), pp. 202–4.

54. For more detailed discussion of *One Day at a Time* see Bonnie Dow, *Prime-Time Feminism* (Philadelphia: University of Pennsylvania Press, 1996), chapter 2; for ratings, see Tim Brooks and Earle Marsh, *The Complete Directory to Prime-Time Network and Cable TV Shows* (New York: Ballantine Books, 1999), pp. 1251–54.

55. Dow, p. 70.

56. *Redbook,* February 1974, p. 30.

57. *Ladies' Home Journal,* October 1977, p. 107.

58. See, for example, Judith Mayne's analysis in "The Woman at the Keyhole: Women's Cinema and Feminist Film Criticism," in Mary Ann Doane et al., eds., *Re-Vision: Essays in Feminist Film Criticism* (Frederick, MD: University Publications of America, 1984), pp. 61–62.

59. Linda Williams makes this point most powerfully in "Something Else Besides a Mother: Stella Dallas and the Maternal Melodrama," in Christine Gledhill, ed., *Home Is Where the Heart Is* (London: British Film Institute, 1987).

CHAPTER 3: THREATS FROM WITHOUT: SATANISM, ABDUCTION, AND OTHER MEDIA PANICS

1. The finest study of this as a cultural and historical phenomenon is Paula Fass, *Kidnapped: Child Abduction in America* (Cambridge: Harvard University Press, 1997).

2. Howard Hayghe, "Working Mothers Reach Record Number in 1984," *Monthly Labor Review,* December 1984, p. 31.

3. *Employment Benefit Plan Review,* October 1988, p. 58.

4. Howard Hayge, "Rise in Mothers' Labor Force Activity Includes Those with Infants," *Monthly Labor Review,* February 1986, p. 43.

5. Joe Schwartz, "Back to Work," *American Demographics,* November 1986, p. 56.

6. Sondra Forsyth Enos, "Work + baby = the new reality," *Ladies' Home Journal,* March 1984, p. 90.

7. Teri Schultz-Brooks, "Single Mothers: The Strongest Women in America," *Redbook,* November 1983, p. 89.

8. Karen Nussbaum, "Issues for Working Families," *Labor Law Journal*, August 1984, p. 466.

9. Hayghe, "Working Mothers Reach Record Number in 1984," p. 31.

10. Nussbaum, "Issues for Working Families," p. 466.

11. Our definition of media panics draws heavily from Stanley Cohen's definition of moral panics. See Cohen, as cited in Simon Watney, *Policing Desire: Pornography, AIDS and The Media* (Minneapolis: University of Minnesota Press, 1996), p. 39.

12. See also Jeffrey Weeks, discussion of moral panics in Watney, p. 40.

13. Ann Mari May and Kurt Stephenson, "Women and the Great Retrenchment: The Political Economy of Gender in the 1980s," *Journal of Economic Issues*, June 1994, p. 535.

14. For a fuller discussion see Tanya Melich, *The Republican War Against Women: An Insider's Report from Behind the Lines* (New York: Bantam Books, 1996).

15. NBC News, September 5, 1984.

16. Robert Lekachman, *Visions and Nightmares: America After Reagan* (New York: Collier, 1988), pp. 60–61.

17. Kathryn Keller, *Mothers and Work in Popular American Magazines* (Westport, CT: Greenwood Press, 1994), p. 131.

18. James Comer, "Kids and Two-Career Parents," *Parents*, January 1987, p. 125.

19. Geraldine Carro, "Mothering," *Ladies' Home Journal*, February 1975, p. 40.

20. Ibid.

21. Geraldine Carro, "Mothering," *Ladies' Home Journal*, March 1975, p. 50.

22. Geraldine Carro, "Mothering," *Ladies' Home Journal*, April 1975, p. 62.

23. Ibid.

24. Geraldine Carro, "Mothering," *Ladies' Home Journal*, May 1975, p. 56.

25. Geraldine Carro, "Mothering," *Ladies' Home Journal*, August 1975, p. 30.

26. Geraldine Carro, "Mothering," *Ladies' Home Journal*, December 1976, p. 30.

27. Geraldine Carro, "Mothering," *Ladies' Home Journal*, October 1975, p. 24.

28. Geraldine Carro, "Mothering," *Ladies' Home Journal*, January 1977, p. 50.

29. Geraldine Carro, "Mothering," *Ladies' Home Journal*, June 1977, p. 54.

30. See the thoughtful, sensitive account in Paula Fass's first-rate *Kidnapped*, pp. 213–21.

31. Cited in Fass, pp. 232–33.

32. Fass, p. 243; NBC News, December 6, 1985.

33. NBC News, March 28, 1984.

34. NBC News, March 23, 1984.

35. Susan Chimonas, "Moral Panics: Towards a New Model" (Ph.D. Dissertation, University of Michigan, 2000), p. 45.

36. Steven Strasser and Elizabeth Bailey, "A Sordid Preschool 'Game,'" *Newsweek*, April 9, 1984, p. 38.

37. ABC News, April 6, 1984.

38. Ibid.

39. Chimonas, p. 130.

40. Hiroshi Fukari, Edgar W. Butler, and Richard Krooth, "Sociologists in Action: The McMartin Sexual Abuse Case, Litigation, Justice, and Mass Hysteria," *The American Sociologist*, Winter 1994, pp. 47–48.

41. Chimonas, p. 89.

42. Paul and Shirley Eberle, *The Abuse of Innocence* (Buffalo, NY: Prometheus Books, 1993), p. 212.

43. Chimonas, p. ix.

44. Eberle, p. 407.

45. Michael J. Weiss, "Child Molesting: What Must be Done to Protect our Children," *Ladies' Home Journal*, November 1984.

46. CBS News, April 6, 1984.

47. NBC News, April 19, 1984.

48. ABC News, May 2, 1995.

49. ABC News, April 21, 1984.

50. CBS News, May 30, 1984; ABC News, May 31, 1984.

51. CBS News and ABC News, June 22, 1984.

52. CBS, ABC, and NBC News, August 8, 1984.

53. ABC News, August 8, 1984.

54. ABC News, August 10, 1984.

55. NBC News, September 5, 1984.

56. CBS News, April 1, 1985.

57. "Disturbing End of a Nightmare," *Time,* February 25, 1985, p. 22.

58. Ibid.

59. ABC News, August 22, 1984.

60. ABC News, November 12, 1984.

61. Ron Givens and Janet Huck, "California: Devilish Deeds?" *Newsweek,* September 16, 1985, p. 43.

62. Eberle, p. 206.

63. CBS News, October 14, 1985.

64. CBS and NBC News, August 24, 1985.

65. See, for example, Melinda Beck and Tessa Namuth, "An Epidemic of Child Abuse," *Newsweek,* August 20, 1984, p. 44; and Aric Press, "The Youngest Witnesses," *Newsweek,* February 18, 1985, p. 72.

66. For a book-length account of the case and the trial, see Eberle, *The Abuse of Innocence.*

67. Chimonas, citing Fukari et. al., p. 49 and pp. 46–47.

68. See Diane Eyer's summary in *Motherguilt* (New York: Times Books, 1996), pp. 10, 251–52.

69. Eberle, pp. 187–202.

70. Ibid., pp. 191, 22.

71. Ibid., p. 353.

72. Michelle Green, "The McMartins: The 'Model Family' Down the Block That Ran California's Nightmare Nursery," *People,* May 21, 1984, pp. 112, 115.

73. Eberle, p. 360.

74. "Peggy McMartin Buckey Dies: Cleared of School Molestations," *The Washington Post,* December 18, 2000, p. B6.

75. NBC News, October 16, 1984.

76. "Disturbing End of a Nightmare," p. 22.

77. ABC News, November 12, 1984.

78. Michael J. Weiss, "Child Molesting: What Must Be Done to Protect Our Children," *Ladies' Home Journal,* November 1984, pp. 114ff.

79. Cited in Keller, p. 130.

80. Cited in Keller, p. 133.

81. Susan Faludi, *Backlash: The Undeclared War Against Women* (New York: Crown, 1991), pp. 42–43.

82. Keller, p. 131.

83. Ibid., p. 135.

84. Janet Staiger, *Blockbuster TV: Must-See Sitcoms in the Network Era* (New York: New York University Press, 2000), pp. 142–44.

85. Cited in Starger, p. 149.

86. Erma Bombeck, *Motherhood, The Second Oldest Profession* (New York: Dell, 1983), p. 2.

87. Ibid., pp. 43, 3.

88. See Andrea Press's discussion of *The Cosby Show* and its relationship to post-feminism in *Women Watching Television: Gender, Class and Generation in the American Television Experience* (Philadelphia: University of Pennsylvania Press, 1991), pp. 44–45.

89. Phyllis K. Bonfield, "Working Solutions for Working Parents," *Ms.*, February, 1986, pp. 9–10.

90. James A. Levine, "The New Fatherhood," *McCall's*, June 1987, p. 122.

91. Keller, p. 128.

92. Rather than jump on the kid about what he or she had done wrong, the Huxtables showed how through mock quiz shows, question-and-answer sessions, and long conversations you could get your kids to admit to the error of their ways. Some interview subjects told Andrea Press that they especially valued this aspect of the show. See Press, p. 106.

93. Keller, p. 129.

94. See Susan J. Douglas, *Where the Girls Are: Growing Up Female with the Mass Media* (New York: Times Books, 1994).

95. Keller, p. 92.

96. Nancy Rubin, "Women vs. Women: The New Cold War Between Housewives and Working Mothers," *Ladies' Home Journal*, April 1982.

97. Keller, p. 97.

98. Prudence Mackintosh, "The Myth of Quality Time," *Ladies' Home Journal*, May 1984, p. 44.

99. Keller, p. 111.

100. Ibid., p. 112–13.

101. Ibid., p. 113.

102. Jean Marzollo, "Don't Call Me Supermom." *Parents*, April 1984, p. 62.

103. Keller, p. 139.

CHAPTER 4: ATTACK OF THE CELEBRITY MOMS

1. Nancy Anderson, "Debby Boone: Now Baby Makes Three," *Good Housekeeping*, January 1981, pp. 78–82.

2. *Good Housekeeping*, February 1995; *Redbook*, February 1995; *People*, September 21, 1998; *People*, May 26, 1997.

3. Richard Dyer, "Entertainment and Utopia," in Simon During, ed., *The Cultural Studies Reader* (New York: Routledge, 1993), pp. 271–83.

4. The notion of advertising making hierarchies seem thrilling comes from John Berger, *Ways of Seeing* (London: Penguin, 1985).

5. Neal Gabler, *Life the Movie* (New York: Alfred Knopf, 1998), passim.

6. Patricia Miller, "Cheryl Ladd: Juggling Sanity and Success," *Ladies' Home Journal*, March 1979, pp. 78–96.

7. Gwen Davis, "Why Goldie Hawn Is Smiling Again," *McCall's*, June 1978, pp. 28, 235.

8. *McCall's*, May 1985; *Good Housekeeping*, November 1984; *McCall's*, October 1986.

9. *Ebony*, May 1995.

10. *People*, September 21, 1998.

11. *Good Housekeeping*, January 1995.

12. Covers of *McCall's*, February 1997, and *Redbook*, April 1997.

13. *People,* July 8, 1996, p. 82.

14. *Ladies' Home Journal,* October 1998.

15. *McCall's,* May 1999.

16. *People,* July 8, 1996, p. 82.

17. Ibid.

18. Delia Ephron, "Hanging Out (and Hanging Up) with Meg," *Redbook,* January 2000, p. 75.

19. Ibid.

20. See Elihu Katz's discussion of Wilbur Schramm's pioneering schema of media texts in "Viewers Work," James Hay et al., *The Audience and Its Landscape* (Boulder, CO: Westview Press, 1996), p. 15.

21. Joshua Gamson, *Claims to Fame: Celebrity in Contemporary America* (Berkeley: University of California Press, 1994), p. 172.

22. Ibid., pp. 29, 38.

23. We draw here, of course, from Stuart Hall's famous "Encoding/Decoding," Simon During, ed., *The Cultural Studies Reader* (New York: Routledge, 1993), pp. 90–103.

24. Zondra Hughes, "The Joys of Being a Stay-at-Home Mom," *Ebony,* May 2001, p. 136.

25. Joy Bennett Kinnon, "The New Motherhood," *Ebony,* May 2001.

26. Diane De Dubovay, "A Royal Welcome for Charles and Diana's Baby," *McCall's,* June 1982, p. 70.

27. And of the President, for that matter. See Mark Herstgaard, *On Bended Knee: The Press and the Reagan Presidency* (New York: Farrar, Straus and Giroux, 1988).

28. James Whitaker, "How Diana Did It," *McCall's,* June 1986, p. 25–26.

29. Dubovay, p. 119.

30. Ibid., p. 121.

31. Beth Weinhouse and Gwen Robyns, "The Princess Who Loves Children," *Ladies' Home Journal,* July 1984, pp. 96–97.

32. Ibid.

33. Susie Pearson, "Diana's Darlings," *Ladies' Home Journal,* February 1990.

34. "Ping-Pong Princes," *People,* September 6, 1993, pp. 60, 64.

35. "The Little Princes," *People,* June 22, 1992, p. 101.

36. Weinhouse and Robyns, p. 96.

37. "Princess Diana's Delighted: Come September Another Babe Will Be Playing at the Palace," *People,* February 27, 1984, p. 64.

38. Douglas Keay, "*GH* Spends the Day with Prince Charles and Diana," *Good Housekeeping,* September 1984, p. 151.

39. Weinhouse and Robyns, pp. 96–97.

40. Ibid., p. 96.

41. Jeffrey Robinson, "Raising the Royal Rascals," *McCall's,* April 1988, p. 13.

42. "Growing Up Royal," *People,* April 25, 1988, pp. 112–14.

43. Penny Junor, "Back to School with William and Harry," *McCall's,* October, 1990, pp. 90–92.

44. Whitaker, p. 26.

45. Ingrid Seward, "Diana's Sons: How They're Coping in a Broken Home," *McCall's,* July 1993, pp. 90–94.

46. Robinson, p. 16.

47. "Growing Up Royal," p. 114.

48. "Di and Her Prince: Everything But Love," *People,* February 11, 1991, p. 77.

49. Susie Pearson, "Diana's Darlings," p. 110.

50. "Once Upon a Time," *People,* July 22, 1991, p. 29.

51. "Love on the Rocks," *People,* June 29, 1992, p. 80.

52. Pearson, pp. 108–109.

53. Ingrid Seward, "Diana and Charles: A Weekend at Home," *McCall's,* September 1988, p. 119.

54. "Bringing Up Baby," *InStyle,* July 2000, pp. 190–97.

55. Glynis Costin, "8 1/2 Months & Counting . . . ," *InStyle,* July 2000, pp. 199–203.

56. "Late Arrivals," *People,* April 29, 2002, pp. 89–90.

57. "Lights, Camera, Cut!" *People,* April 1, 2002, p. 78.

58. Ibid., p. 79.

59. "Teaming With Love," *People,* March 10, 2003, pp. 88–92.

CHAPTER 5: THREATS FROM WITHIN: MATERNAL DELINQUENTS

1. We are indebted to Kris Harrison for reminding us of this framework as laid out in Dolf Zillman and Jennings Bryant, *Selective Exposure to Communication* (Mahwah, N.J.: Lawrence Erlbaum Associates, 1985), p. 449.

2. See Herbert Gans, *Deciding What's News: A Study of CBS Evening News, NBC Nightly News, Newsweek, and Time* (New York: Vintage Books, 1980).

3. The term "mercenary intellectuals" from Jimmie L. Reeves, "Re-Covering Racism: Crack Mothers, Reaganism, and the Network News," in Sasha Torres, ed., *Living Color: Race and Television in the United States* (Durham: Duke University Press, 1998), p. 103.

4. Judge J. S. C. Sorkow, Opinion In the Matter of Baby M, Superior Court of New Jersey, Chancer. Division/Family Part Bergen County Docket No. FM-25314-86E, p. 41, March 31, 1987.

5. S. Moore Hall, *People,* December 8, 1980, pp. 52–54.

6. M. J. Beck, "To My Sister With Love," *McCall's,* September 1981, p. 83; S. King, "I Gave Birth to My Sister's Baby," *Redbook,* April, 1986, p. 34; K. Mills, "I Had My Sister's Baby," *Ladies' Home Journal,* October 1985, p. 20.

7. *Good Housekeeping,* April, 1986, p. 32.

8. "Baby M's Future," *The New York Times,* The Week in Review, April 5, 1987, p. 1.

9. CBS News, January 5, 1987.

10. Robert Hanley, "Baby M's Parents in Emotional Recorded Phone Call," *The New York Times,* February 5, 1987, pp. B1 and B4.

11. Aired on CBS, NBC, and ABC, February 4, 1987; transcript of conversation reprinted in *The New York Times,* February, 5, pp. B1 and B4.

12. Transcript of conversation reprinted in *The New York Times,* February, 5, pp. B1 and B4.

13. NBC News, March 12, 1987.

14. ABC News, February 9, 1987; Robert Hanley, "Whitehead Outlines Her Life Before Baby M," *The New York Times,* February 10, 1987.

15. Iver Peterson, "Feminists See Unfair Maternal Norm in Baby M Case," *The New York Times,* March 20, 1987, p. B1.

16. Robert Hanley, "Dr. Stern Says She Feels She Is Baby M's Mother," *The New York Times,* February 4, 1987.

17. Ibid.

18. CBS News, March 12, 1987.

19. NBC News, April 4, 1987.

20. ABC News, November 1, 1987.

21. This point was made forcefully by the writer Joice Booth, "In Defense of Mary Beth (Kappeler) Whitehead," *The New York Times,* March 17, 1987.

22. G. W. Potter and V. E. Kappeler, *Constructing Crime: Perspectives on Making News and Social Problems* (Waveland Press: 1998), pp. 9–10.

23. "His Research Was Preliminary, But Then the Media Ran with It and Created the Crack Baby Myth: An Interview with Dr. Ira J. Chasnoff," *Reconsider*, www.reconsider.oro/quarterly/2000 Spring/dr_ira_chasnoff.html.

24. Cited in Janine Jackson, "The Myth of the 'Crack Baby,'" *Extra!*, September/October 1998, www.fair.org.

25. Ibid.

26. Reeves, pp. 99, 109.

27. Susan Faludi, *Backlash: The Undeclared War Against Women* (New York: Crown, 1991), p. 428.

28. CBS News, November 12, 1986.

29. In addition to our own viewing of network news coverage of crack babies, and analysis of other media coverage, we are indebted to Jimmie L. Reeves and Richard Campbell, *Cracked Coverage: Television News, The Anti-Cocaine Crusade and the Reagan Legacy* (Durham, NC: Duke University Press, 1994). Their discussion of the crack mother as "she-devil" begins on p. 207. See also Drew Humphries, *Crack Mothers: Pregnancy, Drugs and the Media* (Columbus, Ohio: Ohio State University Press, 1999).

30. Reeves and Campbell, p. 20 and chapter 6.

31. For an excellent discussion of this agenda setting, see Reeves and Campbell, pp. 162–164.

32. ABC News, April 2, 1984.

33. "An Interview with Dr. Ira J. Chasnoff," *Reconsider*.

34. Reeves and Campbell, pp. 208–9.

35. NBC News, February 18, 1986.

36. CBS News, November 12, 1986.

37. CBS News, January 9, 1989.

38. NBC News, October 29, 1988.

39. CBS News, December 13, 1989.

40. ABC News, March 7, 1990.

41. Cited in Jackson.

42. CBS News, January 9, 1989.

43. ABC News, March 7, 1990.

44. ABC News, March 13, 1990.

45. NBC News, October 29, 1988. Reeves and Campell also cite and analyze this story as an exemplar of the crack baby / crack mother genre.

46. Jackson.

47. CBS News, November 12, 1986.

48. Jackson.

49. Cited in Faludi, p. 427.

50. See Reeves and Campbell on the importance of reportorial "disgust" to drug stories, pp. 175–78.

51. NBC News, October 29, 1988.

52. CBS News, March 25, 1989.

53. Cited in Jackson.

54. Marsha Rosenbaum, "Women and Drugs: Twenty-five Years of Research and Policy," The Lindesmith Center, 1996, http://gos.sbc.edu/r/rosenbaum.html.

55. ABC News, July 12, 1989.

56. CBS News, January 9, 1989.

57. ABC News, July 12, 1989; Dan Baum, "Crack Babies," excerpt from "Smoke and Mirrors," http://leda.lycaeum.org/?ID-12943.

58. ABC News, September 17, 1991.

59. David Bailey, " 'Crack babies' may be false image, US report says," March 27, 2001, Reuters, citing study by Deborah A. Frank, MD; Marilyn Augustyn, MD; Wanda Grant Knight, PhD; Tripler Pell, MSc; Barry Zuckerman, MD, "Growth, Development, and Behavior in Early Childhood Following Prenatal Cocaine Exposure, A Systematic Review," *JAMA*, vol. 285, no. 12, March 28, 2001.

60. Philip Coffin, "Research Brief: Cocaine and Pregnancy," The Lindesmith Center/ Drug Policy Foundation, www.geocities.com/Ratspaw_Unlimited/cocaine and babies. html.

61. Jackson.

62. NBC News, July 7, 1989; ABC News, July 12, 1989.

63. Claire E. Sterk, *Fast Lives: Women Who Use Crack Cocaine* (Philadelphia: Temple University Press, 1999); see also Marian Meyers, "Crack Mothers in the News," unpublished manuscript, presented at National Communication Association, 2001.

64. John P. Morgan and Lynn Zimmer, "The Social Pharmacology of Smokeable Cocaine: Not All It's Cracked Up to Be," in Craig Reinarman and Harry G. Levine, eds., *Crack in America: Demon Drugs and Social Justice* (University of California Press, 1997), chapter 7, at www.druglibrary.org/schaffer/cocaine/crack.htm.

65. Coffin.

66. Morgan and Zimmer.

67. Ibid.

68. Coffin.

69. NBC News, September 5, 1992.

70. ABC, July 14, 1988.

71. NBC News, October 24, 1994.

72. CBS News, October 27, 1994.

73. ABC News, October 27, 1994.

74. CBS News, November 2, 1994

75. NBC News, November 3, 1994

76. ABC News, November 3, 1994.

77. CBS News, November 4, 1994.

78. Ibid.

79. NBC News, November 4, 1994.

80. Ibid.

81. "Innocents Lost," *Newsweek*, November 14, 1994, p. 27; NBC News, November 7, 1994.

82. ABC News, November 22, 1994.

83. CBS News, November 9, 1994.

84. NBC News, July 27, 1995.

85. NBC News, July 31, 1995.

86. NBC News, July 25, 1995.

87. ABC News, July 29, 1995.

88. NBC News, July 29, 1995.

89. NBC News, July 31, 1995.

90. Eve Zibart, "The Medea Syndrome: Women Who Murder Their Young," *Cosmopolitan*, August 1996, p. 176.

91. *San Francisco Chronicle*, April 11, 1996, "7-Year-Old Pilot Hopes for Record."

92. *San Francisco Chronicle* April 12, 1996, "Parent Has Total Faith in Children."

93. Knight-Ridder/Tribune News Service, April 11, 1996, "Parents Questioning Judgment in Young Pilot's Crash."

94. NBC News, April 12, 1996.

95. For commentary on the media condemnation of Hathaway, see Katherine Corcoran, Alan Gathright, and S. L. Wykes, *The Bergen Record,* May 26, 1996; David Hinckly, *Daily News,* April 16, 1996, p. 41.

96. Thom Geier, "An American Tragedy," U.S. *News and World Report,* December 2, 1996.

97. CBS News, November 19, 1996.

98. Newsweek, July 7, 1997.

CHAPTER 6: THE WAR AGAINST WELFARE MOTHERS

1. Susan Sheehan, "A Welfare Mother," *The New Yorker,* September 29, 1975, pp. 42–43.

2. Sheehan, p. 44.

3. Quoted in Teresa L. Amott, "Black Women and AFDC," in Linda Gordon, ed. *Women, the State and Welfare* (Madison, WI: The University of Wisconsin Press, 1990), p. 289.

4. This is what academics call "priming."

5. See the work of Patricia DeVine, "Stereotypes and prejudice: Their automatic and controlled components," *Journal of Personal and Social Psychology,* 1989, pp. 5–18.

6. For a powerful critique of how racism has informed welfare policy since its origins, see Kenneth J. Neubeck and Noel A. Cazenave, *Welfare Racism: Playing the Race Card Against America's Poor* (New York: Routledge, 2001).

7. William M. Epstein, *Welfare in America: How Social Science Fails the Poor* (Madison, WI: University of Wisconsin Press, 1997), p. 169.

8. "War on Welfare Dependency," *U.S. News and World Report,* April 20, 1992; "The War on Welfare Mothers," *Time,* cover, June 20, 1994.

9. Laura Flanders and Janine Jackson, "Public Enemy No. 1?" *Extra!,* May/June 1995, p. 14; Muriel L. Whetstone, "The Untold Story: White and Welfare," *Ebony,* August 1995, p. 124.

10. Barbara Ehrenreich, "Welfare: A White Secret," *Time,* December 16, 1991, p. 84.

11. Marieka Klawitter, Robert D. Plotnik, and Mark Evan Edwards, "Determinants of Initial Entry onto Welfare by Young Women," *Journal of Policy Analysis and Management,* 2000, pp. 527–46.

12. Kathleen Mullan Harris, "Work and Welfare Among Single Mothers in Poverty," *American Journal of Sociology,* September 1993, p. 344.

13. Katrina Bell McDonald and Elizabeth M. Armstrong, "De-Romanticizing Black Intergenerational Support: The Questionable Expectations of Welfare Reform," *Journal of Marriage and the Family,* February 2001, p. 214; Gwendolyn Mink, *Welfare's End* (Ithaca: Cornell University Press, 1998).

14. Flanders and Jackson, p. 15.

15. Audrey Vandenheuvel, "Women's Roles After First Birth," *Gender & Society,* v. 11, June 1997, pp. 357ff.

16. *The New York Times,* October 7, 1991.

17. *Reader's Digest,* March 1995.

18. This formulation of agenda setting was coined by B. Cohen and cited in Shanto Iyengar and Donald R. Kinder, *News That Matters* (Chicago: University of Chicago Press, 1987), p. 2.

19. Flanders and Jackson, pp. 15–16.

20. NBC News, February 8, 1990.

21. See, for example, ABC News, June 17, 1988.

22. NBC News, September 27, 1985.

23. NBC News, January 14, 1992.

24. ABC News, January 12, 1995.

25. CBS News, June 14, 1994.

26. This chapter is based, in part, on the viewing and transcribing of approximately 288 network news stories about welfare from 1969 to 1997, 208 of which appeared between 1985 and 1997.

27. Martin Gilens, *Why Americans Hate Welfare* (Chicago: University of Chicago Press, 1999), pp. 124–25.

28. Gilens; see also Kenneth J. Neubeck and Noel A. Cazenave, *Welfare Racism: Playing the Race Card Against America's Poor.*

29. NBC News, October 4, 1972.

30. ABC News, March 3, 1971; for similar commentary see NBC News, January 13, 1970.

31. David A. Rochefort, *American Social Welfare Policy* (Boulder, CO: Westview Press, 1986), p. 100; see also Dorothy Roberts, *Shattered Bonds: The Color of Child Welfare* (New York: Basic Civitas Books, 2002), p. 176.

32. Cited in Sheehan, p. 106.

33. See, for example, NBC News, April 28, 1971.

34. NBC News, October 4, 1972.

35. ABC News, March 3, 1971.

36. Cited in Neubeck and Cazenave, p. 127.

37. CBS News, June 14, 1978.

38. CBS News, November 30, 1978.

39. NBC News, March 16, 1983; ABC News Close Up, August 23, 2002, transcript at www.thehatchergroup.com/stories/WRLIW8_31.htm#ABC.

40. ABC News, April 14, 1994.

41. Rochefort, pp. 114–15.

42. Charles Noble, *Welfare As We Knew It* (New York: Oxford University Press, 1997), p. 121.

43. Ann Mari May and Kurt Stephenson, "Women and the Great Retrenchment: The Political Economy of Gender in the 1980s," *Journal of Economic Issues,* June 1994, p. 538.

44. Affluent America's Forgotten Children," *Newsweek,* June 2, 1986, p. 20.

45. Noble, p. 122.

46. Amott, pp. 290–92.

47. The Working Poor," *The Economist,* May 14, 1983, p. 37.

48. CBS News, October 22, 1985; ABC News, February 12, 1986.

49. NBC News, February 24, 1987.

50. NBC News, August 21, 1987.

51. NBC News, June 17, 1988.

52. CBS News, November 30, 1993.

53. Of course, we may have missed some stories. This was based on a search and viewing of all network news stories listed under "welfare mothers" in the Vanderbilt news archives. See NBC News, October 16, 1969.

54. See, for example, NBC News, December 22, 1985; ABC News, June 26, 1989; NBC News, March 20, 1992; NBC News, September 27, 1985.

55. Heather Boonstra, "Welfare Law and the Drive to Reduce 'Illegitimacy,'" *The Guttmacher Report,* December 2000.

56. CBS News, May 19, 1985.

57. Kristen Luker, *Dubious Conceptions: The Politics of Teenage Pregnancy* (Cambridge: Harvard University Press, 1997), p. 197.

58. R. Kaufmann, A. Spitz, L. Strauss, et al., "The Decline in United States Teen Pregnancy Rates, 1990–1995," *Pediatrics,* 1998, pp. 1141–47.

59. "Mothers Raising Mothers," *U.S. News and World Report,* March 17, 1986, p. 21.

60. CBS News, February 10, 1985.

61. NBC News, December 27, 1994.

62. NBC News, March 21, 1995.

63. For an excellent and scathing discussion of The Moynihan Report, see Ruth Feldstein, *Motherhood in Black and White*, (Ithaca: Cornell University Press, 2000) pp. 142–52.

64. Bill Moyers, "The Vanishing Family: Crisis in Black America," CBS, January 25, 1986; portions also aired on CBS News, January 24, 1986.

65. NBC News, September 27, 1985.

66. ABC News, December 7, 1994.

67. CBS News, February 9, 1994.

68. ABC News, June 26, 1989.

69. Statistical Abstract of the United States, 2000, table 566, p. 360.

70. NBC News, December 28, 1994.

71. NBC News, February 3, 1992.

72. CBS News, February 2, 1995.

73. ABC News, April 14, 1992.

74. NBC News, March 20, 1992.

75. CBS News, July 22, 1988.

76. Roberts, p. 179.

77. CBS News, February 2, 1994.

78. ABC News, February 2, 1994.

79. ABC News, June 14, 1994.

80. Flanders and Jackson, pp. 13–14.

81. Gilens, p. 47.

82. Neubeck and Cazenave, p. 134.

83. ABC News, April 14, 1992.

84. See ABC News, April 14, 1992, and October 22, 1992.

85. NBC News, August 10, 1994.

86. ABC News, February 9, 1995; also cited in Flanders and Jackson, p. 16.

87. "Mothers Raising Mothers," *U.S. News and World Report*, March 17, 1986, p. 24.

88. George Will, "Mothers Who Don't Know How," *Newsweek*, April 23, 1990, p. 80.

89. Roberts, p. 178.

90. We are indebted to Carroll Smith Rosenberg and her introduction to her book *Federalist Capers* for these insights, and to Sonya Rose for her work and comments on gender and nationalism.

91. Smith Rosenberg, unpublished manuscript, *Federal Capers*, p. 33.

92. Noble, p. 128.

93. Douglas J. Besharov, "Welfare Rolls: On the Rise Again," *The Washington Post*, July 16, 2002, p. A17.

94. Pamela Loprest, "Families Who Left Welfare: Who Are They and How Are They Doing?" *Assessing the New Federalism* (Washington, DC: The Urban Institute, 1999), p. 13.

95. Loprest, p. 12.

96. Sheldon Danziger et al., "Does It Pay to Move from Welfare to Work?" Poverty Research and Training Center, University of Michigan, April 2002, pp. 29–30.

97. Sheldon Danziger, "Approaching the Limit: Early National Lessons From Welfare Reform," in B. Weber et al., eds., *Rural Dimensions of Welfare Reform* (Kalamazoo, MI: Upjohn Institute for Employment Research, 2001), p. 3.

98. Loprest, p. 20.

99. "Impact of Recession and September 11 on Welfare Caseloads: Caseloads Up in Most States Between September and December 2001," Center for Law and Social Policy, www.clasp.org.

100. Besharov.

101. Jennifer Mezey, Mark Greenberg, and Rachel Schumacher, "The Vast Majority of Federally Eligible Children Did Not Receive Child Care Assistance in FY 2000," Center for Law and Social Policy, www.clasp.org.

102. Loprest, p. 11.

103. Lisa Dodson, Remarks in Transcript, "Living On and Off Welfare: Family Experiences and Ethnographic Research," symposium at the Brookings Institution, August 1, 2002, p. 9.

104. Ellen K. Scott, Remarks in Transcript, "Living On and Off Welfare: Family Experiences and Ethnographic Research," symposium at the Brookings Institution, August 1, 2002, p. 11.

105. Transcript, "Living On and Off Welfare: Family Experiences and Ethnographic Research," symposium at the Brookings Institution, August 1, 2002, p. 19.

CHAPTER 7: THE "MOMMY WARS"

1. See Susan Faludi's astute account of this in Backlash: The Undeclared War Against American Women (New York: Crown, 1991), pp. 56, 85–87.

2. Elspeth Probyn, "New Traditionalism and Post-Feminism: TV Does the Home," in Charlotte Brunsdon et al., Feminist Television Criticism: A Reader (New York: Oxford University Press, 1997), p. 127.

3. Sharon Hays, The Cultural Contradictions of Motherhood (New Haven: Yale University Press, 1996), p. 132.

4. Audrey Vandenheuvel, "Women's Roles After First Birth," Gender & Society, vol. 11, June 1997, pp. 357 ff.

5. Bonnie Dow, Prime-Time Feminism (Philadelphia: University of Pennsylvania Press, 1996), p. 168.

6. Dow, pp. 168–69.

7. See Dow on this point, p. 152.

8. Howard V. Hayge, "Are Women Leaving the Labor Force?" Monthly Labor Review, July 1994, pp. 37–38.

9. CBS News, March 13, 1989.

10. Ibid.

11. Probyn, p. 128.

12. Tim Brookes and Earle Marsh, The Complete Directory to Prime-Time Network and Cable TV Shows, 1946–Present (New York: Ballantine Books, 1995), pp. 1271–72.

13. Kathleen K. Rowe, "Roseanne: Unruly Woman as Domestic Goddess," in Brunsdon et al., p. 79.

14. Cited in Rowe, p. 79.

15. Cited in Carole Stabile, "Resistance, Recuperation and Reflexivity: The Limits of a Paradigm," Critical Studies in Mass Communication, December 1995.

16. This dialogue was from With Harmful Intent, starring Joan van Ark.

17. CBS News, March 4, 1995, CBS News, March 6, 1995.

18. We are grateful to Liz Kennedy for this observation.

19. "The Confident Parent," McCall's, June 1992 and February 1992, p. 52.

20. Bernice Kanner, " 'Parents' New Parent Backing Revamp," Advertising Age, October 9, 1979, p. 20.

21. Robert Goldman calls these "paleosymbolic moments." "Legitimation Ads, Part I: The Story of the Family, in which the Family Saves Capitalism from Itself," Knowledge & Society, v. 5, 1984, pp. 243–67.

22. Ad in Parenting, September 1999.

23. Ad in *Redbook,* September 1990.

24. Ad in *Good Housekeeping,* May 1990.

25. Ads in *Ladies' Home Journal,* 1995.

26. Cited in Dow, p. 154.

27. Dow, p. 159.

28. Kathryn Keller, *Mothers and Work in Popular American Magazines* (Westport, CT: Greenwood Press, 1994), p. 140.

29. Dow, p. 189, citing Ann Snitow.

30. Probyn, p. 152.

31. Dow, p. 189.

CHAPTER 8: DUMB MEN, STUPID CHOICES— OR WHY WE HAVE NO CHILDCARE

1. ABC News, June 13, 1989.

2. CBS News, April 9, 1992.

3. "A Sour Observation on the Lanham Act," *American Journal of Public Health,* February 1943, p. 174.

4. Margaret O'Brien Steinfels, *Who's Minding the Children* (New York: Simon and Schuster, 1973), p. 67.

5. Sara M. Evans, *Born for Liberty* (New York: The Free Press, 1989), p. 224; David E. Bloom and Todd P. Steen, "Minding the Baby in the United States," in Kim England, ed., *Who Will Mind the Baby* (New York: Routledge, 1996), p. 25.

6. Ruth Carson, "Minding the Children," *Collier's,* January 30, 1943, pp. 46–48.

7. Doris Kearns Goodwin, *No Ordinary Time* (New York: Simon & Schuster, 1994), pp. 416–18.

8. Miriam E. Lowenberg, "Shipyard Nursery Schools," *Journal of Home Economics,* February 1944, pp. 75–77.

9. "Designed for 24-Hour Child Care," *Architectural Record,* March 1944, pp. 84–88.

10. Lora Swartz, Child Service Centers, *Journal of Home Economics,* February 1945, pp. 76–79.

11. Rep. Bernie Sanders, "Corporate Welfare at its Worst," *The Nation,* June 3, 2002.

12. Kim England, "Who Will Mind the Baby?" in Kim England, ed., *Who Will Mind the Baby* (New York: Routledge, 1996), p. 3.

13. England, p. 6.

14. See Childrensdefense.org, which cites, in part, a Harris poll, January 14–18, 1998, and *Parents,* August 1997.

15. Nan Robertson, "Conference on Children Urges Action on Day Care and Racism," *The New York Times,* December 19, 1970, pp. 1, 15.

16. Mary Frances Berry, *The Politics of Parenthood: Child Care, Women's Rights and the Myth of the Good Mother* (New York: Viking, 1993), p. 137.

17. CBS News, May 5, 1971.

18. Tanya Melich, *The Republican War Against Women* (New York: Bantam Books, 1996), p. 27.

19. Jack Rosenthal, "For Nixon, It's an Idea Whose Time Is Not Yet," *The New York Times,* December 12, 1971, Week In Review, p. 4; Berry, p. 137; Joyce D. Miller, "The Urgency of Child Care," *The American Federationist,* June 1975, p. 4.

20. John W. Finney, "Congress Leaders Break Deadlock Over Aid Fund," *The New York Times,* December 11, 1971, p. 1; Jack Rosenthal, "President Vetoes Child Care Plan as Irresponsible," *The New York Times,* December 10, 1971, p. 1.

21. Jack Rosenthal, "President Vetoes Child Care Plan as Irresponsible," *The New York Times,* December 10, 1971, p. 1, p. 20; see also Keller, p. 84.

22. CBS News, December 9, 1971.

23. "Abandoned Commitment," *The New York Times,* December 11, 1971, p. 30; Rosenthal, "For Nixon, It's an Idea Whose Time Is Not Yet," p. 4.

24. See Berry, p. 138.

25. "Dishonest Campaign Against the Child and Family Services Act," *Congressional Record—Senate,* February 19, 1976, pp. 3803–4.

26. Berry, p. 141.

27. Shirley Chisolm, "Day Care Override Urged," *Atlanta Constitution,* April 19, 1976.

28. "Child and Family Services Act of 1975," *Congressional Record,* January 26, 1976, p. 1008.

29. "Child Care Legislation," *Congressional Record,* April 1, 1976, p. 9190.

30. "Dishonest Campaign Against the Child and Family Services Act," *Congressional Record—Senate,* February 19, 1976, pp. 3802–3.

31. "Child and Family Services Act," *Congressional Record,* April 1, 1976, p. 9189.

32. "Child-Care Scare," *Newsweek,* April 5, 1976, p. 77.

33. Robert Signer, "Child Services Bills Stir Storm," *Chicago Daily News,* March 27, 1976, cited in "Child Care Legislation," *Congressional Record,* April 1, 1976, p. 9190.

34. Howard Flieger, "False Alarm," *U.S. News & World Report,* March 1, 1976, cited in *Congressional Record,* March 2, 1976, pp. 5069–70.

35. Geri Joseph, "Smothering Debate on a Family Bill," *The Minneapolis Tribune,* cited in *Congressional Record,* May 5, 1976, p. 12721.

36. Martha McPhee, "Child and Family Services: The Truth About a Misunderstood Bill," *Parade,* June 20, 1976.

37. "Child and Family Services Act, *Congressional Record,* February 26, 1976, p. 4710.

38. "Child and Family Services Act," *Congressional Record—House,* March 2, 1976, p. 5244.

39. "Child Day Care Standards Act—H.R. 9803—Veto," *Congressional Record—Senate,* May 5, 1976, p. 12687.

40. Ibid., p. 12683.

41. England, pp. 8–9.

42. Cited in Ann Mari May and Kurt Stephenson, "Women and the Great Retrenchment: The Political Economy of Gender in the 1980s," *Journal of Economic Issues,* June 1994, p. 534.

43. Bloom and Steen, p. 26.

44. Abbie Gordon Klein, *The Debate Over Child Care, 1969–1990: A Sociohistorical Analysis* (New York: SUNY Press, 1993), p. 40.

45. Berry, pp. 171–72.

46. CBS News, April 4, 1984

47. NBC News, April 19, 1984.

48. ABC News, April 23, 1984.

49. NBC News, August 8, 1984.

50. NBC-September 28, 1984.

51. Bloom and Steen, p. 30.

52. CBS News, October 3, 1987.

53. Berry, p. 180.

54. Berry, p. 183.

55. Klein, p. 47.

56. Berry, pp. 187, 180.

57. Susan Chimonas, "Moral Panics: Towards a New Model" (Ph.D. Dissertation, University of Michigan, 2000), p. 134.

58. Bloom and Steen, pp. 26–27.

59. Klein, p. 32.

60. Klein, pp. 53–55; Bloom and Steen, pp. 26–27; Berry, p. 191.

61. Berry, pp. 191–92.

62. Berry, p. 191.

63. Berry, pp. 185, 191.

64. CBS News, February 23, 1988.

65. NBC News, March 15, 1989.

66. CBS News, August 19, 1991.

67. For interviews with Belsky's critics, see Jennifer Foote Sweeney, "Jay Belsky Doesn't Play Well With Others," *Salon.com,* April 26, 2001, and Carol Guensburg, "Bully Factories?" *American Journalism Review,* July/August 2001.

68. Chimonas, p. 170.

69. ABC News, August 31, 1994.

70. ABC News, April 4, 1997.

71. CBS News, February 6, 1995.

72. ABC News, April 21, 1996.

73. NBC News, April 4, 1997.

74. ABC News, April 4, 1997.

75. ABC News, November 22, 1989.

76. *USA Today,* cited in Guensburg, "From Babies to Bullies," *The Washington Times,* April 25, 2001, p. A18.

77. Guensburg.

78. "Studies Again Raise Child-Care Questions," July 30, 2003, Nytimes.com.

79. Cited in Guensburg, "From Babies to Bullies."

80. Sweeney.

81. Guensburg, "From Babies to Bullies."

82. Cathy Young, "New Squabble Over Day Care," *The Boston Globe,* April 25, 2001, p. A21.

83. Peggy Orenstein, "Bringing Down Baby," *The Los Angeles Times,* April 29, 2001, part M, p. 1.

84. CBS News, January 20, 1992; NBC News, December 12, 1994.

85. Cited in Guensburg.

86. England, p. 11.

87. England, p. 12.

88. See Children's Defense Fund Web site at Childrensdefense.org.

89. Bob Herbert, "Heavy Lifting," *The New York Times,* February 13, 2003.

90. Also at Childrensdefense.org.

91. England, pp. 14–16.

92. Rosalyn Baxandall and Linda Gordon, *Dear Sisters: Dispatches From the Women's Liberation Movement* (New York: Basic Books, 2001), p. 234.

93. Lynne Gaines, "Like Family, not Company," *The Boston Globe,* February 17, 1994, p. 41.

94. *The Economist,* March 17, 1990, p. 60.

95. "Maternity Leave Around the World," International Labor Organization, 1998, www.womenz.org.nz/14%20 weeks%20 PPL/world.pdf.

CHAPTER 9: "MOMS "Я" US

1. James P. Steyer, *The Other Parent: The Inside Story of the Media's Effect on Our Children* (New York: Atria Books, 2002), p. 105.

2. "Toys & Games," *Media Decisions*, November 1977, p. 139.

3. "Do Stores Aim Toy Sections At Kids Or Adults?" *Supermarket Business*, August 1977, p. 26.

4. "Consumer Acceptance of High-Priced Toys Prompts Chains to Add Expensive Playthings," *Supermarket Business*, August 1977, p. 26.

5. Kate Fitzgerald, "Hasbro, Mattel Vie as Toys Rebound," *Advertising Age*, March 9, 1992, p. 41.

6. "Toys—No Longer Child's Play," *The Economist*, December 25, 1982, p. 101.

7. *Toys & Games*, November 1977, p. 140.

8. Nancy Gibbs, "Who's In Charge Here?," *Time*, August 6, 2001, pp. 46, 44.

9. Steyer, p. 103.

10. Stratford P. Sherman, "Where the Dollars R," *Fortune*, June 1, 1981, p. 45.

11. Doreen Mangan, "The Toy Marts," *Stores*, February 1979, p. 6.

12. "Will Success Spoil Toys 'R' Us?" *Chain Store Age Executive*, August, 1979, p. 106.

13. "Prices, Deep Lines Power Toy Supermarkets to Forefront," *Chain Store Age Executive*, November 1979, p. 100.

14. "Brand Report 60: Toys & Games," *Marketing & Media Decisions*, December 1980, p. 136.

15. Sherman, p. 46; "Making It Big With Toys," *Dun's Business Month*, April 1982, p. 77.

16. "Prices, Deep Lines . . . ," p. 102.

17. "Hasbro Industries: Playing Catch-up in Toys by Aiming at Pre-schoolers," *Business Week*, September 15, 1980, p. 86.

18. Ibid.

19. "Brand Report 60: Toys & Games," p. 136.

20. Cara S. Trager, "Parents Don't Just Want to Have Fun Toys," *Advertising Age*, February 14, 1985, pp. 24–25.

21. Richard Rothstein, "What's Hot and New in Toyland for '81," *Drug Topics*, March 6, 1981, p. 55.

22. "Competition Up Over Preschool Toys," *Chain Store Age*, September 1985, p. 72.

23. Ibid.

24. Rothstein, p. 57.

25. Rothstein, p. 58.

26. Trager, p. 25.

27. Ibid.

28. Steyer, p. 105.

29. Ibid.

30. "They May Look Odd, or Even Homely, But 'New Moms' Love These Kids," *Marketing and Media Relations*, Spring 1984, pp. 116–17.

31. "They May Look Odd . . . ," pp. 117–18.

32. "E.T. and Friends Are Flying High," *Business Week*, January 10, 1983.

33. Steven W. Colford, "FTC Toy-Ad Ruling Chips at Regulation," *Advertising Age*, October 8, 1984, p. 12.

34. "Are the Programs Your Kids Watch Simply Commercials?" *Business Week*, March 25, 1985, p. 53.

35. Ibid.

36. James Forkan, "TV Toy Licensing Picking Up Speed in '85," *Advertising Age,* March 4, 1985, p. 38.

37. "Toys the Rising Stars of Children's TV," *Advertising Age,* January 23, 1984, p. 66.

38. Joani Nelson-Horchler, "Could Your Product be a TV Star?" *Industry Week,* October 31, 1983, p. 67.

39. "Advertisers Woo Kids with a Different Game," *Marketing & Media Decisions,* September 1983, p. 73.

40. Jack Feuer, "FCC to Examine TV's Toy Programs As Kids Grow Tired of Genre," *Adweek's Marketing Week,* October 12, 1987, p. 5.

41. Kevin T. Higgins, "Research, Marketing Not Playthings for Toymakers," *Marketing News,* July 5, 1985, p. 14.

42. "Are the Programs Your Kids Watch . . . ? " p. 53.

43. See Susan Jeffords, *Hardbodies* (New Brunswick: Rutgers University Press, 1993), ch. 1.

44. Patricia Van Benthuysen, "Boys Will Be Boys," *Madison Avenue,* December 1985, p. 48.

45. Van Benthuysen, p. 51.

46. "Children: Games Marketers Play," *Marketing & Media Decisions,* September 1985, p. 98.

47. Ibid., p. 96.

48. Noreen O'Leary, "Baby-Boomer Toys Staging Comeback," *Adweek's Marketing Week,* March 2, 1987, p. 49.

49. Higgins, p. 5.

50. Brenda O. Dailey, "Communicating to the Youth Market: The Child's Perspective," *Journal of Advertising Research,* v. 25, 1985–86, pp. RC-7–8.

51. "Advertisers Woo Kids with a Different Game," p. 127.

52. "Children: Games Marketers Play," p. 98.

53. CBS News, April 29, 1987.

54. "Advertisers Woo Kids with a Different Game," p. 127.

55. James Forkan, "Toy Companies Use Tie-ins to Pad Ad Efforts," *Advertising Age,* August 12, 1985. p. 64.

56. "Children: Games Marketers Play," p. 98.

57. James Forkan, "Toy Products Inspired by TV Battle Military for Popularity," *Advertising Age,* March 1, 1982, p. 14.

58. Susan Spillman, "Action Dolls, Other Tie-ins Spark Toy War," *Advertising Age,* August 5, 1985, p. 3.

59. Cynthia Kooi, "War Toy Invasion Grows Despite Boycott," *Advertising Age,* March 3, 1986, p. 44.

60. "Toy Commercials: Fantasy Is Reality," *Television/Radio Age,* November 25, 1985, p. 61.

61. For documentation of the long term effects of viewing media violence and how it engenders violent "scripts," see L. Rowell Huesmann, "Observational Learning of Violent Behavior," in A. Raine et al., *Biosocial Bases of Violence* (London: Plenum, 1997), and Huesmann et al., "Longitudinal Relations Between Childhood Exposure to Media Violence and Adult Aggression and Violence: 1977–1992," *Developmental Psychology,* v. 39, 2003, pp. 201–221.

62. CBS News, February 14, 1986.

63. "Toyland's Elusive Goal—Win Over Both Sexes," *Advertising Age,* February 8, 1993, p. S-2.

64. "'Play' Cosmetics: A Controversial, Booming Toy Category," *Product Marketing,* April 1981, p. 4.

65. "Toyland's Elusive Goal—Win Over Both Sexes," p. S-18.

66. Richard Brandt, "Sega: Lightning Strikes Again," *Business Week,* December 21, 1992, p. 36.

67. Damon Darlin, "Highbrow Hype," *Forbes,* April 12, 1993, p. 126.

68. Rosemarie Del Vescovo, "Preschool Market Heating Up," *Playthings,* September 1988, p. 42.

69. Gary Cross, "Toy Story," *Across the Board,* New York, May 1998, pp. 14–15.

70. Barbara Rowley, "Toy Story: How to Choose the Best Playthings for Your Child, Age by Age," *Parenting,* May 1, 2002, pp. 135ff.

71. Ibid.

72. Robert Ehlert, "Top-Rated Educational Toys," *Better Homes and Gardens,* November 2000, pp. 88ff.

73. Rowley.

74. Ibid.

75. Ibid.

76. Ehlert.

77. See, for example, Diego Ribadeneiva, "Even the Top Students Lag, Colleges Say," *The Boston Globe,* December 20, 1992; Joseph Berger, "Scores in Math Test and Reading Fall in New York Schools," *The New York Times,* June 12, 1992.

78. David L. Marcus, "'Tis the Season for Smart Toys, and They Don't Even Need a Silicon Chip," *U.S. News & World Report,* December 6, 1999, pp. 99ff.

79. Barbara Hall Palar, "Toys That Teach," *Better Homes & Gardens,* November 1993, pp. 36ff.

80. Marco R. della Cava, "The Race to Raise a Brainier Baby: Parents Clamor for Educational Toys," *USA Today,* June 25, 2002, p. D1.

81. Mark Walsh, "Toys 'R' Useful: Stores Cash in on Educational Playthings," *Education Week,* January 16, 2002, pp. 8ff.

82. Della Cava, p. D1.

83. Monica Langley, "Bring Up (Bilingual) Baby—Marketers Rush to Meet Demand for Toys, Tapes and Classes; Achieving Total Immersion," *The Wall Street Journal,* October 6, 1999, p. B1.

84. Della Cava, p. D1.

85. Joe Pereira, "Parents Turn Toys That Teach Into Hot Sellers," *The Wall Street Journal,* November 27, 2002, p. B1.

86. Molly Prior, "Target Signs Exclusive Deal with *Parents* Magazine for Education Toy Line," *DSN Retailing Today,* December 11, 2000, p. 7.

87. Cecile B. Corral, "Educational Toys Boost Sales for the Intelligent Retailer," *Discount Store News,* July 26, 1999, p. 33.

88. Louise Lee, "The Toy That's Leaping Off the Shelves," *Business Week,* December 2, 2002, pp. 46ff.

89. Kate Fitzgerald, "Toy Activity Is Heating Up Early," *Advertising Age,* May 3, 1993, p. 44.

90. Gibbs, p. 44.

91. Steyer, p. 11.

CHAPTER 10: DR. LAURA'S NEIGHBORHOOD: BABY WEARING, NANNY CAMS, AND THE TRIUMPH OF THE NEW MOMISM

1. "Madison Avenue's Audience: Interview with Rena Bartos," *Public Opinion,* August/September 1984, p. 20.

2. Emma Ross, "SIDS May Be Linked to Infection," Associated Press, April 25, 2002.

3. John M. Carroll, MS, and Ellen S. Siska, "SIDS: Counseling Parents to Reduce the Risk," *American Family Physician,* April 1, 1998, www.aafp.org/afp/980401ap/carroll.html.

4. Ibid.

5. Laurie L. Dove, "Baby Beat's Stacie Hansen," *Pregnancy,* June 2002, pp. 56–57.

6. See ad in *Pregnancy,* June 2002, p. 35.

7. See ad in *Pregnancy,* June 2002, p. 91.

8. See ad in *Pregnancy,* June 2002, p. 69.

9. See ad in *Baby Years,* June/July 2002, p. 45.

10. See ad in *Pregnancy,* June 2002, p. 39.

11. See ad in *Baby Years,* June/July 2002, p. 119.

12. "Finding the Right Products for Baby's Skin," *Baby Years,* June/July 2002, pp. 56–57.

13. See ad in *Pregnancy,* June 2002, p. 29.

14. "VIROFREE," *Pregnancy,* June 2002, p. 22.

15. See ads in *Baby Years,* pp. 71, 69.

16. See ad in *Baby Years,* p. 41.

17. See ad in *Baby Years,* June/July 2002, p. 17.

18. See ad in *Pregnancy,* June 2002, p. 83.

19. See ad for "In The Treetop," *Pregnancy,* June 2002, p. 63.

20. Betty Becker, "Creating a Dream Nursery," *Pregnancy,* June 2002, pp. 43–44.

21. "Federal Study: 850,000 Children Home Schooled," Associated Press, August 4, 2001, as reported in the *Detroit News* and the *Dominion Post.*

22. Ibid.

23. Leslie Bennetts, "Diagnosing Dr. Laura," *Vanity Fair,* September 1998, p. 306.

24. Ibid., p. 309.

25. Ibid., p. 308.

26. Mary Eberstadt, "Home-Alone America," *Policy Review,* June 2001, www.policyreview.org/JUN01/eberstadt.html.

27. *America's Children: Key National Indicators of Well-Being,* 2003, Federal Interagency Forum on Child and Family Statistics, www.childstats.gov.

28. For example, *Good Housekeeping,* March, 2001.

29. See Askdrsears.com/about.asp.

30. See Empathicparenting.org/attach.htm.

31. See Askdrsears.com/html/5/T051200.asp#T051205.

32. See Askdrsears.com/html/6/T060500.asp.

33. NBC News, June 20, 2001.

34. *Today,* June 25, 2001.

35. *People,* March 4, 2002.

36. *Newsweek,* July 2, 2001.

37. *People,* op cit.

38. *Time,* January 28, 2002.

39. Anna Quindlen, "Playing God on No Sleep," Newsweek, July 2, 2001, p. 64.

40. "Mail Call: Our Readers on the Tragedy of Andrea Yates and the Toll of Postpartum Depression," *Newsweek,* July 23, 2001, pp. 14ff.

41. Marie Osmond, "I Had Lost All Joy and Hope," *Newsweek,* July 2, 2001, pp. 28–29.

42. Adrienne Rich, *Of Woman Born* (New York: Bantam Books, 1977), p. 283.

43. Ibid., p. 285.

44. Ibid.

45. Anne Lamott, *Operating Instructions: A Journal of My Son's First Year* (New York: Fawcett Books, 1994), p. 20.

46. See http://my.execpc.com/~wmvoice/carols.htm.

47. The term "capitulate" comes from Simone de Beauvoir, who uses it to describe a critical step in the inexorable process of "becoming a woman." Simone de Beauvoir, *The Second Sex* (New York: Alfred A. Knopf, 1952).

EPILOGUE: EXORCISING THE NEW MOMISM

1. Bob Herbert, "Heavy Lifting," *The New York Times,* February 13, 2003, and see Children's Defense Fund Web site at Childrensdefense.org.

2. See the Web site for National Center for Children in Poverty, Nccp.org.

ACKNOWLEDGMENTS

The routines of this book at times have been interrupted by the predictable, and sometimes not so predictable demands of family life and work. But separately and together, we benefited from the wise counsel, moral support, and professional skills of a range of wonderful people who helped us see the project to completion. Our savvy and supportive agent Chris Calhoun steered the manuscript through crucial moments of uncertainty, and found the book a perfect home at Free Press. We are deeply grateful for his talents and his faith in the project. Our editor, Amy Scheibe, brought a passion and intelligence to the manuscript that energized our spirits, and helped make the book more focused and tight. It has been a great delight to work with this terrific editor and her impressive assistant, Steph Fairyington. We are indebted to Martha Levin and Dominick Anfuso at Free Press for their commitment to the book. We also wish to thank Betsy Rapoport for her very constructive and encouraging readings of earlier portions of this manuscript.

Letty Cotin Pogrebin, the pioneering feminist writer; Katherine Arnoldi, an activist on behalf of poor, single mothers and author of *The Amazing True Story of a Teenage Single Mom*; and a prominent writer at a women's magazine who wishes to remain unnamed (but she knows who she is) provided us essential interviews about the media coverage of motherhood. The Vanderbilt Television News Archive at Vanderbilt University provided over forty hours of news footage and did so with extraordinary speed and professionalism. The Museum of Radio and Television in New York was an important source for screening old television shows.

—S.J.D. and M.W.M.

* * *

I wish to thank all those at the University of Michigan who helped make the book possible. The Marsh Center on Journalistic Performance provided a grant that enabled me to analyze the news media's coverage of motherhood, as did a summer research grant from the university's Institute for Research on Women and Gender. Support from the Catherine Neafie Kellogg Professorship as well as research awards from the College of Literature, Science and the Arts funded a great deal of the book's research. Thanks to Terry McDonald and Shirley Neuman for this. And my tireless department chair, Michael Traugott, played a central role in helping me get the time I needed to complete the book, for which I will be eternally grateful. The Undergraduate Research Opportunity Program at the University of Michigan brought me three terrific research assistants, David Horn, Rebekah Parker and Amy Wilmers. Debra Feinberg's research on press coverage of child care was invaluable. Tracie Rubeck, Patricia Kim, Nhi Lieu and TaKeshia Brooks conducted invaluable research on the news media and women's magazines. Special thanks to Tracie and her mother for taping reruns of essential television programs.

I am indebted to my many terrific colleagues at the University. Sonya Rose read portions of the manuscript and provided essential references and comments on the introduction; her own work on gender and nationalism afforded a framework for thinking about how motherhood has been constructed in the news media. Likewise, Carroll Smith Rosenberg's pathbreaking work on gender, race and national identity enriched the chapter on welfare mothers. Kris Harrison offered crucial advice on media effects scholarship, especially on women and self-esteem. The friendship and intellectual camaraderie of Alvia Golden (who also offered editorial comments), Sidonie Smith, Gabrielle Hecht, Gina Morantz-Sanchez, Geoff Eley, Paul Edwards, Guenter Rose, Greg Grieco, Kristen and Richard Beene, Peg Burns, Phil Deloria, Penny Von Eschen, Kevin Gaines, Phil Pochoda, and Mary Kelley have been invaluable sources of inspiration. I wish to thank my great colleagues in the Department of Communication Studies, especially Nicholas Valentino, Travis Dixon, Derek Vaillant, Catherine Squires, and Rowell Huesmann, whose work on media and identity has very much informed my own. The graduate students in Communication Studies have provided various leads, insights and comments while forging away on their own work. Becky Michaels read various chapters with an especially keen eye and proposed crucial changes in emphasis and tone. Joan Braderman also read drafts and offered her typically astute insights and much-needed support.

As with everything I have done, none of it would be possible without the unstinting support of my husband, T. R. Durham. Writing this has reminded me often of the struggles my own mother, now twenty years gone, went through as she sought to raise kids and work outside the home during the 1950s and '60s, struggles I hope no generation of women has to repeat. In her absence, two women have served as surrogate mothers and as abiding friends: Frances Durham, my mother-in-law, and Mary Ellen Brown. Their love for their children, coupled with their down-to-earth approach to motherhood, has been an inspiration to me. I dedicate this book to them. And finally, I dedicate this book to my daughter Ella, whose patience, intelligence, sense of humor, and love, have been a constant source of delight and awe. I could have never written this without her.

—Susan J. Douglas

* * *

Several different lifelines have sustained me while working on this book. I have required regular doses of truth serum from Lynn Morgan, who continues to coax my head out of the philosophical ostrich hole. Joan Braderman provided me the use of her big brain, reading and giving great insights. I would be lost without Mary Russo's uncanny ability to pinpoint the occasional inaccuracy.

At Hampshire College, Marlene Fried and Barbara Yngvesson introduced me to a wealth of perspectives and materials in the courses that we taught together when I was on the faculty there. Joan Landes, Joan Cocks, Kathryn Pyne Addelson, and Jay Garfield have supported my work in innumerable ways. Thanks to Nancy Aronie for the outdoor circle of writing chairs in Chilmark. I am incredibly grateful to my colleagues in the philosophy department at Smith for providing an academic haven. I owe special thanks to the many students who have taught me that when it comes to attitudes toward motherhood, nothing should be taken for granted.

Three able and committed research assistants—Andrew Janiak, Tara Spellman, and Amy Basen—were always able to find what I didn't know I was looking for. Thanks also to Kara McClurken, archivist at the Sophia Smith Collection, for her help locating photographs of what allegedly never existed: feminists advocating on behalf of mothers and children.

I am indebted to the wise counsel of Blaine Garson, who has never taken a prisoner in her life. Molly Whalen forced me to look again, and again. Bill Sax, Lisa Uyehara, Richard Quinn, and Lucinda Scala Quinn, their amazing kids, and other wonderful friends have plied me with food for thought and for the palate. The Tiger maintained the domestic infrastructure, especially its canine center, with unfailing devotion.

Thanks to my remarkable sisters and their mind-blowing families for letting me work on that knoll over Menemsha Pond. For my children Becky, Peter, Jules, Michael, and Cassie I have boundless gratitude for their forbearance, and thank them for bringing me the additional gifts of Peter, Shannon, Lauren, and, of course, Katie. I owe special thanks to Becky for her efforts on behalf of this project.

With the exception of a weakness for televised sports, my husband, Lee Bowie, belies every discouraging "discovery" about the inevitability of sex roles. The background noise of sportscasters and fans has been a small price to pay for the commitment of a man who has never once dropped the ball. I owe him the most.

—Meredith W. Michaels

INDEX

QUESTIONS AND TOPICS FOR DISCUSSION

1. How would you describe the state of motherhood in America today? Do you agree with the authors' premise of the "new momism"—that women are being conditioned to believe they can find true fulfillment only through the perfection of motherhood? How well do they support the arguments and ideas they present in *The Mommy Myth*?

2. What are the tenets of feminism, and how have they been distorted through the years? Do you agree with the authors that "The new momism is the result of the combustible intermixing of right-wing attacks on feminism and women" (p. 24)?

3. The authors cite numerous instances where newscasters reported a story as fact but did not offer evidence or statistics to back it up. Why do you think the American public is so willing to believe what is reported in the media, particularly when no supporting data are offered? Does it surprise you that government officials are the major source of news for the networks?

4. What role has politics played in the rise of the new momism over the last several decades? How have conservative mores in particular shaped the American culture's representation of motherhood?

5. What ignited the enormous popularity of the celebrity mom profile, "probably the most influential media form to sell the new momism" (p. 113)? Why do women continue to be drawn in by the onslaught of celebrity mom profiles?

6. Discuss the ways in which television shows and movies—including *The Cosby Show, thirtysomething, The Simpsons*, women-in-jep films, and *Kramer vs. Kramer*—have impacted our society's attitude toward motherhood in both positive and negative ways. How have the images of motherhood in television shows and movies evolved since the 1950s?

7. The "mommy wars" divided mothers into two camps—the working mother versus the stay-at-home mom. What escalated the mommy

wars? Is there still a divide today between the working mother and the stay-at-home mom? What about women who work out of necessity to support their children? How has the "Martha Stewartization of America" further contributed to the debate about motherhood and added fuel to the mommy wars?

8. In what ways did media coverage of "threats from without" in the 1980s, including dangerous day care and kidnappings, impact the new momism? In the late 1980s, this gave way to "the threat to children from mom herself" (p. 140) with sensationalized stories about Susan Smith, Baby M, and crack babies. What caused this shift in emphasis and what effect has it had?

9. Trace the evolution of the welfare mother in the news media. How was the issue of welfare and, specifically, the welfare mother, used as a cornerstone of the Reagan administration?

10. How has the media's need for heroes and villains enforced the stereotype of the black woman as a bad mother? Have women themselves aided in perpetuating this stereotype?

11. A central point in the book is the failure of the government to institute a national day care program despite legislation having been introduced to Congress on multiple occasions. How did the media's coverage of the McMartin day care scandal reinforce the government's position against national day care?

12. To what degree are advertisers responsible for the new momism, including companies like GE and Johnson & Johnson as well as toy manufacturers and retailers? Have they knowingly or unknowingly added to the cementing of the new momism in our culture?

13. The authors use Dr. Laura Schlesinger—a working mother whose platform is telling other women to quit their jobs and stay home with their children—to exemplify their point that the new momism is "not about subservience to men. It is about *subservience to children*" (p. 299). What do you think of Dr. Laura's message? Does the fact that she herself is a working mother alter your opinion?

14. Has reading *The Mommy Myth* changed your views about mother-hood, the media, or women's roles in society? Susan Douglas and Meredith Michaels view *The Mommy Myth* as a "call to arms" and ask women "to just say no to the new momism (p. 26)." How can women do this? Where do you see the state of motherhood in America ten years from now?

ABOUT THE AUTHORS

Susan J. Douglas is the Catherine Neafie Kellogg Professor of Communication Studies at The University of Michigan. She is author of *Listening In: Radio and the American Imagination,* which won the Hacker Prize in 2000 for the best popular book about technology and culture; *Where The Girls Are: Growing Up Female with the Mass Media;* and *Inventing American Broadcasting, 1899–1922. Where the Girls Are* was widely praised, and chosen one of the top ten books of 1994 by National Public Radio, *Entertainment Weekly* and The McLaughlin Group and the paperback was chosen one of the top books of 1995 by *Choice.* Her journalistic articles have appeared in *The Nation, Ms., In These Times, TV Guide,* and *The Progressive.* She lives in Ann Arbor, Michigan, with her husband and daughter.

Meredith W. Michaels is in the philosophy department at Smith College where she teaches courses on reproductive ethics and feminist theory. Before joining the Smith department, she was a professor at Mount Holyoke and Hampshire Colleges. Her previous books include *Fetal Subjects/Feminist Positions* (1999), with Lynn Marie Morgan, and the top-selling philosophy text *Twenty Questions: An Introduction to Philosophy* (Fifth Edition 2003), with G. Lee Lee Bowie and Robert C. Solomon. She has lectured widely on gender and reproduction, and has written for *Ms.* and *The Nation,* and for other professional publications. She and her husband have five children and live in Amherst, Massachusetts.